Delinquency Theories

Delinquency Theories: appraisals and applications provides a full and accessible overview of contemporary theories of juvenile delinquency.

The book opens with a comprehensive description of what a theory is, and explains how theories are created in the social sciences. Following on, each subsequent chapter is dedicated to describing an individual theory, broken down and illustrated within four distinct sections. Initially, each chapter tells the tale of a delinquent youth, and from this example a thorough review of the particular theory and related research can be undertaken to explain the youth's delinquent behavior. The third and fourth sections of each chapter critically analyze the theories and provide a straightforward discussion of policy implications of each, thus encouraging readers to evaluate the usefulness of these theories and also to consider the relationship between theory and policy.

This text is an invaluable resource for both undergraduate and graduate students of subjects such as youth justice, delinquency, social theory, and criminology.

John P. Hoffmann is Professor of Sociology at Brigham Young University. His research interests include the etiology of juvenile delinquency and drug use over the life course. His research has appeared in *Criminology*, *The Journal of Quantitative Criminology*, and other journals.

Delinquency Theories

Appraisals and applications

John P. Hoffmann

Routledge
Taylor & Francis Group

LONDON AND NEW YORK

First published 2011
by Routledge
2 Park Square, Milton Park, Abingdon, Oxon OX14 4RN

Simultaneously published in the USA and Canada
by Routledge
711 Third Avenue, New York, NY 10017

Routledge is an imprint of the Taylor & Francis Group, an informa business

British Library Cataloguing in Publication Data
A catalogue record for this book is available from the British Library

Library of Congress Cataloging in Publication Data
Hoffmann, John P. (John Patrick), 1962–
Delinquency theories: appraisals and applications/by John P. Hoffmann.
p. cm.
ISBN 978-0-415-78186-2 (hardback) — ISBN 978-0-415-78187-9 (pbk.) 1.
Juvenile delinquency. I. Title.
HV9069.H654 2011
364.3601—dc22
2010043367

ISBN: 978-0-415-78186-2 (hbk)
ISBN: 978-0-415-78187-9 (pbk)
ISBN: 978-0-203-83528-9 (ebk)

Typeset in Baskerville
by Prepress Projects Ltd, Perth, UK
Printed and bound in Great Britain by
CPI Antony Rowe, Chippenham, Wiltshire

Contents

Figures

Tables

Acknowledgements

I have been working on this book off-and-on for several years. The idea of it was planted in my mind by Ronald Akers, distinguished criminologist, developer and advocate of social learning theory, and author of the excellent book *Criminological Theories* (co-authored with Christine Sellers). Ron was interested in a companion book that featured theories of juvenile delinquency given that few texts focused on this important topic. Following his invitation to prepare such a book, I ended up thinking about it for a while and then agreeing to take on the task. However, as often happens, the idiosyncrasies of life were at play and this project took many more years than I had anticipated. If it were not for the support of several people there is no doubt I would never have completed this book. First and foremost, I thank Tim Ireland, collaborator, colleague, teacher, and friend. He helped with the organization and writing of a couple of chapters, reviewed the entire book with a careful and thorough eye, and helped me edit it down to a manageable length. Karen Spence was tireless in finding various bits of information and diagrams that helped illustrate some important issues. I thank her most enthusiastically. The administrative staff of the Sociology Department at Brigham Young University helped me prepare the references. Several reviewers offered many useful suggestions for which I am most appreciative. The staff at Routledge, in particular Gerhard Boomgaarden, Jenny Dodd, and Elisabet Sinkie, as well as Andrew R. Davidson of Prepress Projects Ltd, were incredibly supportive and helpful as they shepherded the book through all stages of production. The final product is so much better than I could have imagined thanks to their hard work. Finally, I thank my family for the warm and loving support I receive every day. In particular, this book is dedicated to my son Brian, who currently lives and serves in Ghana, of whom I am most proud.

1 Theory and delinquency

There are many explanations of why some adolescents become involved in juvenile delinquency. Yet, before considering any explanation, we should ask: Is delinquent behavior simply a normal part of growing up? Studies show that about half of adolescents in the United States are involved in some type of illegal activity before their eighteenth birthday, so perhaps delinquency is, in some ways, normal. However, those youths who get involved in delinquency are also more likely than others to have school, relationship, and employment problems later in life. In addition, delinquency costs U.S. society an estimated $15 billion per year. We should therefore try to understand why some adolescents become involved in delinquency because it may improve the lives of individuals, relationships, and society.

Given this book's title, it should be clear that defining theory and delinquency are necessary if we are to going to study the major explanations of this behavior. In general, *theories* are designed to explain or predict some event or phenomenon. *Delinquency* is defined as the violation of criminal laws by persons under the age of 18 (or younger, depending on the type of crime and the jurisdiction). Both of these statements are deceptively simple and mask many underlying assumptions and realities about the way people behave. For instance, many theories of behavior, whether they involve delinquency or musical tastes, make reasonable claims, yet fail when used to explain the way people actually behave. In addition, the term *delinquency*, similar to the term *crime*, is often not useful. Buying cigarettes one time and killing multiple people both fall under the umbrella of delinquency if committed by a 13-year-old, but should we treat them the same way? Can we explain both behaviors using a single theory? Delinquent behaviors are extremely diverse and it is best to admit that understanding them with theories is a complex exercise. Before studying theories of delinquency, it is therefore necessary to consider some of these concerns.

What is a theory?

As mentioned earlier, a simple definition of a theory is that it is an attempt to explain or predict some event or phenomenon. Many of us claim to have theories of why something occurs. However, we often confuse an opinion with a theory. *Opinions* are judgments or beliefs that are not necessarily based on facts or generalized ideas about truth. I may have the opinion that *American Idol* is the best reality show on television, but others may prefer *The Amazing Race*. My opinion is not a fact, nor is it a theory. There is also some confusion about the differences between facts and theories (Sears, 2005). *Facts* are things that have actually occurred; they are particular truths known by valid observation. I know for a fact that my child was born in May 2000 because I was there to witness his birth. Of course, facts may be disputed: I claim that Michael was smoking cigarettes in the school parking lot, whereas Jennica challenges this because she was in geometry class with Michael during this time. One of us is stating an actual fact; both observations cannot be true.

Theories are more like models: They provide a picture or general representation of how a phenomenon has occurred. Suppose, for instance, that I'm driving home along a deserted stretch of highway and see a pool of water on the road up ahead. I haven't seen any clouds in the sky, nor have weather reports mentioned rain. The next day and each day thereafter I see the same pool of water, yet there has been no reported rainfall. The curious thing is that when I drive past the place where it appears the pool should be, it's not there. So I think I must be seeing a real pool of water that somehow disappears. Perhaps there is an underground spring that bubbles up, but then the water drains quickly into a hole by the time I reach the spot. This is a simple explanation of why I see the pool of water each day, but I could make it more complex by studying the size of the pool, recording the time of day, scanning weather reports, and considering the movement of water on hard surfaces.

The fact that I developed a theory explaining the disappearing pool of water doesn't make it accurate. Most people who have experienced seeing "water" on a stretch of highway know that it is an illusion caused by the way the sun's rays reflect off the dark surface of a road. Nevertheless, my attempts to explain this phenomenon are not unlike the way that people develop theories of all kinds. For example, why do some migratory birds fly in a V formation; why do stars appear to move across the night sky? The more curious among us have tried to explain why these events occurred – in other words, they developed theories to explain an event or phenomenon.

The desire to come up with theories is a normal part of human existence. Some have also studied the process of creating theories. For example, here are some formal definitions of theory used in the social sciences.

A theory is an attempt to explain something or describe the causes of something (Agnew, 2008, p.72).

A theory is a set of logically interrelated statements in the form of empirical assertions about properties of infinite classes of events or things (Gibbs, 1972, p.5).

Theory is a mental activity; . . . it is a process of developing ideas that can allow us to explain how and why events occur (Turner, 2003, p.4).

Theory: A scheme or system of ideas or statements held as an explanation or account of a group of facts or phenomena (*Oxford English Dictionary*, 2010).

Although defining *theory* is a controversial topic in the social sciences (Sica, 1998), these four definitions provide a general sense of how this term is defined. All four note that theories are designed to explain or make sense of some event or phenomenon, much as I tried to do when describing the pool of water. Turner (2003) furthermore defines theory as a process, thus reminding us that good explanations require several steps. Many social scientists also prefer to limit their theories to *scientific* theories, or those that can be tested using scientific methods. Therefore, designing theories falls under the general field of science.

But what is *science*? In general, science is characterized by the idea that we may develop knowledge about how the world actually works, and this knowledge may be altered by carefully observing empirical (measurable) events. For instance, suppose my favorite television program is *Cops*. I've noticed that many of the people who are arrested on *Cops* are young men without shirts. I develop the idea that being male and not wearing a shirt are pieces of knowledge that are tied to being arrested by the police. If so inclined I can represent this idea using the following simple equation:

male + no shirt = arrest by police.

I can then test my crude theory of police arrest by observing not only the television show *Cops*, but also other reality TV shows, talking to the police about people they've arrested, asking those I know who have been arrested whether they are male and wear shirts, and discussing my theory with friends and experts on policing. I might even play the role of a scientific researcher by developing an intricate study of police arrests, complete with a sample of arrestees, a team of expert observers, and statistical techniques to analyze the data these observers collect. In this case, my theory will be proven wrong by testing it against actual events, even though I may not directly observe the sample of arrests. Some people argue that being proven wrong is the key for advancing science and for developing better theories (Popper, 1968): Once we eliminate theories that claim that shirtless young men get arrested, we may focus on other, more important aspects of people who get arrested and develop better theories about them. This approach is known as *falsification*. However, I do not have to discard all the parts of my theory. I will probably find, for example, that males are arrested more often than females, so I should try to develop a better theory that applies to this piece of knowledge.

There are numerous theories of human behavior that have been developed in many different academic disciplines. In general, regardless of the discipline, theories should consist of *concepts* and *statements*. Concepts are the principal elements of a theory and they provide labels for specific phenomena. Statements, which are sometimes called *propositions*, link the concepts together and indicate why concepts are connected. An example of a concept is *self-esteem*, which is defined as the beliefs or feelings people have about themselves. Another example of a concept is *delinquency*, which was defined earlier in the chapter. A theorist who wishes to develop a theory of self-esteem and delinquency must figure out a way to link these two concepts with a statement or proposition. Often, theories are represented visually by graphical models. Figure 1.1 provides a simple model of self-esteem and delinquent behavior. The two concepts are represented as ovals. The statement is represented by the solid arrow connecting the two concepts. We can determine two things about the proposed link between self-esteem and delinquency from the figure. First, the theorist thinks that self-esteem leads to delinquent behavior. If the theorist thought that delinquency affected self-esteem, the arrow would point in the other direction. Second, notice the negative sign above the arrow. This suggests that, as self-esteem decreases, delinquent behavior increases. The next step for the theorist is to describe why these two concepts are linked. A figure cannot fully represent a theory; the theorist usually must also use words (or equations) to describe the links.

How we define concepts often causes a lot of confusion in studies of delinquency. For instance, is self-esteem an easy concept to understand; does the concept mean the same thing to everyone? What about the concept of delinquency; does it mean the same thing in each theory? As you review the theories of delinquency presented in the following chapters, pay attention to how the main concepts of the theories are used.

What makes a good theory?

A good theory should provide clearly defined concepts and statements linking these concepts. A good theory should also offer a compelling explanation of whatever phenomenon it is concerned with. However, how do we know if it provides a compelling explanation? Most observers contend that a good theory should offer the following characteristics: coherence, verifiability, simplicity, significance, scope, and utility (Mithaug, 2000).

Coherence

Coherence refers to whether the theory's statements are logically connected in a way that offers a clear explanation of the phenomenon. The example of the shirtless young men who are arrested on *Cops* does not pass the coherence test. It may be coherent in the sense that most people can visualize the concepts of shirtlessness

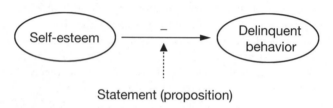

Figure 1.1 A simple model of self-esteem and delinquency.

and arrest by the police, but the statement linking these two concepts offers only a vague explanation of why they are connected. Is there something about shirtlessness that makes young men violent or prone to commit crime? This seems highly unlikely. Do the police target these young men for arrest? Perhaps, but explaining why is difficult.[1] Therefore, unless the statements in a theory are coherent in light of common sense and reasonableness, the theory fails.

Another aspect of coherence is whether the theory is non-tautological. In the field of logic, a *tautology* is a compound proposition that is true for all possibilities of its elementary propositions ("criminology is what criminologists do"). In practical terms, a tautology is a theoretical statement that is always true no matter how the outcome is considered. For example, if my theory claims that delinquent behavior results from the presence of delinquent values among youths, I run the risk of tautological thinking. If I'm not cautious, I could be asserting that delinquency results from delinquency: What is a delinquent? Someone who has delinquent values. And who has delinquent values? Delinquents. However, if I carefully define delinquent behavior and delinquent values as distinct phenomena (see Chapters 6 and 8) and then link them in a coherent way, I can avoid a tautology.

Verifiability

Verifiability refers to whether the theory is supported by empirical evidence or measurable results. This is often called *empirical validity*. A theory is verifiable if research supports its statements. Tests designed to verify theories (or challenge them) should involve research that is well thought out and conducted in a rigorous manner. One of the problems faced by researchers is that measuring social phenomena, such as values, self-esteem, and delinquency, is not an easy task. Most books on research methods discuss in detail how challenging it is to collect good information from people about their behaviors, attitudes, and emotions.

Another key issue for theories is whether they should explain or predict *all* cases of some phenomenon, or simply provide better explanations or predictions than other theories. Should the statements of a good theory of delinquency always be true? When we say that some concept – such as weak emotional attachment to parents – *causes* delinquency, must we always find this link? There is a large literature in the philosophy of science and the social sciences on the issue of *causality* (e.g., Pearl, 2000), with many debates about whether we can ever establish that one concept causes another when they involve human behavior. Perhaps the most well-known, but still controversial, description of causation is by the English philosopher John Stuart Mill (1884). He defined causation based on three criteria:

1   The cause precedes the effect in time.
2   The cause and the effect are associated: As one changes the other also changes.
3   Alternative explanations of the relationship between the cause and the effect can be eliminated.

Some observers have interpreted these criteria as demanding that, for one thing to cause another, the effect must always change with the cause. Others argue that we simply must establish that the cause increases the likelihood of the effect. Most important, we wish to eliminate alternative explanations for the link between the cause and the effect. It is often the case that a third factor causes both.

As an example, suppose my theory predicts that physical abuse by parents causes their children to engage in delinquent behavior. A strict view of causality claims that my theory is correct only if (1) physical abuse comes before delinquency; (2) as physical abuse increases, delinquency also increases; and (3) some other factor does not explain this association (e.g., exposure to lead in the family's diet does not cause both). However, is my theory incorrect if someone finds that some abused children are not delinquent? Most observers now see a good theory as one that offers a good *probabilistic* explanation of the phenomenon. Some researchers simply avoid using the term *causality* to avoid the debate over its meaning. In this book, the term *causal* is not used unless a particular theorist uses it. Rather, using the example of physical abuse, we adopt the following position: A theory that states that parental physical abuse leads to delinquency is not necessarily incorrect if we find a group of abused children who do not engage in delinquent behavior. The important point is whether children who are abused are more likely to be (have a higher probability of being) delinquent than those who are not abused. Of course, we must now make some judgment calls about how much more likely they must be before we consider the theory to be verified. This complicates things because I might be willing to accept one probability as sufficient, whereas another person might want the probability to be higher.

Table 1.1 illustrates four scenarios involving parental physical abuse and delinquency. The first scenario supports a *deterministic* theory: All children who are abused are delinquent, whereas none who are not abused are delinquent.[2] The next set of scenarios show three probabilistic situations. In the second scenario 5 percent of abused children are delinquent, whereas only 1 percent of non-abused children are delinquent. In the third scenario 25 percent of abused children are delinquent and 15 percent of non-abused children are delinquent. In the fourth

Table 1.1 Four scenarios involving physical abuse and delinquency (%)

		Delinquency	No delinquency
Scenario 1	Physical abuse	100	0
	No physical abuse	0	100
Scenario 2	Physical abuse	5	95
	No physical abuse	1	99
Scenario 3	Physical abuse	25	75
	No physical abuse	15	85
Scenario 4	Physical abuse	75	25
	No physical abuse	10	90

scenario, 75 percent of abused children are delinquent and only 10 percent of non-abused children are delinquent. Which piece of evidence, if any, verifies the theory that physically abused children are more likely to be delinquent? A strict determinist would claim that only the first scenario verifies the theory. One observer might claim that the second scenario is persuasive: "Abused children are five times as likely as non-abused children to be delinquent." A second observer might contend that Scenario 4 provides the best evidence: "Three-quarters of abused children are delinquent, but only one-in-ten children who have not been abused are delinquent." This shows the blessing and curse of probabilistic thinking when addressing theories: Asking our theories to predict probabilistically is a better reflection of the complexities of human behavior, yet there are no fixed rules for deciding when a probability is high enough to satisfy our desire to verify a theory.

However, there is another issue that often complicates tests of delinquency theories and has forced some researchers to rethink the way that the delinquency process is envisioned. Although we usually assume that some relationship or behavior leads to delinquency, it is often the case that delinquency affects one of these. For example, learning theories (see Chapter 7) propose that youth learn to be delinquent from their friends, thus delinquent friends lead to delinquency. Research shows, however, that delinquent behavior also leads to associating with delinquent friends. This is an example of a *reciprocal relationship* (Figure 1.2): Factor 1 leads to factor 2, but factor 2 also leads to factor 1. In this reciprocal loop, each factor may be considered a cause of the other.

Relying only on empirical predictions for verification also asks too little of these theories. Two distinct theories may offer similar predictions about who becomes delinquent. Twenty-five percent of abused children may become delinquent, but suppose that we also find that 25 percent of children with low self-esteem become delinquent, thus supporting a theory that links self-esteem and delinquency. How do we decide which theory is better? The better theory will offer a better *explanation* for delinquency, not simply a more precise prediction. In fact, good explanations of delinquent behavior will improve predictions of delinquent behavior (Douglas, 2009). Moreover, we should be prepared to modify our theories when faced with

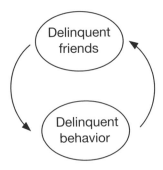

Figure 1.2 Example of a reciprocal relationship.

empirical evidence. In the preceding example, perhaps abuse and low self-esteem are part of a poor family environment, which then increases the probability of delinquency. In general, verification is an essential characteristic of a good theory, but it must be accompanied by other important elements.

Simplicity

Good theories should be as simple as possible, without ignoring the complexities of human behavior (Lave and March, 1975). There are many theories that contain well-defined concepts and persuasive statements, but they lack simplicity because they include concepts or statements that are unnecessary. For example, theories that attempt to account for every conceivable relationship often lack simplicity. It is better to look for a key set of concepts and statements that explain the phenomenon rather than taking an overly comprehensive approach to theory building.

A theory that explains delinquency based on differences in levels of self-esteem is more parsimonious than a theory that explains delinquency based on differences in levels of parental attachment, blood sugar, language skills, fiber intake, *and* self-esteem. Nonetheless, a theory that meets the simplicity goal is not necessarily valid if, say, self-esteem offers a poor explanation for delinquency. In the quest for simplicity, verifiability, coherence, and the other characteristics of a good theory should never be sacrificed.

Significance, scope, and utility

The next three characteristics of a good theory – significance, scope, and utility – are concerned with whether a theory has value. A theory may be highly predictive, coherent, and parsimonious, but may be useless if it addresses a very narrow phenomenon or one that has little concern for society. A theory about why 20-year-old women are more likely than 18-year-old men to play the bass in rock bands may be coherent and verifiable, but that doesn't make it valuable. A significant theory should provide an explanation for all (or at least most) of the key factors that lead to the phenomenon of interest. Are there factors that are well known to predict the phenomenon, yet are left out of the theory? An example from delinquency research involves friends. As mentioned earlier, a consistent empirical finding is that adolescents involved in delinquent behavior are more likely than others to have friends involved in delinquent behavior. A good theory should at least consider the role of friends in its explanation of delinquency. If it does not, then we should question the significance of the theory.

A theory's scope concerns the range of phenomena it explains. Some social scientists argue that social theories should be general enough to encompass numerous human behaviors, from normal to deviant. When assessing delinquency theories, it is a good idea to consider the following question: If the theory does a fine job of explaining delinquency, does it also explain law-abiding behavior? Is it useful for explaining various types of behavior, from shoplifting to auto theft? One of the problems for these theories involves their scope: Delinquency covers a lot of behavioral ground. Is it asking too much to expect them to explain all types of delinquency? Alternatively, should we strive for multiple theories of delinquency that explain various behaviors, such as running away from home, drug use, and violence? It should be clear that there is a delicate balance between scope and simplicity: Although we should strive for simplicity, we must not ignore scope. A theory may be quite parsimonious, with only one or two concepts linked to delinquency. However, if its scope is too narrow, then it risks the curse of having little value. On the other hand, it is not a good idea to develop theories that try to encompass every social phenomenon and then attempt to include every concept that has been linked to these phenomena. Overly broad theories can also be worthless.

Finally, an important question is whether a theory has utility: Does it offer practical solutions to the problem of interest? Can it be used by policy makers? Alternatively, is it so obscure that it is almost impossible to determine what to do with it? A theory's utility is based on all of the other factors: coherence, validity, simplicity, significance, and scope. Public policies must be sensitive not only to whether programs follow good theories, but also to limited resources, political needs, and bureaucratic realities. It is unlikely that a program will be implemented if it is based on a theory of juvenile ant farmers and prostitution, no matter how good the theory. This type of theory is simply too narrow in scope and has little significance to broader issues of delinquency to provide much utility.

Classifying theories of delinquency

There are several classification schemes for theories of behavior. The most basic scheme when addressing delinquency is whether we are concerned with how juveniles behave or with how the public and government agencies react to how they behave. The first topic – how juveniles behave – has led to many theories of delinquency. These will be emphasized throughout this book since they are the most common and have generated the most research. However, we should also remember that the study of delinquency is driven by how delinquency is defined. There are some who argue that delinquency is defined arbitrarily, that those concerned with explaining adolescent behavior should not limit themselves to behaviors that are defined by the criminal justice system and by legislators who create laws. Yet the most common definition of delinquency is that it involves behaviors by persons under the age of 18 (or younger, depending on the type of crime and the jurisdiction) that violate the criminal laws. The boundaries of delinquency are created by lawmakers and may even shift depending on differing state or local laws. A good example involves curfew laws, which make it unlawful for young people to be in public places during certain hours, usually at night. They are an example of a *status offense*: acts that are not legal for persons under a certain age, but that are legal for adults. This may complicate our desire to explain delinquency because status offenses treat particular behaviors differently if committed by adolescents or by adults. Moreover, because the definition of a status offense often changes from one area to another, one might define a group of young people as delinquent if they violate their city's curfew law, even though they would not be violating the law if they lived in a city without a curfew law.

Some researchers prefer to study not the violation of law by juveniles, but rather the creation and enforcement of these laws. This is an important topic that has led to many fascinating studies. Two key questions are (1) why do legislators pass certain laws that are targeted at the behaviors of juveniles and (2) are the enforcement efforts of governmental agencies more likely to be focused on a particular set of juveniles, such as minority youths?

It is wise, then, to remember that many studies of delinquency use arrest or police contact information as the basis for defining this behavior, yet these may be affected by differential enforcement of laws. *Official bias* – the tendency to disproportionately arrest or institutionalize certain adolescents based on something other than their law-violating behavior – is an important factor in delinquency research that cannot be ignored. As you consider the research that tests theories of delinquency, consider also the source of data used to define delinquency. Could it be biased against certain groups of adolescents? Are theories that try to explain differences between groups of adolescents (e.g., males vs. females) tested using data that might also be biased? It is essential that we pay attention to the interplay between theory and research in studies of delinquency. Many of the most prominent theories are based on studies of juvenile behavior; most have undergone revisions because of the results of these studies.

Whose behavior is being explained? Individual-level vs. macro-level theories

Theories of delinquency may be classified into those that address individual-level behavior or those that address macro-level behavior. Individual-level theories seek to explain behaviors by individuals and the factors that affect them. Most of the examples provided earlier are drawn from individual-level theories: Physical abuse leads to delinquency; delinquent friends lead to delinquency. In contrast, macro-level theories attempt to explain delinquency across spatial units, such as neighborhoods or cities. A simple macro-level theory contends, for instance, that neighborhoods higher in residential instability (residents move in and out at a relatively rapid rate) also have higher rates of delinquency due to characteristics of these neighborhoods (see Chapter 5).

Attention to individual-level and macro-level phenomena does not exhaust the ways we can view delinquency theories. In between these two levels are theories of small group behavior. Research on gangs and delinquent peers often uses these theories to understand how groups behave. Since delinquency is frequently a small group activity – groups of youths fight, friends go on a shoplifting spree or steal a car – considering how small group dynamics affect adolescent behaviors is a useful method for understanding delinquency (e.g., Krohn, 1986). As discussed in Chapter 7, social network theories, in particular, have been used to explain the group dynamics that affect delinquency.

Assumptions about human nature

A third way to classify delinquency theories is based on assumptions about human nature. For example, are people naturally inclined to act in the best interests of their fellow human beings? Alternatively, are people naturally selfish and apt only to look out for their own interests unless we design a system to curb these impulses? Do people emerge from the womb as "blank slates" who must be taught everything about how to behave, or are there certain parts of our minds that are fixed before birth and affect how we behave? Do political, economic, and social systems influence the way we act? Is conflict a healthy part of human existence as different groups seek to advance their interests, or should we strive to avoid conflict? Seeking answers to these questions has occupied the minds of great thinkers for centuries and has led to many ideas about human behavior.

In studies of delinquent behavior, answers to these questions have led to a general distinction between *consensus* and *conflict* explanations of crime and delinquency (Bernard, 1983). Consensus theorists view society as, at best, cohesive and made up of individuals who follow – or wish to follow – the accepted rules of behavior. The preferred society is made up of people who agree about proper forms of behavior and support a particular "moral order." When behavior falls outside the proper boundaries established by society it must be eliminated or else society is damaged. Most delinquency theories that rely on legal definitions of unlawful behavior follow a consensus model.

Conflict theorists view the typical society not as a cohesive group designed to curb or encourage certain behaviors, but rather as consisting of separate groups striving to gain, maintain, or manipulate power. A moderate form views conflict as a necessary condition in the production of society. Since most people are naturally drawn to group associations, there tend to be groups in any society that have conflicting interests. The conflict among these groups typically leads to stability. In fact, resolving conflict is a normal way that societies develop.

Delinquency theorists who take a conflict approach admit that certain juveniles are more involved in misbehavior, but then ask what it is about their position in society that affects their behaviors. Perhaps their parents work in lower-wage jobs that provide little autonomy and emphasize authoritarian styles of interpersonal relationships. These parents then treat their children poorly or do not teach them to view other people kindly. The result is a higher likelihood of delinquency among juveniles from lower-status or authoritarian families (see Chapter 10).

The consensus–conflict divide offers only a broad view of how to classify theories of delinquency. A more detailed classification scheme is based on whether we view human nature as being naturally selfish, selfless, or a "blank slate." The philosophical view that human nature is selfish or that self-interest is part of human nature finds its origins in the British philosopher Thomas Hobbes's (1962 [1651], p.113) argument that the scarcity of valued things in the world leads to a constant "war of all against all" and the saying that life in the primordial "state of nature" is "solitary, poor, nasty, brutish, and short." We require a social order that includes fixed laws or else people will destroy each other. This assumption about human nature leads to theories that ask not why people violate laws, but rather: "Why do [people] obey the rules of society?" (Hirschi, 1969, p.10). Since people are naturally inclined toward selfishness and exhibit behaviors that result from this tendency, theories of delinquency should describe the factors that restrain juveniles from committing crime, rather than what factors compel them to commit crime (see Chapter 8).

Suppose we assume, as did the French philosopher Jean-Jacques Rousseau (1974 [1755]), that people are naturally good ("noble savages") and are corrupted only by society's less noble pursuits. We should then assume that people, if left on their own, would choose to help other people and act with selflessness. Unfortunately, the formation of governments often allows certain groups to gain too much authority over the behavior of others. What might a theory that accepts this assumption say about delinquent behavior? It would probably look to the goals people are encouraged to have and also at the means they have for achieving these goals. Some groups, especially those with less power, have fewer means than others to achieve goals, so the theorist would look for ways that they compensate for their social disadvantage (Merton, 1968). Some may turn to crime and delinquency to reach these goals when legitimate avenues are blocked. As we shall see in Chapter 6, juveniles are a group in our society with less power than others and are often not given direct access to certain valuable goals, such as owning a car. They are pushed into delinquency, rather than acting based on their natural impulses.

Another view of human nature is that our minds at birth are a "blank slate" and we must have experiences to learn to function in society. The British philosopher John Locke (1975 [1690]) believed that all our ideas and knowledge come from experience. We have *sensations* that teach us about what occurs in the world external to us, and then we *reflect* on these sensations to learn how we should use our own abilities to operate in the world. Although contemporary studies show that we learn through a more intricate system than Locke envisioned, and that we are not "blank slates" at birth (Pinker, 2002), the idea that we must learn to function in the world through our experiences has led to a denial that human nature is naturally good or selfish. Rather, we have individual natures that depend on what we have learned throughout childhood and into adulthood. Theorists who accept this assumption about human nature have developed several learning theories of delinquency (see Chapter 7).

Although these three assumptions of human nature are broad enough to encompass most theories of delinquency, there are also other assumptions that do not fit neatly under this classification scheme. For example, the British philosopher Jeremy Bentham (1996 [1789]) regarded the main drive behind human behavior as the pursuit of pleasure and the avoidance of pain. The father of economics, Adam Smith (1991 [1776]), believed that the origin of human behavior lay in the pursuit of self-interest. Although this is similar to Hobbes's position, Smith also argued that the accumulation of individuals' self-interested pursuits would be the best economic outcome for the most people. By meeting others' self-interest with our own, we may gain the greatest benefit for all. Contemporary rational choice theorists have suggested that people behave rationally when they select the best means available to reach a goal they think is in their interest. The assumptions promulgated by Bentham and Smith have led to several theories of delinquency that emphasize deterrence and rational choice (see Chapter 2). If people pursue their own self-interests in a rational manner and these interests involve the maximization of pleasure and the minimization of pain, then we should consider that some people may commit delinquent acts as a way either to gain things they view as pleasurable (e.g., money) or to avoid pain (e.g., escaping punishment). Deterrence theorists argue that we must develop ways to make delinquency more painful (or risky) than pleasurable. This might be done through having punishments whose "pain" (not just physical pain, but other types such as deprivation of desired goods) exceeds the pleasure derived from delinquent behavior. Alternatively, it might occur as policy makers take steps to make delinquency more risky, thus reducing the rewards of misbehaviors.

A final assumption about human nature that has led to several theories of delinquency does not focus on people in some hypothetical state of nature. Instead, theorists such as Charles Horton Cooley (1902) and George Herbert Mead (1934) considered the development of one's view of oneself and others through social interactions. Although their ideas are not entirely distinct from learning theories, Cooley and Mead were more concerned with the development of individuals' self-image and how this emerges through the many interactions they have with others. Mead furthermore thought that, because people cannot do all the things they need to to survive by themselves, there is a natural tendency to rely on group participation and cooperation to survive. Therefore, individuals' views of themselves and the roles they play in society depend on how others see them and how they are treated. These assumptions about the role that interactions play in defining us have resulted in theories about *symbolic interaction*. These theories emphasize that how people perceive reality is built through their daily interactions with other people and with groups. They also address how the symbols of everyday life, such as signs, gestures, and language, affect interactions among individuals and groups (see Chapter 9).

Finally, symbolic interaction approaches tend to consider two additional aspects of human behavior: agency and emotions. *Agency* is purposeful action on the part of individuals; we are not passive observers who are pushed around indiscriminately by social and personal forces outside of our control. Rather, we have the capacity to act independently, making our own choices in many situations. *Emotions* are spontaneous feelings that occur as we are exposed to different situations; they are often seen as the antithesis of reason. Both of these have been largely neglected by many delinquency theories, such as social control or social learning (Giordano, 2010; see Chapters 7, 8, and 9).[3]

Theory and context

We have now learned some useful background material about theory and how to classify explanations of delinquency. In addition, it is important to realize that theories of delinquency are influenced by the social context that theorists are part of (Lilly et al., 1994). Our ideas about the natural and the social world are influenced in large degree by current events and shifts in scientific knowledge. Adam Smith, the father of economics, developed his ideas during a time when there was a growing belief in England and in the fledgling American colonies that free trade between nations was vital (Ross, 1995). Therefore, it should not be surprising that he emphasized that, if left on their own to pursue economic gain, the most people would enjoy the greatest benefit. Karl Marx, one of the founders of conflict theory, wrote during a period when capitalism was in overdrive in Europe and many factory workers lived in harsh conditions. His theory that capitalism influenced human nature to emphasize selfishness, but that this would change if the economic system became more egalitarian, was based on observations about social conditions during his lifetime. During the 1960s delinquency theorists focused on economic and social barriers that affected the poor and minorities, so many explanations emphasized how poverty and discrimination led to delinquency.

Thus, it is important to remember that theories are tied to historical conditions. We cannot predict which theories of delinquency will be most widely accepted 100 years from now, but there is little doubt that they will be influenced by the social conditions and ideologies prevalent at that time. This does not mean that we should not trust current theories of delinquency because we should anticipate that they will change with shifting social conditions. Rather, it is wise to consider that explanations of delinquency do not emerge in isolation from broader societal conditions. As you learn about the theories presented in this book, it is useful to use your knowledge of history to increase your understanding of how they may have developed. It is also important that you consider the social context that you grew up in and how this affects your beliefs, opinions, biases, and theories about delinquency.

Conclusions

The goal of this chapter has been to present some important background material that will assist you as you learn about specific theories of delinquency. We have considered definitions of theory, in particular scientific theory, and some of the characteristics that a good theory should possess. A good theory should be coherent, verifiable, simple (but not overly so), significant, and have sufficient scope and utility. There are many policies and programs designed to minimize delinquency, so it is important that we seek good theories to guide these policies and programs.

This chapter also considered several ways of classifying theories of delinquency. The key ways are by placing them into consensus or conflict categories; categories based on whether the theories address macro-level rates of delinquency, individual-level delinquent behaviors, or small group behaviors; and categories based on our assumptions about human nature (Is it naturally selfish, selfless, or a blank slate? Do humans act rationally or do emotions drive behaviors?). All of these schemes are potentially beneficial, since each considers important assumptions about the origins and motivations of human behavior.

Finally, you should consider the historical circumstances that affected the emergence of these theories. Look beyond this book to your own understanding of the social conditions that were present at the time these theories emerged. In addition, adopt a critical eye when considering theories of delinquency. Is the scientific method the best way to understand and explain delinquent behavior? Or are there other methods that are more useful or that overcome some of the limitations of the scientific method? By considering the *social context* under which these theories developed, and the methods used to examine them, we may develop a better understanding of their promise for explaining delinquent behavior.

2 Deterrence and delinquency

This chapter is concerned with one of the oldest theories of crime and delinquency: deterrence theory. A key assumption of this theory is that people, both young and old, make decisions about how to behave based on a rational calculation of its risks and rewards. This may sound simple, but deterrence involves a much more complex set of circumstances than one might think. Consider two U.S. Supreme Court decisions regarding the death penalty for those who commit capital crimes as juveniles – *Stanford v. Kentucky* (1989) and *Roper v. Simmons* (2005). The facts in *Stanford* and *Roper* are quite similar. An adolescent committed a murder, showed little or no remorse, there were aggravating circumstances (such as robbery, sexual assault, or kidnapping), and the trial court sentenced the convicted adolescent to death.[1]

Prior to *Roper* the leading death penalty case for juveniles was the *Stanford* case, decided just 16 years earlier. The court in *Stanford* held that the execution of an offender convicted of a capital crime, who was either 16 or 17 at the time of the offense, is allowed by the U.S. Constitution. Although *Stanford* was a controversial decision, it was the law of the land long enough for 19 juvenile offenders to be convicted and executed for capital crimes (Amnesty International USA, 2005).

One of the arguments raised by the defense in the *Stanford* case was that the death penalty for juveniles "fails to serve the legitimate goal of penology . . . it fails to deter because juveniles, possessing less developed cognitive skills than adults, are less likely to fear death." The Supreme Court rejected this argument, claiming "as the socio-scientific data suggests . . . it is not demonstrable that no 16-year-old is adequately responsible or significantly deterred. It is rational, even if mistaken, to think the contrary." Therefore, the Supreme Court in 1989 suggested that if the threat of death deterred even one 16-year-old from committing a capital offense, then a legitimate societal goal is achieved.

In the *Roper* case the U.S. Supreme Court, by a vote of five to four, broke with precedent and determined that the execution of juvenile offenders who committed capital crimes was unconstitutional. A particularly important part of its decision stated:

> [a]s for deterrence, *it is unclear* whether the death penalty has a significant or even measurable deterrent effect on juveniles . . . [T]he absence of evidence of a deterrent effect is of special concern because the same characteristics that render juveniles less culpable than adults suggest as well that juveniles

will be less susceptible to deterrence. In particular, . . . "[t]he likelihood that the teenage offender has made the kind of cost–benefit analysis that attaches any weight to the possibility of execution is so remote as to be virtually nonexistent." To the extent the juvenile death penalty might have a residual deterrent effect, it is worth noting that the punishment of life imprisonment without the possibility of parole is itself a severe sanction, in particular for a young person (*Roper v. Simmons*, 2005, pp.17–18).

The reasoning of the Supreme Court in the *Roper* case was different from in the *Stanford* decision on the issue of deterrence and how it might affect adolescent decision-making. So which strategy is correct? Can juveniles be deterred from crime or, because of their status as juveniles, is deterrence largely ineffective?

The U.S. legal system relies mainly on the idea that people are rational decision makers. If people are to obey the law, then there must be punishments that outweigh the rewards for breaking the law. This type of thinking also lies at the heart of contemporary theories of rational choice and deterrence, although we shall learn that there are other aspects as well. However, what is meant by deterrence, and what is deterrence theory? Furthermore, how could the *Stanford* court readily accept the role of deterrence in juvenile capital cases, whereas the *Roper* court clearly doubted that deterrence is effective for juveniles who commit murder?

To address these questions, as well as related theoretical issues, this chapter outlines the basic arguments of deterrence theory. We begin with a discussion of the origins of deterrence theory. We then discuss some of the major complexities of deterrence theory, especially how punishment – a core component of the theory – is presumably most effective when it is swift, certain, and severe. We also describe the various forms of deterrence that are thought to affect decision-making among juvenile offenders. A key part of this chapter involves assessing the research on the effectiveness of deterrence: Does it prevent or minimize delinquent behavior? We conclude by evaluating the promises, problems, and policy implications of deterrence theory.

The evolution of ideas about deterrence and delinquency

The starting point for an introduction to deterrence theory is a short book published in 1764 by the Italian philosopher Cesare Beccaria entitled *On Crimes and Punishment*. His work helped lay the groundwork for deterrence theory as a crime control strategy. At the time of its publication the system of justice was quite different from today. Importantly, there was not a separate juvenile justice system, nor was there a distinct notion of juvenile delinquency that was separate from the concept of a *criminal*. Therefore, Beccaria's work applied to the criminal offender in general, with little regard for the age of the offender.

Over time, as the concept of a separate period of life known as adolescence was recognized, a distinction between juvenile and adult offenders emerged. Moreover, during the late nineteenth century, one of the first formally defined juvenile courts appeared in Chicago. From this Chicago court, the idea of a juvenile justice system, separate and distinct from the adult criminal justice system, spread across the country and today remains an integral part of the justice system in the United States. Since the inception of the juvenile court there remains an unresolved debate over deterrence as a crime control strategy for delinquent behavior, however. Even though deterrence theory continues to be the basis for much of the adult criminal justice system, those who organize and study the juvenile system have remained skeptical about its place in evaluating juvenile offenders. In fact, much of the historical emphasis in the juvenile justice arena has been on treatment and rehabilitation rather than on deterrence through punishment.

The foundations of deterrence theory

The rational person

Beccaria saw as the heart of deterrence theory the assumption of a "rational person" who makes choices and reaches decisions based upon a calculation of risk and reward, punishment and pleasure. It is the game that gamblers play on a regular basis: How much risk is involved? How much is the potential reward? If the rewards outweigh the risks, then the person is likely to choose to behave in a certain way. A more general area of research that addresses these issues involves *rational choice theory* (Matsueda et al., 2006).[2]

Clearly, deterrence theory is strongly grounded in choice, and the choice is considered rational and reasonable to the decision maker based upon all available information at the time, or what some economists call the *information set*. The fundamental premise of deterrence theory is that we all choose; that the choices are rational based upon our interpretation of pleasure and pain generated by the situation we are confronted with and the information available to us; and that the decisions are ours to make. Consistent with accepted principles of the criminal and juvenile law, because actors have decided to commit acts they are blameworthy or culpable and deserve punishment.

However, theorists have also noted that the way people judge the costs and benefits of their behaviors is affected by their past experiences and the experiences of others. Suppose that a young person has been caught in the past for trying to shoplift. This may change her calculation of future chances of getting caught shoplifting. Now, suppose she has successfully shoplifted 10 times in the past week. This may create a sense that there is little risk to shoplifting. Similarly, if her two best friends have shoplifted without getting caught, then they may encourage her that the risks are low and the rewards are high. In general, this means that one's judgment of the rewards and risks of delinquent behavior can change over time and is affected by experiences and by one's peers (Matsueda et al., 2006).

Deterrence and punishment

According to deterrence theory the way to prevent future delinquent acts is to adjust the risk (pain) of the act so it outweighs its rewards (pleasure). Generally, deterrence theory has focused on punishment as a way to adjust risk. As the risk of punishment increases to surpass the reward of committing the act, a rational individual will choose not to violate the law. It is through this mechanism of deterrence that delinquency is prevented. In brief, a person is deterred from committing the offense because the risks ("I'll get caught and punished") outweigh the rewards ("I'll get money"; "I'll get back at an enemy").

However, what is meant by the term *punishment?* According to the philosopher Hugo Bedau:

> Punishment under law is *the authorized imposition of deprivations – of freedom or privacy or other goods to which the person otherwise has a right, or the imposition of special burdens – because the person has been found guilty of some criminal violation, typically (though not invariably) involving harm to the innocent* (Bedau, 2003, italics in original).

Observe the careful use of the terms *deprivations* and *special burdens* rather than *pain*. In addition, punishment must be for a violation of rules, it must be directed at a specific offender or offenders, it must be intentionally administered by someone other than the offender, and it must be unwanted on the part of the offender (Newman, 1985). However, for punishment to occur, not only should it satisfy these criteria, but also, according to Beccaria and other scholars, it must have three qualities to be effective as a deterrent: swiftness, certainty, and severity.

Swiftness (celerity)

Swiftness, or celerity, of punishment involves how closely the punishment follows the offense, with more immediate punishments thought to have a greater deterrent effect. Beccaria (1985 [1764], p.55) argued for the promptness of punishment: "The more promptly and the more closely punishment follows upon the commission of a crime the more just and useful it will be." He also contended:

> I have said the promptness of punishment is more useful because when the length of time that passes between the punishment and the misdeed is less, so much the stronger and more lasting in the human mind is the association of these two ideas, crime and punishment (Beccaria, 1985 [1764], p.56).

Certainty

Certainty considers the likelihood of apprehension or the likelihood that punishment attaches for an act. Here, Beccaria argued (1985 [1764], p.58):

> One of the greatest curbs on crimes is not the cruelty of punishments, but their infallibility . . . the certainty of a punishment will always make a stronger impression than the fear of another which is more terrible but combined with the hope of impunity.

Moreover, certainty of apprehension and punishment is more important than either swiftness or severity (see Nagin and Pogarsky, 2001). The wrongdoer must expect punishment for the behavior.

Severity

Beccaria argued that for punishment to be an effective deterrent it must also be severe. However, when considering this final component of effective punishment, he was careful to argue that by severity he did not mean that summary executions for minor violations are an effective deterrent. Rather, by severity Beccaria meant that the punishment must be proportionate to the harm done to society by the offense:

> the purpose can only be to prevent the criminal from inflicting new injuries on its citizens and to deter others from similar acts. Always keeping due proportions, such punishments and such method of inflicting them ought to be chosen, therefore, which will make the strongest and most lasting impression on the minds of men, and inflict the least torment on the body of the criminal. For punishment to attain its end, the evil which it inflicts has only to exceed the advantage derivable from the crime . . . [A]ll beyond this is superfluous and for that reason tyrannical (Beccaria 1985 [1764], pp.42–43).

The end result of deterrence theory is a model that looks roughly like the depiction in Figure 2.1. As portrayed in the diagram, deterrence theory suggests that all that is necessary to prevent delinquency is punishment that is swift, certain, and severe. If these qualities are in place, especially certainty, then delinquency will be held in check.

How to think about deterrence

It is important to realize that deterrence is rather complex. In particular, there are different ways of thinking about deterrence, different methods to determine whether deterrence works, and important questions about whether or not juveniles can be deterred from delinquent behavior in the same way that adults can be deterred from criminal behavior.

What are some types of deterrence?

General deterrence

There are several different ways to categorize *deterrence*. First, there is a distinction between *general* and *specific* deterrence. General deterrence occurs when adolescents contemplating wrongdoing opt not to engage in delinquency because they have seen the consequences of the delinquent act for offenders who have been caught. Suppose that Bryan contemplates breaking into a car to steal a sound-system.

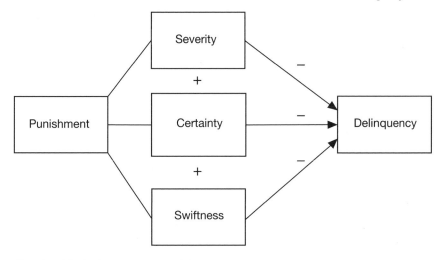

Figure 2.1 The basic deterrence model.

However, during this period of contemplation, the local police department announces a crackdown on theft from vehicles, introduces a no-plea policy for those arrested and charged with larceny from a motor vehicle, and recounts a story of an adolescent recently arrested for such an offense. Bryan, upon hearing the announcement, decides to abandon his crime plan; in the language of deterrence theory Bryan has been generally deterred and a crime has been prevented.

Specific deterrence

Specific deterrence focuses not on preventing delinquent acts in general, but rather on preventing another act from being committed by a particular adolescent. It is targeted at those individuals already involved in delinquency; the objective of specific deterrence is to punish the offender with certainty, severity, and swiftness so that the likelihood of future acts is significantly reduced. Therefore, deterrence theory can be targeted at the general population or it can be targeted at specific offenders. The sentencing structure in New York State, for example, allows for increasing sanctions for repeat offenders even if the offense does not change or the harm done does not increase. Suppose, for example, that Susan is caught in a "buy and bust" operation on the street. She sold a small quantity of crack-cocaine to an undercover operator. This is her first felony arrest so she pleads guilty and receives probation as punishment. A few months later she is caught by police a second time in virtually the same way. However, this time Susan receives a sentence to a secure juvenile institution. Why the increase in severity of the sanction if the act committed and the harm done is identical for both offenses? According to specific deterrence, increasing the sanction the second time is reasonable because obviously the pain of probation was not sufficient to outweigh the pleasure[3] derived from selling crack-cocaine. Therefore, it is necessary to increase the punishment in an attempt to deter future drug-dealing behaviors. If, after the period of incarceration, Susan does not go back to selling cocaine then we assume that she has been specifically deterred from such behavior. On the other hand, what if Susan shifts from selling crack-cocaine to marijuana or to shoplifting? Has she been deterred?

Absolute and restrictive deterrence

Another issue involves the notion of absolute versus restrictive deterrence (Nagin and Paternoster, 1991). In general, it is safe to argue that selling crack-cocaine is a more serious crime than selling marijuana. Suppose that, after a second conviction, Susan shifts away from selling crack-cocaine and instead sells marijuana, which is far less profitable, but far less serious in terms of the presumed "harm" it does to society. Some argue that deterrence has failed in this case as Susan is still involved in street-level drug sales, but others argue that deterrence has succeeded because she no longer sells crack-cocaine.

Absolute deterrence focuses on an "all or nothing" proposition, and only if Susan completely stops selling drugs is deterrence theory supported. Those who embrace, though, the idea of restrictive deterrence would probably celebrate Susan's shift in behavior from a more serious to a less serious offense. If it were not for the punishment for selling crack-cocaine, Susan would continue to sell a dangerous drug. Therefore, Susan has been deterred. Rather than absolute, the deterrence has been restrictive.

Does this example illustrate a success or a failure for deterrence theory? There are no simple answers to this question since people can reasonably disagree on which is preferable, although most would probably choose absolute deterrence as the most desirable goal.

Objective and subjective deterrence

Yet another complexity is whether the risk of punishment in terms of certainty, severity, and swiftness should be objective (what it is in reality) or subjective (what the individual perceives it to be). Much of the research on deterrence theory during the mid-twentieth century focused on objective deterrence (Nagin [1998] provides a review of this research); however, most contemporary research considers what people perceive as risky versus what is actually risky. For example, what is more risky in terms of likelihood of death: flying in an airplane to Miami or driving a car to Miami? Actually, driving is far more dangerous (objective risk), but many people perceive flying to be more dangerous (subjective risk). So, when we consider risk of punishment from the justice system should we consider what juveniles perceive the risk of punishment to be, what the actual risk of punishment is, or both? Similarly, there are different views of what is pleasurable or rewarding.

Research on deterrence and delinquency

Three research strategies have been implemented to ascertain the effects of deterrence on adolescents. The first strategy focuses on research that uses pre-test →

intervention → post-test studies. In this type of study there is a pre-intervention assessment of juvenile delinquency, an intervention, and then a post-intervention assessment to ascertain what proportion of study subjects has stopped offending and was presumably deterred. The second strategy is to assess whether or not deterrence works for adolescents the same way it is supposed to work for adults. This strategy considers the effects, if any, of subjective deterrence on a sample of adolescents to see if their perceptions of risk predict their involvement in delinquency. In these studies, deterrence theory is thought to be supported if, for example, a high perceived risk of apprehension is accompanied by less delinquent behavior. The final strategy is to compare juvenile justice and criminal justice processing. The criminal justice system is generally considered more punitive than the juvenile justice system; thus, if deterrence operates as expected one would see a substantial drop-off in delinquent behavior as the jurisdiction shifts from juvenile to criminal (general deterrence) and, among those enmeshed in the system, one would expect to see lower rates of repeat offending for those in the criminal justice system than those who remain in the juvenile justice system (Levitt, 1998).

Pre-test → intervention → post-test

Although there are several examples of this type of research, we highlight only two studies: *Scared Straight!* and the *Pulling Levers Program*. *Scared Straight!* was a program that began in New Jersey and became quite popular. Many jurisdictions around the United States and in other nations implemented *Scared Straight!* programs with the goal of deterring petty juvenile offenders from a life of crime. There are several good websites with *Scared Straight!*-like themes, and there are also several documentaries based on the original *Scared Straight!* program at Rahway State Prison (now called East Jersey State Prison).

The *Scared Straight!* program takes "at-risk" adolescents who have had contact with the juvenile justice system and sends them on a "field trip" to a maximum security prison to meet with a group of inmates doing 25 years to life for violent crimes. During their "field trip" the adolescents are processed into the prison by gruff guards, walk through the cell blocks where they are taunted by inmates behind bars, and spend time with a group of "lifers." The lifers tell them about life on the inside; they swear, they yell, they intimidate. The developers of *Scared Straight!* envisioned a program so forceful, so compelling, and so frightening that the young offenders would be deterred from subsequent offending. Several documentaries about the program claimed that it was an unqualified success. The most recent, *Scared Straight! 20 Years Later* (1999), revisits the original participants in the 1978 documentary to see how they are doing. All are living conventional lives, with the exception of a few who developed into serious, chronic offenders. Based upon these accounts, it is difficult to believe that *Scared Straight!* is anything but an impressive success that needs to be widely implemented.

However, Finckenauer (1982; Finckenauer and Gavin, 1999) and Petrosino and colleagues (2000) have argued that scientific evidence does not support the claim that *Scared Straight!* is an effective program. In an exhaustive review of research addressing these programs, Petrosino and colleagues (2000) discovered that not only did it appear that *Scared Straight!* had not deterred subsequent involvement in delinquency and crime, but the results from several studies indicated that groups exposed to the "lifers" had higher offending rates and were involved in more severe offenses after the program than groups of young people that had not gone through the program. These researchers concluded that, even when intentions are noble, programs may have unintended consequences and may do more harm than good.

The second pre-test → intervention → post-test program is referred to as *Pulling Levers* (Braga et al., 2001). This program began in response to the substantial number of homicides committed by juveniles in Boston, MA. Kennedy and colleagues (1996) discovered that most of the juvenile homicides were located in specific areas of Boston and many, though not all, juvenile homicide victims and offenders were gang members. A large inter-agency working group considered these findings and began to think about strategies to decrease juvenile homicides. The working group believed that they would not "be able to prevent gang violence unless gang members believe that unpleasant consequences will follow on violence and gun use, and [that they] choose to change their behavior" (Kennedy et al., 1996, p.166). So, the group devised a strategy of zero-tolerance toward youth gang violence. The basic message was something like this:

- We know that you are a gang member and we are watching you and all of your peers.
- If there is a homicide or a shooting that is attributable to one of your gang members we will come down hard on the gang as a whole and not just the shooter.
- Therefore, if one of your members is responsible for a shooting we will crack down in your area of operation. We will make arrests for minor transgressions. We will conduct home searches of probationers and parolees; we will revoke any probationer or parolee in violation of his conditions of release. We will prosecute those arrested on gun and drug charges in federal courts and we will push for maximum penalties. We will disrupt the street-level drug trade, any outstanding warrants will be executed, and everyone in the gang will be punished for the "bad" behavior of one.
- These actions will be swift, certain, and severe.

The message was sent to the gangs and then the working group waited for the next juvenile homicides to occur. One occurred in 1996 and a gang known as the Intervale Posse was apparently responsible. The crackdown began and 20 Intervale members were arrested after an exhaustive nine-month investigation. Ten of the members were prosecuted under federal law, which tends to be more punitive than state law. The working group then sent out another message: "Who's next?" Between 1991 and 1995 the city of Boston experienced about 44 youth homicides per year; after implementation of this deterrence project the number of youth homicides dropped to 15 in 1996. A comparison of youth homicide victimization rates across the major U.S. cities indicated that Boston's reduction was "significantly larger than those in most other American cities at the time" (Braga et al., 2001, p.219).

So how can these discrepant findings between *Scared Straight!* and *Pulling Levers* be understood? Does deterrence directed at certain youth work successfully as indicated in *Pulling Levers* or does deterrence have minimal impact and perhaps even increase the risk of subsequent offending as found in the evaluations of *Scared Straight!*? The answer is not clear and may involve the groups that were targeted and the degree to which the programs were implemented.

Perceptual deterrence among adolescents

A second approach to studying whether deterrence affects delinquent behavior looks at what adolescents perceive the risk of punishment to be and then looks at their delinquent behaviors. If deterrence plays a role in controlling adolescent behavior then one would expect that those adolescents who perceive punishment to be most certain, most swift, and most severe are also least involved in delinquency. Unfortunately, even though there have been dozens of studies of perceptual deterrence (Pratt et al., 2007), few have used adolescent samples.

Nonetheless, in an important study, Nagin and Paternoster (1991) considered whether perceptual deterrence is an effective mechanism among adolescents. They used survey responses from about 1,100 high school students who were followed over a three-year period: tenth, eleventh, and twelfth grades. During each year, the students were asked about their delinquency and their perceived certainty of arrest for theft. The basic model examined in the study is depicted in Figure 2.2.

Nagin and Paternoster (1991) also measured delinquency in two different ways: *prevalence* and *incidence*. The prevalence measure assessed whether or not youths committed any offense in the past year, which was used to judge the presence of an absolute deterrence effect. The incidence measure considered the number of times each student engaged in delinquency in the past year, and therefore was used to ascertain if there is a restrictive deterrent effect.[4] They therefore considered whether perceived risk of arrest at time 1 is an absolute or restrictive deterrent to delinquency at time 2. Their results indicated that those youths who reported

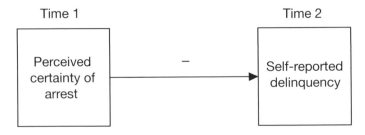

Figure 2.2 Perceived risk and deterrence (based on Nagin and Paternoster, 1991, p.567).

greater perceived certainty of arrest were less involved overall and reduced their offending, thus indicating both an absolute and a restrictive deterrent effect.

More recent studies have attempted to elaborate the role of perceptual deterrence among adolescents by examining factors that might affect these perceptions. Using a large sample of adolescents from across the United States, Pogarsky and colleagues (2005) found, contrary to deterrence theory, that getting arrested did not influence perceptions of certainty and prior offending did not decrease the perceived risks of delinquency. Those who had delinquent friends perceived less certainty than others of getting caught for violating the law. However, those adolescents who had been involved in delinquency *and* reported more moral inhibitions about offending tended to perceive higher risks of future delinquent behavior.

In a similar study, Matsueda and colleagues (2006) determined that adolescents who had been involved in delinquency, but had rarely been questioned or arrested by the police, tended to judge that their risk of getting caught for future offenses is low. On the other hand, those who had been questioned or arrested more frequently were highly likely to think they would get caught for future offending. Over time, youths who judged that they would likely be caught for delinquent acts were substantially less likely to commit delinquent acts. However, perceptual deterrence is not a simple matter of how likely the risks of offending appear to be, but is also affected by beliefs about whether or not delinquent behavior is wrong and whether delinquency enhances a youth's status, and with whom one associates (see also Matthews and Agnew, 2008). In other words, there are many aspects to the perceived risks and rewards of delinquent behavior. Moreover, perceived risks of getting caught are consistently affected by previous experiences. This suggests that evaluations of the risks and rewards of delinquent behavior can change because of previous experiences with rule-breaking and apprehension.

Although these studies suggest that perceived certainty of punishment can deter adolescents in some situations, it remains unclear if this is also the case for severity and swiftness of punishment. A large and sophisticated review of deterrence studies indicated that severity is, at best, only weakly associated with subsequent offending (Pratt et al., 2007). Moreover, a study of college students that compared the three aspects of punishment determined that certainty is the most influential element (Nagin and Pogarsky, 2001). It is important to consider whether or not adolescents are even aware of the particular punishment that may result from their delinquent behavior, however. For deterrence to be effective, presumably there must be knowledge of the specific risks involved in misbehaviors. Yet many youths, especially those who are short-sighted and do not consider the consequences of their actions (see the discussion of impulsivity in Chapter 3 and self-control in Chapter 8), may not be aware of the official sanctions for their behaviors. Thus, as discussed later in the chapter, we may need to change our assumptions about rational decision-making when considering adolescents.

Juvenile justice processing and deterrence

The third strategy used to assess deterrence among adolescents considers whether the justice system itself acts as a deterrent to delinquent behavior. Several studies using this strategy address the effects of *juvenile waiver* (see Redding [2003] for a review of these studies). Juvenile waiver involves the transfer of juvenile offenders from the juvenile to the adult court system. In the two Supreme Court decisions mentioned at the outset of this chapter the defendants were processed through the criminal court rather than the juvenile court; they were treated as adults rather than juveniles. In serious felony cases where the defendant is a juvenile most states have a mechanism in place whereby the juvenile court waives jurisdiction and the defendant is processed through the criminal court. This waiver to criminal court is driven, in part, by deterrence theory. The deterrence argument for waiver is that the juvenile system does not have a sufficiently certain process and it does not have amply severe sanctions to effectively deter some of the most serious juvenile offenders. Therefore, processing serious juvenile offenders through the criminal justice system should be a greater deterrent than processing them through the juvenile justice system.

Fagan (1996) explored whether adolescents processed in criminal court are less likely to reoffend (are more deterred) than those processed in juvenile court. He identified a sample of 15- and 16-year-olds in New York and New Jersey who were charged with either robbery or burglary. The New York State offenders were processed through criminal court whereas the New Jersey offenders were processed through juvenile court. In considering certainty Fagan compared the proportion of those found guilty in New York with the proportion of those found guilty in New Jersey. If deterrence is more likely to be present in the criminal rather than the juvenile system one would anticipate higher conviction rates in criminal court. Interestingly, Fagan found higher convictions rates in criminal court than juvenile court for robbery but not burglary. He also determined that those convicted in criminal court for robbery or burglary are far more likely to be incarcerated than those adjudicated in juvenile court. Therefore, for robbery offenses the criminal justice system appears more certain and more severe, and for burglary the criminal justice system appears only more severe than the juvenile justice system. It stands to reason, then, that youths processed through the adult system should have lower reoffending rates. This was not the case. Those processed through criminal court on robbery charges were *more likely* to be re-arrested and re-incarcerated than those processed through the juvenile system – the exact opposite of what deterrence theory anticipates. Furthermore, no differences in reoffending or re-incarceration were found among those adolescents charged with burglary.

Based on Fagan's (1996) study, it is easy to reach the conclusion that increases in certainty and severity, above and beyond that already present in the juvenile justice system, do not act to further deter subsequent behavior. In fact, in the case of those charged with robbery, increases in certainty and severity may intensify rather than deter the behavior. This is one of the arguments made by labeling theorists (see Chapter 9). Nonetheless, Fagan's study did not address swiftness of punishment, a key component of theories of deterrence.

In contrast, Levitt (1998, p.1159) determined that "harsher punishments for juveniles (within the juvenile justice system) are strongly associated with lower rates of juvenile offending." He reached this conclusion after comparing the proportion of juveniles in custody with the juvenile crime rate over time and across jurisdictions. As juvenile custody rates increase, juvenile crime rates decrease. Levitt (1998) took the analysis one step further and looked at age groups over time to see if as adolescents become adults in the eyes of the law their criminal involvement decreases. He found that jurisdictions that have the most severe criminal sanctions relative to juvenile sanctions see significant reductions in crime as groups of adolescents move into adulthood. However, in jurisdictions where criminal justice sanctions are more lenient relative to juvenile justice sanctions, the transition from adolescence to adulthood results in more rather than less crime. Implied by Levitt's research is that relative severity of sanctions in the juvenile justice system, followed by sanctions that are at least as severe in the criminal justice system, maximizes the overall deterrent effect, at least in the short term. Similar results have been found when researchers have examined arrest rather than custody: When the rate of arrests for violent crimes increases, the number of juvenile offenses such as drug dealing and assault tend to decrease, thus suggesting a general deterrent effect (Mocan and Rees, 2005).

Thus, there is mixed evidence from studies that compare the deterrent effect of the juvenile justice and criminal justice systems. Perceived certainty of punishment may operate consistently as a perceptual deterrent, although it is also affected by several factors. However, the effects of objective certainty and severity are less consistent. Yet there remains a fundamental issue that deterrence theorists must address: Can the assumption of the rational actor be applied to juvenile offenders? The next section highlights two broad lines of research that directly examine this issue: research on adolescent brain development and functioning, and adolescent decision-making in a psychosocial context.

The promises and limitations of deterrence theory

The evidence discussed thus far suggests that perceived certainty of apprehension and punishment appears to decrease subsequent involvement in delinquency. Jurisdictions with more severe penalties for adults relative to adolescents may also provide a general deterrent effect. However, recent research calls into question the overall usefulness of deterrence theory for adolescents.

At the start of this chapter we discussed two Supreme Court decisions that reached opposite conclusions about the role of deterrence among adolescents. When thinking about the applicability of deterrence for adolescents the issue of culpability or responsibility based on an argument of diminished capacity comes to the forefront. Recall that for punishment to operate as a deterrent the person being targeted for punishment must be deserving of punishment. If the person does not deserve punishment then not only is it unjust, it is also unlikely to deter. Moreover, deterrence theory assumes that people are aware of the consequences and risks of their behaviors. This raises an important distinction between *deterrence* and *deterrability*. Deterrability refers to a potential offender's ability to perform the rational calculations that are part of the deterrence process (Jacobs, 2010; Pogarsky, 2002). However, some offenders may not have the capacity for full-blown calculations of risks and rewards. This is especially the case for juvenile offenders, as we shall learn in this section.

It is also important to remember that the bedrock of the juvenile justice system embraces a philosophical and legal orientation that adolescents and adults are not equivalent in the eyes of the law. As a result, the level of procedural protections need not be as great for adolescents as for adults; yet the juvenile system should be less punitive than the adult system. Thus, what are some of the contemporary research findings that might be used to inform our thinking about juvenile culpability, deterrence, and the promise of punitiveness? Studies of the adolescent brain and psychological studies of adolescent decision-making[5] are especially relevant to our evaluation of deterrence theory.

Adolescent brain research

A rapidly growing research area involves the analysis of brain development in humans. Using magnetic resonance imaging (MRI) and other modern scanning techniques, researchers are finding that the frontal lobe of the human brain continues developing through the early twenties (Segalowitz and Davies, 2004). The frontal lobe is important because it helps control reasoning and decision-making (see Chapter 3). This area of the brain develops last, yet holds the "Chief Executive Officer" of our body, the prefrontal cortex, which is responsible for planning skills; the ability to calculate consequences, control impulses, and put thoughts in order; and the ability to think abstractly. However, if this area of the brain does not fully develop until one reaches at least 20 years old, then it stands to reason that adolescents are not fully capable of adult-like decision-making. The implications of this finding for the effectiveness of deterrence among adolescents are important.

Other researchers have found that the childhood brain has an overabundance of "gray matter" that is part of a developmental process referred to as "pruning" (Giedd, 2008). During this process, the brain gets rid of much of the gray matter to allow growth of "white matter." These changes from gray to white matter occur for most people well into their twenties, and white matter is known to help thinking processes and allow the brain to work more effectively.

Researchers have also found that brain functioning in terms of cognitive development continues to change from adolescence to adulthood. In particular, Luna and colleagues (2004, p.1366) concluded, "voluntary/cognitive control of behavior continues to develop through adolescence. These cognitive processes develop in mostly independent streams, though there was a modest, yet significant interrelationship among them."

Current research into brain structure and functioning indicates that even though the brain is changing it does not achieve adult-like performance until well after adolescence (Casey et al., 2008). The implication for deterrence theory is that if adolescents are not able to reason in a fashion that is functionally equivalent to adults then it is unfair to hold adolescents as culpable or responsible as adults. If

adolescents are less culpable than adults, then any sanction that attaches to adolescent behavior should be less severe than any sanction that attaches for similar
adult behavior. Moreover, research on deterrence among adolescents should also
consider this research. If adolescents do not have the same decision-making or
perceptual processes as adults, then the risk–benefit calculations of adolescents
should be considered distinct from those of adults.

These points about brain development do not mean that deterrence has no role
to play among adolescents or that criminal responsibility does not apply to young
people. Rather, it suggests that the way we think about and study deterrence needs
to be sensitive to differences in neurological development and functioning among
adolescents and adults.

Adolescent decision-making

Although research has explored the role of brain functioning in decision-making,
social and behavioral scientists as well as legal scholars have also considered
decision-making in terms of the socio-environmental context experienced by
adolescents. Scott (2000; Scott and Grisso, 2005) has summarized much of the
research in developmental psychology pertaining to adolescent decision-making
and involvement in delinquent behavior. She argued that studies show that adolescent judgment is immature and developing. Three issues apparently affect
adolescent judgment to a much greater extent than adult judgment: peer influences, the tendency to under-assess actual risk while also exhibiting a preference
for risk-taking, and a tendency to give more weight to short-term rather than
long-term consequences (Scott and Grisso, 2005).

Since these three issues, and perhaps others, make adolescent and adult
decision-making qualitatively different, deterrence theory should be modified to
consider how each affects delinquent behavior. We have already learned about
some research that shows that there are peer influences on perceptions of risk
(Pogarsky et al., 2005). Other research has found that adolescents tend to be relatively short-sighted and focused more on maximizing immediate pleasure than
adults (Steinberg, 2004; Reyna and Farley, 2006). In the end, then, deterrence
theory presents a maze of complexity. Furthermore, the empirical literature
directly focused on the effectiveness of deterrence among adolescents is incomplete and much work needs to be done before it becomes clear whether – or how
– adolescents can be deterred from delinquent behavior. Nevertheless, there is
some indication that certain things may deter adolescents better than others.

Policy implications of deterrence theory

Most of the research on deterrence among adolescents has focused on clarifying the role of punishment as a strategy to alter behavior. However, it is obvious
that how punishment is used and how people learn to react to it begins in early
life as parents discipline children. A common finding in studies of delinquency is
that the parents of offenders do not discipline their children adequately. Rather
than relying on consistent discipline strategies that are not too harsh and that

focus on specific wrongful behaviors, the parents of delinquent children often use callous and inconsistent punishment styles (Milner, 2000; see also Chapter 7). Thus, programs designed to teach parents appropriate forms of discipline should be effective at reducing future delinquent behavior. However, teaching how to discipline children is only part of the most effective approaches. The family-based programs that have shown the most reduction in later offending also teach parents to reinforce their children's prosocial behaviors, supervise them better, and communicate with them in a more effective manner (Piquero et al., 2009).

Although addressing the certainty, severity, and swiftness of punishment may offer some additional guidelines for policy development, perhaps a more fruitful approach involves finding ways to reduce the potential rewards and increase the potential risks of engaging in juvenile delinquency. Some observers argue that designing programs that will modify the opportunities to engage in delinquency will be more effective than focusing on punishing juveniles after they have already committed a delinquent act. Since many of those caught for the first time have already been involved in delinquent activities for a substantial period, specific forms of deterrence may come too late.

As an example of a program that was designed to increase the costs and drive down the benefits of offending, consider the Los Angeles Police Department's (LAPD) Operation Cul-de-Sac. It was designed in response to a disproportionate number of drive-by shootings that had occurred in a particular neighborhood. Based on an evaluation of the neighborhood, it appeared that it had a street structure that provided easy access into and easy escape routes from the area. Therefore, drive-by shootings were pretty simple to carry out. Presumably, this made the effort more rewarding, but also less risky. The LAPD slightly modified the street structure in this neighborhood, thereby increasing the difficulty of getting out of the area quickly, which is an obvious goal of those involved in drive-by shootings. Even though this did not increase direct punishment of the perpetrators, the risk of getting caught increased because of a little thought and planning. All the LAPD did was to install concrete blockades on alternating streets. Some of the streets were turned into cul-de-sacs, whereas others were left open to through traffic. Figure 2.3 provides a diagram of the modified street structure.

Lasley (1995) examined the number of drive-by shootings during the intervention. In the community where Operation Cul-de-Sac was implemented there was a dramatic drop in homicides compared with a similar area without the intervention. Thus, without increasing the penalties for offenders and without making more arrests, the LAPD was able to significantly reduce shootings by making the task just a little more difficult to carry out. It therefore seems that one fruitful policy avenue for deterrence theory is to develop strategies that diminish the reward and increase the risk rather than increase direct punishments for delinquents.

Conclusions

There is promising research on deterrence and delinquency. Although conclusions are tentative, it does appear that increasing the perceived certainty of punishment can reduce adolescent offending. Although this may be more of a general than

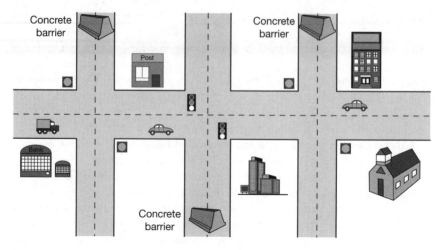

Figure 2.3 Layout of street modifications from Operation Cul-de-Sac.

a specific deterrent effect, it does seem to exist. However, other factors, including some that are part of other theories discussed in later chapters, are more powerful predictors of delinquency. For example, there is likely to be an important relationship between how adolescents evaluate the risks of delinquency and what they believe about delinquency. Adolescents who have internalized beliefs – or have moral inhibitions – that delinquency is wrong also may see such behaviors as more risky. Coupled with research that has shown the effectiveness of programs designed to teach parents to use appropriate punishment and discipline styles, there may be ways to prevent delinquency from occurring in the first place.

3   Biological theories of delinquency

Prologue

Raymond's mother, Sylvia, was raised in a poor neighborhood. When she was 13 years old the city condemned the apartment building she lived in because it was old and filled with lead-based paint. Sylvia became pregnant with Raymond when she was 16. Raymond's father, Gus, was 22 years old and had been in and out of juvenile detention centers for much of his teen years. He left the city soon after Raymond was born and was convicted of murder in California. Sylvia had used cigarettes and marijuana since she was 14, and continued to smoke during most of her pregnancy.

Raymond was born prematurely. He was underweight, but was also aggressive and temperamental. Sylvia tried to discipline him with spankings (often severe), but Raymond didn't seem to care. He got into many fights in school and around the neighborhood. At age 12, he was picked up by the police for punching an elderly woman in the face and stealing her purse. Mental health experts who interviewed Raymond testified that he had no "impulse control." A brain scan revealed that he had what the doctor called "an abnormality in his prefrontal cortex." A juvenile court judge overseeing one of Raymond's many court appearances ordered him to attend therapy sessions to learn to control his temper. By the time he was 20 years old Raymond had a long record of arrests and was serving time in a state prison for attempted murder.

Introduction

During much of the twentieth century, biological research on human behavior was cast in a negative light, especially after the discovery that scientists in Nazi Germany conducted studies designed to "purify" what they considered superior genetic strains. Following their atrocities, scholars favored social explanations of delinquent behavior; research on biological or physiological influences was viewed with suspicion. Nonetheless, the last 15–20 years have seen an explosion of research on biological influences on delinquency. The main motivation for this research is the impressive growth of knowledge about human genetics, brain functioning, and the biochemistry of the human organism.

In this chapter, we shall begin by briefly reviewing some nineteenth- and early twentieth-century research on physiological influences on crime and delinquency. By today's standards, this research was crude and led to some humorous, but also disturbing, conclusions about the differences between offenders and non-offenders. We shall then fast-forward to contemporary physiological and genetic research. This includes a discussion of heredity and genetics, physiological functioning, and environmental risk factors. As we shall learn, studies of the heredity of behavior suggest that there are sets of genes, discoverable only through sophisticated molecular tests, that may be passed from generation to generation and appear to affect various physiological processes that are linked to delinquent and antisocial behavior.

The most important point about this research, though, is its consistent emphasis on the complex interplay between biological and environmental influences on behavior. Biological research on human behavior has often been twisted into a competition identified by the phrase *nature versus nurture* (or biological/genetic factors vs. environmental/socialization factors). In reality, as a vast majority of researchers emphasize, the key is to study the complementary roles of nature *and* nurture (Plomin and Asbury, 2005). Genetic and physiological characteristics interact with complex social environments – in brief, how we are nurtured – to affect behavior, whether it is delinquent or law-abiding. Moreover, the way people react in certain situations, such as when they feel threatened, is influenced by both genetic predispositions and socialization experiences. Hence, contemporary research in this area is often referred to as *biosocial* or *biobehavioral* (Fishbein, 2001; Raine, 2002).

Early research on physiological and anatomical factors affecting crime and delinquency

The nineteenth century saw the emergence of three philosophical and scientific modes of thought that influenced research on human behavior. First, the French philosopher August Comte (2007 [1848]) argued that human behavior was governed by strict laws much like the physical laws of motion described by Sir Isaac Newton. These laws could be discovered by careful observation of human behavior and scientific experimentation. By understanding them, early social scientists thought they could eventually influence human behavior and eliminate social ills. Second, German materialists such as Ernst Haeckel and Friedrich Engels contended that concepts such as the mind or the soul were mere manifestations of physical matter. This view claimed there were no spiritual or metaphysical influences on human behavior; morality and intelligence originated in humans, not in anything beyond them. Third, Charles Darwin's (1871) theory of evolution asserted that natural selection resulted in contemporary animal species, including humans, which had successfully adapted to changing environmental conditions. Thus, there was little need to resort to immaterial explanations of the behavior of animals. It was the goal of scientists, then, to discover natural laws that governed evolution and human behavior (Gibson, 2002).

Motivated by these scientific themes, an Italian medical doctor, Cesare Lombroso, formulated the best-known nineteenth-century theories about what caused criminal behavior (Wolfgang, 1972). His observations of thousands of soldiers, mentally ill patients, and prisoners inspired his theory of *atavism*: criminals were an evolutionary throwback to a more primitive form of human being. He saw such people as "'savages living in the middle of flourishing European civilization,' identifiable by their physical and moral anomalies" (Gibson, 2002, p.25; citing Lombroso, 1876, p.108). Some of the anatomical characteristics of atavists included excessively large or small skulls, thick cranial bones, protruding ears, cleft palates, receding chins, and large jaws. Moreover, Lombroso thought of juvenile delinquents as atavistic. In his view, children were born with an innate drive toward criminal behavior and tended to be cruel, angry, and impulsive; all traits that they had to grow out of as they became adults.

Although he initially thought that atavists made up the bulk of criminals, Lombroso later revised his views to consider several biological and social factors that affected criminal behavior. For example, his famous treatise on crime, *L'Uomo delinquente* (Criminal Man), went through five editions from 1876 to 1897. The first edition emphasized the anatomical differences listed earlier. Later editions, as well as his book *Crime: Its Causes and Remedies* (Lombroso, 1912), though, discussed other factors that caused criminal and delinquent behavior, such as a lack of a moral sense, drunkenness, poverty, immigration, climatological conditions, urban congestion, and even food prices. He also categorized criminals not just as atavists (or *born criminals*, as his student Enrico Ferri called them), but also as epileptics, insane criminals, and occasional criminals. Occasional criminals included "those . . . almost drawn into [crime]" (Lombroso, 1912, p.376), usually because they were protecting another person. They also included what Lombroso termed *criminaloids*. These people had a trace of degeneracy, but not as much as the born criminals. They were motivated to crime and delinquency through environmental factors or opportunities to commit offenses.

Lombroso came to believe that epileptics comprised the largest group of offenders, with born criminals somewhere in the middle. Figure 3.1 is a graph from the fifth edition of *L'Uomo delinquente* that shows Lombroso's presumed distribution of offender types. Notice that he used the term *epileptoids* to characterize a trait underlying all criminals, but he thought that various types of criminals existed. All, with the exception of some occasional criminals and those motivated by passion, had some physiological or evolutionary defect traced, Lombroso believed, to an underlying form of epilepsy.

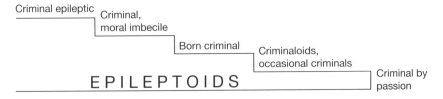

Figure 3.1 Lombroso's classification of criminals. Adapted from Lombroso (1897, p.60).

Although Lombroso focused mainly on adults, others used his ideas to explain delinquency. For example, George E. Dawson, an American professor of psychology, argued that delinquents were degenerate. He also studied anatomical differences among adolescents. In comparing three groups – boys from a reform school, girls from a reform school, and public school children – Dawson (1896) found that, compared with public school students, delinquents were shorter, heavier, had broader and shorter faces, and had more deformed palates. A disproportionate number of delinquent boys had protruding or asymmetrical ears. He concluded that delinquents were an example of imperfectly developed human beings.

Although Lombroso's ideas about anatomical differences between criminals and non-criminals were widely influential, there were also numerous critics. Charles Goring (1913) provided perhaps the most convincing refutation of Lombroso's concept of atavism. He collected meticulous data from 3,000 English convicts and from comparison groups comprising college students, military men, and hospital patients. He concluded that criminals and non-criminals are not physically different: *"no evidence has emerged confirming the existence of a physical criminal type, such as Lombroso and his disciples have described . . .* Our inevitable conclusion must be that *there is no such thing as a criminal physical type"* (Goring, 1913, p.173, italics in original). The only physical differences he detected were that criminals were slightly shorter and lighter than others. However, Goring explained these differences in terms of physical fitness (less physically fit criminals are more likely to be caught) and heredity: Convicted criminals are shorter and they have sons who inherit their short stature. According to Goring, "from these facts the conclusion seems inevitable that the genesis of crime, and the production of criminals, must be influenced by heredity" (Goring, 1913, p.372). He used the term *criminal diathesis* to describe the heritable abnormalities associated with criminal behavior, such as feeblemindedness, alcoholism, epilepsy, and being ill-tempered, and how these led to increased delinquent and criminal behavior across generations.

After Goring's study revealed only minimal anatomical differences between criminals and non-criminals, attempts to study anatomical correlates of crime and delinquency became almost non-existent. Of course, we should recognize that Goring's work also supported biological explanations since he concluded that hereditary explanations were at the core of criminal behavior. Therefore, Goring's research, like the research of Lombroso, Dawson, and others, fed the growing eugenics movement that sought the "elimination" of "degenerate" people, whether they were delinquents, criminals, or the mentally ill (Beirne, 1988).

In the United States, research on anatomy and crime was resurrected by Earnest Albert Hooton's (1939) massive study of more than 17,000 jail, prison, and reformatory inmates (including several hundred 15- to 19-year-olds); patients in mental hospitals; and "civilians" from across the United States. Hooton pointed out that Lombroso's research methods may have been flawed, but there was no evidence that disproved his main conclusion that there were physiological differences between criminals and non-criminals. He found, for example, that criminals and delinquents had deficiencies in height, weight, head circumference, and chest breadth; thinner beards and thicker head hair; straighter hair; low and sloping foreheads; small ears with a tendency toward a rolled helix (the curved fold on the middle part of the ear); and stooped shoulders. He concluded that:

> Criminals are organically inferior. Crime is the resultant of the impact of environment upon low grade human organisms. It follows that the elimination of crime can be effected only by the extirpation of the physically, mentally, and morally unfit, or by their complete segregation in a socially aseptic environment (Hooton, 1939, p.309).

This chilling conclusion was not unusual in the early decades of the twentieth century; it fitted well within the burgeoning eugenics movement, which argued that physical and mental "degenerates" should be prevented from having children, either through involuntary custody in state-run asylums or through mandatory sterilization. Obviously his conclusions were criticized, and these criticisms, as well as the atrocities carried out in Nazi Germany under the banner of eugenics, led most scholars to eventually reject Hooton's findings.

Body types

Another important early study of anatomical differences was conducted by the psychologist William Sheldon (1949). He began his explanation of these differences by focusing on the role played by three layers of embryonic tissue: The *endoderm* produces the digestive system; the *ectoderm* produces the skin and nervous system; and the *mesoderm* produces the bones, tendons, and muscles. During normal growth, according to Sheldon's understanding of fetal development, these three layers are roughly proportional. However, for some, there can be imbalances, with one system developing more than the others. When this occurs, it leads to particular body types and temperamental and personality problems. Table 3.1 provides a brief description of Sheldon's categories. Figure 3.2 shows examples of them.

Sheldon used three numbers, ranging from 1 to 7, to characterize adolescent

Table 3.1 Sheldon's body types and associated temperaments

Body type	Temperament
Endomorph: Tendency to be fat and round; has small bones and smooth skin; the head is large and spherical.	Viscerotonia: Enjoys comfort and luxury items; likes to eat; is lazy but extroverted.
Ectomorph: Tendency to be frail, skinny, and gangly; has droopy shoulders, small bones, and little body mass. The fingers, toes, and neck are long.	Cerebrotonia: Introverted, with poor health and prone to fatigue; tends to avoid crowds, but can be stealthy; sensitive to pain.
Mesomorph: Tendency to be large, strong, and muscular; has thick bones and a heavy chest, with relatively narrow hips. The skin is thick and coarse.	Somatotonia: Tends to be active, dynamic, assertive, and forceful; risk-taker; is more aggressive than the other two types.

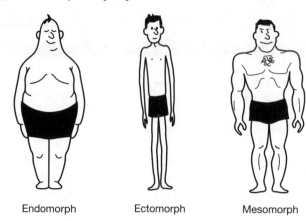

Endomorph   Ectomorph   Mesomorph

Figure 3.2 Sheldon's three body types.

body types. For example, an adolescent with a score of 1–6–2 was identified as an ectomorph, and therefore expected to be skinny and frail looking, but also introverted and sickly. In a study of 200 institutionalized boys, Sheldon found that they had a tendency toward mesomorphy. In an earlier study of 200 college students, he found the average somatotype to be much more prone to ectomorphy, although the distribution was quite close to a balance among the three types. Hence, Sheldon concluded that delinquent boys were more likely to be mesomorphs and, consistent with his view of temperament, aggressive risk-takers. A follow-up study published in 1982 confirmed most of Sheldon's findings, with mesomorphs (and those low on ectomorphy) dominating delinquent and criminal groups (Hartl et al., 1982).

One of Earnest Hooton's students, Sheldon Glueck, and his wife, Eleanor Glueck, sought to expand Sheldon's research on delinquency. In 1940, they began to collect detailed information from 500 boys who had been committed to two correctional institutions in Massachusetts. They matched case by case the 500 "delinquent boys" to 500 boys from Boston public schools on the following characteristics: age, race/ethnicity, neighborhood, and measured intelligence (Glueck and Glueck, 1950). The results of their research revealed numerous social and psychological differences, but they also found differences by body type. The Gluecks (Glueck and Glueck, 1956) determined that 60.1 percent of delinquents and 30.7 percent of non-delinquents were classified as mesomorphs; 14.4 percent of delinquents and 39.6 percent of non-delinquents were classified as ectomorphs. They also proposed that mesomorphs had traits more suitable to delinquent behavior, such as "physical strength, energy, insensitivity, [and] the tendency to express tensions and frustrations in action" (Glueck and Glueck, 1956, p.226). The Gluecks argued that mesomorphic adolescents are more prone to delinquent conduct when these are coupled with temperamental traits such as emotional instability, adventurousness, and a lack of submissiveness. Figure 3.3 provides one of their proposed pathways to delinquency among mesomorphs.

Figure 3.3 Mesomorphy, temperament, and delinquency.

Follow-up research by Sampson and Laub (1997a) supported the Gluecks' finding, but only when delinquency is measured through official records. They found that *extraversion* (the tendency to have one's interests directed predominately towards things outside the self) explained the association between mesomorphy and unofficial delinquency (self-reports and parent-reports), although it did not explain the association with official delinquency. Hence, it is likely that mesomorphy is associated more with how officials, such as the police or truant officers, perceive adolescents than with any true effect of body build on behavior. Mesomorphs, especially those who are extraverted or aggressive, may be perceived as more dangerous and in greater need of state supervision than other adolescents.

Evaluating the early studies of physiology and delinquency

We should be highly skeptical of much of the early research on physiological predictors of delinquency. Almost all of these studies relied on institutionalized adolescents (mostly boys) to identify delinquents. Yet, as demonstrated by Sampson and Laub's follow-up research using the Gluecks' data, physical distinctions tend to show differences only when comparing institutionalized adolescents to noninstitutionalized adolescents. Many, if not most, youths engaged in delinquency are not placed in correctional institutions or mental hospitals, and there are many reasons (some of which have little to do with their behaviors) why only some are identified and institutionalized. Recall from Chapter 1 that official bias, the tendency to disproportionately arrest or institutionalize certain adolescents based on something other than their law-violating behavior, can affect the results of research studies. Therefore, any research – whether biological or environmental – that purports to show differences between delinquents and non-delinquents must first address the definition of who is a delinquent and how they are identified.

Contemporary research on biological factors and delinquency

Minor physical anomalies

One type of contemporary research that addresses anatomical differences examines what are known as *minor physical anomalies* (MPAs). MPAs are small physical deviations found throughout the body. They are known as *congenital disorders* because they are present at birth. MPAs are usually measured on visible areas of the body such as the hands, head, mouth, and ears. Some examples of MPAs include facial asymmetry, lower ear lobes that are connected to the head, a furrowed tongue,

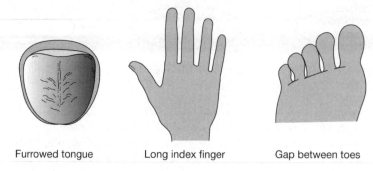

Furrowed tongue   Long index finger   Gap between toes

Figure 3.4 Examples of minor physical anomalies.

an index finger longer than the middle finger, and a large gap between the first and second toe (Waldrop et al., 1978; see Figure 3.4). People with several of these may have developmental problems that originated during the first and second trimesters of pregnancy. They may also indicate a problem with brain development in the womb. There is some evidence that MPAs are linked to specific genes; and they are associated with diagnoses of schizophrenia and other mental health disorders (Gourion et al., 2004).

Recent studies have found that adolescents with more MPAs tend to be aggressive and involved in violent delinquent behavior such as fighting and assault (e.g., Arseneault et al., 2000; Mednick and Kandel, 1988). In particular, Arseneault and colleagues (2000), in a study of 170 adolescent boys living in Montreal, determined that MPAs, especially abnormalities of the mouth (high palate, furrowed tongue), were associated with violent delinquency, but not with non-violent delinquency (theft, drug use).

As mentioned earlier, MPAs may be an indicator for some underlying developmental problem or brain abnormality; and such problems may be especially troublesome for children who grow up in a disadvantaged home environment (Raine et al., 2006). For example, most of the boys in Arseneault and colleagues' study were from poor neighborhoods, which may lead to more difficulties – and consequently more delinquency – for adolescents with developmental problems that underlie MPAs (Mednick and Kandel, 1988).

Puberty and delinquency

Puberty marks the entry into adolescence when children begin to develop secondary sexual characteristics such as body hair and thickening in the chest (boys) and hips (girls); experience changes in sexual organs; develop breasts (girls); menstruate and ovulate (girls); and produce sperm in the testes (boys). It is precipitated by changes in the *hypothalamus* (the area of the brain that regulates many autonomic nervous system functions) that cause the *pituitary gland* (a small gland near the base of the brain that releases hormones that affect growth and reproduction) to release luteinizing and follicle-stimulating hormones that activate the ovaries (girls) or testes (boys) to make sex hormones, such as testosterone and estrogen. The timing of puberty is likely to be affected by one's genetic composition. The average age of onset among girls is about 10.5 years and among boys about 11.5 years. However, some youths experience early or *precocious puberty*.

A subset of precocious girls is at heightened risk of depression, eating disorders, low self-esteem, and hyperactivity. Studies have also shown an association between early onset of menarche (first menstrual period) and delinquency among girls (e.g., Golub et al., 2008). However, this association is limited to girls who attend mixed-sex schools or live in impoverished neighborhoods. Researchers have argued that early-onset menarche leads to interpersonal changes – such as early dating or sexual behavior – that affect delinquency, and that the opportunities to become involved in delinquency are higher in impoverished neighborhoods. Thus, it is unclear whether early-onset puberty causes, in any way, delinquent behavior or is simply a risk factor that exposes girls to peers who are involved in delinquency.

Among boys the association between pubertal timing and delinquency is not well understood. Studies suggest that "off-time" maturing boys (early- or late-onset puberty) are at higher risk of violent behavior, but this seems to be particularly acute for early-onset boys (e.g., Negriff et al., 2008). Felson and Haynie (2002) reported that early pubertal development is associated with more violence, property crimes, drug use, and sexual behavior among seventh- to ninth-grade boys; and that the strength of this association is greater than the association between delinquency and other important predictors (e.g., grades, family problems). However, they also found that physically mature boys have more delinquent friends; and pubertal development is related to delinquency more strongly for boys who are successful academically. Hence, it seems that early-onset puberty or precocious development interacts with various social factors – mostly tied to *opportunities* to commit delinquency – to affect delinquency (Beaver and Wright, 2005). The question of whether pubertal development is also tied to particular genetic susceptibilities to delinquency remains to be seen.

The hereditability of delinquency

The notion that delinquency and criminality are passed down – or inherited – through family lines is not new. Rather, many early researchers believed that, regardless of how various factors affect delinquency, there is something about the physical make-up of delinquents that is inherited. Recall that Goring claimed that "the genesis of crime, and the production of criminals, must be influenced by heredity" (Goring 1913, p.372).

Three strategies have been used most often by contemporary researchers to study the heritability of delinquency: (1) examining parents and children who live together, (2) considering adopted children, and (3) comparing twins. All three types are concerned with the similarity of behaviors among family members. Studies of parent–child criminality that were conducted from roughly 1950 to 1980 reported that about 30–45 percent of delinquents had one or more criminal parents (Ellis,

1982). Of course, it is virtually impossible to separate inherited and environmental factors in this type of study. Are criminal or antisocial parents passing down some physiological trait to their children, or are they simply raising them poorly or providing a model of criminal behavior that is picked up by their children?

Studies of adopted children also suggest that delinquent behavior is passed down along family lines (e.g., DiLalla, 2002) and thus some inherited physiological factor affects this behavior. Yet even the most rigorous studies have problems sorting out environmental and physiological influences on behavior. For example, adoption studies assume there is no selective placement: Children are not placed with parents who are similar in some systematic fashion to their biological parents. Second, researchers assume that biological mothers' prenatal behaviors do not affect the adoptees' behaviors. Yet many studies have found that prenatal exposure to tobacco, lead, and other substances affects fetal and child development and may affect delinquency. Third, several studies indicate that children of antisocial parents elicit more negative responses (e.g., harsh discipline) from adoptive parents than do other children (e.g., Ge et al., 1996; O'Connor et al., 1998). Although this does not discount the possibility of a heritable influence on delinquency, it also suggests that children's behaviors at a young age – and the way adoptive parents react to these behaviors – may contribute to later delinquency.

Finally, many studies indicate a high degree of behavioral similarity among identical or monozygotic twins (e.g., Wright et al., 2008). Since identical twins share virtually identical physiological compositions whereas fraternal (dizygotic) twins do not, comparing whether identical twins are more likely than fraternal twins to be delinquent is presumed to indicate a hereditable link to this type of behavior. However, it is risky to argue that behavioral similarity demonstrates a clear hereditable component to delinquency. Research shows that, on average, identical twins are similar about 84 percent of the time, and fraternal twins are similar about 69 percent of the time (Ishikawa and Raine, 2002). Some observers argue that this illustrates the enduring importance of environmental factors such as family and peer relations.

Moreover, there are two assumptions that affect how we should interpret twin studies: the *equal environments assumption* and the *unbiased by appearance* assumption (Plomin et al., 2000). The equal environments assumption points out that identical twins tend to be dressed alike and they spend more time together. This may explain the greater similarity on delinquency, but only if the way they are treated or their similar social environment also affects delinquency. There is some evidence that, because delinquency is often a shared activity and identical twins share more social experiences, we may be witnessing a bias toward finding a higher similarity rate for identical twins. Again, this points to the complex dynamic of nature and nurture (Rowe, 2002).

The unbiased by appearance assumption notes that, in addition to appearance, identical twins share many more characteristics than fraternal twins. For example, identical twins are more likely than fraternal twins to experience similar parenting styles, have low self-control (see Chapter 8), and associate with similar friends who are delinquent (Wright et al., 2008). Identical twins may also be treated differently from fraternal twins by family members and other adults. Several studies have attempted to measure these shared environmental characteristics (e.g., Rowe, 1986). However, there are many subtle ways that children are treated by parents that affect their behaviors. It is difficult, even with the most careful research design, to measure all of these subtle interactions.

Genetics and delinquency

Recent studies have relied on genetic testing to understand what specific biological characteristics family members share that might contribute to delinquent and antisocial behavior. This approach is particularly promising because it may determine if and how delinquent, criminal, or other behaviors are inherited. *Genetics* is a branch of biology that studies how information encoded in genes affects the development and functioning of organisms. *Genes* are a specific sequence of material in *DNA* or *RNA*. There are about 25,000 genes in the human body. DNA (deoxyribonucleic acid) is the building block of most organisms, including humans. It is a relatively large, complex molecule that is composed of four nucleotides: cytosine (C), thymine (T), adenine (A), and guanine (G). They form base pairs such as AT and GC that connect two strands of the DNA molecule in a twisting, spiral fashion. (This is why DNA is often referred to as a *double helix*; see Figure 3.5.) The ordering of these nucleotides is preserved from generation to generation. DNA is organized into dense structures called *chromosomes*, which are part of every cell in the human body.

There are 22 pairs of chromosomes and two sex chromosomes in humans. During human reproduction, the fertilized egg includes 23 chromosomes from the woman's egg cell and 23 from the man's sperm. These chromosomes carry specific sequences of DNA and thus specific sequences of genes from both parents. In research on *behavioral genetics*, or the study of genetic influences on human behavior, it is important to distinguish two types of genes: *fixed* or *structural* genes and *polymorphic* genes (Ishikawa and Raine, 2002). Structural genes are shared by

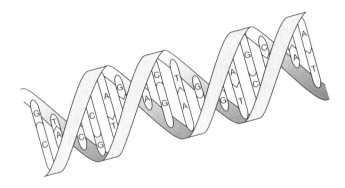

Figure 3.5 The DNA molecule.

almost all humans and determine their basic physiological structure. Polymorphic genes are different across humans and determine their unique characteristics (e.g., eye color, height). About 99 percent of genes are structural and are thus shared with other people within and outside one's immediate family. What determines the unique characteristics of persons are differences in the 1 percent of genes that are polymorphic.

Genes within the DNA of the organism's cells carry chemically coded instructions for the production of specific polypeptides (a complex sequence of amino acids), which then form a protein. These proteins affect the form and functioning of the organism. The human body can make more than 31,000 different proteins. A well-known type, for example, is hemoglobin; it transports oxygen in the bloodstream. Only a few of the 25,000 genes in the human body contain instructions for making hemoglobin. A *regulatory protein* is an important type because it controls the activities of other genes by turning them on and off (Rowe, 2002). Thus, the genes responsible for regulatory proteins are of most interest for studying genetic influences on behavior.

There are several sophisticated methods for identifying genes that are associated with particular outcomes (Plomin et al., 2000). They allow scientists to construct maps (e.g., genome maps or genetic linkage maps) that show, in varying detail, the location of specific genes or sequences of DNA in human cells. If specific genes are found to correlate with certain behaviors, such as hyperactivity or impulsivity (especially among closely related people), then there is evidence that something about the expression of these genes influences behavior.

Genes associated with delinquency or antisocial behaviors are probably not abnormal (Fishbein, 2001), nor are they mutations. Rather, certain combinations of genes increase the risk of delinquency when particular environmental factors are in place. In addition, a person's environment affects the functioning of genes through natural modifications. Research has isolated several genes that may be involved in this process. These genes by themselves do not cause delinquent or other types of behaviors. Rather, particular configurations of genes affect biochemical functions, nervous system responses, and brain functioning. These may then place certain people at risk for delinquent behavior.

Biochemicals: neurotransmitters, enzymes, and hormones

There are three different types of chemicals in the human body that affect how we behave and react to particular situations: neurotransmitters, enzymes, and hormones.[1] *Neurotransmitters* are biochemical substances that are necessary for nervous system functioning since they allow the transmission of nerve impulses from one cell to the next. Nerve cells, also known as *neurons*, are elongated cells with various branches. Some of these branches are the *dendrites* that are responsible for picking up incoming signals from other neurons. The *axon* – the longest branch – is responsible for sending out signals. Axons end at *synapses*, specialized points that are close to the next cell. A typical neuron in the human brain has 1,000–10,000 synapses. When a signal reaches a synapse it releases a neurotransmitter that crosses the *synaptic cleft* and attaches to a protein known as a *receptor site*. When attached, different neurotransmitters send either signals that tell the message to continue to the next neuron (*depolarization*) or signals that tell the message to stop (*hyperpolarization*). Figure 3.6 provides a picture of a neuron and neurotransmitter.

Numerous studies have found that the levels of three types of neurotransmitters – *norepinephrine*, *dopamine*, and *serotonin* – vary among delinquents and non-delinquents. To get a sense of these studies, we shall provide a brief review of research on serotonin. Readers interested in studies of dopamine and norepinephrine may wish to consult DeLisi and Beaver (2011) or Schmidt et al. (2007).

Serotonin is the most widely studied neurotransmitter in research on human behavior, especially psychiatric disorders, but delinquency as well. Serotonin, or 5HT, is a derivative of the amino acid *tryptophan*. Although most serotonin is produced for digestive purposes in the gastrointestinal tract, some acts as a neurotransmitter in the brain. Serotonin's functions in the brain are not entirely understood, but its impact on harmful behaviors has been shown in several studies, with low levels of serotonin or serotonin metabolites such as 5-HIAA – in either the brain or the cerebrospinal fluid (CSF) – associated with higher risks of depression and suicide attempts (Bostic et al., 2005). In addition, high levels of serotonin metabolites in the blood – which are correlated with low levels of serotonin and 5-HIAA in the brain and CSF – are associated with conduct disorders, aggressive behavior, and violent behavior among adults and juveniles (e.g., Schmidt et al., 2007). However, a study of 21-year-old adults conducted by Moffitt and colleagues (1998) found that this association applies only to males, not females.

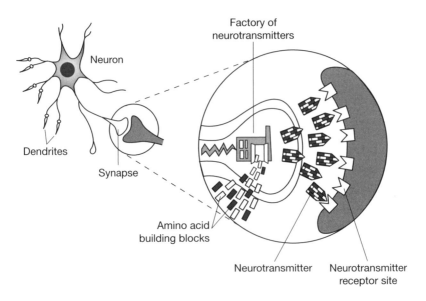

Figure 3.6 Neuron and neurotransmitter in the human cell.

Some researchers hypothesize that low serotonin levels in the brain and CSF increase impulsive behavior, thus enhancing the risk of delinquent activities (Coccaro, 1992). There is also a link between serotonin production and attention deficit hyperactivity disorder (ADHD). Furthermore, levels of serotonin are linked to the tryptophan hydroxylase (TPH) gene, which controls an enzyme that metabolizes serotonin (Åsberg, 1994); the serotonin transport gene (*5-HTT*), which regulates reuptake of serotonin in the neuron's synapse (Zalsman and Apter, 2002); and a serotonin receptor 2C gene (*HTR2C*), which has been linked to impulsivity in males (Evans et al., 2000). One study found that the serotonin transport gene (*5-HTT*) is associated with chronic juvenile offending, even after considering many other influences (Vaughn et al., 2009).

Enzymes

An enzyme is a protein that accelerates a chemical process. Enzymes are necessary for the functioning of cells; they are also required for digestion and other physiological functions. There are more than 2,000 distinct enzymes in the human body. An important class of enzymes is responsible for neurotransmitter functioning either by producing the neurotransmitter or by breaking it down (*hydrolysis*) so its constituent parts may be used again. Thus, the proper balance of enzymes is important. One enzyme in particular, *monoamine oxidase* (MAO), is responsible for metabolizing dopamine, serotonin, and norepinephrine. There are actually two types of MAO – A and B – which have slightly different functions.

Problems arise when our bodies have either too much or too little MAO (the complete absence of MAO is a rare condition that causes severe symptoms such as blindness and mental retardation). When there is too much MAO, the breakdown of neurotransmitters accelerates and communication across neurons is impaired. One byproduct of this rapid breakdown is an overabundance of hydrogen peroxide in the brain, which can devastate cell membranes and cause symptoms of Parkinson's disease. Moreover, the consequent lack of neurotransmitter functioning is likely to lead to depression and possibly schizophrenia. This is why MAO inhibitors such as Marplan® are a common treatment for depression and Parkinson's disease.

When MAO levels are too low, serotonin and dopamine are not broken down sufficiently and accumulate at the neuron's receptor site. This may affect a person's self-control. Yet a lack of MAO may also indicate too little serotonin in the brain. As discussed earlier, low levels of serotonin in the brain and CSF are associated with impulsivity and delinquent behavior.

Ellis (1992) and Raine (2008) have summarized compelling evidence for a link between low MAO levels and criminal/delinquent behavior. Ellis argued that low MAO levels are associated with the following characteristics: sensation seeking, impulsiveness, hyperactivity, extraversion, poor school performance, and defiance of authority. All of these characteristics place adolescents at risk of delinquency. Moreover, MAO tends to be lower in males than in females; this may explain why male adolescents tend to be more involved in delinquency. MAO-B levels, in particular, are also lowest during the 10–15 years following the onset of puberty, so this may account for the increase in delinquent behavior during adolescence and the reduction during the early adult years. In addition, genetically related low MAO levels, when combined with interpersonal risk factors (e.g., delinquent friends, poor relations with parents), predict violent behavior among youths (Guo et al., 2008).

Caspi and colleagues (2002) studied the interaction between child maltreatment and MAO levels. They were able to identify a polymorphic gene that regulated MAO-A activity. Caspi and colleagues found significantly more involvement in antisocial behaviors among those with a combination of low MAO-A activity and severe maltreatment. Figure 3.7 provides a graph of this result. Although they measured antisocial behavior through age 26, there is little reason to think that the results would differ if they restricted the analysis to delinquent behavior only.

Hormones

Hormones send messages from one cell or group of cells to another. Strictly speaking, neurotransmitters such as dopamine, serotonin, and norepinephrine are a specific type of hormone, known as *amine-derived* hormones. However, we shall use the term *hormone* to refer to another type that is secreted by the body's endocrine glands. These hormones travel through the bloodstream and induce certain physiological responses, including in parts of the nervous system (Brain, 1993). Much of the literature on behavioral responses to endocrine hormones has focused on what are known as *steroid hormones*, in particular *cortisol* and *testosterone*.

Cortisol is produced in the adrenal glands (which are located just above the kidneys) and is released in response to physical or psychological stress. Its production

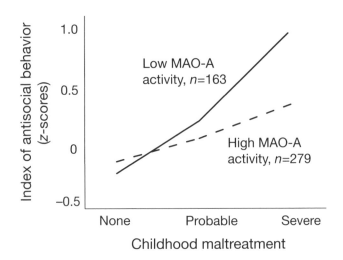

Figure 3.7 MAO-A activity, childhood maltreatment, and antisocial behavior.

decreases when stress ends, which helps the body return to normal functioning. Cortisol also regulates blood pressure and the body's metabolism of fats, proteins, and carbohydrates. When released, it helps break down protein in the muscles into amino acids, which are then used in the liver to synthesize glucose for energy (gluconeogenesis).

Recent studies have suggested there is a link between cortisol and aggressive behavior in children and adolescents (Kobak et al., 2009). One hypothesis is that children and adolescents with low cortisol tend to be less responsive to stress, or *underaroused*, and thus are not as sensitive to punishment or as fearful as others during stressful situations (Popma et al., 2007). Studies of underarousal are discussed in the next section of the chapter.

Another hormone, testosterone, is produced in the male testes, and to a lesser extent in the female ovaries, in the liver, and in a few other tissues. Studies show that aggressive and delinquent males tend to have higher levels of testosterone than other males (e.g., Giammanco et al., 2005). High levels of testosterone may affect delinquency especially among those with low cortisol levels (Popma et al., 2007). However, it is likely that testosterone is associated with delinquency through its influence on temperament and social functioning (Vermeersch et al., 2008). Studies also show that it is associated with greater involvement in delinquency for males and females when family relationships are poor (Fang et al., 2009). Moreover, a study by Tremblay and colleagues (1997) suggested that high testosterone in males is associated with low verbal skills and poor school performance, which then increase involvement with delinquent friends and antisocial behavior. In fact, assessing testosterone levels across adolescence, they found that the most aggressive youths had low testosterone levels at age 13, but their levels increased substantially more than among other youths by age 16.

To sum up, it is clear that there is an association between several biochemicals and delinquency. However, as explained in Chapter 1, an association does not provide sufficient evidence of the mechanisms that link one variable to another. Rather, it is important to consider how physiological changes or differences result in particular forms of behavior. We have seen some possible mechanisms linking biochemicals to delinquency, namely through their influence on personality traits such as impulsiveness and sensation seeking. The next section discusses several additional processes that involve *physiological arousal* and *classical conditioning*.

Nervous system responses and delinquency

The human nervous system consists of two parts: the *central nervous system* (CNS), which includes the brain and the spinal cord, and the *peripheral nervous system* (PNS). The PNS is further divided into the *somatic nervous system* (SNS), which is responsible for sending nerve signals from peripheral parts of the body to the CNS and motor nerve fibers; and the *autonomic nervous system* (ANS), which controls organs, muscles, and glandular activity. The ANS regulates the fight-or-flight mechanism. In particular, the *sympathetic nervous system* – a component of the ANS – controls several functions when a person experiences a stressful situation: Blood pressure and heart rate increase, the digestive system slows down, and norepinephrine, epinephrine, and cortisol output increase. Once the situation eases, the *parasympathetic nervous system* engages. It helps the body return to normal as the stressful situation dissipates.

There are four theories that focus on nervous system responses and delinquency. The first was developed by Mednick (1977), who reasoned that one of the underlying physiological traits that distinguishes delinquents from non-delinquents is how their ANSs respond to stress. In non-delinquents, stressful events such as punishment increase ANS functioning, resulting in a peak level of *physiological arousal*. For children, in particular, such stress reactions can be quite unpleasant. The key to Mednick's theory is how long it takes for the ANS to return to normal following a stressful experience, or what is called *dissipation*. Dissipation times vary across individuals. Suppose the spike of arousal is high and the dissipation time rapid. This is likely to put an imprint on the mind of the child so that he will seek to avoid the stressful event in the future. However, suppose the arousal is less peaked and the dissipation time longer (*underarousal*). In this situation, the child will most likely not be as affected by the stressful event and, if other characteristics are in place, may be more likely to ignore the event in the future. As parents or others punish children for misbehavior, those with normal arousal are more sensitive to the stress of being punished and learn to avoid misbehavior in the future. However, those who are underaroused are not affected as much by punishment, and therefore are less likely to refrain from misbehavior. Eventually, some underaroused children become delinquent because standard forms of punishment do not affect them as much as they do others. Figure 3.8 illustrates normal arousal and underarousal.[2]

The second theory of ANS functioning involves *classical conditioning*. Feelings of distress build up as a child contemplates some misbehavior because, in the past, such misbehavior has resulted in punishment: "It is the association between

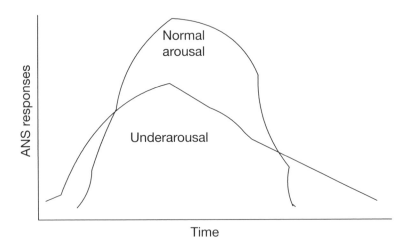

Figure 3.8 Normal arousal and underarousal of the autonomic nervous system.

[misbehaviors such as] stealing and feelings of distress caused by punishment that will deter most children from stealing" (Yaralian and Raine, 2001, p.59). Those youths who are not as sensitive, for whatever reason, to classical conditioning are at higher risk of delinquency because they have not, relatively speaking, formed a strong connection between previous delinquent activities and distress.

A third theory is that low responsiveness in the ANS reflects a low baseline of arousal. If we assume that people have an optimal arousal level that they seek through various activities, then perhaps those with a relatively low baseline of ANS functioning require greater stimuli to reach an optimal arousal state. Delinquency or antisocial behavior may be a way to compensate for low arousal by offering especially thrilling or dangerous activities (Yaralian and Raine, 2001).

The fourth theory involves fearlessness. Raine (1993) argued that some children are relatively fearless, so they are less sensitive to punishment or less deterred by the potential costs of aggressive behaviors such as fighting or assault. He suggested that fearlessness reduces the efficiency of punishment, thus negatively affecting classical conditioning that seeks to discourage delinquent activities.

Two types of physiological measures are used to test these theories: *resting (tonic) heart rate* and *skin conductance activity*.[3] Studies show that delinquents have, on average, lower resting heart rates than non-delinquents, even after taking into account differences in physical fitness, alcohol and cigarette use, and well-known risk factors for delinquency, such as delinquent peers or poor relations with parents (e.g., Armstrong et al., 2009). Raine and colleagues (1990), for example, measured the resting heart rates of a sample of 15-year-old males and then placed them into

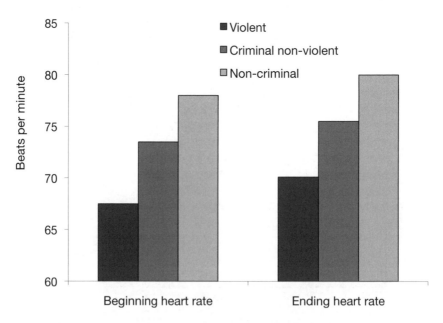

Figure 3.9 Heart rate and criminal behavior (Raine et al., 1990, p.1005).

three categories at age 24: those who became violent offenders, those who became non-violent offenders, and those who did not become offenders. The resting heart rates before and after stimuli are shown in Figure 3.9.

The second physiological measure, skin conductance (SC) activity, assesses fluctuations in the electrical activity of the skin. The notion is that electrodermal arousal may be measured by resting SC levels and fluctuations in SC levels after exposure to stressful events.[4] Several studies have found that delinquents, on average, have lower SC responsiveness than non-delinquents (see Yaralian and Raine, 2001). When presented with aversive stimuli (e.g., loud noises) designed to evoke stress, antisocial and delinquent boys show less responsiveness than non-delinquent or non-antisocial boys. Moreover, the amount of time it takes an SC response generated by aversive stimuli to return to half its baseline level (a measure of dissipation known as *skin conductance half-recovery time*) is substantially longer in those who become criminals than in those who do not (Raine et al., 1996). It is interesting to note, though, that Raine and colleagues (1996) found that low heart rate or low SC adolescents do not become delinquent or highly aggressive when (1) academic performance is high (boys) or (2) depressive symptoms are low (girls). They also determined that low SC response is associated with more aggressiveness only among youth from high socioeconomic status groups. This provides further evidence that physiology (nature) interacts with social circumstances (nurture) to affect delinquency.

There are intricate associations between biochemicals and physiological arousal. For example, during stressful events the ANS increases production of norepinephrine and cortisol, whereas the parasympathetic nervous system uses hormones to restore the nervous system to its previous state. If cortisol production is low, there is likely to be underarousal, with a low peak of responsiveness. Recovery or dissipation may also be longer if there is less cortisol available for normal nervous system resumption. Moreover, dopamine and serotonin are involved in mood regulation, so they may trigger particular responses, such as heightened aggressiveness or impulsivity, in the presence of stress.

Brain functioning and delinquency

The brain is a highly complex organ, with an estimated 100 billion neurons and many more *glial cells* (cells that hold neurons in place, supply them with oxygen and nutrients, and remove dead neurons). Distinct sections of the brain are responsible for various physiological functions. Among the major portions of the brain are the *cerebellum* and the *cerebrum*. The cerebellum is located near the bottom rear of the head. It is responsible for motor control, posture, balance, and some cognitive functions. The cerebrum – the largest portion of the brain – is responsible for higher functions such as thoughts and deliberate actions. The outermost layer of the cerebrum is the *cerebral cortex*. It consists of four lobes that have distinct functions. Table 3.2 provides a brief list of some of these functions. Figure 3.10 shows the location of these lobes.

As mentioned in Chapter 2, studies have shown some important differences in

Table 3.2 Lobes of the cerebral cortex

Lobe	Function
Frontal	Reasoning, planning, parts of speech, movement, emotional control, and problem solving
Parietal	Movement, orientation, recognition, perception of stimuli
Occipital	Visual processing
Temporal	Perception and recognition of auditory stimuli, fear and pleasure, emotional responses, memory, and speech

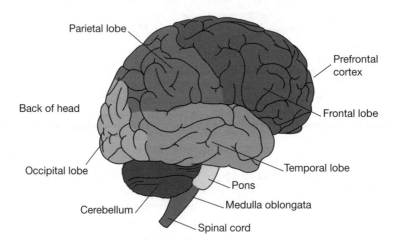

Figure 3.10 Major regions of the human brain.

the brains of adolescents and adults. For example, they tend to use different parts of the brain when analyzing situations or completing tasks. When thinking about fear, adults use the frontal lobe's *prefrontal cortex*, which probably inhibits emotional responses. Adolescents, however, use a part of the brain in the temporal lobe – the *amygdala* – that tends to process emotions and is involved in fear and pleasure responses (Baird et al., 1999). Thus, adolescents tend to have a different response to fear from adults. This may also reflect differences in how they react to stress.

A series of studies by Raine (summarized in Raine, 2008) and others (e.g., Siever, 2008) indicate that dysfunction in the frontal lobe is associated with antisocial and violent behavior. Since the frontal lobe is involved in reasoning, planning, and emotional control, a hypothesis is that dysfunction in this part of the brain affects an adolescent's ability to see the consequences of his action, or causes him to misperceive situations so they seem more threatening (Yaralian and Raine, 2001). Raine (2002) has contended that differences among delinquents and non-delinquents in ANS functioning are associated with problems in the prefrontal cortex. One of his studies also indicates that persistent offenders, in particular, have deficits in spatial and verbal perception, memory impairments, and neuro-cognitive impairments consistent with prefrontal cortex dysfunction (Raine et al., 2005).

There are several sources of frontal lobe dysfunction, including brain injury, child abuse, lesions, and impaired development due to prenatal and postnatal problems. In fact, these various sources have been linked to aggression, delinquency, and antisocial behavior (Raine, 2008). Furthermore, there is likely to be a genetic link, with frontal lobe problems generated by particular genetic strains found in family lines. However, these have not been found yet, so we can only speculate at this point about a genetic origin of frontal lobe dysfunction. Moreover, as with studies described earlier, prefrontal cortex dysfunction probably interacts with social variables to affect delinquency, perhaps by affecting cognitive abilities, impulsivity, and perceptions of social situations.

Environmental risk factors

As mentioned in the last paragraph, there are various causes of frontal lobe dysfunction. Moreover, there are several sources, in addition to genetically inherited factors, of neurotransmitter, enzyme, and hormone differences across individuals. Much of the research on these sources addresses trauma and injury, prenatal and postnatal influences, and environmental toxins. For example, many studies have shown that injury to the brain or trauma induced by child maltreatment is associated with delinquency (Miller, 2002). Post-traumatic stress disorder (PTSD) and other stressors experienced by children and adults are linked to low levels of serotonin, changes in dopamine sensitivity, and hormonal changes (Fishbein, 2001).

Prenatal and postnatal influences

There are numerous factors that affect the development of the fetus in the mother's womb. Some of the key factors involve the mother's diet, use of drugs, and exposure to environmental toxins during pregnancy. Two of the most widely studied prenatal influences on delinquency and antisocial behavior are maternal smoking and alcohol use.

Several studies have shown that cigarette smoking and alcohol use during pregnancy is associated with a higher risk of delinquent behavior, especially for adolescents living in poor neighborhoods (e.g., Brook et al., 2008). However, this may occur because of difficult family factors in addition to maternal smoking (D'Onofrio et al., 2010) or alcohol use during pregnancy, especially binge drinking (Bailey et al., 2004; see, however, Lynch et al., 2003). The mechanisms underlying these associations are likely to involve the effects of these drugs on developing fetuses, especially on portions of their brains responsible for verbal perception and spatial perception. There is also substantial evidence that maternal alcohol and tobacco use affect higher brain functions that occur in the prefrontal cortex: problem-solving skills, judgment skills, ability to plan ahead, and abstract thinking

(Mattson et al., 2001). Moreover, one study indicated that prenatal alcohol exposure leads to deficits in serotonin processing in the neurons of mice (Sari and Zhou, 2004).

A promising hypothesis that links prenatal and postnatal problems and delinquency involves hypothalamic–pituitary–adrenal (HPA) axis functioning. The HPA axis is responsible for regulating the body's response to stress. It includes adrenal gland functioning, which, as we learned earlier, controls cortisol production. Brennan and colleagues (2003) suggested that prenatal stressors such as maternal drug use and birth complications such as breech delivery and forceps extraction damage HPA axis functioning. This may result in lower inhibition and less reactivity to stress, thus explaining the physiological mechanisms that underlie Mednick's theory of underarousal and delinquency.

Environmental toxins

Another type of risk factor that affects delinquency involves environmental toxins. Air and water pollution, lead in paint, and other toxins common in the environment have many negative health consequences for children (Ponce et al., 2005). Of these environmental exposures, lead is the most frequently studied. Lead may be ingested or inhaled. It is absorbed quickly, interferes with cellular functioning, and may cause permanent damage to the neurological system. Exposure to lead during fetal development or in childhood is associated with lower IQ scores, speech problems, attention deficit disorders, and several behavioral problems (Rogan and Ware, 2003). It also reduces the levels of several neurotransmitters, including serotonin and dopamine (Masters and Coplan, 1999).

Several studies have shown that higher levels of lead in the tissues are associated with more delinquency and antisocial behavior (e.g., Chen et al., 2007). A study by Dietrich and colleagues (2001), for example, followed 195 inner-city adolescents from birth until their teenage years. Those subjects who had the highest lead concentration in the blood reported the most delinquent acts, even after adjusting for the effects of several social and family variables. However, it is still unclear precisely how lead exposure, or exposure to other heavy metals such as mercury and manganese (Masters et al., 1998), is associated with delinquency, but it probably involves the damaging effects on neurological development and neurotransmitter functioning.

Promises and limitations of biological research on delinquency

Researchers who study biological mechanisms consistently point out that no single gene (or set of genes), particular neurotransmitter or hormone, or specific brain composition *causes* delinquent behavior. Rather, these interact with environmental influences, including family and peer relationships, to increase the probability of delinquent behavior. There has been important research to support this view. For example, as discussed earlier, Caspi et al. (2002) determined that a strong positive association between low MAO-A activity and antisocial behavior is found mainly among children who were maltreated (see also Guo et al., 2008; O'Connor et al., 1998). In fact, Raine (2008) has coined the phrase "from genes to brain to antisocial behavior" to identify this process that links physiological characteristics to delinquency. He argued that genetic abnormalities impair brain functioning, which can then lead to risk factors for delinquency such as poor judgment, anger control problems, and difficulty in dealing with conflict. Moreover, a person's social circumstances and exposure to substances in the environment affect the way that genes, neurotransmitters, hormones, and the brain operate. The key is to figure out the ways that biological characteristics interact with social characteristics and situations to affect the likelihood of delinquent behavior.

With all the promise shown by biological research, there are still a number of limitations and controversies. First, molecular genetics is just beginning to identify the genes involved in the complex process that may lead to delinquent behavior. Whether a particular set of genes is consistently involved in this process has not been determined. Second, there are several definitional problems associated with biological research on delinquency. Studies use terms such as *aggression, conduct disorder, antisocial behavior*, and other concepts to define their outcomes. It is difficult to compare the results of studies that use different outcomes. As pointed out in Chapter 1, the definition of delinquency relies on legislative decision-making, which is not always uniform as to which behaviors are prohibited. Social and cultural norms play a large part in defining what is and is not acceptable behavior for adolescents (Fishbein, 2001), yet biological studies have not, for the most part, considered the normative aspects of antisocial behavior and delinquency. Furthermore, there is a tendency in some studies to categorize adolescents into discrete groups: delinquent vs. non-delinquent; aggressive vs. non-aggressive. Yet delinquency is a continuum, not an all-or-nothing category.

Third, the samples and methods used in studies are not uniform and are often not generalizable. For instance, many studies use samples of adolescents in juvenile detention facilities. Others use small samples because physiological procedures – such as brain imaging – are expensive to administer. Fourth, many studies have focused on males or show that the associations between physiological functioning and delinquency are stronger for males than for females. However, one large study concluded that biological factors, in general, play a larger role in female delinquency than in male delinquency (Denno, 1990). This raises the question: Are there unique influences on males and females? Perhaps the biosocial interaction that researchers speak of is different for male and female adolescents. If so, then more research is needed that evaluates sex differences.

Fifth, it is overly generous to claim that the research on biology and delinquency constitutes a theory of delinquency. There are many studies demonstrating that physiological factors are correlated with delinquency, and that some of these interact with environmental and social characteristics that are also correlated with delinquency. However, the development of an explanation that meets the needs of a theory is wanting. Some researchers have recently attempted to develop theories that consider various physiological, social, and environmental factors (e.g., Ellis, 2005), but a comprehensive theory has not yet been rigorously examined.

Finally, there continues to be justifiable concern about how the research results demonstrating physiological differences between delinquents and non-delinquents should be used. We are only a little more than a half-century removed from the atrocities of Nazi Germany and the alarming recommendations of the eugenics movement, so many observers are concerned when researchers claim to have found a gene or a particular brain structure associated with delinquency or antisocial behavior. Some argue that people are overreacting and that more knowledge actually guards against the misuse of genetics and biology (Plomin and Asbury, 2005). However, suppose that a set of genes is isolated that predicts delinquent behavior with 90–95 percent accuracy? What should we do with those who carry this set within their DNA? Are geneticists ethically bound to tell parents whose offspring carry this set about the risks? What are the moral and legal implications (Fishbein, 2001; Rowe, 2002)? These are important ethical questions that a society that cherishes freedom and human dignity must ask itself.

Policy implications of biological research

Given the consistent link between maternal behaviors such as smoking and alcohol use and delinquency, perhaps the single most effective prevention strategy involves prenatal health care for pregnant women, especially those at high risk for these behaviors. Educational programs that discuss nutrition and fetal development, prevention of head injuries, home health care visits, and regular visits with a doctor are all effective strategies to ensure fetal and newborn health. For instance, in a study by Olds and colleagues (1998) that included high-risk pregnant women, those who received home visitations from trained nurses had children who, 15 years later, were less involved in delinquency and drug use than those who had standard prenatal care. Prevention of other risk factors such as child maltreatment should also be included in programs designed to curb delinquency.

Moreover, intervention efforts should focus on those children and adolescents at high risk because of physiological factors such as prefrontal cortex dysfunction, underarousal, neurotransmitter deficiencies, or prenatal and postnatal exposure to environmental toxins. There is some evidence, for instance, that biofeedback training can help underaroused youths learn to curb impulsivity and that cognitive–behavioral therapy (CBT) can help at-risk and aggressive youths learn appropriate coping strategies when under stress (Raine and Liu, 1998). It is important, moreover, that intervention efforts be aimed at multiple risk factors – physiological and environmental – rather than simply targeting one or two (Beauchaine et al., 2008). For example, programs that address arousal management, improve social skills, reduce aggression, and enhance positive relations with parents are more valuable than simply training adolescents to control impulsivity or providing them with drugs to modulate deficiencies in serotonin.

Efforts to alleviate impoverished living conditions and exposure to environmental toxins across communities are also recommended as part of prevention and intervention programs (Raine, 2008). There is ample evidence that families living in poverty are more likely to be exposed to environmental toxins such as lead, obtain worse prenatal care, and eat less nutritious foods than wealthier families. Poor nutrition at an early age has been linked to behavioral problems in youths that persist throughout the teen years (Liu et al., 2004). Hence, programs designed to alleviate the problems associated with impoverished living conditions may also reduce delinquent behavior.

Conclusions

This chapter provides an overview of the many studies that have investigated biological influences on delinquency. For about 150 years scientists have explored various aspects of human anatomy and physiology that are related to delinquent and criminal behavior. The earliest studies addressed presumed anatomical characteristics that distinguished delinquents from non-delinquents. Their crude measurement techniques and research methods limited the accuracy of the results and led to some unfortunate conclusions about the biological sources of delinquency. Perhaps the most serious problem was the reliance on "official delinquents" – those from juvenile detention facilities – to distinguish offenders from law-abiders. It should not be surprising that those defined as delinquent had various physical disadvantages considering that many, if not most, came from the lowest socioeconomic groups in society.

Recently, there has been a resurgence of physiological studies. In particular, there is now persuasive evidence that certain neurotransmitters, enzymes, and hormones, underaroused ANS functioning, and prefrontal cortex dysfunction are associated with delinquency and with personality traits such as impulsivity and aggressiveness that place adolescents at risk of antisocial behavior. There is also evidence that many of these physiological functions are linked to specific genetic sequences in human DNA. Most importantly, though, several studies have assessed interactions between physiological and social processes, or between *nature* and *nurture*. Studies that consider both will be the most useful for advancing our understanding of delinquent behavior.

4 Psychological theories of delinquency

Prologue

Tom was a handsome young man with a disarming smile. He was reasonably intelligent, but was chronically absent from school. His parents said that he could not be counted on to stay on tasks. They had started noticing objects missing from their home when Tom was about 10 years old. When absent from school, Tom used to set small fires and was soon picked up by the police. They also found some stolen items, but he lied so convincingly that the police let him go.

His parents called Tom "impulsive" and he was diagnosed with attention deficit hyperactivity disorder (ADHD, attention deficit dominant) at age 13. By the time he was 15, Tom had stolen several cars and forged his mother's name on several checks. His parents took him to many psychiatrists. Following Tom's third arrest for auto theft at age 18, he was sentenced to prison. The psychiatrist-in-residence reported that Tom was an accomplished liar, highly manipulative, and quickly bored by menial tasks. Since he was now considered an adult, the psychiatrist diagnosed Tom with antisocial personality disorder (APD). He prescribed cognitive–behavioral therapy (CBT) to assist Tom in reorienting his thinking about proper forms of behavior (adapted from Cleckley, 1982).

Introduction

In this chapter, we shall describe and evaluate psychological theories and research that have been used to explain delinquent behavior. Psychologists have long recognized that no single theory can explain all types of delinquent behavior (Quay, 1987). Many also avoid the term *delinquency* or *delinquent behavior* because (1) they are legal rather than psychological labels and (2) so many diverse behaviors fall under these terms.

The chapter begins by briefly reviewing some characteristics of delinquents noted by nineteenth- and early twentieth-century scholars. We then examine psychoanalytic theory, especially the ideas that stem from the work of Sigmund Freud. A discussion of personality traits is followed by an assessment of research on intelligence and learning disabilities. After reviewing studies of mental health problems and delinquency, we examine theories of moral development and cognition. Some of the most interesting psychological research on delinquent behavior involves cognitive decision-making and information-processing by adolescents. The final sections consider the promises and limitations of psychological research and the policy options that they recommend.

Early psychological research on delinquency

Among psychologists and alienists (an early name for psychiatrists), two general diagnostic categories of criminals, both poorly defined, were identified in the nineteenth century: *morally insane* and *feeble-minded*. Although these did not encompass all offenders, they were thought to be the basis for many delinquents under state care. Moral insanity included symptoms of "madness" (another poorly defined term) such as irresistible impulses, morbid fascination with unnatural things, moral depravity, moral mania, and violent passions (Rafter, 2004). It eventually was linked to the evolutionary thinking of the late nineteenth century and seen as another characteristic of atavistic children and adults (see Chapter 3).

Many psychologists and physicians assumed that feeble-mindedness was a common cause of delinquency. Although measuring it was difficult, estimates of the percent of feeble-minded delinquents in reform schools ran from 5 to 90 percent among girls and 3 to 80 percent among boys (Fink, 1938). The higher percentages followed the introduction in the early 1900s of the Binet–Simon tests, which were designed to measure intelligence and were early versions of the Stanford–Binet IQ tests that are still used today. The Binet–Simon tests were intended to measure memory, attention, and verbal skills, and, like present-day IQ tests, had an average of 100 that indicated "normal" intelligence. Henry H. Goddard was the first researcher in the United States to administer the Binet–Simon tests to delinquents in state care. He found that 10 of 12 boys and 52 of 56 delinquent girls were "feeble-minded." After conducting more studies, Goddard (1914) concluded that the key heritable trait among delinquents was feeble-mindedness.

William Healy, a Chicago medical doctor, embraced the notion that a minority of delinquents in reformatories or prison populations – perhaps 10–30 percent – were feeble-minded. Moreover, those with mental defects, which included the "feeble-minded," "idiots," "imbeciles," and "morons" (a word invented by Goddard), constituted, according to Healy, the largest single subgroup of delinquents. However, he also stated that:

> One rarely finds personal characteristics as a sole causative factor for criminalism. Defective offenders, in most cases, upon study prove to be individuals who easily succumb to social temptations, easily learn from vicious examples, easily are stimulated to develop criminalistic trends of thought. In morals they prove themselves wanting in resistance when neglected by their families or by society, so that they have to meet undue temptation and suggestion to immorality . . . one must conclude that the development of criminalism is partially the result of environment as well as innate tendencies (Healy, 1915, pp.447–448).

Thus, Healy emphasized that mental defects placed youths at risk of problems, but that delinquency resulted mainly when poor family upbringing and exposure to criminal influences pushed them onto an antisocial path. Furthermore, since Healy found that at most about 30 percent of delinquents showed any sign of a mental defect, he concluded that more frequent causes of delinquency were broken homes, poverty, and poor parenting (Healy and Bronner, 1926).

Searching for the links between delinquency and moral insanity disappeared as psychology became more sophisticated in its views of mental health problems. Moreover, there is no longer research on "feeble-mindedness" and delinquency, although the association between intelligence and delinquency continues to generate research interest. However, early researchers were also influenced by the views of Sigmund Freud on the unconscious mind and how they may be used to understand the psychological bases of delinquent and criminal behavior.

Psychoanalytical theory and delinquency

The famous Viennese psychologist Sigmund Freud (1989a [1923]) was the source of many ideas that gave rise to psychology as a scientific discipline. Freud argued that we cannot understand human nature and behavior until we recognize the existence and power of the *unconscious mind* as a source of most of our motivations, thoughts, and reactions. Although he recognized that the *conscious mind* and the *preconscious mind* (an intermediate stage) also determined thoughts and actions, it was the unconscious mind – where people keep their deepest and most disturbing memories – that most affected these. The unconscious mind is home to three key personality components:

1   The *id* is a source of primal urges and instincts (sexual, hunger) for seeking pleasure and avoiding pain.
2   The *ego* allows awareness of one's external environment, memories, and experiential learning. It also helps keep the impulses of the id partially in check.
3   The *superego* develops through socialization. People learn, primarily from their parents, the norms and morals of society; and this learning constructs, in a sense, the superego.

The id, ego, and superego work simultaneously to influence desires and how people should go about satisfying desires. The ego functions to balance the primitive needs dictated by the id with the moral beliefs of the superego (Freud 1989a [1923]).

Somewhere in the unconscious rests the memory of *the first great crime* when primordial men rose up against their father, slaying him and taking his power. The memory of this crime – which is part of man's evolutionary make-up – is accompanied by a primeval sexual urge for their mothers, or what is labeled the *Oedipus complex*. This complex, exemplified by the Greek myth of Oedipus killing his father and marrying his mother (without his knowledge, though), generates great guilt and remorse (Freud, 1989b [1912]). Since the Oedipus complex remains part of every man's unconscious make-up, these primal urges continue to exist. All men (and women through a similar phenomenon called the *Electra complex*) are thus prone to feelings of great guilt that are *repressed* in the ego and are normally controlled by the superego.

Because the development of the superego varies among individuals, some people experience more unconscious guilt than others. Freud assumed that a crucial way to relieve this guilt is through punishment; hence, those who experience a greater degree of guilt desire punishment to alleviate these feelings. For some, the desire for punishment leads them to commit criminal acts. Thus, guilt is not the result of criminal behavior; it is the cause of this behavior. Criminal acts are not usually directed against the father or mother, but rather they are *displaced* by directing them toward a substitute. Freud argued that when the superego is overdeveloped there is more intolerance for Oedipal impulses. Thus, guilt feelings are more severe and the need for punishment is greater. It is those whose superego indicates oversocialization who seek punishment and thus commit criminal acts (note how this contrasts with the view of deterrence described in Chapter 2). However, an underdeveloped superego also leads to criminal behavior – especially violent acts – because there is little restraint over natural aggressive impulses (Dixon, 1986). This is similar to Hobbes's position that humans have an innate tendency toward aggressiveness.

August Aichhorn used Freud's ideas to argue that, when boys identify strongly with their fathers, unconscious Oedipal urges are resisted. However, when parents fail to socialize children properly the superego does not develop sufficiently to control these urges and aggressive behavior results. When the superego dominates the ego, however, innate guilt feelings lead to delinquent behavior as adolescents seek punishment. Aichhorn (1983 [1925]) blamed various types of parents for the ill-developed superegos of children, especially absent, domineering, weak, alcoholic, and criminal fathers.

Although the unconscious basis of delinquency and the role of psychoanalysis in treating it have been criticized, psychoanalytic researchers continue to argue that deficient childrearing, especially by parents and other adults, affects ego and superego development. When important adult figures overreact to misbehavior or impart a poor self-image on children, the result is a weak or overcontrolling superego. This, in turn, increases the risk of misbehavior as a reaction to guilt impulses or by allowing the adolescent's id to go unrestrained (e.g., Levine and Parra, 2000). However, critics argue that concepts such as the superego are not measurable, nor can we determine if some primeval event really continues to affect our behavior (Hunt, 1993; Shoham and Seis, 1993). Thus, psychoanalytic theories are not scientific theories because they are not based on measurable phenomena.

Personality traits

Many studies of delinquency in the early twentieth century focused on psychological traits that were associated with crime and delinquency. Research discussed in Chapter 3, for instance, identified several traits – such as adventurousness

– possessed by many delinquents. However, a detailed description of personality traits did not emerge until the late 1930s when a psychologist, Starke R. Hathaway, and a psychiatrist, J. C. McKinley, developed the *Minnesota Multiphasic Personality Inventory* (MMPI). The MMPI consists of hundreds of questions that are designed to determine an individual's tendency toward various personality dimensions such as depression, hysteria, paranoia, social introversion, and several others. Hathaway and a colleague, Elio D. Monachesi, used the MMPI to study personality traits of juvenile delinquents. They found three personality traits that characterized delinquent boys: *psychopathic deviation* (rebellious, cynical, selfish, aggressive), *social extraversion* (outgoing, assertive), and *hypomania* (overactive). Delinquent girls were characterized by psychopathic deviation and social extraversion. Delinquent boys and girls also showed a propensity for schizophrenia (bizarre thoughts or behaviour, apathetic) (Hathaway and Monachesi, 1963).

The MMPI has been used in many subsequent studies. Most support the finding that delinquents, especially boys, tend to have psychopathic and extraverted traits (e.g., Basham, 1992). In 1992, a modified version of the test, the MMPI-A, was designed specifically for adolescents. Research using it indicates that male delinquents are high on general maladjustment, immaturity, and psychoticism (Morton and Farris, 2002). Some of the specific personality characteristics that are part of these traits include hostility, dishonesty, rebelliousness, conflicted thoughts, and a tendency to externalize blame.

Eysenck's personality theory

A British psychologist, Hans Eysenck, argued that a person's personality could be assessed along two dimensions: *introversion/extraversion* and *neuroticism/stability* (Eysenck, 1964). He later added a third dimension: *psychoticism/sensitivity* (Eysenck, 1970). In anticipation of social control theories of delinquency (see Chapter 8), Eysenck was interested in "why and how do human beings learn to act in conformity with the dictates of society?" (Eysenck, 1960, p.12) He answered this question by arguing that adolescents' aversion to antisocial behavior develops when they are punished by parents, teachers, and other adults. Subsequently, Eysenck (1996) incorporated many of the physiological mechanisms discussed in Chapter 3 to explain how the personality develops. For now, though, we shall focus on the personality dimensions that he described.

Eysenck's research determined that delinquents tend to be high on extraversion (assertive, sensation-seeking, dominant), neuroticism (anxious, irrational, moody), and psychoticism (aggressive, cold, impulsive, unempathetic). Figure 4.1 shows a picture of these dimensions. Subsequent research indicated that delinquents actually fall into several groupings, but consistent evidence showed that they tend to be high in psychoticism (Heaven and Virgen, 2001) and extraversion (Addad and Leslau, 1989).

More recent studies have expanded Eysenck's three dimensions into the *Five-Factor Model* (FFM). The FFM includes extraversion, neuroticism, agreeableness, conscientiousness, and openness to new experiences (McCrae and John, 1992).

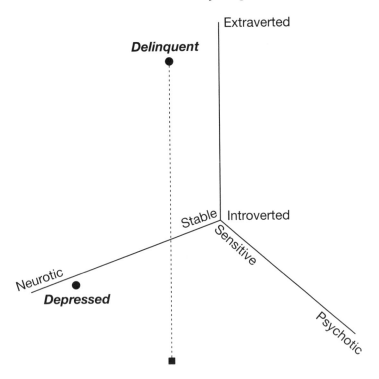

Figure 4.1 Eysenck's personality dimensions.

Table 4.1 shows the characteristics of these factors. Although few studies have used the FFM to examine delinquents, a recent study reported that delinquents are especially low on agreeableness and conscientiousness. Moreover, these characteristics are associated with impulsivity, callousness (insensitivity, lack of empathy), and selfishness (Lynam et al., 2005). The difference in conscientiousness between delinquent and other boys is not surprising since one of its characteristics is "behaves ethically." Moreover, juvenile offenders high in personality traits such as extraversion or psychoticism make up only a minority of overall offenders (Gudjonsson, 1997), so additional explanations are needed to clarify delinquency in general. Aggression, assertiveness, unreliability, or lack of empathy may be predisposing factors for some delinquents, but we must look for other explanations as well.

Impulsivity and sensation-seeking traits and delinquency

Among the personality variables most frequently associated with delinquent behavior are impulsivity and sensation-seeking. Impulsivity involves the tendency to act before thinking through the consequences of the action. Impulsive behavior is seen, for example, when people do not wait their turn or when a child

Table 4.1 Adjectives and descriptors of Five-Factor Model personality items

| Factor | Factor definers | |
	Adjectives	Descriptive items
Extraversion	Active	Is talkative
	Assertive	Skilled in play, humor
	Energetic	Rapid personal tempo
	Enthusiastic	Facially, gesturally expressive
	Outgoing	Behaves assertively
	Talkative	Gregarious
Agreeableness	Affectionate	Not critical or skeptical
	Forgiving	Behaves in a giving way
	Generous	Sympathetic, considerate
	Kind	Arouses liking
	Sympathetic	Warm, compassionate
	Trusting	Basically trustful
Conscientiousness	Efficient	Dependable, responsible
	Organized	Productive; gets things done
	Planful	Able to delay gratification
	Reliable	Not self-indulgent
	Responsible	Behaves ethically
	Thorough	Has a high aspiration level
Neuroticism	Anxious	Thin-skinned
	Self-pitying	Brittle ego defenses
	Tense	Self-defeating
	Touchy	Basically anxious
	Unstable	Concerned with adequacy
	Worrying	Fluctuating moods
Openness	Artistic	Wide range of interests
	Curious	Is introspective
	Imaginative	Unusual thought processes
	Insightful	Values intellectual matters
	Original	Judges in unconventional terms
	Wide interests	Aesthetically reactive

Note: Adapted from McCrae and John (1992, pp.178–179).

immediately grabs a toy from another child. Sensation-seeking involves searching for novel and intense sensations or experiences, and being willing to take substantial risks to attain such experiences (Zuckerman, 1994). Some psychologists think that sensation-seeking is one aspect of impulsivity (Revelle, 1997). In Chapter 3, we learned that specific genes, such as the dopamine D4 receptor, are associated with these traits. Biochemicals, such as MAO, and prefrontal cortex functioning may also influence these personality characteristics.

The association between impulsivity or sensation-seeking and delinquency has been shown in several studies, although the precise mechanisms that lead to this type of adolescent behavior remain unclear (see, for example, Desrichard and Denarié, 2005). Moffitt (1993) argued that impulsivity induces delinquent behavior by interfering with an adolescent's ability to control his behavior and consider the consequences of antisocial activities. The same general process might link sensation-seeking with delinquency, or it may simply be that many delinquent acts involve risks that heighten arousal and associated sensations (see Chapter 3).

Others have suggested that impulsivity and sensation-seeking are related to various types of learning problems and poor school performance, perhaps because of their association with low IQ, deficits in autonomic nervous system arousal, or ADHD (e.g., Avila et al., 2004). Impulsive adolescents are also quick to anger and this may increase their involvement in aggressive behaviors. Furthermore, there is evidence that these traits are more strongly associated with boys' delinquency than girls' delinquency (Colder and Stice, 1998), but more studies are needed to confirm the unique role that personality factors play in affecting male versus female delinquency.

Some psychologists have taken different – sometimes broader – views of personality traits. Impulsivity, sensation-seeking, and other traits – such as aggressiveness – may be part of more general personality domains, such as those defined by the FFM. Alternatively there may be other personality domains that are associated with delinquency. For instance, studies using *temperament inventories* have shown that *emotionality* (child is highly emotional, gets upset easily), *rebelliousness* (refusing to do things), and *callousness* (insensitivity, lack of empathy) are associated with problem behaviors and delinquency (e.g., Pardini et al., 2006; White and Frick, 2010).

Intelligence, learning disabilities, and delinquency

The early 1900s saw substantial attention paid to the presumed relationship between intelligence and juvenile delinquency. One of the reasons for this attention was the introduction, in about 1908, of the Binet–Simon intelligence tests to the United States by the psychologist Henry H. Goddard. He was a proponent of the view that not only was intelligence heritable, but also low intelligence was the key cause of delinquency. After administering the Binet–Simon test to hundreds of children at the training school he operated and to thousands of New Jersey public school students, Goddard concluded that feeble-mindedness was a problem that led to many, if not most, societal problems. In particular, he argued that "morons" (a term he invented), which identified those who scored at least two years below average, but above the seven-year-old level, on the Binet–Simon test, were likely to be delinquents and to eventually have children who would also become delinquents. He concluded, "No feeble-minded person should ever be allowed to marry or become a parent. It is obvious that if this rule is to be carried out the intelligent part of society must enforce it" (Goddard, 1914, p.561). Goddard and several other American psychologists who served on national committees recommended the forced sterilization of "mentally defective" people. Thousands of people in more than two dozen states were sterilized from the 1930s through the early 1960s (Hunt, 1993).

Although Goddard's research has been discredited, there continue to be debates about the association between intelligence and delinquency. Studies indicate that delinquents, on average, score about 6–10 points lower than non-delinquents on standard intelligence tests (Hirschi and Hindelang, 1977; Lynam et al., 1993), especially on measures of verbal intelligence (which assesses the use and comprehension of language) rather than performance intelligence (which assesses visual and spatial perception and reasoning) (Isen, 2010). There are several explanations for this consistent association. First, it may be due to official bias: For various reasons, police are more likely to detain or arrest adolescents who score low on IQ tests. Second, adolescents from lower social status or certain minority groups are disproportionately represented in low IQ and high delinquency groups. Neither of these explanations has been confirmed by studies of IQ and delinquency (Moffitt and Silva, 1988). However, there are other more reasonable explanations.

Third, low intelligence negatively affects school performance, which leads to delinquency as adolescents feel rejected by conventional institutions, are treated poorly by authority figures, or come to prefer unconventional or deviant peers to academically successful students (McGloin et al., 2004). Fourth, low intelligence is an indirect measure of low cognitive abilities, impulsivity, or other personality traits that lead to delinquency (Nigg and Huang-Pollock, 2003). Fifth, as suggested earlier, low intelligence is associated with prefrontal cortex dysfunction, which is also associated with impulsivity, learning problems, and other characteristics that increase the risk of delinquency. All of these characteristics are genetically influenced (Wadsworth and DeFries, 2003), so perhaps there is an underlying genetic explanation for the associations among intelligence, personality traits, brain functioning, and delinquency.

In a study that focused on the fourth explanation, Lynam and colleagues (1993) found that impulsivity and school achievement mediate the relationship between verbal IQ and self-reported delinquency. In addition, a study by McGloin and colleagues (2004) determined that low IQ is associated with a combination of low school achievement *and* deviant peer pressure (adolescents report that their friends pressured them to use drugs or commit criminal acts), which are then associated with more delinquent behavior. Figure 4.2 illustrates these results.

A final possibility is that low intelligence interacts with other factors to place adolescents at risk of delinquent behavior. One study, for example, found that the combination of low verbal IQ *and* family adversity (family stress, low socio-economic status, single or young mother) predicts early-onset offending (police

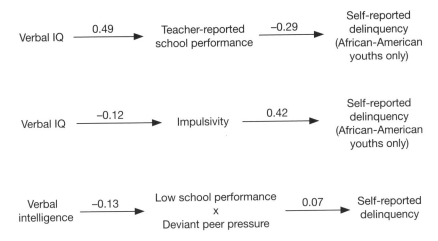

Figure 4.2 Indirect associations between intelligence and delinquency (adapted from Lynam et al., 1993, p.190; McGloin et al., 2004, pp.621, 623).

contact before age 14) (Gibson et al., 2001). On the other hand, Bellair and McNulty (2010) showed that poor cognitive skills (a general term that involves academic knowledge) are related to violent behavior only in neighborhoods that are economically better off. It is therefore clear that low intelligence is a risk factor that may either lead to other problems or combine with other characteristics to affect delinquent behavior. The specific characteristics are still being investigated.

The other body of research that informs our understanding of delinquency and intelligence involves learning disabilities (LDs). LDs are various physical or mental dysfunctions that delay the development or acquisition of knowledge. Adolescents with LDs usually have difficulty sorting and storing information in their minds because of language or sensory processing problems. Most adolescents with LDs score in the average range on intelligence tests. Nevertheless, studies have found that youngsters with LDs are more likely than other youth to be involved in delinquency. This association may be based on (1) personality traits or neurological difficulties, such as impulsivity or ADHD, that lead to both learning problems and delinquency; (2) school problems or failure that are caused by LDs and that lead to delinquency; or (3) differential treatment by law enforcement authorities, who are more likely to detain or arrest adolescents with LDs (Waldie and Spreen, 1993).

One large study determined that adolescents with LDs are twice as likely as other adolescents to be arrested for committing similar offenses (Dunivant, 1982). This may be because these adolescents are less likely to understand the severity of their behavior, have poor verbal skills that place them at a disadvantage when it comes to discussing their activities, or engage in inappropriate behavior when interacting with law enforcement officers (Brier, 1989). Studies have also shown that youths with LDs – especially those with poor reading comprehension – are more likely to return to delinquency following confinement (Rucklidge et al., 2010), and that certain types of disabilities increase aggressive behaviors (Cornwall and Bawden, 1992). However, other studies have found a minimal association between LDs and delinquency (e.g., Malmgren et al., 1999). It is likely that, if there is an association, it is indirect and is channeled through the same factors (e.g., impulsivity, poor school performance, deviant peers) that explain the association between intelligence and delinquency.

Mental health problems and delinquency

Earlier in the chapter, we mentioned that many psychologists avoid terms such as *delinquency* and *delinquent behavior*. Most prefer to use diagnostic categories to study the types of behaviors that other social scientists identify as delinquency. The categories of mental health problems that most closely resemble delinquent behavior are conduct disorder (CD) and oppositional defiant disorder (ODD).

CD and ODD are defined by the American Psychiatric Association (APA) in its compendium *Diagnostic and Statistical Manual of Mental Disorders* (DSM). Now in its fourth edition (APA, 2000), the DSM-IV-TR® (text revision) includes an exhaustive list of mental disorders. Some of the major classifications in the DSM-IV-TR® include mood disorders (e.g., major depression, bipolar), eating disorders (e.g., anorexia nervosa), substance-related disorders (e.g., cocaine-induced psychosis), and anxiety disorders (e.g., phobias, obsessive–compulsive disorder). For each disorder, the manual provides a list of diagnostic criteria designed to help mental health professionals identify problems and design treatments.

Disorders particular to children and adolescents are classified broadly under the category "Disorders of Infancy, Childhood, or Adolescence" (First et al., 2004, p.371). Table 4.2 provides the diagnostic criteria for CD and ODD, disorders that fall under this category. There is a further distinction of CD into childhood onset (before age 10), adolescent onset (age 10 or older), and unspecified onset; and into three severity types: mild, moderate, and severe. Note that CD is given preference over ODD: The defining criteria for ODD specify that CD has not been diagnosed.

Research shows that ODD and CD are persistent disorders, especially among those manifesting more severe symptoms. Those with highly aggressive forms of CD, in particular, tend to have problems that persist into adulthood (Burke et al., 2010; Pardini et al., 2006). Severe CD also increases the risk of *antisocial personality disorder* (APD; previously known as *psychopathy* and *sociopathy*) in adulthood, which is frequently found among adult criminals and is very difficult to treat (DeLisi, 2009).

The prevalence of CD and ODD is generally 5–10 percent among boys and 3–8 percent among girls. Most studies have found that CD is slightly more common than ODD, with a later average age of onset. However, some studies have also shown that there is a progression from ODD to CD for many adolescents (Burke et al., 2002). This is not surprising given the diagnostic criteria: Many delinquent youths begin at an early age acting out in the home by defying their parents or exhibiting bad tempers, and then move on to the types of delinquent activities that characterize CD. Both ODD and CD are more prevalent among adolescents from

Table 4.2 Diagnostic criteria for conduct disorder and oppositional defiant disorder

Conduct disorder	Oppositional defiant disorder
A. A repetitive or persistent pattern or behavior in which the basic rights of others or major age-appropriate societal norms or rules are violated, as manifested by the presence of three or more of the following criteria in the past 12 months, with at least one criterion present in the past 6 months: **Aggression to people and animals** (1) often bullies, threatens or intimidates others (2) often initiates physical fights; (3) has used a weapon that can cause serious physical harm to others (4) has been physically cruel to people (5) has been physically cruel to animals (6) has stolen while confronting a victim (e.g., mugging, extortion, armed robbery) (7) has forced someone into sexual activity **Destruction of property** (8) has deliberately engaged in fire setting with the intention of causing serious damage (9) has deliberately destroyed others' property **Deceitfulness or theft** (10) has broken into someone else's house, building, or car (11) often lies to obtain goods or favors to avoid obligations (i.e., "cons" others) (12) has stolen items of nontrivial value without confronting the victim (e.g., shoplifting, forgery) **Serious violations of rules** (13) often stays out late at night despite parental prohibitions, beginning before 13 years (14) has run away from home overnight at least twice while living in parental or parent surrogate home (or once without returning for a lengthy period) (15) is often truant from school, beginning before age 13 years B. The disturbance in behavior causes clinically significant impairment in social, academic, or occupational functioning. C. If the individual is age 18 years or older, criteria are not met for Antisocial Personality Disorder.	A. A pattern of negativistic, hostile, and defiant behavior lasting at least 6 months, during which four (or more) of the following are present: (1) often loses temper (2) often argues with adults (3) often actively defies or refuses to comply with adults' requests or rules (4) often deliberately annoys other people (5) often blames others for his or her mistakes or misbehavior (6) is often touchy or easily annoyed by others (7) is often angry or resentful (8) is often spiteful or vindictive B. The disturbance in behavior causes clinically significant impairment in social, academic, or occupational functioning. C. The behaviors do not occur exclusively during the course of a Psychotic or Mood Disorder. D. Criteria are not met for Conduct Disorder, and, if the individual is age 18 years or older, criteria are not met for Antisocial Personality Disorder.

Adapted from First et al. (2004).

lower socioeconomic status families and, not surprisingly, in areas with higher crime rates (Loeber et al., 2000).

Research on factors that lead to CD or ODD is quite similar to research on delinquency. For example, Burke and colleagues (2002) reviewed hundreds of studies and identified the following predictors of CD and ODD: certain genetic strains, deficits in neurotransmitter and hormone functioning, frontal lobe dysfunction, underarousal of ANS functioning, prenatal problems, exposure to toxins, low intelligence, reading problems, impulsivity, poor social cognition, impaired moral reasoning, early-onset puberty, child abuse, poor parenting, deviant peers, disorganized neighborhoods, and life stressors. As shown throughout this book, these are key risk factors that criminologists address in research on delinquency.

Nevertheless, it is important to recognize that CD and ODD do not overlap completely with delinquency. Many of the behaviors that determine CD and delinquency are similar, yet youths must show a "repetitive or persistent pattern of behavior" to be diagnosed with CD. Moreover, studies of adolescents in detention facilities have found that only a minority have CD or ODD. One study of youths in a large juvenile detention facility, for instance, determined that 37.8 percent of boys and 40.6 percent of girls were diagnosed with CD and 14.5 percent of boys and 17.5 percent of girls were diagnosed with ODD. However, about half the boys and more than half the girls had mental health disorders *besides* CD or ODD, such as substance use disorder (50.7 percent of boys and 46.8 percent of girls), depressive disorders, anxiety disorders, or ADHD (Teplin et al., 2002). Moreover, about 36 percent of boys and 26 percent of girls did not have a mental health disorder.

A promising area of research that helps us understand problem behaviors involves *comorbidity*: the presence of two or more disorders in an individual. A couple of disorders that are often comorbid among adolescents with CD or ODD are ADHD and PTSD. ADHD, which predicts learning disabilities and school problems, is characterized by a short attention span, overactivity (fidgety, can't remain seated, talks incessantly), and impulsivity. PTSD is caused by exposure to a potentially life-threatening and fear-inducing traumatic event. It is characterized by recurrent memories or dreams of the event, attempts to avoid people or activities that might remind one of the experience, or difficulty sleeping or concentrating because of unpleasant memories of the event (APA, 2000).

The association between ADHD and CD or ODD is complex, but may be traced to biochemical functioning and genetic characteristics. ADHD, CD, and ODD involve similar variations in dopamine and serotonin functioning and in the genes that control these functions (Nadder et al., 2002). Children and adolescents with ADHD are more likely to be diagnosed with a subsequent CD; and those with comorbid ADHD and severe CD are more likely to be diagnosed with APD in adulthood (Burke et al., 2010; Loeber et al., 2000).

Although these disorders are part of a multifaceted condition that some youths experience, an important conclusion is that comorbid ADHD and CD or ODD is associated with impaired developmental pathways that negatively affect personal, educational, and occupational success. It also leads to mental health problems in adulthood. Figure 4.3 illustrates some aspects of these pathways. We shall discuss similar developmental pathways in Chapter 13.

Although few studies have explored the comorbidity of PTSD and CD (e.g., Reebye et al., 2000), there has been substantial research on the association between particular types of traumatic events and delinquency. For example, exposure to family violence increases the risk of mental health problems such as CD among children and adolescents (McCloskey et al., 1995). Perhaps the most frequent traumatic event that children experience is physical and emotional maltreatment by their parents or other adults. Maltreatment is associated with several subsequent mental health disorders, including phobias, panic disorders, depression. Moreover, maltreatment is consistently associated with a higher risk of CD, ODD, delinquency, and adult criminal behavior (e.g., Ireland et al., 2002; Young et al., 2006), especially for adolescents who have academic problems or come from lower socioeconomic status families (Zingraff et al., 1994).

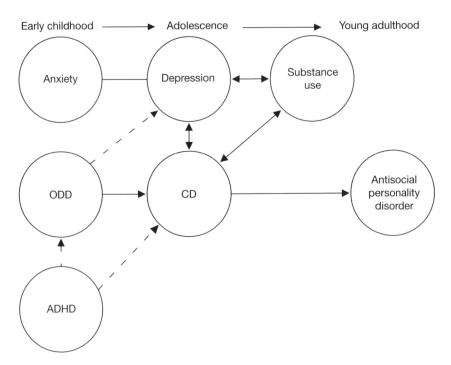

Figure 4.3 Development pathway of CD, ODD, and other mental health disorders. Note: Dotted arrows indicate that ADHD accelerates the onset and worsens the severity of CD or ODD. Lines without arrowheads indicate a relationship, but the direction is not clear. Antisocial personality disorder may also be affected by substance use disorders. The specific roles of maltreatment and PTSD remain unclear, so they are omitted from the figure. Moreover, genetic and neurological influences on ADHD and other disorders, although shown in numerous studies, are not included. (The figure is adapted from Loeber et al. 2000, p.1480).

Moral development and reasoning

The field of *developmental psychology*, which specializes in age-related changes that occur as people age from infancy and childhood to adolescence and adulthood, owes it origins mainly to Jean Piaget, a Swiss psychologist who spent 60 years studying children. He argued that people adapt to their experiences, with their minds going through a series of developmental stages until they reach adulthood (Piaget, 1966 [1932]). Some people go straight through these stages, whereas others get stuck at a stage for longer than normal.

Lawrence Kohlberg, an American psychologist, developed an influential theory of *moral reasoning* that was based on Piaget's ideas. Kohlberg's theory was due to his study of a group of children aged 10–16 who were interviewed every two to five years over a 30-year period. The participants were asked to consider a series of moral dilemmas, such as:

> In Europe, a woman was near death from cancer. One drug might save her, a form of radium that a doctor in the same town had recently discovered. The doctor was charging $2,000, ten times what the drug had cost him to make. The sick woman's husband, Heinz, went to everyone he knew to borrow the money, but he could get together only about half of what it would cost. He told the doctor that his wife was dying and asked him to sell it to him cheaper or to let him pay later. But the doctor refused. The husband became desperate and broke into the doctor's office to steal the drug for his wife. Should the husband have done that? Why? (Kohlberg, 1973, p.64)

Based on responses to this and other hypothetical situations, Kohlberg (1973) argued that there are six stages of moral reasoning, which fall within three levels of general reasoning. Table 4.3 lists these stages.

Because research showed that few people, beyond the highly educated, responded in a way that fell into Stage 6, Kohlberg (1984) later combined it with Stage 5. Moreover, many psychologists criticized these stages because they reflect a male-biased viewpoint (e.g., Gilligan, 1982). Females, they contended, are more likely to reason based on concern for others and empathy, rather than on lofty notions of justice or social contracts. This is not an inferior reasoning process, as is implied by Kohlberg's stages; it is simply different. In a more general sense, why is one stage necessarily higher than another? Is Stage 3 superior morally to Stage 4 (Bandura, 1991)? Alternatively, perhaps a relationship-based perspective is actually more justice-oriented because it is based on concrete social interactions? Moreover, many people develop by either skipping stages or moving up or down a stage depending on their specific life circumstances. Perhaps the most damaging criticism of Kohlberg's theory is that it reflects acceptable thinking and does not correlate with actual behavior. Studies have shown, for instance, that people tend to behave at a lower stage than their reasoning about hypothetical moral dilemmas might indicate (e.g., Wark and Krebs, 1997).

Nevertheless, there has been substantial research on stages of moral reasoning (or *sociomoral reasoning*, as it is often called) among youths. Most studies have found

Table 4.3 Kohlberg's stages of moral reasoning

Level 1. Pre-conventional reasoning	
Stage 1. Naïve moral realism	Motivation is to avoid punishment and obey perceived authority figures
Stage 2. Pragmatic morality	Behavior is based on a desire to maximize one's own benefits and minimize one's own punishment (egocentric)
Level 2. Conventional reasoning	
Stage 3. Socially shared perspective	Relationships with other people are a motivation for behaviors; anticipating approval or disapproval by others motivates actions
Stage 4. Social system morality	Behavior is based on a concern for upholding society's rules and laws because this is the basis of a moral society
Level 3. Post-conventional reasoning	
Stage 5. Human rights and social welfare	Societal laws are based on a social contract between the individual and the community, but, under some circumstances, laws may need to be broken
Stage 6. Universal ethical principles	Behaviors are based on principles of fairness and justice; one's moral principles guide behavior regardless of the circumstances

that delinquents reason at a lower stage of moral development than non-delinquents (e.g., Palmer, 2003; Palmer and Hollin, 2001). However, Raaijmakers and colleagues (2005) found that, although lower stages of moral reasoning predict delinquency, this occurs for older adolescents only as they enter young adulthood (ages 18–20 up to 21–23). However, delinquency also predicts lower stages of moral reasoning from mid to late adolescence (ages 15–17 up to 18–20) *and* during the early years of adulthood (ages 18–20 up to 21–23). Therefore, it appears that not only can moral reasoning move from higher to lower stages, but it is negatively affected by involvement in delinquency as well. This is an example of a *reciprocal association* (see Chapter 1).

Research demonstrating that changes in moral reasoning do not occur only in one direction and can shift as people have different life experiences raises questions about the sources of moral reasoning. Kohlberg (1984) saw the main source as peer relations, with childhood friends providing most of the early opportunities for evaluating moral situations. However, much of the research points to childrearing practices as the main source of moral development. In particular, features of family life such as parental warmth and consistent, yet fair, punishment strategies are positively related to stages of moral reasoning (Wyatt and Carlo, 2002). These aspects of family relationships are also negatively associated with delinquency (see Chapters 7 and 8). However, studies have not looked carefully at whether moral reasoning is also affected by personality factors, genetic characteristics, cultural experiences, or socioeconomic origins. Without more information on its source, theories of moral development provide little utility if we wish to develop an *explanation* of juvenile delinquency. They may be useful for understanding a person's psychological development, but are not especially helpful for explaining behaviors (Dodge and Rabiner, 2004).

Cognitive theories of delinquency

Cognitive psychology involves the study of information-processing mechanisms and mental processes such as planning, problem solving, and decision-making. It differs from psychoanalytic theory because it emphasizes the scientific method of con-ducting research (see Chapter 1) and, unlike *behaviorism* (see Chapter 7), it highlights internal mental states such as beliefs, emotions, and desires. Kohlberg's theory of moral reasoning is one type of cognitive theory because it addresses beliefs and problem solving using emotions and other thought processes. Cognitive theories are useful for understanding human behavior because they force researchers to consider how the processing of information in the mind affects decision-making. To understand delinquent behavior, therefore, psychologists look for differences in the ways that delinquents and other adolescents process information and make decisions. Since some important aspects of adolescent decision-making are dis-cussed in Chapter 2, this section emphasizes research on information-processing.

Cognitive perspectives on misbehaviors focus primarily on how thoughts and information-processing pathways in the mind become impaired in some people, and examine how this may affect delinquent and antisocial behavior. Some key concepts in studies of these cognitive processes include the following:

1   *Memory bias*: Some people emphasize negative over positive memories and experiences. Do delinquents overemphasize the negative?
2   *Attribution*: How do people assign blame or causation for some event? Are delinquents more likely to attribute blame to causes external to them? If so, how does this affect their judgments of their illegal actions? When approached by people in various situations, does a person accurately judge their inten-tions? Are delinquents more likely than other adolescents to attribute hostile or deceitful intentions to others?
3   *Schemas*: These are defined as a mental representation or model of a concept or some piece of knowledge. They have also been referred to as *scripts, nar-ratives, working models*, and *knowledge structures* (Burks et al., 1999). Schemas can be either assimilated to fit new information from the environment, or modi-fied because something differs in the environment (Butcher et al., 2004). For example, a child living in an urban neighborhood links fear with the police,

but then a policewoman helps her, so her schema concerning the police is modified. Do delinquents tend to have unusual or distorted schemas?

Researchers who have developed models of *social information-processing* discuss how information from the environment is processed through six cognitive steps that end in particular behaviors. As described by Dodge and colleagues (e.g., Dodge, 1991; Dodge and Rabiner, 2004), these steps are:

1 *Encoding of relevant stimulus cues*: This involves sensing incoming social information from one's environment. How much information is detected? What is its source? What criteria are used to select certain cues and ignore others?
2 *Interpretation of the cues/attribution of intent*: This includes whether one is interpreting the cues accurately. At this step attribution becomes important.
3 *Generation of goals*: This involves selecting preferred outcomes based on how the social cues are interpreted.
4 *Accessing relevant behavioral schemas from memory*: Given past experiences and knowledge about various situations, what potential social responses are available to the person? Have past experiences that are similar to the current situation resulted in painful or pleasurable interactions? Do memory biases affect the social responses that a person will consider?
5 *Decision-making*: A response is selected from among the various possibilities dictated by Stages 3 and 4.
6 *Behavioral enactment*: After a response is selected it is enacted. Information-processing may continue as the results of the behavior are considered and judged effective or not. Of course, this involves repeating some of the earlier steps, such as interpreting the responses of another person involved in the interaction.

Numerous studies have examined aggression among children and adolescents using the six-step social information-processing model. They have shown that aggressive youths tend to differ from other youths at several steps. In particular, aggressive youths are less attentive to important social cues (Stage 1). For example, they are not as sensitive to facial expressions and have difficulty comprehending the emotions of others. They also tend to be inaccurate when interpreting social cues: Aggressive youths are more likely to attribute hostile intentions to peers and others in social situations (Stage 2). They tend to generate fewer goals, and often consider a disproportionate number of aggressive goals rather than benign or neutral goals (Stage 3). Aggressive youths tend to have memories that are biased in favor of violent or negative experiences. Hence, their schemas often emphasize hostile responses to given social situations (Stage 4). They also anticipate more advantageous outcomes from aggressive or hostile reactions to situations (e.g., "I can win a fight"; "I'll get respect or attention by being aggressive"). It is therefore unsurprising that aggressive youths often decide to enact hostile or aggressive behaviors in what may seem to be unthreatening situations (e.g., Burks et al., 1999; Erdley and Asher, 1998).

Studies have not evaluated all six steps of the social information-processing model using samples of delinquents and non-delinquents. Nonetheless, the following pieces of evidence suggest that this model is useful for understanding delinquent behavior.

- First, aggression is a stable personality trait – aggressive children are highly likely to be aggressive adults – and its presence in childhood is a good predictor of subsequent delinquency and adult criminality (Huesmann et al., 2002).
- Second, the same differences in information-processing among aggressive and non-aggressive adolescents have been found when comparing adolescents with CD and ODD with adolescents without these disorders (Matthys et al., 1999).
- Third, studies have shown that delinquent youth are more likely to have *hostile attribution bias*: They are disproportionately likely to interpret hostile intent on the part of other people during social interactions and generate aggressive responses (e.g., Nas et al., 2005; see, however, Lösel et al., 2007 for contrary evidence).
- Fourth, research has determined that offenders are more likely than others to externalize blame and attribute their behaviors to the intentions of others and to external causes (e.g., Gudjonsson and Sigurdsson, 2004).
- Fifth, the association between perceived experiences such as racial bias and delinquency among African-American adolescents is mediated by beliefs that aggression is a necessary behavioral response (Simons et al., 2003).
- Sixth, studies have shown that cognitive–behavioral therapy (CBT) – which includes teaching adolescents to become better at interpreting social cues and attributing intent, and to consider responses besides aggression when faced with stressful situations – is effective in reducing aggressive and violent behavior among adolescents (Sukhodolsky et al., 2004).
- Finally, research has suggested that female adolescents develop relevant cognitive skills earlier than male adolescents. They also tend to have superior prosocial skills. Hence, differences in information-processing may help explain why boys are more involved than girls in delinquency (Bennett et al., 2005).

An unresolved issue involves the sources of information-processing abilities among adolescents. Some have attempted to link these abilities to personality, arguing that some traits, such as impulsivity, aggressiveness, or neuroticism, may lead to biases in information-processing. For instance, early aggressiveness in children could prevent them from learning how to accurately interpret the emotions of others or increase other people's tendencies to be hostile or negative during interactions with them (Nix et al., 1999). An impulsive personality or an explosive temper also leads some children to attribute such traits to others, thereby increasing their hostile attribution bias (Pardini et al., 2003). If personality traits are a crucial factor for understanding social information-processing among children and adolescents, then there are probably also physiological factors that affect how it develops. There is good evidence, for example, that information-processing tasks involving memory, emotion, and other aspects are affected by prefrontal cortex and amygdala functioning (e.g., Nelson et al., 2005). Furthermore, information-processing functions are impaired by frontal lobe abnormalities (Shimamura, 2002). Given the links among prefrontal cortex functioning, impulsivity, verbal deficits, poor judgment, and delinquent behavior (see Chapters 2 and 3), there are most likely physiological factors that affect delinquency through the cognitive stages of information-processing.

It should also be clear, however, that information-processing is also tied to learning and childrearing. From where do children learn how to manage and interpret information? It is a developmental process, and is affected by how children are socialized and reared from an early age by parents and older siblings, as well as by interactions with peers. From where do children learn hostile attributions and aggressive behavior? They may be affected by physiological mechanisms, yet interactions with parents and peers also play a pivotal role. We shall have much more to say about learning theories of delinquency in Chapter 7. For now, though, it is important to mention that experiences in the family affect information-processing, attributions, and problem behaviors. For instance, Nix and colleagues (1999) examined the attributions and parenting practices among the mothers and problem behaviors among their children over a four-year period (kindergarten to third grade). Figure 4.4 illustrates one of their key results.

Although this study did not assess adolescent behaviors, it suggests that problem behaviors among children are not only the result of their own information-processing steps, but also reflect their parents' cognitive attributions and behaviors. Moreover, children's behaviors can negatively affect parents' attributions, with

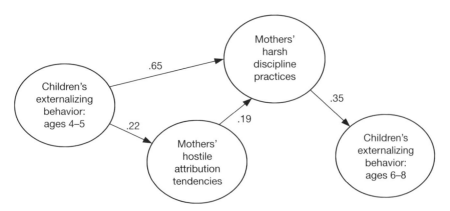

Figure 4.4 Mothers' hostile attributions, discipline practices, and children's externalizing behavior problems. Note: Externalizing behavior includes aggression, threats, fighting, lying, stealing, swearing, lack of guilt feelings, and school problems (ages 6–8 only). Mothers' harsh discipline includes severe or overly strict discipline, arguing, spanking, pushing or shoving, and threats of physical harm. (The figure is adapted from Nix et al. 1999, p.905).

hostility following children's aggressive behaviors. As mentioned earlier, children exposed to violence and maltreated often develop mental disorders such as PTSD and are at higher risk of delinquency. Parents who discipline too harshly may not only place their children on a path toward delinquency, but also impair the development of their information-processing capabilities (Milner, 2000). For example, children exposed to violence or treated harshly develop schemas that emphasize hostility and aggression and tend to attribute hostility to peers during social interactions (Dodge, 2003). We shall learn more about family influences on delinquency in later chapters.

Promises and limitations of psychological theories of delinquency

Psychologists have assembled a vast amount of information about delinquency, antisocial behavior, and mental health disorders. Personality theorists have determined that specific psychological characteristics are associated with delinquency, including low verbal intelligence, impulsivity, sensation-seeking, and aggression. Studies of mental health disorders have found that ODD is a common precursor to CD, and that ADHD and, possibly, PTSD worsen the severity of CD and increase the likelihood of mental health disorders and criminal behavior in adulthood. Cognitive theorists have shown that aggressive youths – and probably many delinquent youths – process social information and reason about morality differently from others. Aggressive youths, for example, tend to exhibit hostile attribution bias, emphasize negative memories, and disproportionately use negative or hostile schemas to evaluate social situations. They also see greater advantage to utilizing aggressive or hostile behavior during social interactions.

It will become clear after reading later chapters that one of the most valuable contributions of psychological research on delinquency and problem behaviors is its frequent emphasis on early childhood conditions. For many years, sociologically oriented criminologists tended to emphasize conditions and risk factors, such as poor family relations, that are present *during adolescence*. Although this is obviously important, it is rare to find sociological theories that directly address how risk factors in childhood affect later delinquency and adult criminality. From psychological research we learn, for instance, that aggressiveness, impulsivity, regulation of emotions, and other traits in *childhood* affect, through various mechanisms, antisocial behavior during adolescence and adulthood (Keenan and Shaw, 2003; Moffitt, 2003). In the absence of attention to early childhood risk factors of delinquency, or the way that childhood problem behaviors develop into delinquency and adult criminality, our understanding of the etiology of these forms of behavior is incomplete.

There are several limitations of the research on personality traits and delinquency, however. With the possible exception of impulsivity, there is a lack of consistent evidence about which personality factors affect delinquent behavior. One important criticism is that personality traits such as aggression and sensation-seeking may also be used to predict successful outcomes. For instance, the most successful athletes and business people are often those who are willing to take risks or be aggressive when pursuing treasured goals. Hence, there may be some definitional problems that psychologists need to work out: What specific types of aggression or sensation-seeking are risk factors for delinquency? What other factors affect the association between personality traits and delinquency? Do environmental conditions, such as neighborhood problems, affect how certain personality traits are channeled into later success or failure (Lynam et al., 2000)?

Although psychological research is more prone than sociological research to consider physiological and genetic factors, there is still a need to study the effects of physiological mechanisms on psychological factors. As mentioned in this chapter and in Chapter 3, there is important research linking impulsivity, aggression, and other personality traits to physiological and genetic characteristics. Yet there have been relatively few studies examining how the social information-processing–delinquency association is affected by brain and nervous system functioning. Dodge and colleagues have presented compelling evidence that information-processing differs in several ways between aggressive and non-aggressive youths. Cognitive psychology and the new field of cognitive neuroscience have shown that information-processing involves various aspects of brain functioning. However, there is little research assessing Dodge's social information-processing theory in terms of frontal lobe or prefrontal cortex functioning, ANS arousal, molecular genetics, neurotransmitters, hormones, or the myriad other physiological mechanisms that have been examined in studies of antisocial and delinquent behavior. Moreover, there continues to be a need for research on early childhood experiences that affect information-processing.

Finally, it is important to ask whether any of the models of delinquency or antisocial behavior used by psychologists constitutes a theory of delinquency. Investigating personality traits is useful for describing the psychological make-up of delinquents. Based on this research, we may claim that delinquents tend to be impulsive, aggressive, disagreeable, callous, and low in verbal intelligence. However, the principal question for a theory of delinquency is why are these personality traits associated with delinquency? Are these characteristics and delinquency the common result of physiological mechanisms that develop prenatally or soon after birth? Are they influenced by genetics? How do they interact with social circumstances to affect delinquency? Why do many adolescents who have these traits not become delinquent or offend only occasionally? A few researchers have attempted to develop theories that answer some of these questions, thus taking us closer to a viable theory of delinquency (Moffitt, 2003). However, substantially more work is needed.

Policy implications of psychological theories

Psychological research on delinquency and antisocial behavior has led to numerous prevention and intervention projects. Most of these have, over the years, emphasized individualized or group counseling of delinquents to delve into their psychological problems and reduce their tendency to misbehave. Many of these programs relied on psychoanalytic theory or personality trait perspectives to understand and treat the sources of delinquent behavior. Unfortunately, though, the results of these intervention programs have been disappointing: There is little evidence that individualized or group counseling, in general, leads to reductions in delinquent behavior (Akers and Sellers, 2008).

Studies of treatment programs for institutionalized offenders have also found that most programs do little to reduce reoffending. Although there is a slight reduction of subsequent arrests among those involved in counseling and skills training while incarcerated, the effects are not notable, with perhaps a 6 percent reduction in rearrests among those participating in these programs compared with those who do not. Nonetheless, programs that emphasize intensive contact with therapists, family counseling, anger management, acquisition of academic and vocational skills, time management, and interpersonal skills work best at reducing reoffending among incarcerated juveniles once they are released (Lipsey and Wilson, 1998).

Some of the most promising prevention and intervention programs involve CBTs. The principal goal of CBTs is to teach cognitively impaired adolescents to learn to interpret social cues better, reduce hostile attribution bias, and gain interpersonal skills. Assuming that many, if not most, antisocial and delinquent youths have problems processing social information and behaving appropriately, CBTs attempt to teach them to monitor their behavior and increase their awareness of inappropriate conduct; reinforce those behaviors that are socially appropriate; and set clear and specific goals that foster interpersonal relations and lessen the likelihood of aggression and impulsivity. Many CBTs also teach adolescents social skills to avoid aggression and conflict situations, and develop prosocial and problem-solving skills (LeBlanc and Le, 1999).

There are a wide variety of CBTs, so it is difficult to judge their general success in reducing aggressive and delinquent behavior. Nevertheless, following an assessment of 30 studies, Bennett and Gibbons (2000) concluded that CBTs have a modest effect on reducing problem behaviors among children and adolescents. CBTs are especially effective among older children and adolescents, but their effectiveness does not depend on the number of treatment sessions or the type of sample (e.g., clinical vs. community sample). Other reviews have also found that CBTs are moderately effective in reducing impulsivity, conduct disorders, and antisocial behaviors among children (e.g., McCart et al., 2006).

Conclusions

Psychological and psychiatric research has generated a wealth of knowledge about delinquency, antisocial behavior, and mental health disorders among children and adolescents. We have not exhausted the types of theories used by psychologists to explain delinquency, however. In later chapters, we shall discuss several other models that draw from psychology, such as those that emphasize social learning, frustration-aggression, or adolescent self-concept to understand delinquent behavior.

Although early psychological research was dismissed by those who argued that a child's social environment, not his mental make-up, was the source of most delinquent behavior, the last 20 years or so have seen a large number of rigorous studies that show that certain psychological characteristics are associated with delinquency. One of the most common results, for instance, is that impulsivity – a personality trait that involves the tendency to act before thinking through the consequences of the action – is consistently associated with delinquent and antisocial behavior.

Another informative line of research indicates that aggressive and antisocial youth tend to suffer from impairments or biases in social information-processing. The research of Dodge and colleagues, in particular, has shown that aggressive youths are more likely than others to exhibit hostile attribution bias and to see hostile responses to social situations as beneficial or preferable to other responses (see Dodge, 2006). Identifying the sources of dysfunctional information-processing requires substantially more research, but the fact that this characteristic is so prevalent among antisocial youth is important information that can contribute to the development of prevention and intervention programs.

The most valuable aspect of psychological research on delinquency and antisocial behavior, however, is its emphasis on childhood experiences that affect later misbehavior. For many years, especially during the mid- to late twentieth century, researchers focused on the period of adolescence and studied risk factors (such as delinquent peers and school relationships) that were associated with adolescent behavior. However, psychological research, especially studies that have followed people from childhood to adolescence, indicates that risk factors that emerge during childhood, such as aggressiveness and learning problems, predict later delinquency with substantial accuracy. As we shall learn in Chapter 13, this general finding has influenced developmental models of delinquency and crime over the life course. For example, those with a substantial number of childhood risk factors often become adolescent *and* adult offenders.

Nonetheless, as with research on physiological characteristics and delinquency, it is important to remember that psychological factors alone do not govern delinquency. Rather, it is more likely – and this has been shown in several studies reviewed in this chapter – that psychological risk factors interact with environmental risk factors (e.g., poverty, disorganized neighborhoods) to increase the risk of delinquency. In other words, impulsiveness, sensation-seeking, emotionality, or impaired social information-processing do not automatically result in delinquent behavior; rather, they are more likely to be channeled toward delinquency and other antisocial behavior among those children and adolescents who live in disorganized families and neighborhoods.

5 Communities and delinquency

Prologue

The Johnson family lived in the Chicago community of Englewood. In the 1950s and early 1960s Englewood was known for its many journalists and community leaders. However, rioting in the 1960s left the community in shambles. The following years were not kind to Englewood; its schools became known as among the worst in Chicago (Williams, 2005). Gang violence was rampant and residents heard a nightly chorus of gunfire.

Teresa Johnson raised two sons in Englewood. One of her sons was killed in the crossfire of a gun fight when he was 10 years old. Her other son, Ron, began to hang around Jesse, whose older brother belonged to a local street gang. Ron and Jesse joined the gang when they were in their early teens, initially as a form of protection; but Ron became second-in-command by the time he was 18 years old. Teresa tried to keep him on the right path, but she worked long hours, so she rarely saw Ron until late in the evening. Her neighbors had little time to watch her children; most either worked long hours or were unemployed and looking for work. Teresa lost her job when the company she worked for moved its operations overseas. For several years, she relied on government payments to feed her family.

A minister at the local church tried to form a community watch group to prevent gang activities, but most people, including Teresa, were too fearful to participate. It was not until the mid-1990s, when the section of Englewood where Teresa lived was designated an Enterprise Zone and a couple of small businesses opened up, that the community began to improve. A community–police relations board was established that monitored police–resident interactions and youth activities. Every Saturday a group of residents cleaned the community park and picked up litter. The State of Illinois and the City of Chicago provided funds to renovate the local community center and the schools. Although violence in Teresa's community decreased, her son was already serving 25 years to life at the Stateville Correctional Center for a gang-related shooting.

Introduction

As noted in Chapter 1, there is a distinction between individual-level and macro-level (group-level) theories. Individual-level theories explain differences in behaviors among individuals. Macro-level theories, by contrast, explain delinquency across spatial units. Many of the earliest sociological studies of delinquency were macro level because they were designed to explain differences in rates of offending across neighborhoods and cities. Interest in explaining differences in these rates was motivated initially as nineteenth-century novelists such as Charles Dickens, as well as social reformers and journalists, took an interest in the plight of the poor in industrialized London. Although they often argued that individual depravity and the failure of parents to control unruly children led to delinquency, most noted that virtually all juvenile delinquents came from the poorest areas of London (Shore, 1999). Similar conclusions were drawn by observers in the United States, especially by a group of researchers affiliated with the University of Chicago in the early twentieth century.

This chapter begins with a brief overview of some early research on whether crime and delinquency varied across urban communities. Next, we shall address some of the early theories about community effects. In particular, which community characteristics might explain differences in rates of juvenile delinquency? Is this tied to the way communities are organized and function? Alternatively, is it tied to the people who live in certain types of communities? We shall first review *types of community* explanations and then *types of people* explanations. We shall then discuss how these two models might be combined to yield better theories of community influences on delinquency. The next section of the chapter asks a different question: Does more delinquency lead to more community problems?

Before evaluating the evidence about the association between communities and delinquency, we shall discuss an area that has been given little attention when assessing this topic: schools as communities. The final section of the chapter addresses policy implications of research and theory on communities and delinquency.

Early research on communities and delinquency

During the nineteenth century, London was the largest city in the world. It became particularly attractive because it offered job opportunities to those seeking work from rural areas of Great Britain and immigrants from Europe, India, and China. However, the resulting urban swell was difficult to manage and the housing and sanitation systems were soon overwhelmed. It even became difficult to find enough space to bury the dead (Porter, 1994). Many observers and reformers began to call attention to the plight of the destitute in London. The slums of London became particularly notorious for their noxious living conditions. The journalist Andrew Mearns (1970 [1883]) gave perhaps the most graphic description of life in these slums:

> Tens of thousands are crowded together amidst horrors which call to mind what we have heard of the middle passage of the slave ship. To get into [their homes] you have to penetrate courts reeking with poisonous and malodorous gases arising from accumulations of sewage and refuse scattered in all directions and often flowing beneath your feet; courts, many of them which

the sun never penetrates, which are never visited by a breath of fresh air, and which rarely know the virtues of a drop of cleansing water. [The] dark and filthy passages [are] swarming with vermin . . . Walls and ceilings are black with the accretions of filth which have gathered upon them through long years of neglect . . . Every room in these rotten and reeking tenements houses a family, often two . . . Here are seven people living in one underground kitchen, and a little dead child lying in the same room (pp.4–5).

Motivated in part by these well-publicized conditions, the nineteenth-century social scientists Henry Mayhew and Charles Booth carefully examined the plight of the poor in London. Mayhew amassed hundreds of interviews with Londoners employed in various occupations such as rat killers, cab drivers, and chimney sweeps as well as pickpockets, thieves, and prostitutes. He published many of these interviews and his detailed observations in a four volume set titled *London Labour and the London Poor* (Mayhew, 1967 [1861]). The first three volumes were devoted to his notes and interviews, whereas the fourth volume analyzed the distribution of crimes throughout England and Wales. Mayhew noted that crime and delinquency rates were highest in the most densely populated counties of England and Wales. Moreover, these high-crime counties also had high rates of illiteracy, illegitimate children, and poverty. Densely populated areas, especially London, became known as "nurseries" of crime, places where a criminal underworld and social underclass cultivated delinquent instincts among poor, urban children (Shore, 1999).

Robert Park, a newspaper reporter turned sociologist, and his colleague Ernest Burgess noticed similar patterns of social problems in early twentieth-century Chicago. Their observations formed the basis for a new discipline called *social ecology*. This discipline applied ecological principles borrowed from the study of plants to understand urban areas. Ecologists had long noted that an area's plant life goes through several stages. First, there is a period of invasion when a new species of plant attempts to gain a foothold. Second, the new plant may become the dominant species in the area. Third, there is a period of succession during which the environment stabilizes with the inevitable presence of the new dominant organism.

Park (1936) viewed urban communities as a kind of "superorganism," which sociologists should analyze for patterns of invasion, domination, and succession. Moreover, it was important to study the development of urban communities and how residents maintain symbiotic associations with one another and with residents of other communities. Park and Burgess were initially interested in the succession of ethnic groups in Chicago communities. They focused on how members of ethnic groups tend to move out of certain communities as they gain the economic means to relocate to more desirable neighborhoods. This left the less desirable neighborhoods open for new immigrants representing other ethnic groups.

Burgess (1925) observed that cities tend to grow from their centers outward, in a pattern of concentric zones. Figure 5.1 provides a diagram of these zones. At a city's center there are the business and industrial districts. Moving outward, one reaches the *zone in transition*: an area where the housing is deteriorating, the poorest

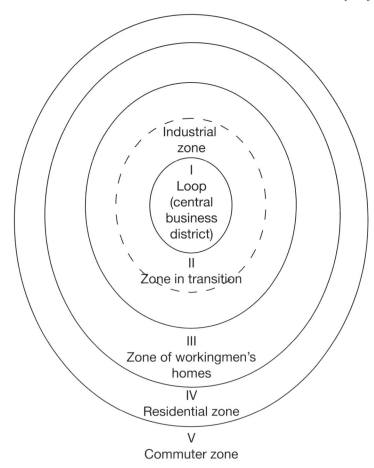

Figure 5.1 Burgess's model of concentric urban zones (adapted from Burgess, 1925, p.151).

residents live, and the industrial district is encroaching. This zone is marked by rapid population shifts since many of its residents leave as soon as they can afford to. The next zone is a residential area dominated by the working class and second-generation immigrants. The residential and commuter zones have better houses, with the commuter zone having the wealthiest residents.

This movement of residents may seem orderly, but it is not. Incoming groups often struggle to gain a dominant status and conflicts arise over different norms and expectations among distinct ethnic groups. This was illustrated, according to Burgess and Park, in Chicago's zone in transition. Its rapid population turnover during the early 1900s resulted in what they called *social disorganization*, a general lack of community and social ties among residents. As a result of these social processes each zone tends to develop a particular set of characteristics that affects the tendency of residents to experience social and behavioral problems.

Social disorganization and delinquency

Two researchers, Clifford R. Shaw and Henry D. McKay, were interested in how the social ecology and concentric zone models could be used to study rates of juvenile delinquency. They collected juvenile court data on the residences of officially identified male delinquents from 1900 to 1933. They then mapped the delinquency rates for specific areas of Chicago during three time periods: 1900–1906, 1917–1923, and 1927–1933. Shaw and McKay found that the highest rates tended to cluster around the central business district in areas on the edges of the business and industrial areas, but decreased as one moved outward. Commenting on these patterns, they wrote:

> Most of the areas characterized by high rates of delinquents, as well as by a concentration of individual delinquents, are either in or adjacent to areas zoned for industry and commerce . . . On the other hand, the areas with the lowest rates are, for the most part, those zoned for residential purposes (Shaw and McKay, 1969 [1942], p.55).

By comparing the distribution of rates over time, Shaw and McKay also observed that the areas with the highest and lowest delinquency rates were roughly the same in 1900 and 1930 even though population turnover had been substantial, if not complete. Moreover, as would be expected if delinquency was determined entirely by individual or family characteristics, the outer areas of Chicago did not experience increasing rates of delinquency as particular groups of residents moved outward. It is also interesting to note that Shaw and McKay, like Mayhew in London, found the same spatial patterns for other social and health problems, such as infant mortality, tuberculosis, and mental disorders.

What might account for the persistent problems found in certain communities? Shaw and McKay explained these results by proposing that the social characteristics of a community persist despite the groups that occupy it. In particular, they discussed several characteristics of communities that led to high levels of delinquency: shifts in the population, especially when it decreased rapidly; high rates of poverty; low home values; low rates of home ownership; and a high percentage of foreign born and African-American heads of households. These characteristics may be placed under three broader categories: residential instability, economic status, and population heterogeneity.

Shaw and McKay saw these characteristics as manifestations of social disorganization: "the inability of local communities to realize the common values of their residents or solve commonly experienced problems" (Bursik, 1988, p.521). In the areas of Chicago that had the highest rates of delinquency and the most gang activity, people tended to move in because they were inexpensive, but then move out quickly because they were undesirable places to live. Many immigrants lived in these areas only long enough to earn enough money to move to more attractive communities. There were also many different ethnic groups living in these areas of Chicago so they had high population heterogeneity. The result was a hodgepodge of people with different backgrounds, languages, and cultural values, which led to communication problems. Since many were trying to move, neighbors did not get to know one another. As Shaw (1951, p.24) wrote, in disorganized communities "the effectiveness of the neighborhood as a unit of social control and as a medium of the transmission of the moral standards of society is greatly diminished." Figure 5.2 provides a general diagram of the social disorganization model.

Studies show that indicators of social disorganization, such as ethnic heterogeneity, are still associated with higher crime and delinquency rates (e.g., Osgood and Chambers, 2000; Pratt and Cullen, 2005). Furthermore, areas with relatively high residential instability have higher crime and delinquency rates, whether these are measured among urban communities or across counties in the United States (e.g., Pratt and Cullen, 2005; Xie and McDowall, 2008). The association between poverty rates and delinquency rates is tenuous, though.

Critiques of the social disorganization model

Subsequent researchers were critical of Shaw and McKay's findings. Lander (1954), for example, studied the distribution of delinquency in Baltimore, MD. He determined that variables such as low rent, overcrowding, and substandard housing were not associated with higher rates of delinquency. Rather, what he termed "anomic" variables such as the percentage of owner-occupied homes and percentage of African-Americans were associated with delinquency across communities. Lander used the term "anomic" to refer to weak social norms in an area or the absence of restraining social factors over the behavior of juveniles.

Of course, Shaw and McKay also suggested that residential instability and ethnic heterogeneity were related to higher rates of delinquency; the percentages of owner-occupied homes and African-American residents were actually key indicators from Shaw and McKay's original model (Kornhauser, 1978). This supports the notion that a community's economic and demographic conditions affect social disorganization. For example, ethnic heterogeneity and population turnover make it difficult for residents to find common ground to solve problems or informally police their communities.

Another early criticism of the social disorganization model involves a thorny methodological issue. In 1950 Robinson (1950) published an article in which he urged caution to those investigating macro-level sources of behavior. It is normally improper to make conclusions about individual-level behavior when relying on macro-level data. For example, we cannot assume that an adolescent who lives in a racially heterogeneous community is delinquent merely because these

Figure 5.2 A general model of social disorganization.

communities have higher delinquency rates. This type of erroneous conclusion is termed the *ecological fallacy*. Robinson was merely warning researchers about this problem, yet many took it as a signal to shy away from macro-level research of any sort, including studies of social disorganization and delinquency. It also motivated an overemphasis on individual-level research on delinquency in the second half of the twentieth century (Bursik, 1988). Nevertheless, the specific mechanisms that define social disorganization did not reflect erroneous inferences from macro-level observations to individual-level conclusions. In fact, the macro level and the individual level are not independent, but may be considered together in a single theoretical model.

Other critics pointed out that Shaw and McKay, as well as many other social disorganization researchers, relied on official police records to measure delinquency rates. As noted in Chapters 1 and 3, this risks official bias. For example, studies have shown that the police are more likely to make arrests in certain urban areas, disproportionately target African-American youths for arrest, and are more likely to make contact with and arrest suspicious persons in racially heterogeneous communities (e.g., Kirk, 2008). It is not uncommon for people – including police officers – to brand certain communities as dangerous; these tend to be communities that are also socially disorganized (Sampson and Raudenbush, 2004).

Finally, Shaw and McKay did not sufficiently account for the changing nature of communities. They generally assumed that a community's characteristics tend to influence the residents rather than the reverse. However, Shaw and McKay could not have anticipated the rapid changes that occurred in U.S. cities following World War II. After the 1940s and 1950s, in particular, there were more immigrants from other areas of the world than during earlier periods; housing reform efforts began to take hold; and the industrial districts of cities began to contract as many businesses moved out of urban areas.

This criticism of Shaw and McKay's work does not, however, invalidate social disorganization theory. Rather, it simply encourages researchers to consider how urban communities might change over time in such a way that the same areas labeled socially disorganized a generation ago may move towards organizing, especially as the population stabilizes. In general, then, it remains accurate to say that communities that experience residential instability and high ethnic heterogeneity tend to have higher rates of juvenile delinquency. But why is this so? Two general explanations attempt to answer this question: *socialization* models and *social control* models.

Is it socialization or social control?

Socialization models suggest that bad communities will affect even good people. That is, people are naturally inclined to act kindly toward one another and parents normally teach their children to be law-abiding. However, living in a community where people are forced into conflict or cannot get along because of different cultures and expectations leads even good people to do bad things. Social control models, on the other hand, suggest that residents must actively control unruly behavior. In certain communities this is hard because there is a lack of relation-ships or shared understandings about how to control bad or violent behavior. We shall learn later in the chapter that this distinction is not as clear-cut as it may seem. For example, socialization could go either way: It is necessary to bring out the good in people *and* curb their bad desires.

Criminologists who favor socialization models tend to focus on *criminal* or *delin-quent values*. In particular, they argue that adolescents who live in disorganized communities observe law-abiding and law-violating behaviors and learn that there are conflicting sets of values. Given the preponderance of delinquent values and activities in these communities, there is a high probability of being exposed to delinquent peers and groups (Gibson et al., 2011). As Shaw (1951, p.24) noted, the "transmission of the moral standards of society" is difficult in disorganized communities. By contrast, in organized or stable areas there tend to be a dominant set of values that is consistent with the conventional values of society. Adolescents in these areas learn these values and thus avoid delinquent behavior. Others have observed that disorganized communities are infused with little hope and few opportunities for residents; this tends to foster oppositional values and "codes" that encourage behaviors such as delinquency and early sexual experimentation (e.g., Anderson, 1999).

Researchers who favor social control explanations argue that adolescents in disorganized neighborhoods lack supervision and community activities to occupy their time. Their parents must work long hours or are often single and hence have little time to spend with their children. Moreover, because many adults do not know one another, there is little joint supervision of adolescent activities. Delinquency is a natural outgrowth of unrestrained natural urges that result when there is a lack of supervision and guidance (Kornhauser, 1978; see also Chapter 8). Moreover, the lack of control in a community is also a form of *attenuated culture*: Residents of disorganized areas do not follow the conventional values of society (e.g., working hard in school, putting off having children until marriage) and, consequently, there is less motivation to control the behaviors of others (Warner, 2003). A weakening of conventional values or lack of motivation to take part in conventional society among residents of disorganized communities leads to a lack of social control; and it is this lack of social control that fosters delinquency. Studies suggest that socially disorganized neighborhoods tend to have more unsupervised youths and residents who are less likely to intervene when they see trouble. These characteristics predict higher rates of delinquency (e.g., Elliott et al., 1996; Sampson and Groves, 1989). Figure 5.3 illustrates these two explanations.

Types of communities or types of people?

Whether the link between communities and delinquency is due to differences in socialization or social control is not yet clear. A closely related question that is also difficult to answer is whether problems in disorganized communities, or the disorganization itself, are due to the types of people who live in these communi-ties or the structural characteristics of the communities.[1] Do some communities

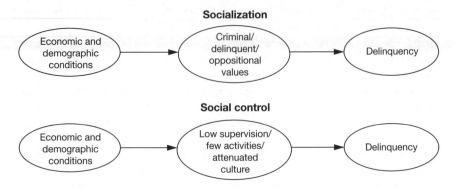

Figure 5.3 Socialization and social control models.

have more delinquency simply because they are populated by more delinquents (or dysfunctional families that put children at risk of delinquency)? Alternatively, do the structural characteristics of communities increase the risk of delinquency among adolescent residents regardless of the types of adolescents or families who reside in them? As mentioned earlier, Shaw and McKay focused on persistent characteristics of communities that affected delinquency rates, thus accepting a type of community explanation. Another question is whether certain communities attract more delinquents because they are run-down or have residents who are unwilling to prevent unruly behavior. However, it is difficult to decide which explanation is more valid because families and adolescents are not distributed randomly across communities; rather, families live in particular communities not only on account of their personal preferences, but also because of constraints due to income, race, and ethnicity.

Although we have already discussed how residential instability and ethnic heterogeneity can affect the behaviors of residents, we shall now consider two additional community characteristics that recent studies have addressed.

Broken windows and incivilities

Most people do not like to live in communities with substandard housing, walk streets that are littered with garbage, or see physical signs of neighborhood deterioration. Some who experience such an environment become complacent and add to the problem by littering or failing to keep up the neighborhood's appearance. A neighborhood's physical appearance might even contribute to delinquency if it attracts vandalism, theft, or gangs. Wilson and Kelling (1982, p.31) suggested that the effects of physical decay and disorder are even more subtle:

> disorder and decline are usually inextricably linked . . . Social psychologists and police tend to agree that if a window in a building is broken *and is left unrepaired*, all the rest of the windows will soon be broken. This is as true in

nice neighborhoods as in run-down ones. Window-breaking does not necessarily occur on a large scale because some areas are inhabited by determined
window-breakers whereas others are populated by window-lovers; rather, one
unrepaired broken window is a signal that no one cares and so breaking more
windows costs nothing. (It has always been fun.)

Wilson and Kelling argued that, if a sense of apathy about a community's
physical appearance takes root, then, eventually, residents become less likely to
control adolescents who misbehave, thus allowing petty offenses, the formation
of gangs, and greater fear of crime and delinquency among residents. This will
increase the likelihood of "criminal invasion": potential delinquents and criminals will be emboldened by the lack of control in the community. This "broken
windows" hypothesis has generated substantial interest among academics, public
policy experts, and police departments.

The solution to community-level delinquency and crime, according to Wilson
and Kelling, is to fix broken windows, cart off abandoned cars, remove graffiti,
and clean up litter. Moreover, when physical disorder is not tolerated, this sends
a message to potential offenders that their behavior will also not be tolerated. It
also brings residents together with the signal that their community is a safe and
orderly place to live (Kelling and Coles, 1996). These ideas led the New York City
Police Department to adopt a program of low tolerance for petty offending and
disorderly behavior in the late 1980s. Some observers claim that this led to the
general reduction in crime and delinquency rates in New York City and cities that
adopted this program in the 1990s.

However, critics argued that other factors led to lower crime and delinquency
rates during this period, including fewer young people of an offending-prone
age, the waning of the crack-cocaine problem, and a more robust economy that
reduced the number of people using public assistance programs (Harcourt, 2001).
Proponents countered that an influx of immigrants actually increased the number
of young people in New York City during the 1990s; cocaine use continued to be
high; and the city experienced a recession in the 1990s even as the crime rate was
falling (Corman and Mocan, 2002; Kelling and Coles, 1996).

A similar area of research involves *incivilities*. Incivilities are community problems such as garbage on the street, abandoned buildings, poor street lighting,
empty lots with substantial litter, and graffiti (Wilcox et al., 2004). These are signs
of *physical decay* or *disorder*. Moreover, incivilities include behaviors that create
fear or trepidation among residents, or what researchers identify as *social disorder*.
These include public intoxication, loud and crude language, street-level drug
sales, and groups of young people causing problems on the street (Sampson and
Raudenbush, 2004).

The association between incivilities and delinquency or crime is unclear. Some
studies indicate that neighborhoods with more physical decay have higher rates of
crime and delinquency, whereas other studies have found inconsistent effects (e.g.,
Wilcox et al., 2004; Gau and Pratt, 2008). In an enlightening study, Sampson and
Raudenbush (1999) determined that physical disorder and social disorder are not

associated with victimization reports (violence, burglary, or theft) once the proportion of immigrants, mixed land use, and what they term *collective efficacy*[2] within communities is considered. Disorder measures are associated only with robbery rates. Sampson and Raudenbush also found that residents base their reports of community disorder as much on the presence of minorities and impoverished residents as on the actual presence of graffiti, litter, dilapidated buildings, and gang activity. Thus, certain communities get a reputation for disorder that is based on the people who live in them; and this may affect perceptions of delinquency or crime more than the number of broken windows or abandoned cars.

Public housing

In the 1950s and 1960s, many cities erected large buildings to provide apartments for low-income residents. This type of public housing was often known simply as "projects." Many of these buildings were demolished in the 1990s, partly because they gained a reputation for delinquency, drug dealing, and violence. Numerous jurisdictions passed laws to evict residents of public housing facilities who were convicted of criminal activities (Rodney, 2004). Another form of public housing involves *Section 8* facilities. The Section 8 program was designed to encourage private construction companies to build homes for needy families. Today, there are also voucher programs intended to assist families who cannot afford housing.

Studies have found that fear of crime and rates of violent victimization are relatively high in public housing projects (e.g., Griffiths and Tita, 2009). However, other research has determined that actual rates of delinquency in housing projects tend to mirror rates in surrounding communities (e.g., Santiago et al., 2003). Moreover, the same characteristics, such as residential instability and poverty, which influence crime and delinquency rates in general, also affect them in public housing projects. In more detailed research, Ireland and colleagues (2006) noted that adolescents who live in public housing for long periods are not at higher risk of participating in violent crime; rather, those whose families move in and out of public housing report more participation in violent offenses such as assault and robbery. This suggests that it is not the type of housing that affects delinquency, but rather the uncertain living arrangements that some adolescents experience. Moreover, factors such as overcrowding and poverty are much better predictors of delinquency rates than residence in public housing units (Weatherburn et al., 1999). However, regardless of which community characteristics are associated with delinquency, it is still unclear whether adolescents who are delinquency-prone are simply more likely to live in socially disorganized communities. Thus, the next section discusses types of people explanations.

Types of people explanations

Jencks and Mayer (1990) outlined several ways that the types of people who live in disorganized communities might influence delinquent behavior. First, an *epidemic* or *peer influence model* suggests that children and adolescents are socialized, at least partly, by the role models they are exposed to in their communities. If children are raised in communities where other children and adolescents assault one another or steal from neighborhood stores then they are likely to adopt these sorts of behaviors. On the other hand, if children grow up in communities with peers who do well in school and stay out of trouble, they will probably adopt more conventional behaviors. Some researchers have termed this a *contagion model* because, much as people are susceptible to catching the flu when exposed to someone who is ill, children may "catch delinquency" if exposed to delinquents.

Second, a *collective socialization model* focuses on adults in a community. Affluent adults are thought to provide role models of conventional behavior and be less likely to tolerate misbehavior, even among children who are not their own. They are also more likely to intervene when a child is misbehaving. They usually work at steady jobs and do not engage in illegal or deviant activities, at least not visibly. Hence, affluent adults provide positive role models for youth. As the concentration of affluent adults in a community increases, the risk of delinquency decreases and rates of delinquency are lower. In contrast, if there are few affluent adults to provide conventional role models, such as in areas with high numbers of adults without jobs (Hoffmann, 2003), the risk of being exposed to unconventional adults – or those who are unwilling to intervene when observing misbehavior – increases.

A combination of the peer influence and collective socialization models forms the basis for the explanation that was ultimately adopted by Shaw and McKay (1969 [1942]) after they had conducted many interviews with youths from disorganized communities. They argued that, if there is a preponderance of delinquent values and activities in a community, then there is a high probability that youths will be exposed to peers and adults with delinquent values. Shaw and McKay's explanation led some to label this approach *subcultural*. Subcultural theories focus on the values and norms that arise in disorganized areas that, typically, are in opposition to more conventional values and norms promulgated by society. The challenges of urban life (e.g., overcrowded conditions, poverty) lead people to develop coping mechanisms that include greater tolerance for or reliance on deviant behaviors.

There are various studies that support peer influence and collective socialization models. Research has found that youths who grow up in impoverished and disorganized areas often report values and attitudes that are conducive to delinquency (e.g., Anderson, 2008; Stewart and Simons, 2010) and more delinquent peers (Gibson et al., 2011). Disorganized communities may also include a preponderance of adults who lack conventional societal values, which impairs their motivation to exercise control over misbehaving adolescents (Warner, 2003). However, a great majority of residents of disorganized, inner-city communities adhere to the values and norms of the broader society, including those that emphasize education and employment (Small and Newman, 2001).

Third, an *institutional model* focuses on adults from outside the community, including teachers, recreation and community center staff members, and police officers. Although some of these adults may live in the community, many commute to work. If better teachers tend to avoid working in disorganized communities, then children may get an inferior education and become involved in delinquency. If community workers and police officers treat adolescents in disorganized areas poorly or differentially arrest them for law violations, then this will affect their life chances and expose them to the juvenile justice system.

Peer/epidemic, collective socialization, and institutional models assume that children and adolescents must learn, from parents and other community residents, how to behave within or outside the law. Hence, they all share, to a certain degree, the assumption of learning theories of delinquency (see Chapter 7). The key issue, then, is to understand how adolescents learn conventional and unconventional behaviors, adopt values conducive to these behaviors, and what role significant others play in this learning and adoption process. We shall review research on this topic in Chapter 7.

A final model assumes that exposure to affluent adults does not decrease delinquency; rather, it may lead to a higher likelihood of delinquency for some who reside in disorganized communities. Based on social psychological principles about how people compare themselves with others, a *relative deprivation model* argues that, when affluent neighbors reside in the same community as impoverished residents, a heightened sense of unfairness results. As poor adolescents see people in their community who have money or valuable things, they also want them but do not have the same access to them through legitimate means. Moreover, a sense of frustration may build when experiencing poverty amidst affluence. Some poor adolescents might work harder to achieve the education or occupational goals that will allow them to gain valuable material items. Others may simply give up. However, according to this model, a substantial number of youths channel their sense of unfairness and frustration toward delinquent behavior. Violating the law may be a way to gain desired material items or to lash out against an inherent sense of unfairness (see Chapter 6).

There have been several studies of the effects of relative deprivation on delinquency. One study found that those who see themselves as having relatively few economic means are more likely to be involved in delinquency and drug use (Stiles et al., 2000). Other studies indicate that adolescents from less affluent families are more likely to engage in delinquency if they live in affluent communities than if they live in poor communities (Jarjoura and Triplett, 1997). Moreover, neighborhoods that experience gentrification – the revitalization of property in run-down communities – tend to have higher rates of robbery and larceny than other neighborhoods, although these tend to decrease in the long term (Covington and Taylor, 1989; O'Sullivan, 2005).

Combining types of community and types of people explanations

Some researchers contend that types of community and types of people explanations of delinquency need not be independent. For example, consider that some communities are neglected by city and state officials or lose desirable jobs over time. Consequently, these communities cannot provide their residents with much.

They tend to have fewer parks and more bars and liquor stores than other urban communities. There are fewer conventional outlets for youths after school. Many parents struggle to earn enough money to raise their children, which leads to less time available not only to supervise their children, but also to spend time together and provide positive socialization experiences. In general, as we look at the individual-level predictors of delinquency (e.g., impulsivity [see Chapter 4], stress [see Chapter 6], poor family relations, or low self-control [see Chapter 8]), we should ask whether they are more likely to be present in disorganized than in other communities. Hence, we should not only look at the types of youths who live in certain communities and speculate about why they misbehave, but also consider what it is about the community that undercuts their ability to succeed through conventional means or magnifies the individual-level factors that motivate delinquent behavior.

As an example of how macro-level factors influence the socialization of children, McNulty and Bellair (2003) examined racial/ethnic differences in delinquency across a number of communities. They pointed out that many studies have found that African-American adolescents report more violent behavior than Caucasian adolescents. What explains this difference? Is it some family-based risk factor, such as low supervision, or something else? McNulty and Bellair discovered that African-American youths report more violence because they are more likely to live in communities that have high rates of unemployment and more poverty, not because they tend to be raised in dysfunctional families. Hence, the type of community may affect the ability of families and community members to socialize youths to avoid delinquency and seek conventional lifestyles.

There are also several specific ways that communities affect the association between individual-level risk factors and delinquency. Some of these were discussed in Chapters 3 and 4. For example:

- Cigarette smoking and alcohol use during pregnancy are associated with a higher risk of delinquent behavior, especially for adolescents living in poor communities (Gibson et al., 2001).
- The association between early onset of menarche and delinquency among girls is limited to those who live in poor communities (Caspi et al., 1993).
- The positive association between impulsivity and delinquency exists primarily in poor communities; there is no association between impulsivity and delinquency in high-status communities (Lynam et al., 2000).

In general, not only do adolescents in disorganized communities experience more risk factors than adolescents residing in better-off communities (e.g., Kroneman et al., 2004), but also the link between risk factors and delinquent behavior tends to be magnified in disorganized communities. As discussed earlier, parents of children who experience these risks often do not have the resources to cope with their children's incipient misbehavior. Parents in disorganized communities experience many difficult life circumstances, including social isolation, lack of employment opportunities, low income, and a lack of access to community resources (Moore, 2003). Their children often attend poor schools that lack the resources to provide adequate educational opportunities. In brief, living in these communities makes childrearing more difficult and, consequently, socialization suffers.

An example of this is found in a study by Beyers and colleagues (2003). They determined that the association between parental supervision and delinquency was more pronounced in communities with high residential instability than in other communities. Figure 5.4 provides an illustration of one of their key findings. Similar studies have shown that residing in disadvantaged communities is detrimental to quality parenting, which then leads to associating with delinquent peers and a higher risk of delinquent behavior (e.g., Furstenberg et al., 1999). Moreover, this process may affect boys more than girls (Kroneman et al., 2004).

Collective efficacy

An important theoretical model that emphasizes whether some communities are better able to control the behaviors of adolescents or not uses the concept *collective efficacy* to link community characteristics and crime and delinquency. Researchers studying urban communities have addressed community social control (the capacity of community residents to regulate other residents' behaviors) and social integration (social ties, friendships) as separate phenomena. Studies of social control focus primarily on crime and deviance, whereas studies of integration focus on community satisfaction. For example, as explained earlier, a lack of informal social control in communities is thought to result from community disadvantage and consequently affect delinquency rates (Sampson, 2000). On the other hand, having more friends in one's community is associated with a greater sense of community satisfaction and leads to residential stability (Austin and Baba, 1990). Sampson and colleagues (1997) surmised that these two phenomena were actually indicators of an important, underlying concept that is a key feature of

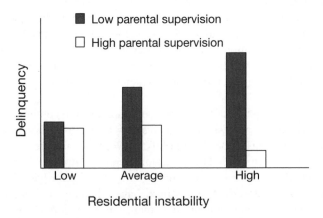

Figure 5.4 Parental supervision, residential instability, and delinquency (adapted from Beyers et al., 2003, p.46).

communities: collective efficacy, or mutual trust combined with the shared willingness to intervene for the community good. Social control, especially when it is informal (e.g., provided by residents rather than the police), does not normally occur unless there is trust and social ties among community residents. It is unlikely that someone will intervene when observing delinquent behavior unless she believes that her neighbors will back her up or provide support if things become dangerous. A general model illustrating the role of collective efficacy is shown in Figure 5.5. Note that neighborhood conditions, such as economic disadvantages and residential instability, are thought to decrease collective efficacy, which, in turn, creates conditions where delinquency is allowed to occur. Collective efficacy, however, says little about adolescents' motivations to commit delinquent acts. Rather, the model assumes (although not always clearly) that a lack of community social cohesion and informal control permits delinquency to occur.

Few studies have addressed the association between collective efficacy and delinquency. Most research on collective efficacy focuses on crime, sexual behavior, or educational outcomes (e.g., Almgren, 2005; Browning et al., 2004). In one notable exception, Maimon and Browning (2010) examined the association between collective efficacy and violent behavior among youths in Chicago. Higher collective efficacy was directly related to less violent youth behavior. Moreover, neighborhoods in which youths spent more time hanging out with friends, going to parties, and going out on weeknights experienced more violent behavior by these youths. However, in neighborhoods with high levels of collective efficacy, this effect was relatively weak. This suggests that collective efficacy may affect adolescent behaviors, but more research is needed to show how generally applicable it is as an explanation of delinquency.

Effects of crime and delinquency on communities

Another important issue is the impact of delinquency on communities. For example, suppose that a well-kept, yet poor, neighborhood finds itself overrun – perhaps because of a police crackdown in an adjacent neighborhood – with rival gangs that are trying to control the city's cocaine and methamphetamine trade. The neighborhood is an area that the police and city officials tend to ignore, perhaps because it has few politically active residents or business owners. Over time, the gangs gain a foothold. How will the residents react? Perhaps some – and

Figure 5.5 Community composition, collective efficacy, and delinquency (adapted from Sampson et al., 1997, p.919).

these will probably be the better-off residents – will move to more organized areas of the city or to the suburbs. Others may become fearful of crime and shelter themselves in their homes, coming out only when necessary. Greater fear of crime may feed a decrease in neighborhood satisfaction, trust, and social cohesion. This type of "spiral decay" (Skogan, 1990) has been shown to lead to more poverty, a depressed housing market, a lack of new businesses, racial segregation, social isolation, and less collective efficacy (Oh, 2005; South and Messner, 2000). In general, then, it is likely that crime and delinquency are reciprocally related with declining community conditions. When crime and delinquency increase, more social disorganization tends to result. This is followed by conditions in a community, such as low social cohesion and less informal control, which foster an environment conducive to more crime and delinquency.

Schools as communities

Adolescents spend a large portion of their waking time in school. Thus, schools function as communities in which they experience socialization and social control. Relationships among students, or between students and teachers, are similar to the social ties that determine the cohesiveness of a neighborhood. Values such as hard work and an achievement-oriented outlook mirror the conventional values that social disorganization researchers address as they consider subcultures or inconsistent values in certain communities. In addition, there is clearly variation in the way that schools are organized (Gottfredson, 2001).

Payne and colleagues (2003) argued that a *communal school organization* – which includes participation by students, informal social relations, administrator support for teachers, and common norms and values – is similar to collective efficacy. When teachers, students, and administrators get along, when they are dedicated and involved, and when morale is high, students are less likely to misbehave because there is joint monitoring of behavior by all members of the school community. Payne and colleagues found that a communal school organization is associated with less teacher victimization. It is also indirectly associated with less delinquency and student victimization because students are more committed and happier in these schools.

Although other studies have shown that school characteristics are associated with delinquency (e.g., Gottfredson et al., 2005; LeBlanc et al., 2008), it is not entirely clear whether the types of students or independent characteristics of schools are better able to explain delinquent behavior. Moreover, the impact of schools on delinquency is likely to be influenced by characteristics of the community surrounding the school (Bowen and Van Dorn, 2002), with schools in disorganized neighborhoods experiencing more delinquent behaviors by students.

The promises and limitations of community theories

The idea that community characteristics affect crime and delinquency has existed for more than 100 years. Social reformers in London and sociologists in Chicago concluded that the conditions of urban life in the nineteenth and early twentieth centuries led to mental illness, the spread of disease, and increasing crime. Living in sordid conditions had a profound effect on people, many of whom lost hope in the future. Sociologists from the University of Chicago were especially instrumental in collecting information on communities with which to assess people's lives in urban areas. The term *social disorganization* stemmed from the realization that the structural conditions of communities affected the life chances and behaviors of residents.

The concern with social disorganization led to important research on how community conditions affect rates of crime and delinquency. In particular, there is substantial evidence that unemployment, ethnic heterogeneity, and residential instability decrease the ability of residents to informally control the activities of community residents, especially adolescents and young adults, and impair the ability to socialize children and adolescents so they develop conventional values or avoid delinquent behaviors. In addition, these and other community characteristics diminish social ties among community residents because they lead to less trust, fewer community organizations, and more fear of problem behaviors. The combination of more control and more social ties is known as collective efficacy.

Nevertheless, the evidence concerning the role of informal control, social ties, and collective efficacy is not conclusive. Perhaps the most glaring limitation of research on social disorganization and collective efficacy is that most studies have assessed only official crime rates or victimization experiences among adults rather than youths. Furthermore, additional research is needed on how community conditions translate into collective efficacy. What process, for instance, determines trust or close relationships among residents? Is trust based primarily on familiarity with residents or length of residence in a community? Research has shown that friendships are less restricted by community boundaries than in the past; how does this affect social cohesion and trust? Is the ability or motivation to intervene affected mainly by social ties with other residents or are other factors more consequential, such as age, gender, social class, employment, or previous experience with crime? Some community gangs may actually contribute to social organization by protecting residents from criminals or delinquents from outside the community, but can we claim that they also add to the sense of collective efficacy? These and many other questions remain unanswered.

Research on communities has also not attended sufficiently to how residents respond to delinquent behavior. As discussed earlier, several studies have determined that, as crime increases, property values decrease, more houses are abandoned, and disorder increases. However, research analyzing short-term effects has shown that, in some communities, perceptions of crime and victimization experiences are associated with more attempts at problem solving, such as organizing community groups or helping neighbors deal with problems (Woldoff, 2002). Hence, increases in crime or delinquency do not automatically herald more community disorder or diminished collective efficacy. Rather, residents frequently band closer together in a signal of greater social cohesion. A question that remains is whether there are identifiable factors that affect how community residents respond to the threats posed by crime.

It is also important that researchers consider how the association between delinquency and individual- and family-level factors is affected by community-level characteristics. For example, we learned in previous chapters that there are certain biochemicals (e.g., MAO-A) and environment toxins (e.g., lead) that place youth at risk for delinquency. If we assume that a social control assumption is valid, then perhaps residents of neighborhoods with low collective efficacy find it especially difficult to control the behaviors of youth with these risk factors. Given the finding that children in inner-city neighborhoods are exposed to substantial levels of lead and other heavy metals from the environment, this proposition is reasonable. However, we also cannot ignore the effects of these environmental risk factors on whether youths are socialized to behave in a lawful manner.

Finally, researchers need to develop more sophisticated methods for investigating how people decide where to live. People base this decision on many personal and perceived community characteristics, including racial composition, economic status, affordability, schools, and family ties. Studies are needed that examine the joint influences of residential choices, social ties, and constraints on families (Sampson et al., 2002). There is some evidence that adolescents who move from impoverished neighborhoods to more affluent areas decrease their involvement in some types of delinquency (e.g., Kling et al., 2005, 2007; Sharkey and Sampson, 2010). However, over the long term, involvement in delinquency and drug use may actually increase. Therefore, it is clear that more work on how families end up in certain types of neighborhoods – and its consequences – is needed.

Policy implications of community research

Since much of the research discussed in this chapter addresses factors that affect crime and delinquency rates across communities, policies should focus on helping communities become more organized (Reiss, 1986). If a lack of social cohesion among residents or weak informal controls causes delinquency, empowering residents to intervene when misbehavior occurs is an important step (Novak and Seiler, 2001). If unemployment and the relocation of skilled jobs from urban to suburban areas affect delinquency rates, then efforts to revitalize local economies are needed. Some have argued that investing in employment is only part of the solution; there must be similar investments in education (Brown and Richman, 1997). History shows that the revitalization of communities is expensive and laborious, however; finding sufficient resources in a free-market economy is difficult. If the key is increasing collective efficacy even when communities are impoverished and experience residential instability, then an effort to increase social ties and community groups should be a priority. However, we should also not ignore the possibility that socialization experiences of young people may differ in disorganized communities. Thus, programs to help parents who do not have sufficient economic or social resources for successful childrearing may also be needed.

Numerous programs have been designed to revitalize urban communities or provide poor families assistance with childrearing. Many include steps to increase involvement in schools, develop community organizations such as block clubs and neighborhood watch groups, and increase access to social services. They also attempt to raise awareness of community problems among local politicians and state legislators. Federal programs designed to increase community investment and create *Empowerment* or *Enterprise Zones* to augment the economic status of inner-city neighborhoods are part of this general effort (Brown and Richman, 1997). Early evaluations of these federal programs have not yielded consistent evidence, however; in some communities Empowerment Zones have led to the creation of more jobs, but they are usually low-paying (O'Keefe and Dunstan, 2001), in others, there is little evidence that they have affected the local economy (Pulsipher, 2005).

Research suggests that the greatest potential for success occurs when (1) delinquency prevention programs are part of a larger effort to mobilize the community and successfully enroll residents in community organizations that serve various functions; and (2) when they take place in communities that are already at least partially cohesive and stable (Bursik and Grasmick, 1993). Unfortunately, the communities that need the most help to decrease delinquency often suffer the most from conditions that make prevention and intervention programs less effective.

It is still too early to tell what role collective efficacy might play in policy efforts to decrease delinquency. Programs that increase the economic and educational viability of communities, and that encourage participation in community organizations, would seem to have the side-effect of increasing collective efficacy. In addition, Cancino (2005) has argued that the following steps be used to enhance collective efficacy: increase the use of police–citizen collaborations (e.g., citizen patrols, community policing); encourage residents to become more active in local politics; and ensure that residents participate in block associations and neighborhood organizations.

There are several encouraging programs that have followed this advice. For instance, the Ten-Point Coalition, which tries to improve trust between police and residents, organizes community leaders to monitor youth activities, uses "reverse stings" to arrest drug purchasers from outside the community, and encourages community events at parks has led to lower rates of violent delinquency in Boston (Sampson, 2001). The question that remains, however, is whether implementing these steps is most difficult in the communities that need them most.

Conclusions

Communities do matter for understanding delinquency. Residential instability, economic disadvantages such as poverty and a shortage of jobs, a lack of community cohesion and trust, and problems maintaining social order and control are signs of social disorganization and affect the ability of residents and authorities to reduce delinquent behavior. The combination of trust and informal social control – or collective efficacy – is negatively affected by these conditions. Yet they also impair the family and community's ability to socialize young people to pursue conventional goals and avoid delinquent behavior.

Nonetheless, substantially more research is needed to fully understand the mechanisms that undermine the ability of community residents to socialize children and adolescents or to intervene when delinquency occurs. For example, understanding how trust and the motivation to intervene develop is not a simple issue. There are numerous aspects in addition to demographic and economic conditions that may destabilize residents' trust and informal control efforts. These include factors that are often outside the control of community residents, such as economic investment, housing programs, construction projects, and political will or motivation. It is not surprising to find that poor residents have significantly less political power than more affluent residents of urban areas; unfortunately, this often translates into less efficacy outside the community as well as within.

6 The stresses and strains of adolescence

Prologue

It had been an awful year for Katie. Her parents went through a bitter divorce and she was forced to move to another school, leaving friends and a neighborhood she loved. On top of that, her mother told her that she had to spend her college fund. This shattered Katie's dream of going to college. The promise of government grants didn't help her feel any better.

The neighborhood they moved into was pretty rough. Katie heard gunshots one night in front of the house. It was a scary place to be. Katie wanted to call her dad, but her mother said the phone bills would be too high. Katie felt lonely, lost, angry, and that she had lost control of her life.

On her first day at a new school, another girl bumped into Katie in the lunchroom, forcing her to drop a tray of food. That was it; Katie couldn't take it any more. She grabbed a plastic fork and stuck it in the girl's arm. She then shoved her over a table. Katie was suspended for three days. The police came to her house and said the girl's mother wanted Katie arrested for assault. Katie was scared but still angry and moody. It wasn't long before she got into another fight. Fighting helped her feel better and gain a sense that she had control of her life again. Soon her mother stopped trying to get her to behave. Besides, she was too busy working two jobs since her ex-husband rarely paid child support. Before long, after Katie's third arrest for assaulting another student, she was expelled and ended up with a six-month sentence to the juvenile correctional facility. She was also ordered to attend an anger management course.

Introduction

One of the primary cultural demands in American society is to make money. Accumulating wealth is a major sign of success. The allure of America is its reputation as a land where anyone with the right drive and determination can become wealthy. Many students spend four or more years in college laboring through difficult, often tedious tasks, because education is a pathway to wealth and prestige. Education is not normally an end in and of itself; it has evolved into a means to an end. Higher education for many is the primary vehicle utilized to begin the process of accumulation of money – to live the American Dream. However, what happens if hard work and determination do not result in a better life? Suppose that the only work available is in a low-paying job? Moreover, how much wealth is enough? Is it possible that much of the crime in American society is a reaction to the cultural ethos to make as much money as possible?

William Finnegan (1990) of *The New Yorker* magazine spent several months in New Haven, Connecticut, observing and interacting with a young man living on the margins of society whom he calls Terry Jackson. Terry is from a downwardly mobile family, living in a fractured community and an economically devastated city. On a daily basis, Terry is confronted with the demand to obtain material goods: Television tells him what is important, the city mall displays attractive items, and Yale University regularly reminds him that there are two Americas – one for the privileged and another for the under-privileged.

In a relatively short period of time, Terry abandons his low-paying jobs in the food service sector to pursue a career as a street-level drug dealer. He uses the money he earns to buy Gucci pants, leather shirts, thousand-dollar shoes, and gold chains that proclaim to everyone that he has money. At the core of Finnegan's story is a message that links the cultural ethos of accumulation of wealth to the decision to deal drugs in the ghetto.

Similar stories are told by Sullivan (1989) in an ethnographic study of Brooklyn neighborhoods and in Hagedorn's (1988) research on up-and-coming gangs in Milwaukee. These reports demonstrate how difficult it can be for youths who live in disadvantaged areas of the United States. They are consistently bombarded by media and cultural messages that the accumulation of money and consumer goods is valued in society, yet their opportunities to obtain these valuable items through legitimate work are frustrated by an educational, employment, and economic system that does not serve them well.

This chapter is concerned with what happens when youths are exposed to various situations that may cause them to feel uncomfortable or stressed. Do youths who adopt the view that accumulating material possessions is important but do not have the means to get them legally tend to turn to delinquency? What about youths who are exposed to various stressful events, such as family conflict or the death of a friend? Does experiencing these stressful events lead to delinquency? Strain theory was developed to answer these questions. Its original form focused mainly on the importance of accumulating material goods and the limited means of achieving this goal for many people, but it has been revised to deal more broadly with a variety of stress-inducing experiences that may provoke anger, hostility, or other emotions. After considering early and more contemporary versions of strain theory, we consider the promises and limitations of this theory, as well as what it might say about policies designed to reduce delinquency.

Early versions of strain theory

The sociologist Robert K. Merton is largely recognized as the originator of what became strain theory. In his influential article, "Social Structure and Anomie,"

Merton (1938) argued that deviance is not an inborn characteristic; rather, it flows from certain social forces. These social forces shape people differently, so that some are at greater risk for involvement in deviance than are others.

Imagine that society is divided into two dimensions that theoretically work together to generate a balanced and stable environment: culture and structure. The cultural dimension tells people what is important and how to achieve it legitimately. As already indicated, a key cultural demand is the accumulation of wealth. Those who make vast quantities of money are praised and afforded celebrity status. For example, Bill Gates, Warren Buffet, and Donald Trump are household names, mainly because they are among the richest men in the United States and are thought to characterize an American ideal of economic success.

Clearly, making money is not the only culturally defined goal. There are others, such as a good home life and a good education. Nonetheless, making money tends to fall fairly high on a list of important goals. Just think of the mortgage crisis of 2008 when millions of Americans suffered from financial problems because they could no longer afford the homes they had bought. Although we could accuse them of being greedy and consciously buying more house than they could afford, the cultural environment supported their decision and certain unscrupulous people took advantage of the goal that people should own their own homes.

According to Merton (1968), the cultural mandate to pursue wealth is communicated to all who either are born here or otherwise arrive in the United States. Regardless of their social class or background, people tend to define status and success primarily in terms of money and material goods. However, the culture not only defines the goals, it also defines the acceptable means of reaching goals. Merton referred to acceptable measures as "institutionalized means." For example, formal education and occupational opportunities that flow from a good education are considered as legitimate approaches to the accumulation of wealth. Merton also discussed how persistence, hard work, and deferral of gratification facilitate access to legitimate means of financial success. These are key components of the culture: the primary goal and the primary means to achieve the goal.

However, culture is only one dimension of society. The other dimension is its social structure, which has many different aspects. For example, a patriarchal social structure places primacy upon the male head of the family, whereas a matriarchal social structure places primacy upon the female head of the family. However, the aspect of social structure that received the most attention in Merton's work concerns the class or economic structure.

It is undeniable that there are many poor people living in the United States. The number of children and adolescents living below the federally established poverty level (a family of four making less than $22,000 a year was living in poverty in 2009) hovers around 14 million. Nevertheless, the poor and the rich get the same message – make as much money as possible.[1] However, the economic structure in American society actually makes it difficult for the poor to achieve economic success. They tend to have limited access to the best medical care, the best schools, and many of the resources that would ease the trials of everyday living. Government assistance helps, but it offers only limited means of supporting people in the lower economic rungs of society. As a result, accumulation of wealth for the poor is full of hurdles. Whereas our culture emphasizes making money, the social structure tips the playing field unfairly toward the middle and upper classes.

According to traditional strain theorists, this cultural–structural "malintegration" or "disjunction" is the source of much crime, deviance, and delinquency. One key hypothesis is that the likelihood of delinquency increases in an environment where there is a significant emphasis upon a cultural goal, but the social structure inhibits pursuit of this goal. This disjunction between cultural goals and access to legitimate means is often referred to as *strain* (Featherstone and Deflem, 2003). For instance, a young person may recognize that the best way to achieve the American Dream is through higher education, but if college attendance is not available then access to an institutionalized means is blocked. This person, faced with a disjunction between goals and access to institutionalized means, experiences strain, and strain increases the likelihood of a deviant adaptation.

We all experience strain, but those who experience it more often and for a longer duration tend to come from the lower economic rungs of society. A disproportionate number of the lower class are excluded from the conventional opportunity structure, and, as a result, "the greatest pressures toward deviation are exerted upon the lower strata" of society (Merton, 1968, p.168). Moreover, since many people in the lower classes are "armed with little formal education and few economic resources" (Merton, 1968, p.199) they tend to reject legitimate means and may adopt illegitimate means as they seek culturally driven goods.

Merton argued that strain can result in one of five adaptations: conformity, ritualism, rebellion, retreatism, and innovation. These adaptations are presented in Table 6.1.

Conformity is, by far, the most typical outcome. In fact, much of our cultural ethos focuses on self-reliance and independence to reach cultural goals, especially when institutionalized means are available. Therefore, even if one is falling short of the American Dream, the cultural demand for self-reliance mandates that people use conventional means to reach it. Ritualists differ from conformists on the expectation of achieving the cultural goal. Whereas conformists remain convinced that the cultural goal is worth striving for, ritualists have learned that reaching this goal is unlikely, but they continue to play by the rules anyway.

Those who rebel toss aside both the cultural goals as well as the institutionalized

Table 6.1 Merton's adaptations to strain

Adaptation	Cultural goal	Institutionalized means	Example
Conformity	Yes	Yes	Upper management
Ritualism	No	Yes	Educator
Rebellion	No/yes	No/yes	Old World Amish
Retreatism	No	No	Drug addict
Innovation	Yes	No	Thief

means. They establish new goals and new ways to attain those goals. The Old World Amish represent rebels. They reject the cultural goal of accumulation of wealth and the means to achieve that wealth. Instead, they embrace a different set of goals and means and as a result remain largely separate from mainstream American life. Retreatists adapt to strain by dropping out of life. Many float through life, some searching for the next thrill, the next high. Retreatists are the drug addicts, the alcoholics, and the reclusives who reject the goals and the means.

The adaptation of innovation receives the greatest amount of attention in criminology because it refers specifically to delinquent and criminal behavior. A number of individuals are confronted with the cultural goal to accumulate wealth, but their place in the social structure severely limits their legitimate opportunity to do so. Confronted with the pressure to accumulate wealth and material goods, yet without legitimate strategies, these individuals innovate – they develop illegitimate means to pursue cultural goals. Figure 6.1 captures a basic causal diagram of Merton's strain theory.

In this model, those lowest on the economic ladder experience the most strain. This strain then affects one's likelihood of responding in a deviant manner. However, one of the shortcomings of this perspective is the question why one strained individual opts for rebellion, another for ritualism, and still a third for innovation? It is here that the theory needs elaboration and further theoretical development because the processes linking strain to crime and delinquency remain largely unexplored in Merton's theory.

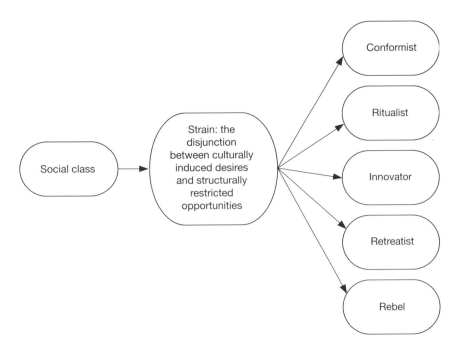

Figure 6.1 Merton's basic strain model.

Adolescents, schools, and middle-class status

Albert Cohen (1955) observed that much juvenile delinquency serves no apparent purpose and certainly does not make adolescent offenders wealthier. He also criticized Merton for presenting a theory that implies that the conditions leading to delinquency take place in the absence of interactions with others. Moreover, Cohen was dissatisfied with Merton's definition of strain. Practically speaking, adolescents in Merton's world need to realize early on that their access to the legitimate means is restricted and that alternative strategies are required to accumulate wealth. Cohen thought that this future orientation gives far too much credit to adolescents. Most of them are more concerned about the present.

As an alternative, Cohen argued that adolescents are subjected to formal evaluation of ability in school with little regard for individual differences or backgrounds. In fact, schools actively encourage students to compare themselves against "all comers." Evaluations of school performance represent a universal standard by which adolescents are judged. In this competitive atmosphere, those unable to achieve status in school experience frustration or strain. Adolescents who experience this frustration are not evenly distributed in the social structure, however. Lower-class children are the most likely to experience frustration because of their ascribed position. Those from the "most disadvantaged classes . . . lack the requisite personal qualifications resulting from their class-linked handicaps" to achieve status in school (Cohen, 1955, p.86).

Cohen used the concept of "reaction-formation" to explain the process by which strained juveniles reject the culturally derived impulse to achieve middle-class status. The inability to advance toward this status or live up to "middle class measuring rods" frustrates lower-class adolescents. A reaction-formation takes place to mitigate the frustration, and the culturally mandated goals become unimportant as they are relegated to the unconscious mind. Reaction-formation allows the incipient delinquent to reject the legitimacy of conventional goals and norms, and begin to develop alternative sources for status. Thus, delinquents are like the classic rebel in Merton's theory.

Cohen furthermore argued that the process of moving from status frustration to delinquency involves mutual conversion via "exploratory gestures." A group of similarly frustrated adolescents comes together and begins to tentatively experiment with alternative standards for status. As a delinquent subculture begins to appear, the group must be willing to recognize the new status structure, because "[s]tatus, by definition, is a grant of respect from others" (Cohen, 1955, p.136). Figure 6.2 illustrates Cohen's modifications to the strain perspective.

Cohen's model addresses specifically the development of rebellious behavior: through a process of reaction-formation with similarly situated peers a delinquent gang forms that values everything antithetical to the middle class and awards status in the group for behavior that opposes the middle-class way of life. Delinquency represents this oppositional behavior.

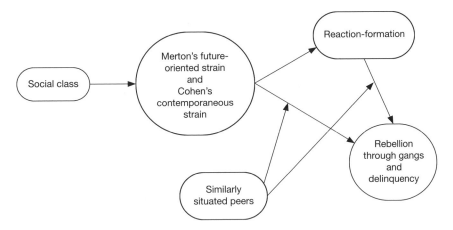

Figure 6.2 Cohen's elaboration of strain theory.

Delinquency and opportunity structures

Soon after Cohen developed his model, Richard Cloward and Lloyd Ohlin (1960) attempted to shift the theoretical focus back to innovation, clarify the intervening mechanisms that link strain to innovation, and argue that not only are legitimate opportunity structures important, but so also are *illegitimate opportunity structures* (Hoffmann, 2008). Some youths, for example, have more access than others to opportunities to deviate or become involved in delinquent behavior.

Cloward and Ohlin (1960) argued that the main legitimate pathway to follow to achieve wealth is education. Therefore, strain occurs when there is a desire for money but access to a good-quality education is blocked. Furthermore, an adolescent's social class, in part, determines access to higher education. They maintained that the possibility for lower-class adolescents to secure higher education is often limited because of structural impediments, including high costs, discrimination, economic hardship, and poor secondary education (Sullivan, 1989). Therefore, although lower-class adolescents embrace the cultural mandate to acquire money and material goods, they cannot gain sufficient access to higher education in order to pursue them. Thus, lower-class adolescents disproportionately experience strain (the pressure to deviate). However, why do they choose innovation? Cloward and Ohlin recognized that, although strain creates pressure for deviance, it alone cannot determine the form of the deviant response. To link a strained adolescent specifically to innovation Cloward and Ohlin incorporated much of Cohen's (1955) discussion of peer influences. They also claimed that a process of alienation serves to direct strained adolescents toward delinquency and interaction with other delinquents. This occurs in three ways.

Frustration, anger, and hostility[2]

According to Cloward and Ohlin (1960), the *alienation process* begins with blaming others for adversity. Adolescents who experience strain can attribute the adversity to either personal shortcomings or social obstacles. Blaming oneself, or what is called "internalization of blame," places pressure upon an individual to change oneself rather than the system (Cloward and Ohlin 1960, p.112). However, blaming other people or institutions (externalization of blame) results in frustration, anger, and hostility directed at others and the social structure. These are important mechanisms in the pathway that leads strained youths to delinquency. According to Messner (1988, p.39):

> Merton's theory of deviant motivation . . . involves a rather simple social psychological model. Individuals who are relatively deprived become frustrated and angered, which drives them to do things that they normally would not do [references omitted].

Withdrawal from legitimate norms

In addition to experiencing frustration and anger, adolescents who externalize blame

> may become alienated from the established set of social norms. [They] may even become convinced that [they are] justified in evading these norms in pursuit of success-goals (Cloward and Ohlin, 1960, pp.111–112).

Cloward and Ohlin maintained that lower-class adolescents (and in particular lower-class African-American adolescents) may be at greater risk of feelings of anger and alienation because our cultural ethos encourages an egalitarian view of economic success, even though the reality is that many compete but relatively few will succeed.

Many lower-class adolescents perceive themselves to be as qualified as middle- or upper-class adolescents but they tend to remain stationary while others are moving toward or achieving various forms of success. As a result of observing similarly qualified adolescents succeed, lower-class adolescents may conclude that the system is unfair. Therefore, they are more likely to attribute adversity to the social structure rather than themselves. This tendency to experience feelings of hostility directed at, as well as alienation from, society is reinforced by highly visible discriminatory barriers to opportunity.

Access to illegitimate opportunities

Cloward and Ohlin (1960) saw their theory as identifying a specific source of strain and linking it to a specific deviant adaptation: the formation of a serious delinquent subculture. However, they also argued that the type of delinquency adolescents engage in is the result of their access to illegitimate opportunities (see Cullen, 1988). Some youths have greater opportunities to, say, steal cars, whereas others may have more opportunities to shoplift. It depends on what opportunities are available to them. If there are no cars around to steal, perhaps shoplifting, getting drunk, or fighting is a more viable option. Another source of illegitimate opportunities involves peers. Some youths may have no friends, so they have little opportunity to join a gang. Others may have several like-minded friends who help them put together a gang that sells drugs or gets into fights with other gangs. Thus, opportunities to engage in delinquent acts are an essential component of Cloward and Ohlin's theory and dictate the types of delinquency (e.g., stealing vs. selling drugs) that adolescents engage in. Figure 6.3 provides a depiction of Cloward and Ohlin's strain theory.

Research on traditional strain theory

Probably the most common criticism of strain theory is that, compared with other individual-level theories of delinquency (e.g., differential association theory; see Chapter 7), it does not receive consistent empirical support. For example, a number of studies have shown that adolescents who experience strain in the form of the disjunction between wanting to obtain material goods and presumed opportunities to obtain these goods through legitimate means are only slightly more likely to report delinquent behavior (e.g., Burton et al., 1994). Moreover, Hirschi (1969) argued that delinquency results when adolescents do not have suf- ficient commitments to legitimate means of gaining valuable goods; the pressure they may feel from their culture to obtain these goods has little to do with whether

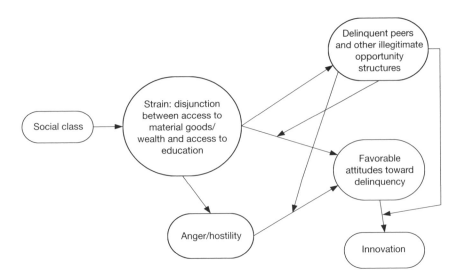

Figure 6.3 A final version of traditional strain theory.

they get involved in delinquent behavior. However, many, if not most, studies of traditional strain theory have suffered from one or more of four limitations.

Measuring strain

A variety of strategies have been developed to measure strain. Numerous studies, most of which were published some time ago, measure strain as a discrepancy score between aspirations (what an adolescent wants) and expectations (what an adolescent expects to get). This discrepancy score typically focuses on (1) occupational aspirations, (2) educational aspirations, or (3) economic aspirations. These are combined with some type of occupational or educational expectation (e.g., Farnworth and Leiber, 1989; Greenberg, 1999). For example, a strained person reports that attending college is very important, but does not expect to actually attend college. Alternatively, adolescents are considered strained if having a lot of money is important but they do not expect to have a good job that will pay well.

Studies using these types of measures have rarely found support for strain theory, but many have looked only at the difference between educational aspirations and expectations (see Burton and Cullen, 1992). Focusing only on educational goals and expectations misses the heart of strain theory, though, because, as Merton argued, economic goals are the most important cultural aspiration. As an alternative approach, Farnworth and Leiber (1989) presented a new way to create the discrepancy score. They argued that:

> economic wealth is a dominant goal in our meritocratic society and education is the conventional means for attaining wealth . . . therefore we propose the operationalization of juvenile strain as the dysfunction [sic] between economic goals and educational expectations (pp.264–265).

Using survey data on adolescents, they found that an economic–educational discrepancy score is associated with multiple measures of delinquency, thus suggesting that Merton and Cloward and Ohlin's theoretical arguments have merit (see also Hoffmann and Ireland, 2004).

Sampling concerns

Many tests of strain theory are conducted with largely middle-class samples primarily drawn from high schools (e.g., Elliott and Voss, 1974). However, as suggested by Merton and by Cloward and Ohlin, the most important groups for strain theory involve lower-class adolescents. Traditional strain theorists are also not particularly concerned with middle-class, suburban crime but rather focus on serious crime perpetrated by adolescents living in urban areas. However, most of the empirical assessments of strain theory focus on middle or high school adolescents and fairly minor forms of delinquency. Additionally, studies that focus on serious crime among urban adolescents provide support for various strain theory propositions (e.g., Short, 1964; Spergel, 1967).

Access to illegitimate opportunity structures

As mentioned earlier, Cloward and Ohlin (1960) argued that opportunities available to strained adolescents influence *the type* of delinquent behavior they engage in.[3] However, this fairly straightforward argument has been largely ignored in the empirical research on strain theory. The idea is that some of the adaptations to strain include the formation of various types of gangs that focus on violence or drug distribution. Although the unique types of gangs that they discussed probably do not exist (see Hagedorn, 1988), whether strain requires the presence of illegitimate opportunities to affect delinquency has yet to be fully considered or explored (Cullen and Wright 1997; Hoffmann and Ireland, 1995). Studies examining the availability of illegitimate opportunity structures usually consider self-reported interaction with delinquent friends or exposure to adult criminals (e.g., Menard, 1997). These studies suggest that, when strain is coupled with delinquent peers or exposure to adult criminals, the likelihood of delinquency increases, thus tentatively supporting Cloward and Ohlin's model.

Have studies tested the theory or only a limited number of propositions?

The final issue involves proposition testing versus theory testing. Much of the research on strain theory has simply examined the relationship between a single measure of strain and delinquent behavior. Far too often, the contextual or intervening mechanisms proposed by Merton, Cohen, or Cloward and Ohlin receive scant attention (see Baumer, 2007). However, as depicted in Figure 6.3, there are a number of interrelated propositions that contribute to strain theory. For example, the class-based argument hypothesizes that strain is most severe for youths on the lowest social rungs of society. Strain theorists also argue that, compared with strained adolescents in the middle or upper classes of society, lower-class adolescents suffering from strain are more likely to respond with delinquent activities. However, this has not been examined adequately by researchers.

Finally, Cloward and Ohlin clearly indicated that delinquent peers facilitate delinquent adaptations and foster the rejection of normative values. In a study that includes peers, Menard (1997, p.169) found that "delinquent peer group bonding and anomia are useful for distinguishing between conforming and nonconforming adaptations." However, Menard did not utilize a measure of strain as the discrepancy described by Cloward and Ohlin. Although some studies have considered peer groups, none has estimated all the pathways shown in Figure 6.3 (e.g., Elliott and Voss, 1974; Paternoster and Triplett, 1988).

In general, then, it is clear that the issues surrounding strain theory are complex from both a theoretical and an empirical standpoint. However, this does not mean that testing whether strain theory offers a valid model of delinquency is hopeless. Since its intricacies have not yet been fully examined, it is premature to dismiss traditional strain theory (Baumer, 2007). Yet it has recently been revitalized and broadened to consider contemporary research on how the stresses experienced by adolescents affect their behaviors and the way that strain may lead to delinquency.

The revitalization of strain theory

In an attempt to revitalize the strain perspective, Robert Agnew (1992) presented what he identified as a *general strain theory* (GST). The introduction and development of GST has, in turn, generated dozens of studies designed to analyze its core concepts and broaden it to address additional concepts that are associated with delinquency. As outlined earlier, *strain* traditionally refers to a structurally induced inability to access legitimate means or legitimate opportunities to achieve monetary goals. Agnew (1992) took this view of strain and generalized it to include a variety of negative relations rather than just negative relations that are the result of striving for unattainable but culturally mandated goals. He also considered the role that negative emotions, such as anger, play in the pathways that lead from strain to delinquency. The types of strain included in GST are a broad assortment of events and situations placed into three general categories: (1) blockage of positively valued goals, (2) presence of negative stimuli, and (3) loss of positively valued stimuli.

Blockage of positively valued goals

Agnew argued that traditional strain represents one facet of a more general type of strain that he refers to as the blockage of positively valued goals. Also placed under this umbrella is strain that results from the discrepancy between "expectations and actual achievement" and between "just/fair outcomes and actual outcomes." This has been elaborated to address goal blockage in term of masculinity and autonomy goals as well as economic goals (Agnew, 2001). In general, adolescents value certain goals such as good grades, being treated well by others, having consumer goods, and getting a good job or into a good school. When they perceive that their ability to achieve these goals is blocked by unfair disadvantages or other barriers, they feel strained.

Presence of negative stimuli

Agnew's (1992, 2001) second category of strain emphasizes relationships in which others present the adolescent with negative stimuli. These include aversive situations or environments (e.g., physically abusive parents, overly critical teachers) as well as negative life events (e.g., criminal victimization, family turmoil). Agnew (1992) argued that experiencing negative stimuli increases the likelihood of delinquency as adolescents attempt to escape from the aversive situations, exact revenge on the source of the stimuli, or attempt to cope with the resulting negative emotions with drugs or alcohol. For example, if youths are physically or emotionally abused by parents or guardians, they may attempt to escape these negative environments by running away from home, getting involved in gangs that provide alternative family structures, or using drugs and alcohol to help them feel better or escape the emotional trauma of the abuse.

Loss of positively valued stimuli

Drawing from research on how people react to stress, Agnew (1992, p.57) suggested that "numerous examples of such loss can be found in the inventories of stressful life-events," and events such as the loss of a boyfriend/girlfriend, death or serious illness of a family member or friend, moving, and divorce or separation of parents all represent losses of positively valued stimuli. When families are disrupted through separation or divorce, for example, youths may feel the stress of the break-up and become frustrated as they feel they have little control over the situation. This stress and frustration cause an emotional overload that is channeled into some type of negative outcome such as delinquency, drug use, or emotional withdrawal.

Additional strain issues

There are two other issues that Agnew addressed to complete the GST. First, the duration, the frequency, and the recency of strain, as well as the actual number of strains or stressors that occur at any one time, will, in part, determine the effects of strain on delinquency. Second, Agnew (2001) claimed that researchers need to consider the difference between measuring strain subjectively and objectively. Whereas subjective strain measures assess the degree to which individuals are not being treated as they would like, objective measures of strain assume that individuals experience an event or condition that is disliked, because it is usually disliked by members of his or her group (Agnew 2001). Sole reliance upon objective strain measures "may cause researchers to underestimate the support for strain theory because objective strains sometimes create little subjective strain" (Agnew 2001, pp.321–322). Thus, it is important to carefully delineate the various sources of strain in an adolescent's life, as well as their frequency and duration, to get a full picture of how they may affect delinquency or other behaviors.

Linking strain to delinquency

Not all strained individuals turn to delinquency; some may react to strain with conventional behaviors. Agnew theorized that individuals respond to strain with a variety of cognitive, behavioral, or emotional adaptations. Within each of these adaptive strategies there exist both deviant and conventional options. For example, experienced or anticipated strain might result in an emotional response in the form of "meditation, biofeedback, and progressive relaxation," or it might result in illicit drug use or violence (Agnew 1992, p.70).

The question for GST is *why* a particular strained individual adapts with delinquency rather than some other behavior. To answer this question, Agnew identified negative affect as an important intervening concept between strain and delinquency. Negative affect includes a variety of negative emotions including anger, frustration, guilt, depression, worthlessness, and anxiety (e.g., Broidy and Agnew, 1997). Agnew contended that including negative affect in strain theory distinguishes it from other individual-level explanations of delinquency. He also argued that whereas other affective states might lead to deviant behavior, such as social withdrawal or suicidal thoughts, anger, in particular, increases the likelihood of delinquency:

> Anger results when individuals blame their adversity on others, and anger is the key emotion because it increases the individual's level of felt injury, creates a desire for retaliation/revenge, energizes the individual for action, and lowers inhibitions, in part because individuals believe that others will feel their aggression is justified (1992, p.60).

Note that, similar to Cloward and Ohlin, Agnew thought that externalization of blame is important for understanding why some youths become angry in the presence of strain. However, he also pointed out that adolescents may or may not be accurate in placing blame on another; it is their perception that is important. Once angered, constraints that inhibit certain behaviors are lowered, allowing for the possibility of delinquency in response to the anger or in an attempt to remove the strain. Thus, adolescents who go through a parental divorce may become depressed or withdrawn. However, if they become angry because they blame one or both parents, the reaction may be to lash out at others in an attempt to alleviate their frustration.

GST and moderator effects

Agnew (e.g., 1992, 2006) also identified various factors that inhibit or enhance a delinquent response to strain. For example, individuals high in self-efficacy (which involves a sense of being able to control life situations to produce desired effects) or self-esteem might be strained, but are not generally inclined to become angry or direct their reactions at other people. Instead, a sense of control or feeling good about oneself often leads to other coping strategies as alternatives to delinquency.

Characteristics of the environment in which adolescents live may also encourage or hinder a delinquent response to strain. For example, the presence of a delinquent peer group is likely to exert a substantial influence on those strained adolescents who have restricted access to conventional means because these groups act to "reinforce the adolescent's delinquency, and instill delinquent values" (Agnew and White, 1992, p.478). Conventional peers may help reduce the effects of strain if they provide a supportive environment or can facilitate the removal of stimuli that produce negative emotions such as anger and frustration. Disorganized neighborhoods (see Chapter 5) also provide an environment conductive to violent behavior or other delinquent behaviors. When there are models of deviant behavior, or when the neighborhood itself is stressful, it is more likely that strained adolescents will get involved in delinquency (Agnew, 1999).

Research on general strain theory

Many studies have examined the validity of GST since it was introduced. However, it can be a difficult theory to test since there are numerous sources of strain and several factors that presumably enhance or diminish the likelihood that strain results in delinquency. Moreover, this difficulty is heightened by Agnew's (1992) proposal that a measurement strategy is needed that takes into account the magnitude, duration, recency, and clustering of strain. A comprehensive approach that includes the various sources and characteristics of strain is needed to fully understand the effects of strain on delinquency, but identifying all of these is complex.

Although the results are not entirely consistent, there is general evidence that the introduction of strain – especially stressful life events – in an adolescent's life is associated with a higher risk of delinquency (see Hoffmann, 2009). Moreover, certain negative experiences, such as physical and emotional maltreatment of children by their parents and exposure to violence in the home, are consistently related to delinquency (Bender, 2010). However, there is also substantial variation in the degree to which strain is associated with delinquency. This may reflect the complexity of the theory and the difficulty in judging which particular aspects of GST are most influential. Nonetheless, there have also been several attempts to identify how general strain results in delinquency.

GST, negative affect, and delinquency

As mentioned earlier, an important proposition of GST is that youths experiencing strain are more likely to become angry or frustrated, and anger or frustration increases the likelihood of a delinquent response. Generally, the research on negative affect as a mediator between strain and delinquency has received mixed support (e.g., Aseltine et al., 2000; Piquero and Sealock, 2010). For example, using a random sample of adolescents, Aseltine and colleagues (2000) found that stressful life events, family conflict, and peer conflict – all considered measures of strain – lead to anxiety and anger, and anger leads to aggression, but there is no mediating effect on delinquency. Rather, stressful life events alone are associated with increasing involvement in delinquency. Family conflict leads directly to marijuana use, but has no influence on delinquency. Peer conflict leads to anxiety, but not delinquency or marijuana use. Figure 6.4 shows the model that Aseltine and colleagues examined.

In a more thorough analysis, Broidy (2001) collected self-report data on the blockage of positively valued goals, unfair outcomes, negative stimuli/loss of positive stimuli (stress), anger, and both conventional and delinquent behaviors from a sample of college students. She showed that experiencing blocked goals decreases rather than increases anger – exactly the opposite of what GST predicts. However, experiencing unfair outcomes or stress increases anger, which is consistent with GST. In addition, Broidy found that anger increases the risk of self-reported delinquency. Therefore, at least among this non-random sample of college students it

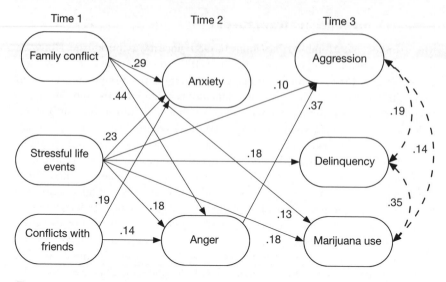

Figure 6.4 A test of general strain theory. Note: Only significant path coefficients are shown. Dashed lines indicate correlations. The correlations among variables are omitted in Times 1 and 2 (source: Aseltine *et al.*, 2000, p.267).

appears that there is some relationship between strain and anger, and that anger increases the risk of delinquency.

Community-level strain

Agnew (1999) elaborated general strain theory in a manner consistent with much earlier work by Cloward and Ohlin by addressing how stressful environments may reinforce the effects of individual-level strain. He also pointed out that some communities are much more violent than others, and it is these types of communities that tend to reinforce the effects of strain. In other words, if we were to expose a group of youths to the same degree of strain and place some in a violent neighborhood and others in a safe middle-class neighborhood, we could expect those experiencing strain in the former type of neighborhood to be especially likely to react with delinquency.

There have been few tests of whether community-level strain affects the association between individual-level strain and delinquency. However, recall from Chapter 5 that some research suggests that schools are an important "community" for adolescents. Two studies using different data sets indicate that when a school includes many students who are aggressive and violent, or experience strain in their lives, other students are likely to be delinquent (Brezina et al., 2001; Hoffmann and Ireland, 2004). In general, then, there may be stressful schools that foster delinquency among students. Hoffmann and Ireland (2004) also found, however, that youths who experience many stressful events are more likely to commit delinquent acts regardless of the level of stress or delinquency in their schools.

Promises and limitations of strain theory

Strain theory is unique as an explanation of delinquency because it addresses specifically how social and psychological factors that result from the culture and social structure may push adolescents toward delinquency. Moreover, GST is distinct in claiming that various goal blockages and unpleasant experiences induce delinquent behavior when other choices are not available or when the social environment is conducive to deviance (Agnew, 2006). Rather than claiming that learning must take place (see Chapter 7), strain theory exemplifies the way that life can push people down a road not of their own making: a road that results in delinquent behavior. GST, in particular, offers an interesting model of adolescent behavior since the teenage years are a period of high risk of stresses and strains. Given the link between being treated poorly, such as when adolescents are abused physically or emotionally by adults, and delinquency, as well as the general finding that negative emotions such as anger and frustration are common correlates of delinquency, it is not surprising that strain theory continues to generate substantial interest as an explanation of delinquency.

Nevertheless, some observers have argued that the line of theory building and research that started with Merton has been a misguided venture (e.g., Kornhauser, 1978). Strain theory has been accused of missing the important point that delinquency results not from pressure to achieve culturally induced goals, but rather from a failure to be socialized to use conventional means to achieve these goals. Strain theory is seen as an overly sociological model that does not give sufficient credit to influences arising in the family, schools, or communities. It has also been accused, somewhat unfairly (see Bernard, 2001), of arguing that there is substantial variation in the norms of society; that some groups justify illegal methods whereas others sanction only conventional, law-abiding methods. Instead, even hardcore delinquents tend to believe in a moral order (Hirschi, 1969). However, as discussed in Chapter 7, there is substantial cultural variation and pressures to deviate from the norms of society in some environments. When legitimate access to valued goods, such as wealth, is blocked, such as in some impoverished or disorganized neighborhoods, residents may have little choice but to turn to illegal activities.

This raises a more important criticism of strain theories, in particular traditional strain theory. Bernard (1987) argued that Merton's model and its offshoots are actually macro-level models that do not propose that individuals are strained and therefore turn to delinquency. Rather, there is real blockage in the social structure that restricts access to valuable goods and, when this occurs, some groups have little choice but to find illicit ways to get these goods. Individuals do not have to manifest strain for this to occur, nor do they need to be angry or frustrated. Rather, reacting to social conditions with illegal activities is simply a rational choice in a world with limited opportunities.

Moreover, it is not clear why some youths are angry when presented with stressful situations, whereas others react by accepting the situation, overcoming it through willful action, or emotionally withdrawing. Aggression and anger, which are not the same trait but are closely related, often show up well before stressful situations. As discussed in Chapter 4, aggression is a relatively stable trait that begins early in life. However, is strain a necessary condition for anger to turn into delinquency? Alternatively, when we see strained youths becoming angry and then delinquent, is this merely a consequence of anger? Perhaps, some youths learn that the proper response to stress is aggression or violence, whereas others are taught to cope with stress in other ways. Thus, newer versions of strain theory such as GST may be a form of learning theory (see Chapter 7).

Finally, one of the continuing difficulties for evaluations is how to measure strain. Each of the models from Merton (1938) to Agnew (1992) addresses the rather evident conclusion that adolescents experience strain and stress as a general condition of life. However, measuring strain remains problematic at best. Similarly, how should negative or noxious stimuli be measured? What about the removal of positively valued goals? These may vary tremendously among youths; some may value personal relationships whereas others may value their cars, iPods, or new shoes. This has implications for how strain is experienced. For example, going through a family break-up is normally considered stressful for adolescents and parents, yet it may also reduce an abusive situation. It is also reasonable to consider that experiencing violent victimization is a stressful situation, but is likely to be interpreted differently by adolescents in wealthy areas compared to those in violent, inner-city areas. In general, then, much more work is needed to fully determine what strain is and how it affects adolescents.

Policy implications of strain theory

The implications of strain theory for reducing delinquency are varied. However, it is obvious that one effective strategy is to reduce strain. For example, programs might be designed that reduce the blockage of positively valued goals by creating greater access to educational and economic opportunities. This was the goal of *Mobilization for Youth*, a program established in the 1960s by the Kennedy administration that was influenced by Cloward and Ohlin's research. It was initially set up on the Lower East Side of Manhattan and provided job training and remedial education, and tried to help those in need understand the welfare and health systems that were designed as safety nets for the poor. However, after President Kennedy was assassinated and Lyndon Johnson took over, the community action groups that formed the basis of *Mobilization for Youth* were gradually disbanded as Johnson's War on Poverty was seen as a better and broader effort to combat inner-city problems (Lemann, 1988).

Perhaps the most promising objective is to reduce blocked opportunities to higher education. For example, Stafford loans and Perkins loans are federally subsidized programs designed to help make college more affordable, and can be especially beneficial to poor students and their parents. Greater access to educational opportunities can also be started much earlier in an adolescent's life – through Head Start programs for example. This program provides funds to local agencies that teach mainly disadvantaged preschool children reading and math skills so they can be successful as they enter the school system (U.S. Department of Health and Human Services, 2006).

Although greater access to quality education is one policy derived from strain theory, one might also work to limit the loss of positively valued stimuli or the persistent exposure to negative stimuli among adolescents (Agnew, 2006). For example, research indicates that child maltreatment, such as abuse and neglect, increases the risk of delinquency, as does exposure to violence in the home and in the community. Therefore, policies designed to limit exposure to violence should reduce strain, which in turn should reduce involvement in delinquency.

A second broad strategy, according to some strain theorists, is to reduce access to illegitimate opportunities. Hoffmann and Ireland (2004) claimed that there are two broadly defined illegitimate opportunity structures: physical and social. Most studies of strain theory focus on social illegitimate opportunity structures; for example, interactions with similarly situated peers. However, it is also possible to consider strategies such as target hardening to decrease opportunities to engage in crime irrespective of the level of strain experienced by adolescents. Focusing on delinquency prevention by implementing effective security measures (e.g., better lighting; see Chapter 2 for other examples) might reduce opportunities for potential delinquents.

Finally, policies that are directed at reducing anger or negative affect might offer effective strategies for reducing delinquency. If strain increases the risk of anger and frustration, which in turn increases the risk of delinquency, then a strategy designed to reduce anger among adolescents might also reduce delinquency. This simple notion has spawned a litany of anger management programs around the country for adolescents and adults involved in the justice system (e.g., Amendola and Scozzle, 2004).

Conclusions

Finding its origins in sociology, strain theory initially addressed how cultural conditions and social structural impediments lead some people to use illicit means to obtain valuable goods. Yet it has evolved into a more sophisticated social-psychological theory that draws our attention to how experiencing stresses and strains leads some adolescents toward delinquency. The empirical support for Agnew's general strain theory is impressive, especially the consistent finding that negative life events and the removal of valuable things, whether emotional or tangible, are consistently associated with delinquency.

However, the results of studies that include anger or other negative emotions, or the role of social-psychological conditions such as self-efficacy, are less impressive. It is still unclear if anger is a prerequisite for delinquency, even the more violent forms (Felson, 1992). It is also not known yet whether strain that leads to anger or negative affect produces delinquent responses. Thus far, the evidence suggests that these intermediate steps do not need to exist for delinquency to occur. However, it is also clear that more research using better measures of strain and other variables is necessary before we can draw any definite conclusions.

Finally, as discussed in Chapter 5, schools and neighborhoods matter for delinquency and some are more stressful than others. How stresses and strains at the community level translate into strain at the individual level or motivate delinquency is still unclear. However, this might be a key for strain theory for it may be how strain is experienced at both the macro and individual levels – as well as what illegitimate opportunity structures are available – that ultimately affects who becomes delinquent and who does not.

7   Learning to be delinquent

Prologue

Jessica and Marc grew up together. When they were toddlers, their mothers shared babysitting responsibilities. Marc's father had a wicked temper and drank heavily. He would often yell at Marc and his mother. On occasion he would spank Marc severely. Jessica's mother and father divorced when she was three years old. She saw her father only about once a year because he moved to another state shortly after the break-up.

Marc was an aggressive child, who lost his temper and punched other kids when he didn't get his way. Most kids in school avoided him because they were scared or didn't know how he'd react when they tried to talk to him. But Jessica continued to be his friend. Marc also made friends with an older boy, John, who bragged about how he had smoked cigarettes since he was 10. Marc and John began to spend most of their free time together, which seemed all right with Marc's parents. His father didn't like him around (they always fought) and his mother wanted to protect Marc from his father's violent temper.

By the time Marc was 13 and John was 15 they had gained a reputation for fighting and stealing. Jessica, who had remained friends with Marc, used to hear them laughing about beating up some kid. Nevertheless, Jessica and Marc started dating when they were both 14 years old. Marc tried to pressure Jessica into having intercourse with him, but she resisted. However, when they were 16, Jessica began to drive Marc and John to another part of the city to buy crystal meth. She was also with them when they stole a car from a local garage. All three were arrested for auto theft. Marc and Jessica were placed in a new state program for families that was designed to teach them what the administrators called "prosocial, family management, and life skills." Jessica and her mother successfully completed the program and her juvenile record was expunged. Marc's father, however, refused to participate because, he said, "He got into the mess and I'm not going to bail him out." Although his mother went to weekly counseling sessions, Marc lost interest after a few weeks and dropped out of the program. He was arrested a few months later for shooting a drug dealer in the back. His friend John drove the getaway car.

Introduction

How does one learn to do anything? This is a simple question, yet it is surprisingly difficult to answer. In Chapter 1, we discussed one of the classic philosophical assumptions about human nature: Humans are blank slates at birth. This assumption was described most famously by John Locke, the seventeenth-century English political philosopher. Locke (1975 [1690]) argued that all our ideas and knowledge come from experiences. We have *sensations* that teach us about what occurs in the world around us, and then we *reflect* on these sensations to learn how we should operate in the world. Contemporary studies show that we learn through a much more intricate system than envisioned by Locke; we are not "blank slates" at birth (Pinker, 2002). Rather, our brains develop in such a way as to favor certain experiences and emotions, which then affects how we learn to behave and think. Nonetheless, the idea that we must learn through our experiences has led to the idea that our individual natures depend upon both our physiological structures and what we have learned throughout childhood and into adulthood.

The assumption that learning is at the core of human nature has led to a number of individual-level theories about how delinquent behavior – or its antecedents, such as aggressiveness – develops. Learning theories suggest that delinquent behaviors are motivated and acquired through the same processes as other behaviors, whether these are learning to play a sport, write an essay, or discuss foreign affairs. As discussed in Chapter 5, recent scholarship has also addressed how community conditions may affect the learning process and motivate learning values that are conducive to delinquent behaviors.

Although ideas about how juveniles learn to engage in delinquency have existed for many years, it was the pioneering work of Edwin Sutherland that organized them. His work also motivated many studies of how youths learn to become delinquents. Sutherland developed a theory of *differential association*, which consisted of a series of propositions about learning delinquent and criminal behavior. Subsequently, criminologists, in particular Ronald L. Akers, used the theory of differential association as a source for a *social learning* theory of crime and delinquency. Much of this chapter addresses differential association and social learning theories, as well as contemporary research based on these theories.

Differential association

Sutherland's theory of differential association was one of the most widely studied theories of criminal and delinquent behavior in the twentieth century. Sutherland was motivated to develop a theory of crime and delinquency for several reasons. First, in 1921 the chairman of the Sociology Department at the University of Illinois encouraged Sutherland to write a textbook outlining contemporary knowledge about criminology. Second, in 1932 a prominent research report argued that a general explanation of delinquent and criminal behavior was needed, but that social scientists were poorly prepared to develop such an explanation. Third, while working at the University of Chicago in the early 1930s, Sutherland interviewed a professional thief, Broadway Jones, on several occasions. Sutherland was persuaded by Jones's stories of learning the ways of theft and deception (Sutherland, 1973 [1942]).

After considering the evidence, Sutherland concluded that specific factors, such as the desire for money, could not explain behaviors. Rather, abstract principles and processes that could be linked to specific types of behavior were needed. He also argued that behaviors could not be understood unless theories focused on learning through interaction and communication. Therefore, Sutherland developed a systematic description, composed of seven propositions, of how criminal and delinquent behaviors are learned. He expanded these seven propositions to nine in his later work (Sutherland, 1947).

The nine propositions are as follows:

1 Criminal behavior is learned. Negatively, this means that criminal behavior is not inherited.
2 Criminal behavior is learned in interaction with other persons in a process of communication. This communication is verbal in many respects but includes also "the communication of gestures."
3 The principal part of the learning of criminal behavior occurs within intimate personal groups. Negatively, this means that the impersonal agencies of communication, such as movies and newspapers, play a relatively unimportant part in the genesis of criminal behavior.
4 When criminal behavior is learned, the learning includes (a) techniques of committing the crime, which are sometimes very complicated, sometimes very simple; (b) the specific direction of motives, drives and rationalizations and attitudes.
5 The specific direction of motives and drives is learned from the definition of legal codes as favorable and unfavorable.
6 A person becomes delinquent because of an excess of definitions favorable to violation of law over definitions unfavorable to violation of law. This is the principle of differential association. It refers to both criminal and anti-criminal associations and has to do with counteracting forces. When persons become criminals, they do so because of contacts with criminal patterns and also because of isolation from anti-criminal patterns.
7 Differential associations may vary in frequency, duration, priority, and intensity. This means that associations with criminal behavior and also associations with anti-criminal behavior vary in those respects.
8 The process of learning criminal behavior by association with criminal and anti-criminal patterns involves all of the mechanisms that are involved in any other learning.
9 Though criminal behavior is an expression of general needs and values, it is not explained by those general needs and values since non-criminal behavior is an expression of the same needs and values. Thieves generally steal in order to secure money, but likewise honest laborers work in

order to secure money. The attempts by many scholars to explain criminal behavior by general drives and values, such as . . . the money motive,
. . . have been and must continue to be futile since they explain lawful
behavior as completely as they explain criminal behavior (Sutherland,
1947, pp.6–7).

These learning principles were current at the time Sutherland was writing,
even if they now appear simplistic (Warr, 2001). Interaction and communication
played key roles in his ideas about learning. In particular, differential association
highlights interactions with other people and how these lead to learning techniques and motives for behaviors, and, most importantly, *definitions* about violating
the law. Although Sutherland did not clearly indicate the pathways that lead to
delinquency, later research tended to assume that people learn criminal behaviors
from friends, family members, and other intimates. They learn not only how to
commit certain acts, but also when it is appropriate to commit these acts. Learning
techniques and motivations are not sufficient to explain behavior, however. Rather,
people also learn not to commit certain acts, in particular why they are wrong. In
general, definitions that favor or do not favor delinquent behaviors are part of
the thought processes of any individual. When these definitions favor delinquent
behavior in a certain situation, then it tends to occur. One possible model of this
process is provided in Figure 7.1. Note, though, that the order of learning the
definitions versus the techniques was not clearly articulated in Sutherland's theory.

Sutherland also suggested that associations that are more frequent, of longer
duration, and more intense are more influential. However, a criticism of his theory
is that that he did not make clear whether definitions and associations are distinct. Presumably, definitions are similar to beliefs about appropriate conduct (see
Chapter 8). Also, these definitions are preceded by associations with other people,
in particular close associates such as family members or friends. However, he failed
to discuss whether definitions also influence associations, such as when delinquents
are attracted to other delinquents because they share similar beliefs and goals.

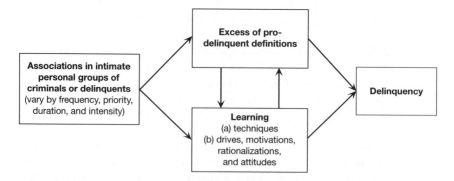

Figure 7.1 Differential association and delinquency.

Sutherland also discussed how definitions of acceptable behavior vary across social and cultural groups, as well as across different societies. In some cultures, for instance, people overwhelmingly support the law and thus associating with others will undoubtedly lead to individual definitions that favor adherence to the law. In other cultures, though, there are many people who oppose certain laws or do not see them as valid. Therefore, differential association may involve culturally prescribed normative behaviors that have a profound effect on the learning of definitions. Sutherland thus developed a sociological learning theory because the acquisition of definitions and behaviors is affected by the norms of a person's cultural or social group (Gaylord and Galliher, 1988).

Research on differential association

Early research on differential association theory tended to focus on the relationship between peer delinquency and delinquent behavior. These studies usually considered a strong relationship between delinquency among one's friends and one's own delinquency as evidence in favor of differential association. Some studies were more careful and looked at more intense or frequent relationships. Most studies found a strong association between close friends' delinquency and one's own delinquency (e.g., Jensen, 1972). However, critics noted that most of these studies examined delinquency at only one point in time. However, delinquents may be attracted to other delinquents, so they naturally gravitate toward one another. Some criminologists used the adage "birds of a feather flock together" to describe this association (see Chapter 8). Another problem with these studies is that they failed to consider the essential issue of definitions. Was it true that associations preceded definitions? Alternatively, did favorable definitions regarding delinquency precede the associations. Most importantly, what are definitions?

Efforts to be more faithful to differential association have yielded favorable evidence, although they have also extended it in an important way. For example, longitudinal studies (data are collected over time) indicate that peer delinquency has a significant effect on one's own delinquency at a later time (Warr, 2001, 2002). However, the effect of one's own delinquency on subsequent peer delinquency is even stronger (e.g., de Kemp et al., 2006). In general, peer delinquency and delinquency are part of a reciprocal loop, as shown in Figure 7.2, with the path from delinquency to associating with delinquent friends especially strong. Note, however, that Sutherland did not argue that peer delinquency and delinquency are directly related. Rather, according to the way he listed the propositions, he thought that close associates affect the acquisition of definitions about the law. Therefore, it is just as important to look at what adolescents believe about the law as it is to look at their peers' behaviors.

As pointed out by critics, but also by Sutherland, attempting to assess these definitions is difficult (Cressey, 1960; Matsueda, 1988). Should researchers try to develop a measure of the ratio of pro-law violation and anti-law violation definitions or is some other mathematical function or relationship needed? Suppose these definitions balance out? What does this predict about delinquent behavior?

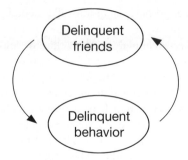

Figure 7.2 Delinquent friends and delinquent behavior.

Although researchers have not developed satisfactory answers to these questions, several studies have shown that definitions – measured by questions such as whether respondents think it is okay to break the law – affect the association between friends' delinquency and one's own delinquency (e.g., Hochstetler et al., 2002). They have found, for instance, that pro-delinquent definitions mediate the association between delinquent peers and delinquency, and adolescents who report both delinquent friends and pro-delinquent definitions are particularly likely to engage in delinquency. A study by Mears and colleagues (1998) also determined that definitions explain the well-known gender gap in delinquency: Girls are less delinquent than boys not because they have fewer delinquent peers, but mainly because girls are less likely to have pro-delinquent definitions.

Moreover, in support of Sutherland's ideas about the frequency and priority of associations, one study established that adolescents' favorable attitudes toward delinquency combine with their best friends' aggression to predict greater involvement in subsequent delinquency (Vitaro et al., 2000). However, other research has found that friends' behaviors are more important than their attitudes in predicting delinquency, even after considering one's own attitudes (Warr and Stafford, 1991). Thus, modeling or imitating friends' behaviors is an important aspect of learning to be delinquent.

Studies have also generally failed to look at Sutherland's ideas about the influence of direct models of delinquent behavior. Based on his interviews with the professional thief, Sutherland argued that training is important. Initial delinquent and criminal behavior may therefore be viewed as an apprenticeship, in which youths are taught how to commits acts, whether they are techniques for using drugs or stealing car radios. A study by McCarthy (1996), for instance, verified the role of what he termed *tutelage*: Most adolescents involved in theft or selling drugs reported that they had been approached by friends offering to help them commit delinquent acts. In another study, Conway and McCord (2002) determined that adolescents who had no record of violent offending were more likely to commit violent acts in the future if their first offense involved a violent co-offender. They argued that "lessons of violence" could be learned "on the street" from delinquent peers.

Social learning theory

One of the key problems with differential association theory is that it was based on incomplete learning principles. Sutherland failed to articulate specific learning processes, mentioning in the eighth proposition only that "The process of learning criminal behavior by association . . . involves all of the mechanisms that are involved in any other learning" (Sutherland, 1947, p.7). Scholarship that was unavailable in Sutherland's time has shown that learning involves a more intricate process than he described. The attitudes and behaviors of friends and family members, as well as the frequency and intensity of associations, certainly matter, but the way they affect delinquency involves many aspects of learning.

In response to this criticism, several criminologists attempted to revise differential association using contemporary theories of learning. Perhaps the most influential model of learning during the mid-twentieth century was B. F. Skinner's (1953) principles of *operant conditioning*. This model assumes that people learn to change their behaviors in response to events that occur in the surrounding environment. One of the key ways this occurs is when a stimulus–response (S–R) pattern is rewarded. People can be conditioned to respond in a specific way to a certain stimulus if their reactions are reinforced. Examples abound in childrearing practices: Children are taught that saying "please" will gain them a treat more efficiently than grabbing it off the shelf; they are usually taught that sharing is more likely to meet with approval from parents than keeping all the toys. A *reinforcer* is something that increases the likelihood of the desired response. Thus, reinforcements such as parental approval or a tasty treat are persuasive and link certain behaviors to certain outcomes. In addition, punishments reduce the likelihood of an inappropriate response, such as when an unpleasant experience (e.g., spanking) follows some behavior.

Two sociologists, Robert Burgess and Ronald L. Akers, used the principles of operant conditioning to reformulate differential association. Consistent with Sutherland's presentation, they listed seven propositions to articulate their *differential association-reinforcement* theory:

1 Criminal behavior is learned according to the principles of operant conditioning.
2 Criminal behavior is learned both in non-social situations that are reinforcing or discriminating and through that social interaction in which the behavior of other persons is reinforcing or discriminative for such behavior.
3 The principal part of the learning of criminal behavior occurs in those groups which comprise or control the individual's major source of reinforcements.
4 The learning of criminal behavior, including specific techniques, attitudes, and avoidance procedures, is a function of the effective and available reinforcers, and the existing reinforcement contingencies.
5 The specific class of behaviors which are learned and their frequency of occurrence are a function of the reinforcers which are effective and available, and the rules of norms by which these reinforcers are applied.

6 Criminal behavior is a function of norms which are discriminative for criminal behavior, the learning of which takes place when such behavior is more highly reinforced than noncriminal behavior.
7 The strength of criminal behavior is a direct function of the amount, frequency, and probability of its reinforcement (Burgess and Akers, 1966).

Akers (1985) later modified these propositions by substituting the word *deviant* for *criminal*, so as to contend that the theory applies to a variety of deviant behaviors. He also renamed it *social learning theory* to focus on its status as a learning theory and to highlight the fact that differential association may be seen as simply one component of his theory.

Akers (1998, 2001) also updated the theory by including more recent scholarship on learning principles and by elaborating its main assumptions, addressing more clearly its key concepts, and restating it in a more general form. Although he assumed that the same learning processes dictate delinquent or conforming behavior, what matters most is the balance of influences on behavior. These influences include differential association, differential reinforcement, imitation, and definitions. Table 7.1 provides a description of these concepts.

The following statement provides a concise description of social learning theory:

> The probability that persons will engage in criminal and deviant behavior is increased and the probability of their conforming to the norm is decreased when they differentially associate with others who commit criminal behavior and espouse definitions favorable to it, are relatively more exposed in-person or symbolically to salient criminal/deviant models, define it as desirable or justified in a situation discriminative for the behavior, and have received in the past and anticipate in the current or future situation relatively greater reward than punishment for the behavior (Akers, 1998, p.50).

Akers was also persuaded by more recent work on learning theory, especially by the research of Bandura (1986), that observational learning and vicarious reinforcement are important. Direct reinforcement of behavior provides only a limited picture of the way children and adolescents learn. They also have much more control over their thought processes and motivations than implied by operant conditioning and its progeny. Hence, as shown earlier, Akers included an emphasis on imitation or modeling, as well as on anticipated reinforcement and self-reinforcement of behaviors. In addition, even though Sutherland argued that the media were a rather weak modeling source, Akers argued that technological advances since Sutherland's time (e.g., the widespread availability of television, movies, music videos, and video games) have magnified media influences. The effects of media on delinquency are discussed later.

Finally, Akers (1998) sought to link social structural influences – such as community characteristics (see Chapter 5) – and social learning in a single model.

Table 7.1 Definitions of key concepts in social learning theory

Concept	Description
Differential association	The process whereby one is exposed to normative definitions that are relatively more favorable or unfavorable to illegal or law-abiding behavior. Its interactional dimension is direct associations with others who engage in certain acts and indirect associations and identification with reference groups. Its normative dimension is the different patterns of norms, values, and attitudes to which a person is exposed through these associations.
Differential reinforcement	The balance of anticipated or actual rewards and punishments that follow or are consequences of behavior. Reinforcers and punishments can be non-social (e.g., effects of drugs), but most often they are social. Social rewards may be symbolic, such as when they are defined by ideological, political, or religious goals.
Imitation	The engagement in behavior after observation of similar behavior by others. It is more important for the initiation of behavior than for the continuation or cessation of behavior.
Definitions	The attitudes or meanings a person attaches to a particular behavior. These include general beliefs, such as norms; values that favor conventional or delinquent behavior; and specific definitions, such as that stealing is always wrong, but drinking alcohol at after-school parties is acceptable. Definitions favorable to delinquency may be positive or neutralizing. Positive definitions are beliefs or attitudes that make the behavior desirable, whereas neutralizing definitions excuse or justify delinquent acts (e.g., "I have a bad temper that I can't control").

Source: Akers (2001, pp.194–196).

He argued that the individual's social context provides a learning environment in which associations and reinforcements occur. Cultural traditions and norms that are prevalent in the social environment affect learning and dictate with whom youths interact. A prevalence of conforming peers and reinforcers in one's local environment is likely to lead to a preponderance of definitions that favor conforming behavior; these minimize the risk of delinquent behavior (Akers, 1998; Jensen and Akers, 2007). However, certain social contexts may enhance learning conditions conducive to delinquency. Economically and socially disadvantaged neighborhoods, for example, tend to have a greater concentration of delinquent peers, thus increasing the chances that youths will have more friends who are delinquent (Gibson et al., 2011).

Research on social learning theory

Research on social learning theory is generally supportive of several of its main elements. As noted earlier, many studies find that delinquent peers and pro-delinquent definitions are positively related to delinquent behavior. Akers (2001) argued that studies showing a reciprocal loop (see Figure 7.2) between delinquent peers and delinquency also support social learning theory because such a loop shows the effects of reinforcement. Moreover, research demonstrates that criminal or deviant behavior among parents and siblings is associated with delinquent behavior among adolescents, thus indicating that definitions and models that encourage delinquency are found in the home as well as among peers (e.g., Brauer, 2009).

The best evidence that social learning theory provides a valid explanation of delinquency comes from studies conducted by Akers and his colleagues (summarized in Akers, 1998, 2001). Their research on delinquency and smoking (tobacco or marijuana) has shown that key aspects of social learning – differential reinforcement, differential associations, and pro-delinquency definitions – are positively associated with these behaviors. For example, Akers and Lee (1996) demonstrated that smoking and social learning variables are related over time, as depicted in Figure 7.3. The strongest influences run from the social learning variables to smoking, with no evidence that smoking increases reinforcement, associations, or definitions that support cigarette use. There is also evidence from other studies that non-social reinforcers, such as the pleasure of intoxication or the thrill of committing a risky activity, affect the likelihood of drug use and delinquency (e.g., Brezina and Piquero, 2007).

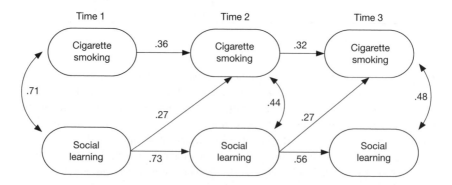

Figure 7.3 Social learning variables and adolescent cigarette smoking (adapted from Akers and Lee, 1996, p.333, and Akers, 1998, p.229). Note: Social learning combines measures of differential reinforcement, differential associations (peers), and definitions about smoking (adolescents' and parents' attitudes). Only significant path coefficients are shown.

Coercive processes in the family and among peers

A similar social learning theory has been developed by Gerald Patterson and colleagues. This theory emphasizes how early parent–child interactions affect delinquency and antisocial conduct later in a child's life. In most families, children are taught to not get upset when they do not get their way, to talk through problems rather than react aggressively, and to be patient and ask for a desired object instead of simply grabbing it. Yet, in some families, parents yell or use physical means to get children to obey. Some parents also use psychological control rather than a more authoritative or calm approach to discipline their children. These parents provide models of aggression and coercion; and children learn that physical means of discipline and control are appropriate. Moreover, in many of these families, parents withdraw when the child reacts in a negative way, such as leaving the room when a child yells back or throws a temper tantrum. Such interactions tend to intensify over time. As children engage in more antisocial behavior, positive interactions between parents and children decrease and negative interactions increase. Parents in these families often fail to monitor their children's activities, allowing them to engage in undetected misbehaviors. Moreover, many of these children do not learn important problem-solving skills, such as how to negotiate verbally to gain some desired object or how to defuse a tense situation (Patterson and Dishion, 1985).

As children enter adolescence, those who have learned to rely on coercive and negative reinforcement strategies are typically rejected by conforming peers at school and in their neighborhoods. Therefore, they tend to gravitate toward peers who share their style of interaction. These peers then provide positive reinforcement for coercive strategies, which translate naturally into deviant forms of behavior, such as fighting and stealing.

A useful contribution of this theory is that it helps explain the differences between early-starter and late-starter delinquents. Patterson and colleagues argued that *early starters* (i.e., those who begin in late childhood) and *late starters* (i.e., those who begin during adolescence) may be distinguished based on childrearing practices. Early starters typically have parents who use coercive discipline strategies and thus they follow the pathway toward delinquency outlined earlier. However, late starters have parents with marginal, yet crudely effective, childrearing skills, but have begun to associate with delinquent peers, perhaps in the pursuit of fun and adventure or because of family problems. Late starters are usually involved in offending only during adolescence, whereas early starters tend to continue offending in adulthood (Patterson and Yoerger, 1997). Figure 7.4 provides a depiction of early-starter and late-starter models of delinquency.

Research on coercive processes

Patterson and colleagues have provided substantial empirical support for their model. Children from families that engage in coercive and negatively reinforcing behaviors in the home often become delinquents during adolescence. They

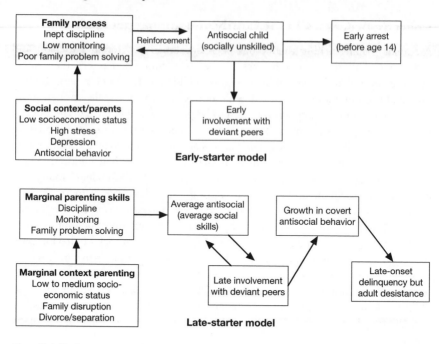

Figure 7.4 Early-starter and late-starter models of delinquency (adapted from Patterson and Yoerger, 1997, p.150).

also tend to make friends during adolescence with others who engage in these behaviors, spend more time with such friends, and have a high proportion of these friends among their network of peers. Delinquents and their peers are inclined to engage in frequent discussions that positively reinforce breaking rules (Patterson et al., 2000; Dishion et al., 1997). These peer interactions further reinforce delinquent and other antisocial behaviors (Wiesner et al., 2007). However, much of this research has been conducted with relatively small samples of families. This is not surprising given that these researchers' studies involved time-intensive observation of family and peer interactions. Nonetheless, it is not clear whether their observations generalize to various types of families and adolescents.

A role commitment/role-taking model of delinquency

Another attempt to elaborate a social learning theory of delinquency rests on the assumption of George Herbert Mead (1934) that interactions with others result in self-images and self-labels that affect how we subsequently behave (see Chapter 1). Mead was concerned with how the many interactions people have with others – both personally and symbolically – affect how they see themselves. He believed that there is a natural tendency to rely on group participation and cooperation to survive. As people gain access to and participate in various groups, they learn how to behave within the group context. These observations have resulted in several theories about *symbolic interaction* (see Chapter 9). This approach emphasizes how people perceive reality as built through their daily interactions with other people and with groups. Symbolic interaction also addresses how the symbols of everyday life, such as signs, gestures, and language, affect interactions among individuals and groups.

Karen Heimer and Ross Matsueda (1994) used Mead's ideas to argue that delinquency results when adolescents learn to see themselves as they think others see them: as rule breakers and deviants. *Role-taking* is the outcome of a combination of self-perceptions and the real or perceived perceptions of others. Significant others who affect these self-perceptions include parents, teachers, other adults, and peers. They may also be affected by the symbols that adolescents are exposed to through the media. More directly, role-taking includes five processes that affect delinquent behavior:

1   *The specific meaning of the self as reflected appraisals (as a rule violator) affect delinquent behavior.* Delinquency results when an adolescent is labeled or takes on the role of a delinquent. Reflected appraisals imply that adolescents learn to see themselves in a particular way based on how others (might) see them. For example, do they think that others, such as parents or peers, see them as deviants or as law-abiding citizens?

2   *Attitudes toward delinquent solutions affect delinquent behavior.* Attitudes are derived from the community or social groups, but often do not furnish satisfactory solutions to presumed problems. Thus, adolescents may develop their own attitudes that justify delinquent behavior or, when they are dissatisfied with legitimate solutions (e.g., telling an adult that another youth is harassing them), they may adopt deviant solutions (e.g., carrying a knife as protection).

3   *Anticipating the reactions of significant others to delinquent behavior.* When adolescents consider a delinquent activity, they first consider how others will react. If they anticipate that peer groups will react favorably whereas parents will fail to react (perhaps because they are unaware of the activity), then delinquency is more likely. On the other hand, if they anticipate that parents will disapprove – especially if they expect to get caught – then delinquency is unlikely.

4   *Associating with delinquent peers.* These associations directly and indirectly affect delinquent behavior. Indirectly, they facilitate involvement in a pro-delinquent reference group, thus providing pro-delinquent attitudes and motives. Directly, they increase the likelihood of group delinquent activities by providing encouragement and opportunities.

5   *Delinquency can occur as habitual responses to situations through prior experiences.* When adolescents are continually confronted with challenging situations that, in the past, were successfully resolved through delinquent behavior, then the behavior may become habitual. Thus, prior experience with delinquency increases the chances of future involvement with delinquency (Heimer and Matsueda, 1994, pp.366–368).

Heimer and Matsueda argued that theories such as differential association and labeling theory (see Chapter 9) are particular cases of their role-taking model.

Differential association, in particular, discusses attitudes and peer groups, but does not sufficiently emphasize role-taking, especially adolescents' views of themselves, anticipation of the reactions of others, and how group processes affect delinquency. Figure 7.5 provides a depiction of their model.

Research on a role commitment/role-taking model

Heimer and Matsueda (1994) have determined that delinquent behavior is positively affected by delinquent peers, delinquent attitudes (adolescents did not think the behaviors are wrong), and reflected appraisals (adolescents perceived that their friends and parents thought they were troublemakers); yet negatively affected by perceived disapproval of delinquency by their parents. The delinquent role-taking variables (high on reflected appraisals and delinquent attitudes, low on anticipated disapproval) are affected mainly by parents' appraisals (parents responded: My son gets into trouble; my son breaks rules), expectations that youth would not be successful academically, and delinquent peers.

Tests of their theory also indicate that parental appraisals of youths as delinquent affect their own perceptions of themselves as rule violators, which then lead to delinquency. This process may be more consequential for boys than for girls. However, prior delinquency is more likely to result in negative appraisals for girls (e.g., Koita and Triplett, 1998).

Peers, networks, and delinquency

As we have learned, examining the association between peers and delinquency is not easy. Researchers have assumed that differential association or social learning theory is supported if associating with peers at one point is associated with delinquency at a later point. However, if delinquent behavior precedes associating with delinquent peers, then some other theory – such as social bonding theory – is supported. However, most studies using data collected over time have shown that the association between delinquent peers and delinquency operates in both directions.

Warr (2001, 2009) observed that peers may be a particularly important influence on adolescent behavior for at least three reasons. First, adolescents seek to

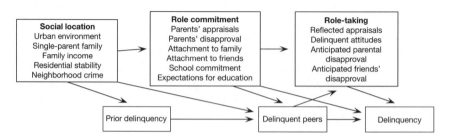

Figure 7.5 Role commitment, role-taking, and delinquency (adapted from Heimer and Matsueda, 1994, p. 374).

avoid ridicule by their friends, so they may go along with their activities to avoid some of their friends laughing at them. Second, many youths attach great importance to loyalty. Being loyal means not telling about your friends' activities, but also participating with them in illegal activities in order to show that you are a true and reliable friend. Third, engaging in delinquency with friends can demonstrate one's courage or strength and thus enhance one's status in the group.

In general, there are three areas of research that have elaborated the role that peers play in the etiology of delinquency: (1) the types of peers that are important, (2) peer rejection, and (3) social networks. First, studies of peer relationships have elaborated Sutherland's notion about the frequency, intensity, priority, and duration of associations. For example, if we compare delinquent behaviors among adolescents and their friends, the similarity is much more consistent among best friends than among other types of friends (e.g., teammates, next-door neighbors) (Vitaro et al., 2000). Furthermore, studies have shown that time spent with peers in *unsupervised* activities is strongly associated with delinquent behavior, thus suggesting that low parental supervision or monitoring may allow peer influences to emerge (Mahoney and Stattin, 2000). Research has also shown that, when a friendship between two delinquents is longer in duration, both tend to continue or increase their involvement in delinquency, perhaps through mutual reinforcement (Brendgen et al., 2000).

Another issue that is particularly important for adolescents involves romantic partners. Being involved in a romantic relationship can actually decrease involvement in delinquency (McCarthy and Casey, 2008). However, this may depend on the behaviors of those romantic partners. Haynie and colleagues (2005) found that adolescent girls engage in significantly more minor forms of delinquency when their boyfriends are also involved in delinquency. This association persists even when accounting for delinquency among their other friends. However, there is little influence of romantic partners' behaviors on boys.

A second topic involves peer rejection. Coercive process theory suggests that most youth do not wish to associate with peers who use coercion, whether physical or psychological, to get their way (Patterson et al., 2000), so conventional peers tend to reject them. Hence, coercive youths tend to gravitate toward others who behave as they do. This serves to reinforce their interaction styles, which then lead to and reinforce deviant and delinquent behaviors.

Several studies have explored the association between peer rejection and various forms of misbehavior (e.g., Dishion et al., 2010). Peer rejection occurs in several ways, including through gossip, aggressive behavior against adolescents, or moral disapproval of adolescents' behaviors. Whether peer rejection eventually influences delinquency, however, depends on how adolescents react to the rejection. Researchers have highlighted the effects of *rejection sensitivity* as an antecedent to delinquency. Rejection sensitivity refers to defensive expectations that adolescents have to social situations that may lead to acceptance or rejection by a peer group (Downey et al., 1998). If adolescents anticipate that they will be rejected by peers, perhaps because of past experiences, then they are often extra sensitive to social situations with peers. Even a modest slight may then be taken as a sign of rejection; the reaction is often hostility and aggression. Research has supported the notion that adolescents highly sensitive to peer rejection are more likely to be aggressive, misbehave at school, and commit violent offenses (e.g., Guerra et al., 2004). Nonetheless, rejection sensitivity tends to lead to more delinquent behavior only among those adolescents who are already aggressive (Guerra et al., 2004). Hence, it may be part of a pattern of coercive interactions that those adolescents described by Patterson engage in.

The third topic that concerns peers is the effect of social networks. Social networks are relationships among several individuals. They are analyzed by studying interpersonal connections that run from intimate family relationships to casual acquaintances. Most research on peer associations and delinquency is based on crude measures of relationships and interactions; this typically involves asking adolescents about their closest friends or studying one adolescent and one peer. Social network studies of delinquency, on the other hand, explore interactions with various peers, as well as family members and adults. In a seminal article, Krohn (1986) assumed that social networks constrain certain behaviors but encourage others. He also explained that delinquents tend to have fewer relationships in their social networks with conventional adults and peers. Figure 7.6 represents two simple social networks that illustrate these concepts.

As youth become more engaged with delinquent peer networks their involvement in delinquency tends to escalate (Sarnecki, 2001). At a certain point, perhaps when all fellow members of a network are delinquents, an adolescent is almost certain to be involved in delinquency (Haynie, 2002). Furthermore, networks that have more personal interconnections among members strengthen the association between delinquent peers and delinquency (Ennett et al., 2006). It thus appears that delinquent networks provide reinforcement, encouragement, and opportunities for delinquency. They are also likely to facilitate the acquisition of pro-delinquent attitudes and definitions. In addition, isolation from conventional peer networks may put some adolescents at risk (Kreager, 2004). Yet even a small network of conforming peers may reduce the risk of delinquency.

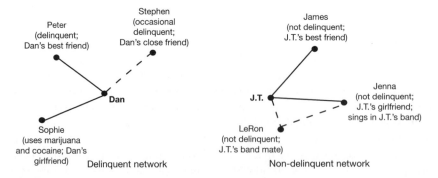

Figure 7.6 Social networks: delinquent and non-delinquent. Note: A solid line indicates a close relationship; a broken line indicates a casual relationship.

Media and delinquency

Recall that Sutherland's third proposition declared:

> The principal part of the learning of criminal behavior occurs within inti-
> mate personal groups. Negatively, this means that the impersonal agencies of
> communication, such as movies and newspapers, play a relatively unimpor-
> tant part in the genesis of criminal behavior.

This statement certainly supports a social network approach to delinquency, even
though the concepts underlying social network analysis were not available to
Sutherland. It also indicates that media influences are not particularly important.
However, the media in Sutherland's time were, relative to the early twenty-first
century, limited in their ability to reach a wide audience or to provide influential programming (Warr, 2001). Television and movies have become much more
widely available and thus it is likely that their influence has grown.

Do media depictions of delinquency and violence provide models that youths
imitate? Studies of media influences on delinquency have been controversial.
Early studies that found a positive association between viewing violence on television or in the movies and aggressive or violent behaviors were criticized because
of methodological problems and limited samples (Freedman, 2002). More recent
studies that have followed children into adolescence and adulthood indicate that,
regardless of family and neighborhood factors, watching more hours of television
or movies (especially shows with violent content) is associated with aggression,
physical fights, robbery, and threats to injure (e.g., Anderson et al., 2003). For
example, Johnson and colleagues (2002) compared 14-year-olds who watched one
hour or less and those who watched three or more hours of television per day.
They concluded that those who watched more television were more than four
times as likely to have assaulted another person or gotten into a physical fight that
resulted in injury by age 16 or 22.

Recent studies have also indicated that exposure to violent video games
increases the risk of aggressive behavior among adolescents. In particular, playing these games increases aggressive thoughts and feelings, which may translate
into aggressive and potentially violent behaviors (Anderson et al., 2010). However,
these studies have rarely assessed actual violent behaviors, so whether a correlation with aggression establishes a link with violent delinquency or adult crime is
unlikely given the present state of the evidence (Ferguson and Kilburn, 2010).

A comprehensive review of the evidence by Savage (2004) carefully considered
many of the major studies that have purported to find an association between
violent media and violent behavior among adolescents. She listed some key limitations of these studies, including:

* limited measures of violence, with most studies simply assuming that aggression is strongly associated with violent delinquency or adult crime;

- an overreliance on peer-nominated aggression (e.g., researchers have typically asked students to nominate aggressive classmates); and
- a failure to consider previous aggressive tendencies among study subjects.

The third criticism is the most important: It is likely that aggressive children who become violent delinquents prefer to watch violent programming and play violent video games. Therefore, it may simply be that the association between viewing violent programming and violent behavior is explained by the preferences of viewers. In answer to the question of whether a link between media violence and delinquency has been established, Savage concluded, "not so far" (Savage, 2004, p.124). Thus, it is clear that additional studies of media effects that examine delinquency and consider the many other learning components that affect it are needed.

Promises and limitations of learning theories

Differential association was one of the premier theories of delinquency in the twentieth century. However, a key criticism is that it was not based on modern theories of learning. Sutherland's claim that delinquent and criminal behavior resulted from the same learning processes as other behaviors was an advance over previous theories of delinquency, yet it was vague. Subsequent social learning theories overcame this imprecision by using contemporary models of learning, drawing mainly from operant conditioning principles and more recent advances such as social cognitive theory and research on modeling (Akers, 1998).

Nonetheless, Sutherland's theory continues to be under-studied and may still offer important information about delinquent behavior. Perhaps the most obvious limitation of research on differential association is that most studies focus on peer relations. The theory clearly does not ignore the influence of siblings, parents, or other adults as models of behaviors. There are many studies that have shown an association between criminal behaviors among parents and siblings, and delinquent behavior among adolescents (e.g., Snyder et al., 2005), yet few have explored how differential association might offer an explanation for this association (Warr, 2001).

Social learning theory was an important development. It is general enough to explain many forms of deviant behavior in addition to delinquency, and empirical studies have generally supported its main principles. An early criticism that continues to have supporters is that, contrary to the assumption of social learning theory, delinquency typically precedes associations with delinquent friends. Learning to be delinquent does not require peers; rather, the lack of parental attention, affection, and training in prosocial behaviors – or perhaps even peer rejection – is sufficient to motivate delinquency (Gottfredson and Hirschi, 1990). Social learning theory has also been criticized for ignoring learning during early childhood; most studies focus on learning processes during adolescence. In addition, critics argue, few delinquent activities require much learning; they are simply the result of low self-control and innate aggression (see Chapter 8).

As noted by Akers (2001), however, social learning theory is not limited to a one-way path from delinquent peers to definitions to delinquency. The reciprocal loop between delinquency and delinquent peers, for example, is a predictable part of social learning theory because it demonstrates reinforcement. Moreover, as shown in Patterson's research, learning clearly takes place in the family as some children model aggressive and coercive behaviors from parents and siblings. Reinforcement of these behaviors also occurs in the family. It is therefore consistent with social learning theory to find that some forms of delinquency precede delinquent peer associations and that family influences predominate in early childhood.

The key for social learning theory, then, is not that it requires verification by additional studies, but rather it should be elaborated by drawing on more recent theories of and research on learning among humans (see Siegler, 2005). For example, the principles of operant conditioning, although informative, do not function the same way for all individuals. Rather, as we learned in Chapter 3, some children and adolescents are not as affected as others by punishment or negative reinforcement strategies; in brief, they are *underaroused*. When parents punish children for misbehavior, those with normal arousal are sensitive to the stress of being punished and learn to avoid misbehavior in the future. However, those who are underaroused are not as affected by the punishment, and therefore are less likely to refrain from misbehavior. Eventually, some underaroused children become delinquent because punishment does not affect them as much as others (Yaralian and Raine, 2001).

In Chapter 4 we learned about cognitive theorists who argue that, in order to understand delinquency, we must consider differences in the way that delinquents and other adolescents process information and make decisions (see also Chapter 2). If delinquents are somehow different from other youths in the way their minds use information or react to certain situations, then this has important implications for learning theories. Children and adolescents learn through reinforcement of certain attitudes and behaviors, but the way reinforcement is processed affects their capacity to be taught to act in certain ways.

Cognitive neuroscience studies have also shown that learning is affected by the composition of several biochemicals as well as the structure of certain portions of the brain (see Chapter 3). We are not true blank slates at birth whose minds must be imprinted with the antecedents of every type of behavior. Rather, our brains develop in ways that affect our capacity to process information and learn new things (Pinker, 1999). We may also use our individual agency to override what we have learned and arrive at decisions about how to behave or think. The next step for a social learning theory of delinquency is, therefore, to consider recent research on learning and agency.

Finally, more research is needed that assesses how definitions and attitudes function across families and communities. As mentioned earlier, both Sutherland and Akers argued that their theories are useful for explaining variations in delinquency rates across communities. Akers (1998; Jensen and Akers, 2007) maintained, for example, that the local community provides a learning environment in which associations and reinforcements occur. Norms and customs that are prevalent in the community constrain or encourage with whom youths interact. A preponderance of conforming peers or adults in a youth's local environment will probably lead to a preponderance of prosocial definitions and beliefs, thus lessening the chances of delinquency. Several studies of community effects on delinquency – as well as social network studies – offer support for this position. In Chapter 5 we learned that a great majority of residents of disorganized, inner-city communities adhere to the values and norms of the broader society, which largely oppose delinquency (Small and Newman, 2001). Nonetheless, studies have found that youths who grow up in impoverished and disorganized areas often report values and attitudes that are conducive to delinquency (e.g., Stewart and Simons, 2010; Warner, 2003). In addition, communities with high levels of crime provide pro-delinquent models for youth and opportunities to interact with adult criminals (Stewart and Simons, 2010). Research that explores the various learning opportunities for adolescents across different types of communities would therefore help elaborate a learning theory of delinquency.

Policy implications of learning theories of delinquency

Learning theories have probably influenced more prevention, intervention, and rehabilitation programs than any other theory of delinquency. This is appropriate given the substantial evidence that programs that focus on family interaction, peer associations, and attitudes about delinquency may be the most effective among the various alternatives (e.g., Greenwood, 2008). Akers and Sellers (2008. p.109) reviewed several programs and concluded, "[the] principles of social learning theory have been applied to a range of prevention and treatment programs . . . [T]here is also some evidence of success, and generally such programs are more effective than alternative approaches." In addition, a review of the correctional treatment literature found that

> social learning theory draws the clearest and most convincing support from extant research on rehabilitation . . . Consistent with this approach, treatment interventions that target for change antisocial attitudes and antisocial peer associations tend to achieve meaningful reductions in offender recidivism (Cullen et al., 2007, p.340).

Programs that use learning theories as the basis for prevention or intervention have focused on various periods in the life of children and adolescents. Programs for infants and young children usually focus on teaching parents effective skills to raise their children, including correct disciplinary measures and learning to monitor youth activities (e.g., Forgatch et al., 2009). Programs for elementary school children often include family, peer, and school-based components. An example of this type of program is the two-year Montreal Prevention Treatment Program (PTP) (Tremblay et al., 1996). It begins in kindergarten and includes social skills training in the school with parent training in the home. The children participate in multiple sessions designed to emphasize prosocial skills. Small groups of aggressive and non-aggressive boys learn through role-playing, peer modeling, and reinforcement of prosocial behaviors. Their parents also participate in sessions that teach them to supervise their children better, provide them with positive reinforcement of prosocial behaviors, and use effective punishment strategies. Children who participate in the program are significantly less likely to be involved in delinquency up to six years later.

There are many programs that are designed for youths who have already been arrested or gone before a juvenile court. An example of an effective program is Multidimensional Treatment Foster Care (MTFC). Based explicitly on a social learning model, MTFC includes training parents to manage adolescent behavior by providing consistent discipline, supervision, and reinforcement of prosocial behaviors. Adolescents are initially placed in foster homes with adults who are specially trained to teach youths about rules, expectations, and limits on their behaviors. Their behaviors at school are also closely monitored. An evaluation that compared youth who participated in the MTFC to those who lived in traditional group homes indicates a reduced risk of arrest among the MTFC group (Chamberlain, 2003).

In general, the success of prevention and intervention programs appears to rest on a multifaceted approach. Focusing on only one aspect of learning or on only one learning environment is not effective. For example, there is evidence that programs led by peer leaders (who are usually older youths), such as those that emphasize resisting peer pressure to misbehave, are not effective (Greenwood, 2006). Similarly, programs that use community leaders or police officers to teach youths about the risks of delinquency and drug use make little difference. The principal lesson is that effective programs focus on most, if not all, of the learning environments that affect children and adolescents. Programs that address family, school, and peer influences, such as those that include both parent and child training at home and in school, are more effective than those that only consider peer influences or that are implemented only in schools (e.g., Smit et al., 2008). Unfortunately, comprehensive prevention and intervention programs are expensive, so they are not widely available.

Conclusions

There is substantial evidence that delinquent behaviors are affected by the same learning principles that govern other behaviors. Children learn to behave based on their experiences with parents, siblings, peers, and adults. Those who are taught that coercion and aggression are appropriate forms of conduct will most likely act accordingly. When behavioral models are reinforced by parents, siblings, and peers then acquisition of the models becomes highly likely. Nonetheless, learning is also affected by individual traits, such as cognitive functioning and mental health. Reinforcement functions differently even within the same family. Some children are quick to respond to punishment or rewards, whereas others are slow to respond, perhaps because of their unique physiological compositions.

Learning theories have provided much useful information for explaining delinquent behavior, and perhaps more importantly, for preventing it. Their emphasis on the types and sources of learning has increased our knowledge of why some adolescents violate the law. They also provide valuable guidance for designing prevention and intervention programs. Teaching children and adolescents to manage their emotions and what constitutes acceptable behavior may be difficult in many situations, but is feasible given what we know about how they learn. Moreover, understanding how children learn is essential for developmental theories of delinquency, such as those that discuss the process that leads some children to go from aggression or impulsivity to delinquent behavior during adolescence and criminal behavior during adulthood (see Chapter 13).

8 Control theories of delinquency

Prologue

Parker and Emily started seeing each other when they met in a drug treatment program. Soon, Emily, who was 19 at the time, found out she was pregnant, so she moved in with Parker. They went into debt as Emily decided that they needed to give their new baby everything that she didn't have growing up. Her hasty purchases included a couple of cribs and lots of new baby clothes. After their baby boy, Michael, was born, Emily continued to buy clothes and toys, pushing them farther into debt.

Emily and Parker tried to be good parents, but they still liked to go out and party. They left Michael home alone for hours or asked a neighbor to look in on him when they were gone. Michael, like his parents, had a short attention span, but also an aggressive nature. His parents held him back a year before beginning school hoping he would calm down. They also spanked him occasionally for wrongdoing, but let him do what he wanted most of the time.

Michael didn't like school much. One school counselor said he was impulsive and insensitive. A parent from the neighborhood thought that Michael "lacked a conscience." Michael told his parents that he hated school; there were too many rules and the teachers were mean to him. His parents ignored him, though; they were having too many problems with their marriage. They fought over money and Parker's frequent periods of unemployment.

About a year later Parker and Emily divorced, and Michael was arrested for stealing a neighbor's bicycle. He claimed that no one was using the bike, so he just borrowed it. No one got hurt; what was the problem? His father soon abandoned the family, moving across the country to be with a new girlfriend. Michael saw his father maybe once a year. Although Emily tried to treat her son well and take an interest in his life, she was busy with work and trying to take some college classes. It was hard to concentrate on work, school, and her son, so Michael was often left on his own. When he was 15, he began to sell drugs so he could save up for a sports car. But most of the money he made was spent on an iPhone and video games. He was arrested a couple of times before turning 16. Eventually, he was sent to a juvenile correctional facility, convicted of drug distribution and possession of stolen property.

Introduction

The theories discussed so far have been based on a couple of common assumptions about human nature. Theories that discuss how the strains of adolescence lead to delinquency (see Chapter 6) focus on external forces that push otherwise normal youths toward delinquency. Theories that address learning to be delinquent (see Chapter 7) assume that we must be socialized to cooperate, follow the law, or become delinquent. As discussed in Chapters 3 and 4, there are actually many complex biochemical and cognitive processes that also affect behaviors.

However, Thomas Hobbes, a seventeenth-century philosopher, tutor to the future King Charles II of England, and exile during the English Civil War, thought that humans are by nature uncooperative and rather unpleasant. Left to their own devices, and not restrained somehow, humans are more likely than not to fight for survival; to take what they can get without thinking about the effects on other people. So why are most people law-abiding and cooperative? Hobbes (1962 [1651]) suggested that a social order is needed to tame natural human impulses so that civilization can exist and flourish. Without the boundaries that a social order establishes, humans will battle constantly, with the strong dominating the weak. One of the founders of sociology, Émile Durkheim (2006 [1897]), made a similar argument: Families, schools, and governments are needed to regulate human behavior; they control the tendency of humans to desire more and more material goods.

This assumption became the building block for several notable theories of human behavior. In particular, when asked why a social order is needed, some theorists argue that the main role is to regulate human behaviors so that people are compelled to cooperate rather than fight it out to gain essential resources. Hobbes was clearly motivated by the English Civil War, which resulted in the execution of a king. He feared that, without a strong central government represented by a monarchy, people would revert to their natural instincts and eventually annihilate one another.

This assumption also became the cornerstone for a number of theories about crime and delinquency. What was needed was not a theory about why youths are pushed into delinquency. Instead, some delinquency theorists contend that we must try to understand what prevents adolescents from committing unlawful acts. Thus, a group of explanations of delinquency became known as *social control theories*. Theorists who take the Hobbesian assumption as their starting point try to explain the mechanisms that restrain individuals from becoming involved in deviant, delinquent, and criminal behavior. Taking their cue from Durkheim, the mechanisms that these theorists discuss are usually located in social institutions like families and schools.

In this chapter, we shall discuss a couple of prominent social control theories. We shall then address a recent innovation that has motivated many studies over the past 20 years: *self-control theory*. It posits that a single mechanism is the basis for most delinquent lifestyles. After evaluating some general issues involving social control theories, we shall discuss some of the policy implications that stem from them.

Early social control theories

Several social control theories were designed in the first several decades of the twentieth century. These explained, for example, the emergence of urban gangs (Thrasher, 1927), the role of the family in controlling adolescent behavior (Nye, 1958), and the effects of external factors (e.g., poverty) and internal factors (self-esteem, ego control) that influence delinquency (Reckless, 1961; Reiss, 1951). Rather than discussing each of these, we shall focus on two theories that have influenced numerous studies of delinquency over the past few decades.

Drift and delinquency

David Matza (1964) observed something important about delinquent behavior: Those who commit delinquent acts do not do so constantly. Rather, most people who commit delinquent acts are law-abiding much of the time. In addition, Matza argued that most assumptions about human behavior go too far because they do not consider that people have free will to act in particular ways of their own choosing. Using these two underlying ideas about behavior, Matza thought that the alternative was somewhere between free will and determinism: Behavior is not completely free or completely determined. Instead there are various levels of freedom that are affected by one's social position and social circumstances.

Matza also thought that most theories predict too much delinquency. If delinquents are so different from non-delinquents, then one would expect them to break the law all the time. This is clearly not the case; rather, delinquency tends to be transient and intermittent. As an alternative, Matza (1964) proposed that delinquents are in a state of what he called *drift*. Drift occurs when social controls have been loosened and when youths have not developed a sufficient sense of freedom. Matza thought of freedom as a sense that adolescents had command over resources and their personal destinies.[1] Adolescents who are not emotionally prepared to deal with the world, yet are not in an environment with adequate social controls, are likely to drift into delinquency. Yet these adolescents are also involved in conventional activities. They are, generally speaking, in a state of flux, "committed to neither delinquent nor conventional enterprise. Neither [of these conditions] is precluded" (Matza, 1964, p.28). The situation of drift is therefore somewhere between absolute control and absolute freedom.

Matza also noted that a lack of social control is not sufficient to explain delinquent behavior. It occurs only when what he called "will" is present. There are two conditions that trigger the will to motivate delinquent behavior: preparation and desperation. Borrowing from learning theories, Matza contended that preparation involves learning through experience. An adolescent does not automatically become a thief; rather, he must learn the techniques of theft. Once a youth learns the techniques, future law violation becomes more likely. However, this occurs only if the youth is somewhat adept at theft. If he gets caught early then he is often discouraged from trying it again. Deterrence also works on some youths who may be in a state of drift but fear getting caught should an opportunity to break the law exist.

Desperation occurs among those who sense they have little control over their environment. By successfully committing a delinquent act, some youths regain a sense of control over their lives; they feel they have the ability to direct their own destinies. Thus, drift leads to delinquency in the presence of preparation or desperation. However, sufficient deterrence – that is, the fear of getting caught (see Chapter 2) – might also be present for an adolescent and diminish the likelihood of delinquency.

Matza accepted the idea that society is organized on a consensual model of order, with most people agreeing that order is necessary and that certain methods are needed to maintain it. Matza also argued that most adolescents, whether delinquent or not, accept mainstream norms and values. This is a common assumption of social control theories of delinquency (Kornhauser, 1978). However, how do delinquents then justify or try to understand their own illegal behaviors? There must be some mechanism that allows them to feel comfortable with what they have done. For instance, youths who steal food must have some way to justify taking someone else's property without paying for it. Perhaps some say they are hungry or that food stores make so much money from marking up products anyway that they will not miss one or two items.

Matza, along with his colleague Gresham Sykes, systematically documented several of the techniques that youths use to justify their illegal activities. They called these "techniques of neutralization" (Sykes and Matza, 1957). In particular, there are five general techniques used by delinquents:

1 *Denial of responsibility*: This is meant to deflect blame from adolescents to forces beyond their control. Delinquent acts, for example, might be accidental or due to unaffectionate parents, wicked friends, or impoverished living conditions.
2 *Denial of injury*: This involves the excuse that "no one got hurt." Some adolescents see their behaviors as harmless pranks.
3 *Denial of the victim*: Delinquents may see themselves as modern-day Robin Hoods. The victim, who may have been injured, had it coming. Alternatively, perhaps a delinquent denies that there is a victim, so, for instance, if someone steals from a large chain store, there is really no "victim" except a faceless corporation that has probably ripped off a lot of customers anyway.
4 *Condemning the accusers*: This involves defining those who condemn you as hypocrites. They are just as bad, if not worse, than the delinquent, so they have no right to judge someone else.
5 *Appeal to higher authorities*: This includes justifying delinquent behaviors by saying they are required by someone else or some group. Adolescents' friends may expect them to be involved in delinquent activities such as theft, assault, or drug sales. The norms of the group outweigh the norms of society.

Techniques of neutralization – or *neutralization theory*, as they are often called – allow drifting adolescents to justify or excuse most of their behaviors, even as they retain their self-image as upstanding people. They still claim that they follow the moral order; it is just that sometimes the rules do not apply to their situation. Either they are forced into particular illegal behaviors or they are doing no worse than other people in society, many of whom get away with their behavior. Not only do these techniques offer excuses for their actions, but they also diminish the guilt and shame that youths might feel otherwise. Since techniques of neutralization must be learned in some way, some scholars claim that they are part of the learning process of delinquency (see Chapter 7). In fact, the techniques may simply be part of the definitions in favor of delinquent conduct that are a key element of differential association theory.

Research on techniques of neutralization

An interesting thing about neutralization theory is that it has been used widely both inside and outside criminology. The neutralization techniques come in handy for understanding all sorts of deviant behaviors, from violating religious norms to gambling (Maruna and Copes, 2005). For example, a person who loses a lot of money but continues to gamble may excuse this behavior by saying that the casino games are unfair and it's now time to try to get the money back. Nevertheless, a common area of research is the study of neutralization techniques among adolescents.

As described by Maruna and Copes (2005), there are two general ways that neutralization theory has been examined: (1) by asking offenders to discuss informally why they committed delinquent acts (usually as part of a qualitative research design), and (2) by comparing delinquents with non-delinquents in terms of their likelihood of using neutralization techniques to justify their behaviors. Other researchers have used experiments to study techniques of neutralization among college students (Fritsche, 2005). Unfortunately, the first approach has not been used much to study the motivations and decision-making processes of delinquents. Rather, this research has focused on adult offenders, especially sexual offenders, white collar criminals, and other adults. By far the most common way – yet this may be the most unsatisfactory method – has been to ask youths about their use of neutralization techniques.

Most of this research examined if there is an association between neutralization techniques and delinquent behavior among samples of adolescents. When asked at only one time point, there is a weak association between these techniques and delinquency (e.g., Mitchell et al., 1990). However, this type of study usually consists of asking about current beliefs and previous delinquent behavior. Yet the most important question for the theory is whether it predicts future delinquency. It is not a useful explanation of delinquency if adolescents merely use the techniques to justify previous delinquent acts, for it is unremarkable that youths use excuses to rationalize questionable behavior. This seems to be a normal human tendency (Maruna and Copes, 2005).

Studies using data collected over time indicate modest support for the theory: Adolescents who agree with neutralization statements at one time are slightly more likely to be involved in delinquent behavior at a later time (e.g., Shields and Whitehall, 1994). However, a problem with this research is that it does not consider earlier delinquency; it is likely that delinquency that occurred before the adolescents participated in the study affects later techniques of neutralization (Maruna and Copes, 2005).

Some observers have argued that techniques of neutralization, regardless of which theory they are linked with, are actually better suited as a technique of escalation of or desistance from delinquent behavior. Maruna (2001) suggested, for example, that, when delinquents begin to use and accept techniques of neutralization, it implies that they have begun to accept the moral order upon which society rests and perhaps serves as motivation to give up their delinquent lifestyle. If it is true that most delinquency is transient and part of a general process of drift, then, as youths accept techniques of neutralization, they may begin to move away from delinquency and toward conformity and commitment to conventional institutions (Maruna and Copes, 2005). Of course, it would be useful if studies collected information on changes in neutralization techniques over time to see if, as adolescents begin to adopt excuses for their delinquent behavior, they also decrease these behaviors over time.

However, in a study that turns neutralization theory on its head, Topalli (2005) interviewed active street offenders and determined that they often adhere to values or "codes of the street" that sanction illegal activities. They then have to apply techniques to neutralize when they are being "good" or acting in a way that most people in society would consider conventional. For example, Topalli found that some offenders violate the urban street value of not snitching on other offenders, but then rationalize this behavior by "blaming the victim" or claiming that it is legitimate retribution for some action ("He snitched on me earlier" or "he threatened to attack my girlfriend, so it was one way to stop him"). Another so-called "code of the street" mandates retaliation for some perceived wrong, such as when a drug dealer is ripped off. However, some of the offenders neutralize the need for retaliation by appealing to the value of mercy or by minimizing the harm against them, which Topalli termed "denial of seriousness" ("That stuff is beneath me; it's not worth my time to pay attention to that stuff").

As Topalli (2005, p.823) explained, neutralization theory could be made more valuable by focusing on different values in society and then determining how members who adhere to these different values justify their behaviors:

> Reconceptualizing neutralization theory in this way allows for a more thorough and inclusive understanding [of] the behavior of criminals [and delinquents]. For those attached to conventional society, neutralizing allows them to engage in offending without relinquishing their image of themselves as good. For those dedicated to street culture, the process allows them to drift (see Matza, 1964) into a state in which the pressures of criminal life can be temporarily abandoned to allow for conventional behavior without sacrificing intrinsically valuable hardcore self-concepts.

As mentioned earlier, though, this way of viewing neutralization theory does not determine whether it is a control theory or a learning theory. In Topalli's description, it seems more the latter than the former.

Social bonding theory

In the 1970s and 1980s no social control theory received as much attention as Travis Hirschi's theory of social bonds. This is because not only was it described in a manner that led to straightforward empirical tests, but it also appealed to many observers who thought that explanations of delinquency too often blamed the general social and cultural structure of society. Moreover, previous control theory principles, such as Sykes and Matza's techniques of neutralization, seemed closer to learning theories. Hirschi's theory offered an internally consistent individual-level alternative to learning and strain theories that also prescribed some straightforward policies to curb delinquency.

In his path-breaking book, *Causes of Delinquency*, Hirschi (1969) began with the explicit assumption derived from Hobbes that humans are by nature uncooperative and rather unpleasant. A social order is needed to curb the natural tendencies of humans or else we would be left with constant battles over material goods. This leads to a simple idea: There is no need to identify the factors that motivate youths to commit delinquent acts. Rather, we should ask: Why do youths conform to the laws? What is it that impedes them from following their natural instincts and fighting or stealing? Social control theories should therefore be concerned with identifying the factors that prevent delinquency and lead to social conformity.

Hirschi argued that the sources of conformity were grounded in what he termed *bonds to society*. In particular, and this is what made his theory so attractive, he clearly articulated four elements of the social bond:

1 *Attachment*: This includes affectionate relations with others, such as family members, friends, school teachers, and communities. Without sufficient attachments, adolescents are free from morally imposed restraints on their behavior. If they do not care about the wishes or feelings of other people, then deviation from what is generally accepted as proper behavior becomes much easier.
2 *Commitment*: This involves the time and effort invested in conventional activities. When adolescents consider committing delinquent acts, they must also consider what effect their involvement might have on other commitments. For example, if students are committed to extracurricular activities, stealing or beating someone up might jeopardize their status as club or team members. As commitments to conventional roles increase, there is more to lose by being involved in delinquency.
3 *Involvement* is based on the saying "idle hands are the devil's workshop." Adolescents who are involved in conventional behaviors do not have the time to devote to delinquent activities. As their time is spent on homework, sports, or school clubs, there is simply not enough time to steal or fight.

4 *Beliefs*: These are the moral principles held by adolescents. Adolescents who feel a moral obligation and respect the norms of society tend toward conformity. However, if such beliefs are not held, then it is easy to break rules. In general, the techniques of neutralization described earlier are unnecessary. A lack of beliefs frees adolescents to pursue delinquent ends as a natural consequence of a weak bond to society.

Hirschi also contended that there are three relationships among the bonds that affect delinquent behavior. First, those who are more attached to conventional society also tend to be involved in more conventional activities. For instance, those who are attached to their schools are likely to get involved in school activities. Second, adolescents who are more committed to conventional institutions are more involved in activities. As commitment to the local community increases, for example, there is often more involvement in community activities. In addition, more involvement leads to greater commitment. Third, adolescents who are more attached to conventional society are also more likely to accept its norms. Thus, moral beliefs are increased by greater attachment to, say, families and schools. Figure 8.1 provides a diagram of Hirschi's theory.

Research on social bonding theory

As part of his initial description of social bonding theory, Hirschi (1969) included a thorough empirical evaluation with information he collected from students in Richmond, CA. The information included questions about family, school, and peer relationships; involvement in activities; commitments; beliefs about behaviors; and delinquent acts (these included mainly minor delinquent activities, such

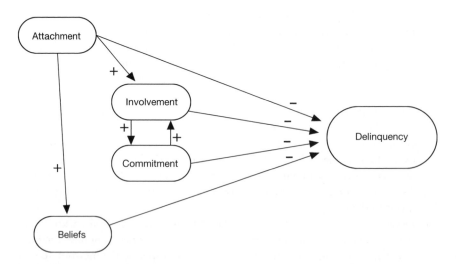

Figure 8.1 Hirschi's social bond theory.

as stealing items, taking cars, and getting into fights). Consistent with his theory, Hirschi found that adolescents who report greater attachment to parents (they wanted to be like their parents; there was good communication) and schools are less delinquent. However, even though Hirschi argued that attachments to delinquent peers also diminished delinquency, he found that the opposite was true: Those adolescents who say their friends are involved in delinquency also tend to be involved in delinquency. As discussed in Chapter 7, this finding has been shown consistently in the delinquency literature, with close friends, siblings, and romantic partners having strong influences on delinquency (Haynie et al., 2005; Warr, 2002). Hirschi countered by arguing that "birds of a feather flock together," meaning that incipient delinquents with poor bonds tend to gravitate towards one another. As mentioned in previous chapters, this continues to be an important issue in delinquency research, with the bulk of the evidence suggesting that delinquency leads to stronger associations with delinquent peers (e.g., Matsueda and Anderson, 1998). Nonetheless, as discussed in Chapter 7, adolescents who become enmeshed in relations with delinquent friends also tend to get involved in delinquency at a later time.

Hirschi also determined that adolescents who are more involved, committed, and have stronger beliefs in conventional norms are less delinquent. In opposition to traditional strain theory (see Chapter 6), youths with high aspirations for success, regardless of their expectations or sense of blocked opportunities, are less delinquent than other youths. Hirschi argued that this shows a weakness of strain theory: It does not matter whether they have low expectations or a sense of blocked opportunities, delinquents with low aspirations – or commitments – are more delinquent than those with high aspirations. However, in a later reanalysis of Hirschi's data, Greenberg (1999) determined that the highest likelihood of involvement in delinquent behavior was indeed among those who reported high aspirations and low expectations, as predicted by traditional strain theory.

A subsequent analysis of these data by Costello and Vowell (1999) was designed to compare social bond theory to differential association theory (see Chapter 7). They identified social bonds as a combination of attachment to schools, attachment to friends, attachment to parents, supervision, and conventional beliefs. They also measured definitions favorable to law violation (a measure of differential association) and friends' delinquency. The results of their analysis are shown in Figure 8.2. This diagram illustrates their preferred model. It accounts for

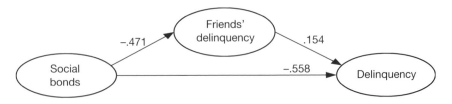

Figure 8.2 A test of social bond theory (adapted from Costello and Vowell, 1999, p.832).

delinquency better than a model that includes definitions favorable to law violation (a differential association model; but see Matsueda and Heimer [1987], who
came to the opposite conclusion). However, they used the same survey questions
to measure beliefs (a part of social bonds in the diagram) and definitions, so it
is unclear whether social bond theory and differential association theory can be
compared well, or if beliefs and definitions are simply two sides of the same coin.
The principal difference between these two theories is in the assumptions they
make about human nature and motivations, so empirical analyses cannot fully sort
out which, if either, is correct.

Several studies have attempted to determine the relative contribution of each
bonding element. Researchers have also described particular types of bonds,
such as school attachment, parental attachment, parental monitoring/supervi-
sion, communication, family conflict, and peer relations (e.g., Cernkovich and
Giordano, 1987; Mack et al., 2007). In fact, a meta-analysis conducted more
than 20 years ago indicates that, of a large number of family factors, parental
supervision, parental rejection of children, and parent–child involvement are the
strongest predictors of delinquency (Loeber and Stouthamer-Loeber, 1986). The
consistent role of low parental supervision as a predictor of delinquency has been
shown in studies ever since (see, for example, Sampson and Laub, 2003), although
this research has been criticized because parents' knowledge of their children's
whereabouts does not predict delinquency as well as children's *disclosure* to their
parents of where they go and who they are with when away from home (Kerr et
al., 2010). School attachment and involvement in school activities are also associated consistently with lower levels of delinquency (e.g., Gottfredson, 2001).

There is a key criticism of social bond theory that has led some scholars to
question its validity, however. Evidence suggests that the bonds between adolescents and social institutions, such as families, schools, or religious organizations,
are associated mainly with contemporaneous involvement in minor forms of
delinquency. Research using data collected over time shows only weak support for
the idea that attachment, involvement, commitment, or beliefs affect subsequent
delinquency (Agnew, 1985, 1991). For example, Agnew (1985) conducted a test
of Hirschi's theory using parental attachment, school attachment, involvement in
school activities (e.g., time spent on homework), commitment to educational goals,
and peer attachment as measures of social bonds. He then looked at delinquency
one year later. The results of his analysis are shown in Figure 8.3.

Agnew found only weak evidence that social bonds are associated with subsequent delinquency. In fact, one of the associations – between school involvement
and delinquency – was in the opposite direction from that predicted by social bond
theory. Along with other evidence that indicates that bonds and delinquency have
only a weak association (Greenberg, 1999), these results have led some researchers
to call for a move away from social bonding theory. However, Agnew also determined that delinquency is negatively associated with subsequent social bonds.

Research over the past 20 years or so has pointed to important institutions
that were mentioned only briefly, if at all, in the initial presentation of the social
bonding theory. For example, an institution that numerous studies have linked

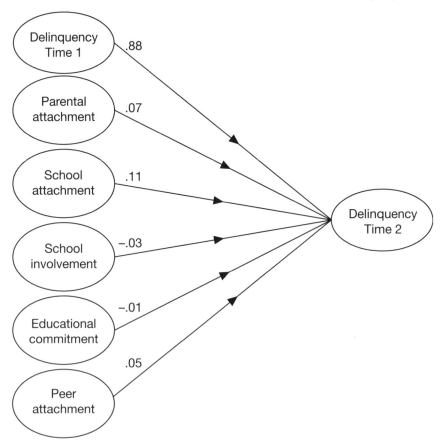

Figure 8.3 A longitudinal test of social bond theory (adapted from Agnew, 1985, p.56).

to delinquency involves religion or spirituality. In general, adolescents who participate in religious organizations, who report strong religious beliefs and regular practices, or who associate with religious peers are less involved in delinquency (e.g., Bahr and Hoffmann, 2008; Baier and Wright, 2001).

Bonds to religious organizations may prevent delinquency in several ways. First, individuals who become attached to a faith community may not wish to risk their associations by engaging in unlawful and prohibited behaviors. Second, involvement in religious activities allows less time for delinquent behavior. Religious involvement also provides social support that shields adolescents from opportunities to become involved in delinquency. Third, commitment to religious organizations and beliefs provides existential meaning that may make delinquency less attractive. Finally, the belief systems of most religious groups discourage or prohibit unlawful conduct in most situations. Thus, involvement in delinquent behavior may jeopardize one's standing in the group and may even result in ostracism (Bahr and Hoffmann, 2008). As with any of the bonds discussed earlier, it remains unclear whether religious affiliations and commitments simply bond adolescents to the group, thereby diminishing their natural tendency to misbehave, or the adolescents actually learn proper roles and appropriate conduct in religious settings (Akers and Sellers, 2008).

Finally, the associations between religious bonds and delinquency may not be uniform, but might be affected by the religious climate of the school or community. Two competing models have been proposed. First, the *moral communities* hypothesis suggests that individual-level religious bonds have a stronger preventive influence in areas with a strong religious climate (Stark, 1996; Wallace et al., 2007). According to Stark (1996), a proponent of this idea, such an environment reinforces religious commitments and attachments. Second, the *secular hypothesis* proposes that religiousness has a greater impact in communities populated by people with low religious bonds; it is in these communities that individual-level bonds to religious organizations and beliefs emerge as especially important for preventing delinquency (Tittle and Welch, 1983). However, research reviews indicate that community-level effects are independent of individual-level influences of religiosity on delinquency; in other words, neither the moral communities hypothesis nor the secular hypothesis is supported by empirical studies (Baier and Wright, 2001).

Self-control theory

About 20 years after Hirschi introduced his social bonding model, he teamed up with Michael Gottfredson to offer a dramatic modification of – some might say a replacement for – his theory. It was a much simpler theory because it traces the source of delinquency and conformity to a single characteristic: self-control. Before presenting their definition of self-control, Gottfredson and Hirschi (1990) identified a distinction that had rarely been considered in delinquency research: the difference between *crime*, or the criminal act, and *criminality*, or the individual propensity to commit criminal acts. Crimes vary because of differences in opportunities to commit them, so, in order to explain them with a theory, we would need to examine and understand variation in opportunities. What was more interesting to these theorists, however, was criminality. What explains the observation that some people have a propensity to commit illegal acts that seems to occur in adolescence and adulthood? The key aspect of their lives is self-control: "the differential tendency of people to avoid criminal acts whatever the circumstances in which they find themselves" (Gottfredson and Hirschi, 1990, p.87).

The main elements of self-control can be traced to the nature of delinquent or criminal acts. Gottfredson and Hirschi (1990, p.89) described six of these:

1   These acts provide immediate gratification.
2   They provide an easy source of gratification.
3   They are risky and exciting.
4   They offer few long-term benefits.

5 They do not require much skill or foresight.
6 They usually result in pain or loss for a victim.

From these characteristics, they inferred that those with a propensity to be delinquent or criminal are, among other things, adventuresome, physical, unstable socially, unable to delay gratification, self-centered, and insensitive. They also tend to look for immediate gratification through smoking, drinking, using drugs, and having sex. Gottfredson and Hirschi summarized this type of person as those "who lack self-control [and] will tend to be impulsive, insensitive, physical (as opposed to mental), risk-taking, short-sighted, and nonverbal, and they will tend therefore to engage in criminal and analogous acts" (Gottfredson and Hirschi, 1990, p.90). These characteristics appear early and persist throughout the life course. In fact, this type of person sounds quite similar to someone with an antisocial personality disorder or one who is impulsive (see Chapter 4; DeLisi, 2009), although Gottfredson and Hirschi have rejected such a characterization. Moreover, some critics have argued that self-control is actually only a modest repackaging of some early social control theories' emphasis on internal control (Akers, 1991).

In recent discussions of self-control theory, Hirschi (2004, 2008) has tried to move it closer to his original ideas about social bonds. He has argued that low self-control is akin to a lack of inhibitions and that delinquency occurs when inhibiting factors, such as strong bonds to institutions such as families, are weak or absent. Delinquent behavior is more likely to occur among youths who do not have inhibitions. However, whether delinquent behavior occurs or not also depends on the situation youths find themselves in. When immediate inhibiting factors are not present in a particular situation, then those with a lack of self-control tend to commit selfish acts, including delinquency (Piquero and Bouffard, 2007).

However, where does self-control come from? Gottfredson and Hirschi argued that it develops early in life (roughly before age eight) if parents provide a nurturing environment where children's behaviors are supervised and punished appropriately. Parents who care more for their children are likely to correct them for breaking rules; this leads children to develop the ability to delay gratification, become sensitive to others' feelings, and become less likely to use force to gain valuable possessions or attain goals. However, children whose parents fail to provide a proper childrearing environment are at risk of developing little self-control (Gottfredson and Hirschi, 2003). Thus, "self-control is acquired; neglect tends to leave the child in a 'natural' state" (Hirschi, 2008, p.69), which involves low self-control. What types of parents are more likely to raise children with low self-control? Those who also have low self-control (Gottfredson and Hirschi, 1990; Nofziger, 2008, 2010).

This argument is not unlike the model of coercive reinforcement developed by Patterson and colleagues (1992; see Chapter 7). The key difference between their theory and self-control theory is that Gottfredson and Hirschi were explicit that low self-control is the natural outcome of a lack of nurturance, discipline, and training. Hence, it is not a process of socialization, but inadequate socialization, that causes a lack of self-control. Moreover, Hirschi has situated self-control theory in the rational choice perspective and claimed that self-control determines whether or not deterrence affects behaviors (see Chapter 2):

> In self-control theory . . . we are all potential offenders . . . But some are more short-sighted than others, and some are more likely than others to assume that luck is on their side. Some people are less likely to attend to the long-term natural consequences of crime. Their choices are therefore unlikely to be altered by changes in the certainty or severity of legal sanctions (Hirschi, 2008, p.69).

Research on self-control theory

Self-control theory has generated significant research attention. The theory promises a relatively simple method for empirical testing. If self-control is the key concept that predicts delinquency and other risky behaviors, then it should be associated consistently with these behaviors regardless of the learning environment, the community context, or how much strain adolescents experience.

Gottfredson and Hirschi recommended that behavioral measures, ideally through direct observation, be used to measure self-control. Following their advice researchers have directly observed seat belt use, measured previous involvement in deviant and risk-taking behaviors, or asked parents and teachers to rate youths on their restlessness, inattentiveness, and other qualities that seem to tap into low self-control (see, for example, Marcus, 2003).

It is relatively well accepted, however, that adolescents involved in delinquency also tend to be involved in other types of risk behaviors, such as drug use, risky driving, unsafe sex, gambling, problems in school and in relationships, and other activities that do not conform to societal expectations (see Dunlop and Romer, 2010; Junger and Deković, 2003). In fact, studies indicate that traditional bonding mechanisms, such as parental monitoring, predict lack of involvement in a variety of adolescent risk behaviors (e.g., DiClemente et al., 2001). However, the overlap among behaviors is certainly not complete and many delinquency items are not highly correlated. For example, property, violent, and drug offenses are often only modestly correlated (see, for example, Greenberg et al., 2002). It is also not clear from this evidence whether these overlapping and correlated behaviors result from low self-control or from some other mechanism.

In an attempt to overcome the potential measurement problems of self-control, researchers have tried to develop survey items that measure tendencies that identify low self-control. The best known example of this was developed by Grasmick and colleagues (1993; Tittle et al., 2003). In the original representation, they formulated 23 items that tapped into tendencies such as shortsightedness, aggressiveness, and risk-taking. Here are examples of five of these items:

- I often act on the spur of the moment without stopping to think.
- I do not devote much thought and effort to preparing for the future.
- I often do whatever brings me pleasure here and now, even at the cost of some distant goal.

- I am more concerned with what happens to me in the short run than in the long run.
- I frequently try to avoid projects that I know will be difficult.

They then examined the association between these items and the use of fraud or force. Responses that identified low self-control were only modestly related to criminal behavior; opportunities to commit crime and factors that were not measured in the study had the greatest influence. In research on delinquency, however, several studies of self-control support the hypothesis that it consistently predicts delinquency (e.g., Higgins, 2009; Rebellon et al., 2008). In fact, a meta-analysis that combined the results of 21 studies of self-control and crime/delinquency indicated that there is a consistent negative association, regardless of whether it was measured by behaviors or by the way people describe themselves (Pratt and Cullen, 2000). In addition, as shown by Hay and Forrest (2008), the presence of low self-control and opportunities to commit delinquent acts work together to increase the likelihood of these acts. Nevertheless, the presence of self-control does not completely eliminate the effects of other variables such as definitions in favor of delinquency or delinquent peers. Rather, these variables also predict criminal and delinquent behavior at least as strongly as self-control.

In a study that further demonstrates that self-control is not a sufficient predictor of delinquency, Hay (2001) used survey questions to measure self-control, parental monitoring, disciplining of children, and acceptance and involvement by parents. As shown in Figure 8.4, he found that low self-control is associated with delinquency and drug use, but that so too is a combined measure of parental monitoring and discipline. However, he also determined that monitoring, fair discipline, and

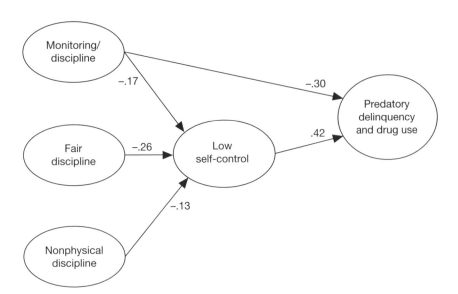

Figure 8.4 A test of self-control theory (adapted from Hay, 2001, pp.722–724).

nonphysical discipline predict self-control to a modest degree. Studies suggest that low self-control is also related to rejection by conventional peers and associating with delinquent peers (Chapelle, 2005). Indeed, youths who report a combination of low self-control and delinquent peers are much more likely to be involved in delinquency (McGloin and Shermer, 2009).

In general, then, there is evidence that low self-control, whether measured through behaviors such as dangerous driving or tendencies such as shortsighted-ness, is associated consistently with delinquency. Gottfredson and Hirschi (1990) claimed that the source of self-control is in the childrearing practices of parents and that it is a stable trait that persists throughout one's life. Studies have not taken a sufficiently long-term perspective to fully test these claims, although research by Boutwell and Beaver (2010) indicated that the mother's and father's level of self-control is associated with their child's level of self-control. Neglectful parents also tend to have children with low self-control (Rebellon et al., 2008). Other studies suggest that low self-control occurs more frequently in poor, disorganized neighborhoods (Pratt et al., 2004), although this may be explained by relatively poor parenting in these neighborhoods (Gibson et al., 2010). Moreover, since low self-control is similar to impulsiveness (see Chapters 3 and 4), research that focuses on this psychological characteristic is germane. However, Gottfredson and Hirschi (1990) rejected the notion that biology – or what they referred to as *biological positiv-ism* – determines criminality. Still, the similarities between research on self-control and impulsiveness should not be ignored and there is clearly room for studies that draw strength from our understanding of both concepts.

Promises and limitations of social control theories

Control theories offer a parsimonious way of understanding delinquency. By assuming that it is human nature to take what one wants, these theories redirect our attention from explaining delinquency to explaining conformity. Since most people conform to societal expectations most of the time, the goal for control theorists is to determine which factors prevent people from pursuing their own selfish desires. The key is control through societal institutions and conventional socialization in the family.

Although compelling from a theoretical point of view, especially because empirical testing seems relatively straightforward, the simplicity of control theo-ries is also seen as a weakness. According to this view, delinquency cannot possibly result from such a simple matter as bonding or self-control. Rather, a much more complex process must be necessary to explain delinquency. Self-control theory has also been criticized as being tautological (Akers, 1991; see Chapter 1). That is, Gottfredson and Hirschi asserted that low self-control is the main cause of delinquency and other behaviors; however, they define self-control with reference to the propensity of youths toward criminality. If self-control is measured only by the propensity to commit delinquent acts then we cannot clearly separate self-control from criminality. Some research has tried to measure self-control using involvement in risky behaviors such as smoking or heavy alcohol use, but these fail to distinguish self-control because it is supposed to underlie all these behaviors, including delinquency. Hirschi and Gottfredson (2000) have offered a spirited defense that self-control theory has the qualities of a good, testable theory, even if measurement problems currently exist.

Moreover, the relatively modest empirical support for social bonding theory has led some observers to claim that it should be modified or rejected. For example, some maintain that the bonds articulated by Hirschi should be studied more carefully because they often have reciprocal effects with delinquency or with other variables (e.g., Liljeberg et al., 2010). This issue is taken up in Chapter 12 when we discuss theoretical elaboration. Others contend that changes in bonds over time should be studied because a decrease in bonds may predict increased delinquent behavior, yet an increase in bonds, especially those that accompany life course transitions, such as marriage or entering the workforce, may herald desistance from delinquent and criminal behavior (Sampson and Laub, 2003).

Another important issue is whether the family variables at the core of social bonding and self-control theory are control variables or they gauge the learning environment of the home. Perhaps adolescents who develop strong self-control, have strong relationships with parents, or are supervised closely by parents learn that delinquency is not a wise or preferable choice in their families. They learn that any delinquent action on their part is likely to be detected and they will be punished. Thus, family factors may tap into the learning environment of the home instead of simply the control attempts by parents (see Chapter 7 and Akers, 1998). Studies that link school attachment to delinquency may similarly be identifying a learning environment rather than a social control process, as students are socialized from a young age to behave at school. The problem of sorting out the effects of bonds from the effects of learning has led several researchers to consider combining aspects of social bond and social learning theories into a single integrated model. This line of reasoning is pursued in Chapter 12.

Other criticisms of social bonding and self-control theory include: (1) they generally fail to address the behaviors of significant others, and (2) genetic characteristics may account for the association between bonds or self-control and delinquency. Similarly to research on peers and delinquency (see Chapter 7), studies indicate that, if parents or older siblings are involved in criminal or delinquent behavior, this increases the likelihood that adolescents will also engage in delinquent behavior (see, for example, Snyder et al., 2005), even when family attachments are strong. Moreover, a recent study indicates that genetic characteristics explain most of the association between parenting variables and self-control (Beaver et al., 2010). Again, this implies that learning or biological theories are more valid than social control theories since adolescents may learn how to violate the law partly from their family members, and genetic risk factors – rather than family socialization practices – might account for adolescents' levels of self-control.

Policy implications of control theories

The policy implications of social bonding and self-control theory are relatively straightforward. In fact, according to Gottfredson and Hirschi (1990, pp.272–273), "policies directed toward enhancement of the ability of familial institutions to socialize children are the only realistic long-term state policies with potential for substantial crime reduction." This requires not merely parents, but also "responsible adults committed to the training and welfare of the child" (p.272).

More generally, if we accept that social bonds are essential, policies that encourage children to bond with their parents through affectionate relations, consistent discipline practices, and commitment, or that encourage involvement in lawful recreational activities, offer a simple way to ensure that children conform to the expectations of society. For example, a program called *Sure Start* offered parenting classes to adults from socially disadvantaged areas in Wales. The classes and supplementary home visits were designed to improve parent–child relations, teach parents effective discipline practices, increase the confidence of parents, and provide parents with support as they raised their children. At a six-month follow-up, misbehavior and conduct disorders had decreased for children in the *Sure Start* program relative to a control group of children (Hutchings et al., 2007). Other studies have also shown that policies that show parents how to develop better relations with adolescents lead to less delinquency (e.g., Farrington and Welsh, 2003). Many of these programs are not based strictly on social control or self-control theories; they usually adopt a learning framework to promote parenting that is designed to socialize children to treat others fairly and with respect and to avoid using coercive means to get desired objects (e.g., Spoth et al., 2001).

Many school-based prevention programs also encourage adolescents to develop stronger bonds to conventional institutions. These programs attempt to make schools safer for students, encourage strong social bonds between students and teachers, and provide extracurricular activities so that students are more involved in schools. For example, Gottfredson et al. (2004) found that participation in after-school programs is associated with less delinquent behavior among middle school students. However, this diminished delinquent behavior is not due to greater supervision by adults in charge of the programs or greater levels of involvement in conventional activities. Rather, students enrolled in after-school programs have more positive relations with peers and fewer intentions to use drugs. The effects are especially pronounced when these programs emphasize the development of social skills and character development.

Neutralization theory has also influenced several prevention policies and, in particular, is at the heart of many cognitive–behavioral therapy programs (see Chapter 4). Some of these programs are designed to teach delinquents to take responsibility for their actions rather than excuse their behaviors by denying the victim or condemning their accusers (Maruna and Copes, 2005). By shifting adolescents' cognitive orientations from those that accept coercion or force to gain what they want to those that emphasize cooperation and persuasion, they can be taught to adopt a more conventional and less risky interaction style.

Neutralization theory has also served as a basis for the principles of *restorative justice* (Braithwaite, 1999). Restorative justice is a program that is designed to bring together juvenile offenders and victims to discuss reaching a mutual understanding of the damage caused by the offense. When offenders meet their victims face-to-face and learn about the consequences of their acts, it is difficult to deny that there is a victim, condemn a condemner, or appeal to a higher authority such as one's friends. Any shame for the offense is shifted to the offender, who is compelled to take full responsibility for the delinquent act (Braithwaite, 1999). A study by McGarrell and Hipple (2007) suggested that face-to-face meetings between young first-time offenders and their victims led to several positive outcomes. Most importantly, participants have lower re-arrest rates at a six-month follow-up than those who do not participate in the program. However, it is not clear whether overcoming the neutralization techniques used by offenders was part of the program, or simply discussing the offense with their victims and learning about the pain and suffering they caused helped prevent future delinquent behavior.

Conclusions

Control theories are attractive because they do a fine job of isolating the roots of delinquency in the natural tendencies of humans and the need for a social order. Instead of emphasizing the problems caused by the culture and social institutions, control theories point out the benefits of institutions such as families, schools, and religious organizations. Their key argument is that we need these institutions to function well so that children are raised to be cooperative, kind, and law-abiding. If these institutions are fragile or do not share the same social goals, then youth are freed from conventional constraints and, often, turn to delinquency and similar behaviors.

Social bonding and self-control theories are also attractive because they are parsimonious. Parsimonious theories are preferred because they allow straightforward empirical testing of their core propositions. Hence, there have been dozens of studies of social bonding theory since it was introduced in the late 1960s. Following the introduction of self-control theory in its full form about 20 years ago (Gottfredson and Hirschi, 1990), there have been more than 100 published research articles, as well as several dissertations, designed to examine its role as an explanation of delinquent behavior. Regardless of the eventual judgment of its validity, this clearly denotes an important idea for delinquency research.

However, what can be concluded at the present time about social bonds and self-control? Many studies attest that bonds to conventional institutions and self-control among adolescents are associated with less involvement in delinquent behavior. Adolescents who have poor relations with parents, weak attachments to schools, and less involvement in conventional activities are more likely to be involved in delinquency. The strength of the association between self-control and delinquency is particularly impressive. Adolescents who manifest low self-control, whether in their behaviors or their tendencies, tend to be involved in delinquent behavior and, later, adult crime. However, studies that demonstrate these associations tend to ask adolescents about their current state of mind, attitudes, and beliefs, and then look at their associations with current or past levels of delinquent conduct. Studies that take a longer view and examine the effect of bonds or self-control on subsequent delinquent behavior show less support for these theories. There is also evidence that learning remains important and that we should not ignore the idea that adolescents can learn to bond with conventional institutions. Perhaps they can even learn self-control.

Finally, control theories are attractive because they offer straightforward prevention and intervention programs. For example, many policies are based on deterring juveniles from starting or continuing to engage in delinquent acts. However, according to self-control theory, the most likely delinquents – those with low self-control – are too shortsighted and impulsive to be deterred by traditional prevention programs or law enforcement methods. Hence, the main goals are to encourage more effective childrearing practices that inculcate self-control and to enhance crime prevention through decreasing the attractiveness of crime to delinquents (Gottfredson and Hirschi, 1990). In the end, however, it appears that at least the first of these goals cannot be achieved without reliance on valid learning principles.

9 Labeling, symbolic interaction, and delinquency

Prologue

Marcie was living in a working-class neighborhood with her parents and brother when disaster struck. Her father, who worked in a coal mine, was killed when the carbon monoxide detector failed and he collapsed from lack of oxygen. By the time they found him, he had already suffered massive brain damage, and he died a few days later. Marcie, then 13, went through periods of depression and anger. When a couple of girls at school made fun of her father's death, she stabbed one of them twice, sending her to the emergency room for 10 stitches. Marcie was arrested for assault and kicked out of school. Although she was placed in a juvenile diversion program and given grief counseling, she also had to attend an alternative junior high school for "troubled" youth. Marcie's mother, who was on medication for severe anxiety, had little time and seemed to take no interest in Marcie's problems. Some of the neighborhood kids began to call her "ho" and "skank" because the school she attended was also for pregnant teenagers. Marcie rarely backed down from these kids and began to threaten them with a knife that her brother gave her.

Marcie became friends with Laurie, who had been kicked out of school for vandalism and fighting. Laurie introduced Marcie to marijuana and cocaine. They also spent their afternoons shoplifting clothes from local stores. Marcie didn't feel good about the drugs or stealing, but when she tried to talk to her mother or older brother, they told her, "You've got to grow up." She began to think, "To hell with them; I'll do whatever I want." When they were 15, Marcie and Laurie stole a car and drove to a city about 100 miles away. They slept in the car and shoplifted at convenience stores to eat. Marcie considered going home, but thought there was little for her there. She didn't like school and knew that her reputation as a shoplifter would make it impossible to find a job. Laurie – who had developed an addiction to crystal meth – talked her into exchanging sex for drugs and money from men who hung out at a city park. Marcie was soon arrested for prostitution, but sent home with her mother's assurance that she would be supervised and sent back to school. She ran away several more times. Marcie was eventually arrested and sentenced to a juvenile facility for slashing a girl with a knife.

Introduction

Most of the theories discussed in earlier chapters addressed some of the factors that either push adolescents into delinquency or prevent them from becoming delinquent. Suppose, however, that we shift our focus and ask the following questions: Why do we identify some activities as deviant or delinquent? Why are some youths called delinquent or said to have a conduct disorder whereas others who misbehave are called well-adjusted or normal? If we say that children are temperamental and difficult or adolescents are troublemakers, does this affect their subsequent behavior? These are some of the questions that scholars from the symbolic interactionism school have asked and attempted to answer.

As mentioned in Chapter 1, symbolic interactionism is a field of inquiry that focuses on interactions among individuals. An underlying assumption is that, by interacting with others, we create our own perceptions of reality; we define the meaning of things (Blumer, 1969). We use symbols, which include verbal and non-verbal forms of communication, to interact with others and to reach a common understanding of what is real and what is not. Symbolic interaction researchers study interactions, symbols, and language to determine how these influence people's perceptions of themselves and their behaviors. An important goal is to make sense of how people define or understand the meaning of various situations and conditions.

Symbolic interactionism is not a theory of behavior: It does not attempt to explain some phenomenon or identify its causes. Rather, symbolic interactionism is a general research approach that provides information about how human beings think and behave (Blumer, 1969; Ulmer, 2011). It typically employs inductive methods to develop theories. *Induction* is a research approach that uses observations to generate general concepts (Ragin, 1994), which may then be used to construct a theory. Studies using symbolic interactionism are typically designed to explore people's social worlds using direct observation, informal conversations, and in-depth interviewing. Some even argue that we cannot understand people's actions or thoughts unless we are willing to become part of their social world. Nevertheless, quantitative studies using information from surveys also provide important information about symbolic interactions (Ulmer and Wilson, 2003).

Several scholars have argued that the origins of most of the prominent theories of delinquency may be traced to symbolic interactionism. For example, to develop his theory of differential association, Sutherland used Mead's ideas about the importance of social interactions and Thomas's notion that how situations are defined affect the outcome of those situations (see Chapter 7; Gongaware and Dotter, 2005). Nonetheless, the most notable theory of delinquency that stems from symbolic interactionism is labeling theory. As we shall learn, labeling theory is concerned with the effects of societal reactions on delinquent behavior. When a youth is defined as delinquent by others, what effect does this have on subsequent behavior? Research on self-image and delinquency is also based on symbolic interactionism.

The ideas underlying symbolic interactionism are old, since even the ancient Greeks were concerned with interactions and how they affect social situations

(Fine, 1990). Nonetheless, two social scientists, George Herbert Mead and Charles Horton Cooley, are considered among the principal founders of symbolic interactionism (Turner et al., 2002). In general, they argued that the symbols we attach to objects are defined through our interactions with other people. Moreover, rather than being the passive outcome of external influences, behavior is influenced by people's decisions and judgments. These, in turn, are affected by social relationships. Moreover, social interactions affect people's self-images and self-concepts. Cooley (1902) referred, for instance, to the importance of the *looking-glass self*. The reactions of others to our behavior provide us with a sense of who we are. We also tend to imagine other people's reactions to and evaluations of our behaviors. Our "social self" – the roles we utilize in our interactions with others – influences how we characterize ourselves. It also defines how others see us: Are we considered shy, boisterous, affectionate, intelligent, or slow? Briefly, then, our self-image is influenced by and influences our interactions with others. In addition, we tend to adapt to the roles in which we place ourselves and others place us. These roles change as we grow older, enter new environments, or associate with different people. Moreover, certain people have a stronger effect on our self-image. For example, parents exert a strong influence on the self-image of young children, whereas peer groups affect the self-image of adolescents.

In studies of deviance and delinquency an important concept that has grown out of symbolic interactionism is *stigma*. In general, a stigma is a distinguishing characteristic. In the social sciences, it is usually considered a negative label that is affixed to certain people or groups. Thus, it provides a way to set apart some set of persons from others who are considered more conventional (Shoham, 1979). The label of delinquent may be considered a stigma because it is often used to distinguish groups of adolescents and place them in a category denoting an undesirable or troubled person.

Stigma and its association with delinquent behavior may be studied in two ways. First, how does it affect the initial delinquent act? Are adolescents from socially stigmatized groups more likely to commit delinquent acts? If they are, is it because stigmatization limits their life chances, or affects the way other people treat them or the way they see themselves? We learned in earlier chapters that low socioeconomic status is associated with violent delinquency. Is this association due to stigmatization and how this affects the opportunities of adolescents? Second, how do formal labels affixed by the juvenile justice system (e.g., arrest by the police or adjudication as a delinquent by the courts) or the informal labels affixed by peers (e.g., loser, slut, or gangsta) affect subsequent behavior? Are juveniles who are defined by others as delinquents or troublemakers likely to adopt this role and become more heavily involved in delinquent behavior? In general, does a social stigma – or a *label*, as it is often called in studies of delinquency – that is affixed by others result in behaviors that are stereotypically associated with the stigmatized group?

It is not difficult to find examples of the effects of social stigma in fiction and in autobiographies. Perhaps the most telling description is by Jean Genet, the French playwright and philosopher. One of his most famous characters, who was based on Genet himself, grew up in an orphanage and in a foster home with a peasant family. He believed that the family members and fellow residents of the village thought the worst of him, so he recalled living up to this stigma. If others saw him as a thief then he would steal; if others saw him as evil then he would behave accordingly (Genet, 1964 [1949]). He remembered when, as an adolescent, he was caught stealing by the school headmistress. When asked why he had done it, Jean replied, "Because all the others think I'm a thief." Many literary works, such as Nathaniel Hawthorne's *The Scarlet Letter* (1851), or movies such as *Shrek* (2001), offer compelling and sometimes amusing descriptions of the effects of social stigma.

The next section of this chapter reviews early sociological work on the association between social stigma or labeling and delinquency. We shall then consider contemporary research that distinguishes the effects of formal and informal labeling. A subsequent section assesses research on self-image, in particular self-esteem and self-concept, and delinquency. The final two sections of the chapter provide a general evaluation of symbolic interactionism as well as what policy steps such an approach recommends.

Symbolic interaction and labeling

Labeling theory refers to the idea that adolescents will live up to whatever labels others place upon them. Moreover, labeling theorists study why certain activities are labeled as delinquent whereas other, similar forms of behavior, are not. In Chapter 1, we discussed status offenses: Acts that are not legal for persons under a certain age, but that are legal for adults. An example of a status offense is curfew laws, which are often applied only to children and adolescents. Labeling theorists might study why a particular municipality passes curfew laws whereas others do not. Are adolescents in some municipalities more likely to be labeled as delinquents, thus motivating the presumed need for curfew laws? Are certain neighborhoods more prone to receive the label *criminal, delinquent,* or *violent?* We learned in Chapter 5 that certain communities may be labeled as disorganized or dangerous; these tend to be communities with impoverished residents, dilapidated buildings, and residential instability, regardless of the prevalence of crime (Sampson and Raudenbush, 2004). Researchers who take a conflict approach often argue that extralegal factors, such as race, poverty, or power, affect the labeling process and the way adolescents are treated by the justice system (see Chapter 10).

A more common goal of labeling theory is determining the effects of labels on adolescents. This aspect of labeling theory is influenced heavily by symbolic interactionism. In particular, it draws upon the work of Mead, especially his work on the social self. Mead (1934) argued that how we view ourselves and others is affected by myriad interactions that include language, gestures, and the roles we adopt in particular environments. He also distinguished between the "me" self and the "I" self. The "me" self is how we think we are seen by others in social situations. The "I" self is our actual behavior in social situations. Mead thought that the "I" self could only be defined after the "me" self was understood. Of course, these self-images can change as people are involved in different social situations throughout their lives. Eventually, through numerous interactions, people develop a sense of the *generalized other.* An awareness of the attitudes of others with whom they associate on a regular basis.

> The organized community or social group which gives to the individual his [or her] unity of self may be called "the generalized other." . . . It is in the form of the generalized other that the social process influences the behavior of the individuals involved in it and carrying it on, i.e., that the community exercises control over the conduct of its individual members; for it is in this form that the social process or community enters as a determining factor into the individual's thinking. In abstract thought the individual takes the attitude of the generalized other toward himself (Mead, 1934, pp.154–156).

By honing a sense of the generalized other, an individual may become a *unified self.* Nonetheless, one still takes on particular roles that depend on how the generalized other is perceived. For example, the generalized other is usually seen differently when adolescents are in a classroom from when they are playing video games.

Dramatization of evil

An early application of both the conflict and symbolic interaction aspects of labeling theory was Frank Tannenbaum's (1938) discussion of the *dramatization of evil.* He noted that adolescent activities are often seen in one of two ways. First, children may be involved in harmless pranks. Because they are exciting, even dangerous, some youth are drawn to certain of these activities. Second, community members find some of these activities to be troublesome. Some adolescents who are involved in dangerous activities may be seen as troublemakers, rather than typical youths having fun. As they get older and the activities become more widespread, adults in the community become more rigid and thus are more likely to condemn the activities. The activities are given negative labels. At some point, various adolescents are also given negative labels, or what Tannenbaum described as a definition that they are "evil."

Adolescents are aware when such labels become attached to them. Some then make the transition from a conventional state to a delinquent state. Their "me" state falls in line with the label the adults have given them. Even when they do good or routine things, the labelers tend to say they had ulterior motives ("Oh, Daniel just helped Ms. Fields take her groceries home to see what he could steal from her apartment"). A period of antagonism and conflict occurs between those who are labeled and their labelers. Labeled adolescents perceive the injustice that has been wrought; others are also involved in behavior that is just as bad but they are not called delinquents. The solution for the labeled adolescent is to lash out – directly or indirectly – at the labelers and become what the label dictates.

Tannenbaum thought that delinquent gangs offered refuge for labeled boys. The gang furnishes something of a community or family for adolescents labeled as delinquent. The conflict that occurs between the gang and others in the community is the glue that holds the gang together. As community members or the police attempt to force the gang apart, bonds among the labeled adolescents become stronger. The result is a self-fulfilling prophesy: Adolescents become what the label dictates – troublemakers, delinquents, and gang bangers.

Primary and secondary deviance

Another attempt to describe the labeling process was provided by Edwin M. Lemert (1951). He discussed two forms of deviance: *primary* and *secondary*. Primary deviance involves the actions that lead to the initial label as a delinquent or troublemaker. Secondary deviance involves adopting a new role, or social self, which affects delinquent behavior. Lemert argued that most theories of deviance failed to recognize the distinction between the forms of deviance. There are many sources of primary deviation, including psychological conditions or social situations. However, most primary deviant behaviors do not lead to the adoption of a deviant role.

Nevertheless, if the person continues to be involved in deviant activities and if the reaction from others is particularly harsh, then the person may actually go through a transformation and adopt a deviant role. Lemert (1951, p.76) wrote:

> When a person begins to employ his deviant behavior or a role based upon it as a means of defense, attack, or adjustment to the overt and covert problems created by the consequent societal reaction to him [or her], his deviation is secondary.

The example from the life of Jean Genet involves secondary deviance. Lemert also emphasized that the role must be reinforced by others, mainly through their reactions to the person's behavior. In this respect, secondary deviance is the acquisition of a social role that may even become a person's unified self. This process is complex, but is consistent with the symbolic interactionism notion of a long-term dynamic process that occurs when labels are applied and reinforced over time.

The delinquent role as a master status

Howard S. Becker (1973) contributed to labeling theory by focusing on different types of status traits. He emphasized two status roles in people's lives: *master* and *auxiliary*. The particular characteristic that best discriminates between roles that people play is the master trait. For example, medical doctors go through a specific training program before they are allowed to practice medicine. Furthermore, there are certain traits that people tend to associate with a master status. For many years, and even to this day, certain occupations have been considered "male" and "female" occupations. Moreover, certain types of people are expected to work in certain types of occupations.

Becker claimed that the role of criminal or delinquent often has the characteristics of a master status. In addition, this type of master status tends to overwhelm other roles that people might have. An honors student who is caught robbing a store will most likely be identified and subsequently labeled as a delinquent. The delinquent status also carries many auxiliary traits, such as poor character, untrustworthy, and suspicious.

Becker also argued that once a master status as delinquent becomes affixed to an adolescent, a self-fulfilling prophesy occurs. Since delinquents are judged as disreputable, their opportunities for participating in conventional activities become limited. They often find only unconventional or illegal channels open to them. In the words of Lemert, they have little choice but to adopt secondary deviance. Nonetheless, Becker also recognized that the pathway to a delinquent master status is not inevitable for those labeled delinquent. Some youths may be deterred from delinquent behaviors if they are caught and punished effectively. Family members and friends may also help them resist a delinquent label. Why some youths are deterred whereas others live up to the label of delinquent is not clear, however.

The labeling process often leads to associations with others who have been given similar labels. This may be because conventional peers reject incipient delinquents, so they tend to gravitate toward other delinquents. Whatever the cause, associating with others who share a delinquent label reinforces the label since groups provide a sense of belonging and a network of friends. As Tannenbaum noted, the delinquent group functions something like a family, a system of social support, and as the source of one's self-concept.

Retrospective interpretation and role engulfment

Edwin M. Schur (1971) explained that there are several steps to the labeling process. In particular, he was interested in the process by which a label is affixed to an individual. There are several important parts of this process, in particular *retrospective interpretation* and *role engulfment*. Retrospective interpretation "involves the mechanisms by which reactors come to view the deviators or suspected deviators 'in a totally new light'" (Schur, 1971, p.52). For example, when an honors student is labeled a delinquent, perhaps because he robbed a convenience store or assaulted a woman, people often reinterpret his past actions in a new way. Whereas previously he may have been thought of as a model child who worked hard in school, people may now recall certain events from his past that were, at the time, out of character. His success in school may be reinterpreted as manipulative or as evidence of an evil genius.

Role engulfment concerns a shift in attention from the labelers to the labeled person. It occurs as adolescents become enmeshed in a delinquent role. As mentioned earlier, they may come to identify with the role and behave in ways that are consistent with the role. Like secondary deviance or the unified self, role engulfment does not appear suddenly. Rather, it occurs over time as interactions with others reinforce the label. Why some youths adopt the role is not clear, however. Perhaps it requires a consistent set of interactions that reinforce the role, with a relative absence of interactions that might allow the adolescent to resist the label.

Formal and informal labels

There have been numerous studies of labeling and delinquency (e.g., Bernburg et al., 2006; Paternoster and Iovanni, 1989). Before discussing some of the results of these studies, it is important to consider that some observers question its status as a theory. For instance, it is not clear whether the concept of a label or stigma is defined precisely enough to allow empirical studies, how these labels are applied or adapted by adolescents, or whether it really matters if we label certain acts as delinquent because some are so heinous (e.g., forcible rape, armed robbery, murder) that those who commit them are clearly troubled and in need of intervention by the justice system (Gibbs, 1975).

Following the claims of symbolic interactionists, however, perhaps labeling is not a theory, but rather a complementary way of viewing human behavior from a standpoint that had not been considered previously (Becker, 1973). Nonetheless, it has been the subject of numerous empirical tests, many of which assume that being arrested results in a delinquent label. These tests offer, at best, only modest support for the proposition that labeling leads to more delinquency. Rather, there is evidence that some of those who are arrested reduce their involvement in delinquency, perhaps because deterrence has functioned effectively (see Chapter 2), whereas others become more involved in delinquency (e.g., Bernburg et al., 2006).

Nonetheless, much of this research has focused on *formal labeling*, which refers to labels that are presumably applied by the juvenile justice system. A more recent emphasis is on *informal labeling*. These labels are applied not by the justice system (police, courts), but rather by family members, peers, teachers, or other adults in the community. Addressing informal labels is more faithful to symbolic interactionism since how the self develops and how adolescents see their roles in society are heavily influenced by early socialization experiences (Shoham and Rahav, 1982). For example, whether an adolescent sees himself as a good or a bad kid is affected more by the way he is treated by his parents and peers than whether he is picked up by the police.

In addition, although they are related, there is a difference between how adolescents are perceived by others and how they think they are perceived by others (Gecas, 1982). Therefore, it is important to distinguish between the labels that parents or peers apply to adolescents and the labels that adolescents apply to themselves *based on how they think others see them*. In an illustration of the process through which informal labeling affects delinquency, Zhang (1997) found that parental labeling of youths as "bad kids" or those who "get into trouble" and youths' perception of labeling by adults, in particular teachers, uniquely affect delinquent behavior. Furthermore, youths' perceptions of informal labeling by parents, peers, and teachers are affected by parents' labels of them as bad kids and troublemakers. Figure 9.1 provides a depiction of these results.

The figure also shows that prior delinquency affects labels. This is not surprising since the youths most likely to be perceived as troublemakers or delinquents are those who have violated the law. The model represented is also similar to Heimer and Matsueda's (1994) theory of role-taking, role commitment, and

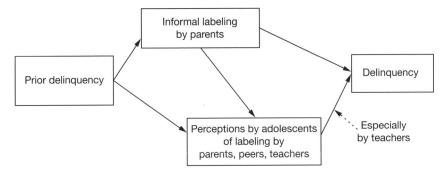

Figure 9.1 Informal labeling and delinquency (adapted from Zhang, 1997, p.135).

delinquency discussed in Chapter 7. Their learning theory, which was based explicitly on symbolic interactionism and differential association, indicated that parental appraisals of youths – which are the same as parental informal labels – affect reflected appraisals by youths of how they are perceived by others. When parents label youths as delinquents, youths tend to incorporate this role into their lives and act accordingly.

This research supports the symbolic interactionist notion that one's social roles are created by others' perceptions and our own perceptions of how others see us. As suggested by Mead's research many years ago, some adolescents consciously take on the role that they perceive from others. When the role includes traits such as "bad," or "troublemaker," some youths live up to this role and engage in delinquent behavior. Of course, this is not a deterministic process; rather, informal and formal labeling increases the probability that youth will engage in delinquent behavior. Some youths, however, are able to resist or cast off the label and conform to social rules and norms (Paternoster and Iovanni, 1989), although it is not clear how this is done.

Does labeling affect conventional opportunities?

Even though some criminologists have dismissed labeling theory because of the weak empirical support for the association between formal labels and delinquency, others have recognized its value in describing a process that culminates in delinquency and adult crime. This process is complex and may take place over a long period of time. A key part of this process, though, is the effect that formal or informal labels have on conventional opportunities such as education, peer associations, family relationships, and occupational choices. Sampson and Laub (1997b) have provided a detailed description of this process. They argued that involvement in the juvenile justice system prevents some youth from taking advantage of conventional opportunities for success. Early delinquency leads to contact with the justice system, which then affects subsequent opportunities. For some adolescents, a "snowball" effect occurs, with delinquency and formal adjudication leading to school problems, difficulty finding work, probation or incarceration, and weakened bonds to conventional society. Hence, Sampson and Laub have linked the labeling process to social bond theory (see Chapter 8), with labels negatively affecting bonds to conventional institutions (see also Chapter 13).

Studies have provided substantial support for the idea that labeling affects conventional opportunities. For example, De Li (1999) determined that adolescents who had been "convicted" of a delinquent offense were more likely to be unemployed, had lower conventional achievement (less schooling, low job status), and were more involved in delinquency a few years later. He concluded that labeling restricts future opportunities for success in conventional society. In a similar study, Bernburg and Krohn (2003) found that adolescents who had been arrested or involved with the juvenile justice system were less likely to graduate from high school, more likely to be unemployed, and more involved in crime and drug selling during early adulthood. These results occurred regardless of earlier involvement in delinquency. Thus, youths who were caught appeared to have a decreased chance of conventional success during adolescence and young adulthood compared with those who were not delinquent or who were delinquent but had not been identified by the juvenile justice system. Figure 9.2 provides a depiction of one of Bernburg and Krohn's key results.

Other studies have shown a similar pattern of associations: Contact with the police or the juvenile justice system negatively affects later educational or employment opportunities (e.g., Lanctôt et al., 2007). Moreover, it is not just the police or court system that furnishes labels as deviant or delinquent; the mental health system also supplies deviant labels that may affect later chances for educational, economic, or personal success (Link and Phelan, 2001).

Studies also suggest that labels affect interpersonal relationships with parents, peers, and adults. For example, deviant labels may influence rejection by conventional peers. They often lead to subsequent delinquency as labeled adolescents associate with delinquent peers (Bernburg et al., 2006; Emler and Reicher, 2005), who may be similarly labeled. These associations then reinforce and motivate additional delinquent behavior. Formal labels may also be affected by parenting practices. In a provocative study, Stewart and colleagues (2002) determined that

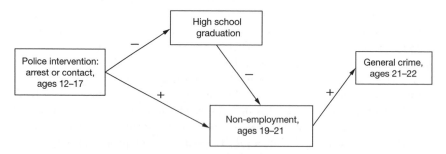

Figure 9.2 Effects of police intervention on general crime (adapted from Bernburg and Krohn, 2003, p.1311).

poor parenting practices were associated with formal labels (e.g., youths had been arrested, gone to court, or were convicted), which led to greater involvement in delinquency and poor parenting practices at a later time. It seems not only that youths from troubled families are more likely to be formally labeled, but also that, once they are labeled, family relationships deteriorate even further. Of course, it is not clear if this reflects some process besides labeling, such as a poor learning environment in the home or low self-control (see Chapters 7 and 8).

Finally, although the emphasis is on labels applied to individuals, in some situations delinquent, criminal, or deviant labels may be applied to families. A study by Hagan and Palloni (1990) illustrates the consequences of these types of labels. They found a consistent association between a parent's conviction for a criminal offense and a son's delinquency, regardless of other factors such as peer associations, parenting behaviors, and measures of intelligence. Moreover, when both the parent and the son had acquired formal labels, delinquent behavior became especially likely. Thus, the labeling process may affect entire families. This does not discount, though, the possibility that there is a genetic component to delinquency and crime that is passed down from parents to children (see Chapter 3) or other intergenerational processes that developmental theorists have described (see Chapter 13).

Self-esteem, self-concept, and delinquency

Another set of studies that has grown out of symbolic interactionism involves the way adolescents see themselves. Rather than asking if adolescents have a self-image as a troublemaker or delinquent, or perceive others as thinking of them in these terms, this type of research asks whether adolescents think of themselves as capable and significant. Most of this research focuses on either *self-esteem* or one's *self-concept*. Self-esteem refers to individuals' thoughts about themselves as good and capable, or bad and incapable (Baldwin and Hoffmann, 2002). It is normally measured by asking youths what they believe about themselves (e.g., liked vs. disliked by others; a success vs. a failure). Although similar, self-concept is closer to Mead's ideas about the social self. It is usually characterized by a vague sense of who we are physically, emotionally, spiritually, and socially (Gecas, 1982). Self-esteem and self-concept are influenced by our interactions with others, especially as they are learned and adopted through family and peer associations.

In studies of delinquency, an important hypothesis is that high self-esteem or a strong self-concept is associated with less delinquent behavior. There are a couple of reasons why such an association might exist. First, those with high self-esteem may see less need to act out or to use delinquent behavior as a way to gain material objects. A strong self-concept, especially if it involves an adolescent's self-perception that he or she is emotionally and socially capable, may also minimize the need for delinquency. Second, those with high self-esteem may be less sensitive to peer pressure or be more accepted by conventional peers. Nonetheless, there is mixed support for the idea that high self-esteem is associated with less delinquency or that low self-esteem leads to involvement in delinquency (e.g., Jang and Thornberry,

1998; Vermeiren et al., 2004). One argument is that many delinquent youths have an over-heightened sense of self-esteem or egotism. They become aggressive and violent when they think they have not been treated with respect or if they feel dishonored in some way because their high self-esteem is threatened (Baumeister et al., 1996). Others point out that there are different types of self-esteem that may affect involvement in antisocial behaviors. For example, secure self-esteem, which is the general sense that one is capable and competent, is distinguishable from defensive self-esteem, or the importance of maintaining a self-image as competent in light of some external threat to one's well-being. Research suggests that defensive self-esteem is associated with aggressive behaviors (Sandstrom and Jordan, 2008).

There is empirical support, however, for a *self-enhancement hypothesis*. According to Howard Kaplan (1980; Kaplan et al., 1986), adolescents behave in ways that maximize their positive attitudes while minimizing their negative attitudes about themselves. In general, they seek ways to enhance their self-esteem so that it remains high. Delinquent behavior may provide a means to heighten self-esteem, perhaps because it furnishes marginalized or labeled youths with a way to feel they have accomplished something, or it is a way to lash out at those who have victimized or hurt them in some way. In a series of studies, Kaplan and colleagues have found that delinquent behavior leads to higher levels of self-esteem (Kaplan et al., 1986; Stiles et al., 2000).

In a study that followed a group of adolescents over time, Jang and Thornberry (1998) found that self-esteem was enhanced not by delinquency, but rather by associating with delinquent friends. In fact, in one of their analyses, delinquency actually led to lower self-esteem over time. As they explained, some delinquents are sensitive to people's condemnation of delinquent behavior, so they come to see themselves as having low self-worth or as failing to live up to societal expectations. On the other hand, delinquent peers may enhance self-esteem by providing acceptance, friendship, and social support for behaviors that others tend to condemn. Figure 9.3 provides an illustration of one of Jang and Thornberry's empirical models.

Studies of self-concept and delinquency also provide mixed support for the notion that a positive self-concept is associated with less delinquent behavior. Several studies have found that institutionalized adolescents have lower self-concepts than others. In particular, they perceive that they are held in lower regard than others and that they are poor family members and individuals. However, they also tend to see themselves as physically capable (e.g., Bynum and Weiner, 2002). It is difficult to determine, however, whether institutionalized adolescents have low self-concepts because they are institutionalized or because their delinquent behavior is somehow affected by their self-concept.

In a study of high school students, Marsh and colleagues (2001) determined that those who felt victimized in school by other students had substantially reduced self-concepts over time. However, troublemakers – those who got into fights and misbehaved at school – tended to have higher self-concepts over time, perhaps because of a self-enhancement effect. Since many youths in this study may have

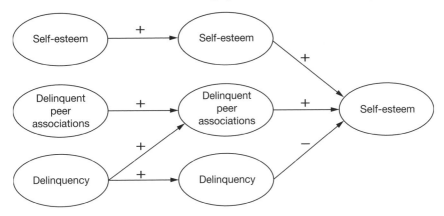

Figure 9.3 Self-esteem, delinquent peer associations, and delinquency (adapted from Jang and Thornberry, 1998, p.589).

been troublemakers *and* felt victimized, perhaps self-concept is affected by how they respond to victimization. Some youths may withdraw and report less self-confidence, whereas those who fight back gain a more positive self-concept.

Promises and limitations of labeling and symbolic interaction theories

For many years, criminologists have compared labeling theory and deterrence theory to see which perspective provides a more valid explanation for delinquent behavior. They were seen as opposing theories, with different assumptions and predictions. Deterrence theory was based on the assumption of rationality, with youths consciously selecting choices that would maximize their benefits and mini-mize their losses (see Chapter 2). By being arrested or processed in the juvenile justice system, youths would see that engaging in delinquency was a poor choice; they would thus be deterred from continuing this sort of behavior. On the other side, labeling theorists assume that the social self and the roles people take on are influenced heavily by how others treat them and how they are characterized. If adolescents are given the label of delinquent or troublemaker, and this label is rein-forced through social interactions, they will begin to adopt the role of delinquent and behave accordingly. Bringing them into the juvenile justice system makes the likelihood of a delinquent label quite high and more delinquent behavior is liable to result. Unfortunately, the research literature has not determined which view is more accurate. For some youths, entrance into the juvenile justice system acts as a deterrent, whereas for others it may function as a labeling process that results in more delinquent behavior.

As we learned in Chapter 2 and in this chapter, however, recent studies have taken a much more intricate view of deterrence and the labeling process. For exam-ple, there is now much more attention to the role of informal labels. Adolescents may perceive the arrest and adjudication process differently depending on various characteristics, including their socialization experiences or reactions of their parents. It is likely this perception affects the likelihood that formal labels result in more or less delinquency. However, the symbolic interactionist roots of labeling theory indicate that labels applied by or perceived from parents, peers, and teachers are the most consequential. It is therefore more faithful to labeling theory if the focus is on informal labels. It is the research on informal labeling that provides the most consistent empirical support for labeling theory.

However, research has also shown that labels are not directly associated with delinquency. Rather, informal and formal labels limit access to conventional pathways for success by negatively affecting educational achievement, occupational success, relations with family members, and associations with peers. This supports the notion suggested years ago by symbolic interactionists: The labeling process is a long-term, dynamic pathway that affects the life course. Only recently have researchers taken this view seriously and considered the enduring consequences of labeling for conventional opportunities.

The goal for research should be to explore in greater detail how labeling affects these outcomes. For example, is the effect of labeling on education due to poorer academic skills among delinquents who are labeled, learning disabilities, time away from school due to arrest and incarceration, or getting suspended or expelled for bad behavior? Is the association between labeling and lack of occupational success caused by poor work habits, impulsivity, or deficiencies in education? Why do labeled youth tend to band together? Is it because they share a similar outlook on life, have been treated poorly or rejected by conventional peers, or simply like to have fun in the same ways?

There is also too little attention to how labels are resisted or discarded. Some youths are clearly deterred by involvement with the police or the juvenile justice system. Others have become quite successful in school or in their occupations even after being informally labeled by adults and peers as troublemakers during childhood and adolescence. Some may resist these labels and discontinue their involvement in delinquent behaviors perhaps by having an "internal moral conversation" that focuses on how to develop better relations with others or relabel themselves as law-abiding citizens (Vaughn, 2007). However, what characteristics do these people have that others do not? Are parents and peers instrumental in helping them shed negative labels? What role does their agency play?

In a theoretical sense, labeling theory has been "adopted" by two other delinquency theories: social learning/differential association theory and social control theory. For example, the labeling process may be seen as a part of the learning process. Children learn to define themselves in a certain way based on their reinforcement experiences with family members, peers, and adults. In describing a theory of role-taking and role commitment (see Chapter 7), Matsueda and Heimer (Matsueda, 2001; Heimer and Matsueda, 1994) suggested that Mead's ideas may be used to elaborate differential association theory. They argued, much like labeling theory, that role-taking is the outcome of a combination of self-perceptions and the real or perceived perceptions of others. As suggested by differential association and social learning theory, perceptions and attitudes are learned from others, experiences affect subsequent behavior, and peer associations provide motivations and justifications for action (Akers, 1998).

Recent elaborations of social control theory have also claimed that the labeling process affects and is affected by social control (see Chapters 8 and 13). Recall that Sampson and Laub (1997b) argued that official labels affect opportunities for conventional involvement in society. The social controlling aspects of institutions such as education and family may be less effective when youths are labeled as delinquents. This is because labeled youths have impaired access to these institutions and often accumulate other disadvantages. A lack of educational opportunities and success impedes occupational choices and relationship or marriage opportunities. These weak ties to society limit legitimate avenues, so those who have the label of delinquent or criminal may be forced to continue to pursue illegitimate means to gain money or material goods.

Although these two "adoptions" may not be entirely inconsistent, their advocates often emphasize learning or social control and downplay the other theory's contributions. Nonetheless, as we shall learn in Chapter 12, there have been several attempts to combine seemingly distinct theories into a unified whole that can better explain delinquency. Several of these *integrated theories* include aspects of labeling, learning, and social control.

A characteristic of labeling that is frequently ignored by researchers is that delinquency is often attractive to some youths because it is fun and exciting. Delinquency has too often been viewed as the grim outcome of a labeling process. However, some youths may actually adopt the role of a delinquent because they enjoy its rewards and find satisfaction in deviant behaviors. Katz (1988) has argued that many adolescents who steal or fight get "sneaky thrills" because they are part of a performance that enhances their self-concept as competent people who can get away with behaviors that others consciously avoid (see Chapter 11). By fighting, robbing, or stealing, some youths gain a sense of superiority over others. They think of themselves as stronger and more capable than other adolescents because they can get what they want without payment or even much effort. Brezina and Aragones (2004), furthermore, contended that some youths use *positive labels* to get away with delinquency. It is part of the "sneaky thrills" attraction to be perceived by adults as a good kid and then engage in misbehaviors such as smoking, stealing, or drug use. In fact, positive labels allow more delinquent opportunities because adults are less likely to supervise or be suspicious of adolescents who are thought of as good kids.

Although recent attention to the labeling process has yielded promising information, there are other branches of sociological and psychological theory that may offer additional insights for understanding how labels affect delinquency. For instance, Stryker's (1994) identity theory focuses on defining the importance of multiple identities and predicting when a particular role will become most important. It suggests that the likelihood of role behaviors increases as the importance of the identity also increases. However, what determines which identity is most important? According to social network analysts, *identity salience* increases as one is involved more deeply in a particular social network. Hence, as individuals develop more social ties they also perceive their group identity as more important. This increases the likelihood that they conform to the group's behavioral expectations. Yet people also have mutually exclusive (basketball player and guitarist) and overlapping identities (basketball player and student-athlete) that may take on a more significant role in certain situations. Thus, how a delinquent identity is shaped or reinforced by social networks is an interesting issue for labeling theorists.

Studies of group membership also indicate that some stigmatized groups encourage the maintenance of high self-esteem or a strong self-concept even when it is threatened by people outside the group (Crocker and Major, 1989). Group membership allows adolescents to reject labels from other people. Hence, membership in a delinquent peer group may allow adolescents to increase or maintain their self-esteem or self-concept because they are living up to the behavioral expectations of their group. However, it may also help reinforce role-taking and their identity as a delinquent if law-violating behaviors are a key part of group membership. Studies of labeling and its association with delinquent peers or gangs could benefit from considering social identity theory, research on group influences, and social network concepts.

Finally, it is curious that, even with its roots in symbolic interactionism, few studies of labeling and delinquency have adopted the most common research techniques used to examine symbolic interactions. As mentioned earlier, these techniques typically include direct observation, informal discussions, and in-depth interviewing. Yet most studies rely on survey data from adolescents to test the propositions of labeling theory. Those studies that do use observational methods and in-depth interviews, however, have led to useful elaborations of the labeling process and how it affects delinquency (e.g., Brezina and Aragones, 2004). A particularly valuable result of this research involves understanding the effects of living in a neighborhood that is labeled as criminal or dangerous. Many youths living in such neighborhoods think that their access to conventional opportunities for success is severely limited. They therefore see little choice but to take on delinquent roles and engage in unlawful behavior (see Chapter 5). The need to maintain respect through violence is a common value or code that many youths in these neighborhoods learn to adhere to because there is little else that allows them to feel worthy and capable (e.g., Jimerson and Oware, 2006).

Policy implications of labeling theory

The influence of labeling theory was felt during the late 1960s and 1970s as juvenile justice reform efforts became popular. The emergence of juvenile diversion programs is one example. These were designed to remove adolescents from the typical justice system process and place them in specialized treatment programs. Diversion also included simply releasing adolescents into the hands of their parents. One of the goals of these programs was to avoid placing the negative label of delinquent on adolescents. However, most of the diversion programs used in the 1970s and thereafter were still run by the juvenile justice system, with some administered by the mental health system, so the potential for labeling continued to be high.

Evaluations of juvenile diversion programs have yielded mixed results. Many studies found little reduction in reoffending among juveniles in these programs compared with juveniles who are put through the normal process of arrest, hearing, and sentencing (e.g., Rose, 1997). However, some programs seem to work better than others, such as those that utilize individualized counseling or that emphasize that youths should consider themselves accountable for their actions (Patrick et al., 2004). However, other factors, such as the type of offense (e.g., violent vs. property), number of prior offenses, family support, drug and alcohol use, and peer associations, also influence the effectiveness of diversion programs.

A diversion program that is gaining popularity is the teen court. Teen courts are generally for younger, non-violent juvenile offenders. Youths from the community serve as a jury in a "sentencing forum." The courts typically offer lessons in life skills and are designed to provide offenders with positive peer contacts (Herman, 2002). Evaluations of teen courts have been mixed, with some studies indicating that they reduce reoffending among participants and others finding they increase reoffending (e.g., Norris et al., 2010). However, they may have the secondary effect of creating a better impression of the legal system among participants, although this result has not been consistent across studies (e.g., LoGalbo and Callahan, 2001). Still, it is important to keep in mind that teen courts are designed primarily for first-time offenders; most are in early adolescence. Whether it would be effective for older youths or those who have had repeated contact with the juvenile justice system is not yet known.

Another policy that is linked to labeling and symbolic interaction involves the restorative justice programs that were described in Chapter 8. Although it is common to link these programs to neutralization theory, they are also seen as a potentially effective juvenile diversion program. By taking youthful offenders out of the juvenile justice system and placing them in a program that emphasizes healing the rifts caused by delinquency before they become too wide, restorative justice has the goal of helping youths to avoid labels or being treated by others as delinquents or troublemakers (Braithwaite, 1989).

However, it is difficult to evaluate the effects of programs that are based on labeling theory principles because the labeling process is complex and can involve many stages. Although diversion programs are predicated loosely on labeling theory, they still tend to be part of the juvenile justice system. In fact, teen courts may foster a greater propensity to label because peers are part of the process and may come to recognize young offenders as budding delinquents. In addition, the labeling process involves not only the juvenile justice system, but also, as emphasized by the idea of informal labeling, parents, teachers, peer groups, community leaders, and even the community itself. Thus, diverting youths within or even away from the juvenile justice system is likely to have little actual effect on labeling if other societal entities that affect the acquisition of labels are not also considered (Matsueda, 2001).

Conclusions

Symbolic interactionism is a rich tradition in the social sciences that has led to many interesting findings and theories about human behavior. Rather than seeing people's behaviors as determined wholly or mainly by external influences such as parents or peers, or social institutions such as schools, symbolic interactionism highlights the effects of one's self-image and how it is influenced by the numerous interactions people have throughout their lives. Its value for understanding delinquency has been realized mainly through its effect on the development of labeling theory. Simply put, labeling theory assumes that adolescents who are identified or defined by others as delinquent, and who adopt this definition as their primary self-image, will live up to the role and engage in more delinquency. However, it has not been clear exactly how these labels are applied. Are youth who are arrested or formally processed through the juvenile justice system labeled? Alternatively, does labeling take hold only if adolescents themselves come to identify with the label? An affirmative answer to this latter question risks a tautology: We can know adolescents are delinquents if they think of themselves as delinquents. Moreover, many youths may behave in such a way as to deserve the label. Therefore, which comes first, the label or the behavior? Perhaps it does not matter, yet sorting out the effects of labeling from the effects of other variables that predict delinquency (e.g., low self-control, impulsivity, poor family relationships) is difficult if labeling is simply the consequence of repeated involvement in delinquent behavior.

Nonetheless, recent efforts that focus on informal labels and that link labeling to impaired life opportunities offer a promising direction for this theory. If parents, peers, and adults think of an adolescent as delinquent and he or she incorporates such an image as a key part of the self, then more delinquent behavior is likely. On the other hand, parents and peers may play an important role in an adolescent's ability to resist negative labels. There is also the important, but often neglected, role of agency. Some youths may be able to resist being labeled or shed a delinquent label through their volition. Furthermore, negative labels make it more difficult for youths to take advantage of conventional opportunities for success, such as education and legitimate occupations. Limited conventional opportunities may force reliance on illegitimate opportunities through delinquency and crime.

10 Conflict and radical theories of delinquency

Prologue

Jimmy was born in a Baltimore neighborhood near Johns Hopkins University, one of the finest universities in the United States. However, Jimmy and his family did not benefit from living so close to this prestigious institution. Their neighborhood was riddled with violence and drug trafficking. Jimmy's mother, Teresa, had even been interviewed by David Simon, a city reporter for the *Baltimore Sun* whose work was the basis for the acclaimed HBO drama *The Wire*. She claimed that one of her stories inspired the character Patrice, who appeared in the fourth season. This didn't matter much to Jimmy; he still had to live in a rough neighborhood.

At age 11, Jimmy was diagnosed with a learning disability. Unfortunately, the funds that his school had been promised to hire a special education teacher had been diverted to help build a new school in Bolton Hill, a wealthy neighborhood a few miles away. So Jimmy was placed in a regular class. He stopped going to school in eighth grade, though, because he couldn't read and had a hard time following the teacher. Teresa and her live-in boyfriend, Buck, tried to force Jimmy to go to school but they soon gave up. Jimmy began to hang out with a gang called the Mass Money Murder Gangsta Crips (MMMGC) because his cousin was a member. He liked the way gang members watched out for one another. Jimmy started running drugs for the gang, but soon began to sell. His cousin used to say, "If we keep selling stuff pretty soon we'll be rich enough to live over in Bolton Hill." Jimmy gained a reputation for being a little crazy, especially after he shot a couple of rival gang members for looking at him "funny." He laughed when Buck told him he could find work at a loading dock. Why should he work for $7.50 an hour when he was making $100 a day?

Jimmy became a lieutenant in the MMMGC at age 19. He also served six months at the Baltimore City Correctional Center for possession of marijuana. It wasn't long before Jimmy was caught with a shipment of handguns from New York City. He shot two cops trying to escape; both died. He was sentenced to death and currently lives in Baltimore's supermax prison.

Introduction

Most of the theories discussed so far have something in common: they rely on a consensus model of social order. Some theories, such as Sutherland's theory of differential association (Chapter 7), may assume that there are many norms and values and that conflicts over which to accept lead to delinquency. However, this conflict is not normal; consensus is the preferred way to construct a society (Collins, 1990). Moreover, many of the theorists whose ideas motivated early models of behavior – such as Thomas Hobbes – presumed that consensus was normal (or desired) and that conflict between groups over which values were appropriate was abnormal. Yet there are several theories of social order that assume that society rests on conflict between groups; others see consensus and conflict as part of a natural social order. Neither conflict nor consensus should, some theorists claim, be *privileged* over the other. Thus, *conflict theorists* study which groups have the most economic, political, and social power and how this power is used to develop laws. They also try to explain how members of groups commit illicit acts in order to gain power or oppose more powerful groups.

There are actually two perspectives that are based on conflict assumptions. Traditional *conflict theory* identifies competing groups and investigates how they transform their interests into criminal laws. According to this view, conflict is not necessarily detrimental; it is simply a natural part of societies. Based on the writings of Karl Marx, *radical theory* originally addressed the sources of conflict within the economic structure, but it now considers various forms of inequality in society (Lynch and Michalowski, 2006). Two other traditions that discuss conflict among groups – postmodernism and feminism – are addressed in the next chapter. There are other perspectives that are often placed with conflict and radical theory[1] but are rarely used as models of delinquency.

Thus, this chapter addresses how conflict theory and radical theory have been used to understand illegal behavior. Each section begins with a broader review of these theories. Next, some explanations of delinquency that have been influenced by conflict and radical theory are discussed. The chapter also includes an evaluation of these theories and their policy implications.

Conflict theory

Traditional conflict theory contends that social order stems from conflicts between groups in society. Collins (1990, p.68) has described four themes that underscore this model:

1 Individuals and social organizations are stratified; there is inequality among groups and individuals. Inequality allows domination of one group over others.
2 Most events may be understood by examining the interests of groups and individuals, especially those in a dominant social or economic position.

3 Groups with more resources can reach or maintain a dominant position. These resources can be monetary, natural, or ideological (e.g., defining which ideas are considered best).
4 Changes in society are caused mainly by conflict among groups.

Of course, all societies are made up of groups; we are not simply individuals seeking only our own interests. The number of groups in any particular society may be few or many, however; this depends on how they are defined. For example, some groups are defined by ethnicity, age, or gender. Others are defined relative to competing groups (Democrats vs. Republicans). Through group interactions, values develop that affect the behavior of group members. The essential observation is that those groups with the most power relative to other groups tend to have their interests represented by the norms and laws of the society or culture. Thus, groups with less power are usually involved in more norm violations since they may not support these norms.

Conflict theory is normally used to study the formation of laws and how group interests influence the creation and enforcement of these laws. The laws that are in the interests of dominant groups are those that are enforced forcefully, whereas those that serve less powerful groups tend to be enforced weakly. This idea has influenced the *threat hypothesis*: groups involved in behaviors that jeopardize the interests of dominant groups are more threatening to these groups and are therefore subject more often to the criminal justice system (Mosher, 1999). As an example, consider laws against robbery and environmental contamination. Some claim that environmental crimes cause much more harm than robbery, yet robbery laws are enforced much more than environmental laws (Lynch and Stretesky, 2001). This is because many successful companies have an interest in lax enforcement of environmental laws. They may lose money when environmental protection laws are enforced, whereas those who are directly harmed by contamination tend to be poor and members of minority groups (Gibbs and Melvin, 2008). By contrast, robbery threatens the economic system that serves the interests of the wealthy.

Much research on conflict theory studies whether or not arrest or imprisonment rates are higher for members of groups with less power (e.g., Keen and Jacobs, 2009). This research has led to many debates about the criminal justice system. However, conflict theorists ask that we take a step back and examine not only if the laws are enforced differently for more or less powerful groups, but also if inequality in society actually pushes members of certain groups to engage in criminal behavior. Unfortunately, there are relatively few studies of conflict theory and juvenile delinquency. In what follows, we review a traditional and a more innovative theory of delinquency, each of which is influenced by conflict theory.

Turk's conflict model

Austin Turk (1964) discussed how conflict among groups in society influenced young people's behaviors. He argued that youths by their very nature are in a disadvantaged social position relative to adults: They have less authority. There is also always some conflict between the cultural norms of adults and youths. Turk contended that youths in urban areas are more likely to be seen as delinquent. They are supervised less and often find themselves in conflict with authority groups. Low supervision is the key for Turk's theory because it allows youths the freedom "to elaborate cultural and social patterns conflicting with the expectations of adults, in particular those adults who are dominant in the larger social structure, i.e., whose attitudes are most likely to be reflected in legal definitions and actions" (Turk, 1964, p.219).

He also noted that the cultural norms of youths are often different from those of adults, and, when the discrepancy in norms is greatest, the most delinquent behavior tends to result. The greatest potential for discrepancies of norms is among those from relatively higher socioeconomic status groups. Turk thus assumed that the highest levels of delinquency were among youths from urban areas and relatively well-off socioeconomic groups who adhere to norms that are most at odds with conventional adults. This sounds remarkably like some of the strain theories discussed in Chapter 6, although Turk argued that there were macro-level implications of his theory that went beyond strain theory. Moreover, his theory was one of intergenerational conflict as much as it was of socioeconomic or political conflict (Turk, 1964, p.229), so perhaps it complements theories that address the latter type of conflict. However, it is unclear whether it helps explain most delinquent behavior.

Power-control theory

John Hagan's power-control theory is concerned with two important concepts: (1) from a conflict perspective, it considers power relationships in society; and (2) from a social control perspective (see Chapter 8), it considers family control of adolescent behavior. In conflict terms, especially from a Marxist perspective (see the discussion later in this chapter), power is derived from the economic relationships between those with the most authority in the economy and the workers. Those who control the economic machine tend to have political and social power. These economic relationships affect how power and control are used by individuals. Since traditional delinquency theories examine individual-level control efforts, especially by parents over children, the task for power-control theory is to link these two concepts to understand how each promotes or discourages delinquent behavior.

Rather than try to explain delinquency in general, Hagan (1989; McCarthy et al., 1999) developed power-control theory to explain gender differences in delinquency. Most research indicates that males are involved in more delinquency than females. However, it is not clear why this is the case. Hagan argued that we needed an explicit model that accounted for these gender differences.

What are the mechanisms that lead to gender differences in delinquency? Power-control theory begins with the conflict theory assumption that those in the upper classes of society hold the most power or authority. Class, however, is defined not just by income or upper, middle, and lower class. Hagan proposed that classes depend on social relations among their members. Importantly, classes are distinguished by the power and control relations people have in the workplace. According to this model, there are four general classes of workers:

1 *Employers*: They are the owners and control workers by hiring and paying them.
2 *Managers*: They are not the owners, but they have some control over employees.
3 *Workers*: They are not in supervisory positions; rather, they take the orders and do most of the day-to-day labor.
4 *Surplus population*: They do not own or sell their labor. They are the unemployed and people outside the workforce.

Power-control theory assumes that power relations in the workplace affect power relations in the home. This affects how children and adolescents are subject to social and behavioral control practices. Parents in positions of power at work tend to have most of the power in the home. Implicit in this statement is that greater participation by females in the workforce leads to more power in the home. Therefore, Hagan identified types of families based on the work arrangements of parents. In *patriarchal families* the father works outside the home in a position of power and the mother is not employed. In *egalitarian families*, both parents work outside the home in positions of authority. Of course, these are two extremes; there are several other types of families that fall in between. The distribution of power among parents affects how they control their children's behaviors. In patriarchal homes, mothers provide the principal controlling force over children. Because of traditional socialization practices daughters are controlled more than sons in these types of families. However, in egalitarian families the control efforts are much more even. Also, since mothers have more power relative to fathers in these families, daughters tend to acquire more freedom – and less control – relative to sons. This relative degree of freedom has important implications for delinquency.

Hagan (1989) viewed delinquency as a form of adolescent risk-taking. The task for power-control theory is to explore risk-taking in different family types. Since daughters in patriarchal homes are controlled more than their brothers, they are socialized to avoid risks. Sons, however, since they are socialized to have relatively more power and are less controlled, tend to be risk-takers. Less control in the home leads to less fear of getting caught, which increases the likelihood of delinquency, presumably because deterrence is not as effective. Therefore, this theory anticipates that the greatest gender difference in delinquency occurs in patriarchal families, with the least difference in egalitarian families.

Power-control theory addresses primarily behavior that is the "product of calculation" (Hagan, 1989, p.159). Violent behaviors or those that are considered more serious (e.g., armed robbery) are left to other theories. It is concerned, therefore, with minor forms of delinquency such as petty theft and vandalism. These are the types of offenses that are the product of adolescent risk-taking in general.

Extensions of power-control theory have addressed two types of maternal control in the family: relational control and instrumental control. Note that this distinction continues to assume that mothers provide the greatest control efforts in families. Relational controls are indirect, focusing on affectionate ties between mothers and children. Instrumental controls are direct, addressing supervision and monitoring (see Chapter 8). As implied earlier, these control efforts are affected by the type of family and the gender of the adolescent. They then affect preferences for risk-taking and perceived risks among adolescents, ultimately leading to a higher or lower probability of delinquency (Hagan et al., 1990). Figure 10.1 provides an illustration of power-control theory.

Hagan and colleagues (2002) also argued that these power and control relationships affect the propensity for youth to take different routes to conventional and deviant behavior. In patriarchal homes with less instrumental control, males tend to get involved in physically aggressive forms of delinquency, and in drinking and drug use. Females, as they are exposed to more relational control in patriarchal families, are inclined toward relational aggression (e.g., treating friends poorly) and depression. In general, by examining the type of family and the relative levels of control in these families, we may understand how gender affects delinquency and other behaviors. Hagan also predicted that, as the patriarchal family structure continues to decline in the western world, participation in delinquency will become more equal by gender.

Research on conflict theories

Most conflict theories do not explain delinquency specifically. Rather, they are concerned with how power differentials in society create conditions under which

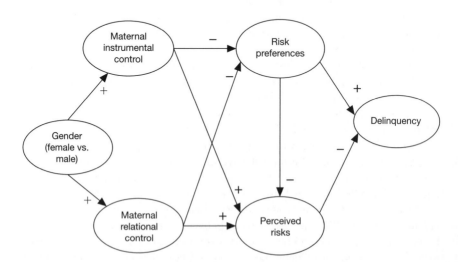

Figure 10.1 Power-control theory of delinquency (adapted from Hagan et al., 1990, p.1030).

particular laws are passed or enforced, and how people or groups with less power are disproportionately targeted by the juvenile and criminal justice systems. As mentioned earlier, a common way to evaluate conflict theories is to determine whether laws that are passed affect low-status people more than high-status people. How might this apply to children and adolescents? One rather obvious observation is that, since there are *status offenses* that focus on adolescent but not adult behavior, the conflict between adults and youths has led to the passage of laws that mainly affect a low-status group. Do laws that restrict alcohol or cigarette use, require adolescents of a certain age to go to school, or limit work hours provide evidence of conflict theory? This seems doubtful. More persuasive evidence that societal conflict affects delinquency is if laws are enforced primarily among adolescents from low-status groups, such as the poor.

For example, Sutphen and Ford (2001) examined the effects of a new curfew law and determined that it did not lead to more arrests or less reported crime. However, police citations for curfew violations were issued mostly in poor neighborhoods and in neighborhoods with more African-American youths. Moreover, parents of minority adolescents were more likely to receive a citation when their children were found violating the curfew law. The authors concluded that police differentially enforce the law against juveniles from less powerful ethnic groups.

Broadening the scope of this research, several studies using data from the 1960s, 1970s, and 1980s found that African-American and low socioeconomic youths were more likely to be arrested and processed through the juvenile justice system (see, for example, Bishop and Frazier, 1988; Sealock and Simpson, 1998). However, a large study of juvenile arrests from the early 2000s did not show differential patterns of arrest by race or ethnicity (Pope and Snyder, 2003) (although minority youths may have disproportionate contact with the police; Huizinga et al., 2007), thus casting doubt on conflict theory. Arrest is only part of the picture, though. Some studies of sentencing and incarceration show that there is some bias by race/ethnicity, with African-American and Hispanic juvenile defendants slightly more likely to be charged and incarcerated. However, offense severity and past offending record are the most important aspects (e.g., Huizinga et al., 2007). Still, it remains important to ask why youths from lower-status groups are more likely than youths from higher-status groups to commit serious violent offenses, as well as be victims of violent crimes (Browning, 1999). Is conflict between groups, such as the conflict of values discussed by differential association theory, a major cause of juvenile violence? Alternatively, are other factors, such as self-control, mainly to blame?

Research on power-control theory

In general, Hagan's (1989) own research supported the main propositions of power-control theory. He determined that the discrepancy between male and female delinquency is much greater in patriarchal families than in egalitarian families. The same is true of risk-taking preferences, with a greater preference for risk associated with larger gender differences in delinquency, but mainly because risk preferences help determine risk perceptions. Moreover, males are more delinquent than females in the employer class group because they are relatively less relationally controlled by mothers and perceive fewer risks of getting caught. However, relational control is also directly associated with delinquency. Figure 10.2 shows the results from one of Hagan's studies. Note that the strongest direct predictor of theft is the perceived risk of getting caught, which indicates that deterrence theory (see Chapter 2) may also have an important place in a power-control model.

Subsequent research attempted to expand the theory by addressing how beliefs about childrearing and gender roles affect the amount of control among males and females (McCarthy et al., 1999). In patriarchal families, parents tend to accept traditional gender roles, whereas in more egalitarian homes mothers are assumed to expose female children to more liberal views about gender roles, thus affecting their risk-taking propensities. The key difference in later tests of power-control theory is that they included beliefs about gender roles explicitly in the empirical model.[2] The results showed that mothers in patriarchal families are more accepting of traditional beliefs about gender roles. These beliefs have little influence on risk preferences in patriarchal families, whereas they do affect risk preferences in egalitarian families. They also found that male delinquency is relatively low in egalitarian homes mainly because patriarchal beliefs are also low.

Other researchers who examined power-control theory generally failed to find support for it. One study found that both male and female adolescents in patriarchal families are lower on risk-taking and less delinquent overall than adolescents in egalitarian families (Singer and Levine, 1988). Another determined that class of the family and delinquency are not related (Jensen and Thompson, 1990). In general, there is little evidence outside Hagan's studies that the types of families

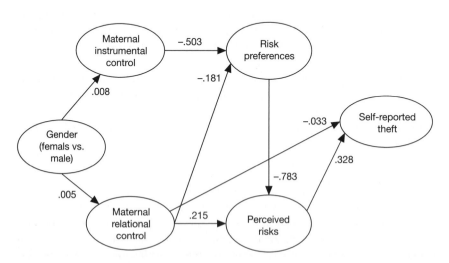

Figure 10.2 A test of power-control theory (adapted from Hagan et al., 1990, p.1030).

envisioned by power-control theory explain the gender gap in delinquency (e.g., Morash and Chesney-Lind, 1991).

Nevertheless, some studies support certain aspects of power-control theory. Blackwell (2000), for example, attempted to broaden power-control theory by including measures of embarrassment and shame in the model. She determined that females in patriarchal families are more likely to think they would get caught; they also tend to say they would feel shame if they were involved in delinquency. Females in more egalitarian families report relatively less potential embarrassment. Perceptions of both shame and embarrassment are directly related to delinquency. In general, Blackwell found that, in addition to risk preferences and perceptions, shame and embarrassment are useful components of a power-control model. In another study, Blackwell and Piquero (2004) argued that male and female adolescents have different levels of self-control (see Chapter 8) that partly depend on whether they live in egalitarian or patriarchal families.

Promises and limitations of conflict theories

It seems clear that whether conflict theory is a useful explanation for delinquency depends on how the conflict and groups are defined. Unfortunately, concepts such as conflict, groups, power, and authority are rarely defined well, resulting in imprecise models of delinquency (Liska, 1987). Furthermore, although some models provide a useful way to describe how groups in a society develop different norms and values, there are clearly laws for which there is consensus. Laws against murder and rape, for example, do not appear to have developed as a result of conflict among competing status groups. Nevertheless, anthropological studies of various cultures indicate that some accept violence more than others, with even what we define as murder not out of bounds for some groups (Whitehead, 2004). Perhaps it is best, therefore, to admit that both consensus and conflict occur in most societies, and sometimes one or the other leads to the development and enforcement of laws against delinquency.

Power-control theory is perhaps the only conflict model of delinquency that has been subjected to rigorous research. The support for its key propositions is tenuous. Nevertheless, the way that power-control theory seeks to understand the relationship between power differentials at work and in the home is important for understanding adolescent behaviors. It is also a useful theory because it offers specific predictions that may be tested empirically. For example, are females from patriarchal families less involved than females from egalitarian families in delinquency? Are gender differences in delinquency linked to control efforts by mothers? Is control in the home really affected by power in the workplace? It is sweeping to assume that mothers who stay at home are more subservient to husbands who exercise power in the workplace, or that this translates into gender-based differences in how children are socialized. Yet these are empirical questions that can be answered by research. Moreover, power-control theory specifically addresses gender differences and expressive forms of delinquency. Thus, its scope is well specified and parsimonious.

There are several additional issues that power-control theorists should consider. For instance, there are other sources of family control beyond affection and supervision that are related to delinquency. Studies suggest that consistent discipline and psychological control are associated with delinquency (see, for example, Chapter 4). These theorists should also consider in more detail racial/ethnic differences, single parents, relations between fathers and adolescents, peer relations, and actual childrearing practices, rather than just perceptions of what is the appropriate role of mothers and fathers. Studies indicate that, even in egalitarian families, husbands continue to lag behind their wives in the amount of housework and childrearing duties they engage in (see, for example, Bittman et al., 2003). These husbands may believe in norms that emphasize gender equality, but this does not mean they practice equality. Therefore, power-control studies should examine actual household behaviors rather than simply accepting the survey responses of parents and adolescents.

Radical theories of delinquency

Radical theory is broader than traditional conflict theory because it is concerned with how different forms of inequality – whether economic, social, racial, or gendered – affect delinquency and crime. This had led to some notable attempts to examine how inequality affects involvement in delinquency. Moreover, radical theories are interested in the historical and cultural aspects of crime and delinquency. It is not enough to study whether, say, poor youths are more involved in violent delinquency. Rather, radical theories are interested in the power that members of these groups possess, their position in the socioeconomic hierarchy, and what opportunities they have to be successful. These, in turn, affect their likelihood of involvement in delinquent behavior (Lynch and Stretesky, 2001).

Most radical theories trace their roots to the writings of Karl Marx. Marx (1999 [1867]) argued that the principal form of conflict in society results from an association between the *social relations of production* and the *material modes of production*. This latter term identifies the economic system employed by a society. Examples of modes of production include feudalism, socialism, and capitalism. The mode of production can be divided into (1) the *means of production*, such as the tools, machines, types of labor, and institutions most commonly found in the economic system; and (2) the relationships among people and groups who are part of the means of production. For instance, under English feudalism the lords controlled the local economy; they owned the land (or it was leased to them by the king) and decided how it would be used. The serfs, villeins, and peasants worked the land as tenant farmers or laborers, but were beholden to the lord and had to give him a substantial proportion of whatever they produced. Hence, the power relations in feudalism were designed to support the monarchy and the nobility.

Under a capitalist system, groups are defined by their class affiliation. A group's class depends on its relation to economic production. Some individuals or groups own the means of production, whereas others sell their labor. This simple classification of laborers and owners, Marx argued, can be used to study many things about a society. Owners wield a great deal of power over laborers. They determine the way that labor is used, which products are manufactured, and what will be done with the products. They also control the profit that makes up the difference between what something costs to produce and how much it is sold for. Workers, on the other hand, have few choices beyond selling their labor.

The main conflict under capitalism arises because the owners are motivated by profit and the workers by the need to earn a decent wage. Since profit is maximized by keeping the costs of doing business low, owners are motivated to pay the lowest wages possible. Workers, however, wish to keep wages rising. The main force driving capitalism is therefore the exploitation of labor (Marx, 1999 [1867]). Exploitation occurs when the owners attempt to increase profits by extracting more and more *surplus value* from their workers. Surplus value is the value of the commodities that workers manufacture beyond what they are paid in wages and the other costs of production. For example, if an automobile is valued at $20,000 when it leaves the factory, but it costs only $15,000 in wages, insurance, benefits, materials, and so forth, then the surplus value is $5,000.

Radical theorists criticize traditional conflict theories because they fail to identify which groups have the greatest political and social power; for radicals these are, of course, the owners. The other classes in a capitalist society are the managers employed by the owners, small shopkeepers, self-employed artisans, wage laborers, the unemployed, and those outside the economic system. Marx thought that members of this last group had the highest offending rates.

The behavior of groups can be understood by where they fall in the economic system. Those who benefit most from the capitalist system – the owners – are motivated to defend it; their values focus on keeping their profits high and their companies protected. Owners are inclined to fight against threats to the economic system; thus, laws to provide a minimum wage or health insurance for workers are resisted, whereas laws against theft or those that protect private property are supported.

There are two additional components that underlie a Marxist view of crime and delinquency: the *base–superstructure* and the *dialectical perspective* (Marx (1979 [1859]). The base involves relationships people have with one another that are determined by where they fall in the economic hierarchy. The political, social, and cultural institutions develop from the base. These institutions and the ideas that support them are the superstructure. The superstructure protects the base, mainly through propagating an ideology that lends credibility to the notion that capitalism is the premier economic system. The superstructure also dictates the legal and education systems. The laws support the base of society by protecting private property and punishing those whose actions threaten the capitalist system. The education system provides the knowledge and skills that provide labor so that the capitalist productive machine can operate. Most importantly, people's consciousness is influenced by the superstructure and the base: Laborers, for example, feel less powerful and influential in the world, but are taught to accept this condition as a natural part of life. They are discouraged from questioning the capitalist system; rather, they are taught that through hard work they will have opportunities for wealth and property. Marx considered these arguments to be part of the illusion of capitalism's superstructure.

A second component involves the method of analysis in Marxist thought: *dialectical analysis*, which uses a comprehensive and interdisciplinary approach, such as by considering the wider historical, political, psychological, and social forces that affect what occurs in a society. A single discipline cannot be expected to have the breadth necessary to explain why social changes or large-scale historical movements occur. Thus, radical theorists should consider what various disciplines have to say about crime and delinquency. They also should consider different levels of analysis. As mentioned in Chapter 5, most theories of crime and delinquency look at behaviors from only one analytic perspective, such as at the macro or the individual level. Radical theories use a dialectic approach to analyze the wider social, political, and economic forces that affect individual-level relationships.

Instrumental and structural Marxism

There are two general methods used by Marxist theorists to study crime and delinquency: *instrumental Marxism* and *structural Marxism*. The main thesis of instrumental Marxism is that the state and its laws are instruments that the owners use to control workers and maintain the economic structure of society. Quinney (1974), for example, argued that criminal laws serve the ruling class by preserving and protecting the capitalist order. The laws are used primarily to repress the poor and keep the owners prosperous.

Most instrumental Marxist views of crime and delinquency are extreme; they are like conspiracy theories, with the owners and politicians controlling a kind of "Matrix" to suppress the workers and create laws that will protect their property (Greenberg, 1976). However, it is difficult to imagine that the ruling class is this well organized. Moreover, there are laws that are clearly not designed to favor the ruling class. Environmental laws and antitrust laws are examples of legislation that often work against the interests of owners of prosperous companies (Lynch and Michalowski, 2006). Rather than focusing on conspiratorial theories of how laws protest the ruling class, most radical theorists prefer the ideas of structural Marxism.

Structural Marxists[3] argue that visible events are explained by their underlying structures. Although the economic system predominates, the individual components of a society should be considered in relation to larger social, historical, political, and cultural structures. Since capitalism must include a support structure in order to survive, certain laws are necessary to protect the capitalist system as a whole (Milovanovic, 2003). Antitrust legislation, environmental protection acts, and minimum wage stipulations help safeguard the capitalist system. The laws show people that the social order under capitalism works well to promote the health, safety, and well-being of all members of society. However, underlying this ideology of egalitarianism is the true function of the law: to support an economic system that exploits workers and keeps the owners in positions of power.

One of the traditional criticisms of radical theory is that it fails to offer an explanatory model of crime and delinquency. However, radical theorists have answered this criticism by describing four ways that the inequality that stems from a capitalist system causes crime and delinquency:

1   The capitalist system drives the conflict between labor and capital, which means that capitalism is a long sequence of historical systems based on inequalities between owners and workers.
2   Through the inequalities between labor and capital, society becomes stratified into social classes characterized by inequalities in wealth, status, and power.
3   This stratification influences material conditions of life which offers persons in different classes vastly different opportunities and choices in life.
4   Among these opportunities are the possibility of becoming involved in delinquency and crime (Lynch and Michalowski, 2006).

Any exploration of the causes of delinquency must consider not only the individual and micro-social processes that lead to misbehaviors, but also the relationships caused by the capitalist economic structure.

As evidenced by power-control theory, conflict and radical theory ideas have been linked fruitfully to issues of control in families. Moreover, the stresses and strains that adolescents experience (see Chapter 6), the opportunities for advancement that are curtailed by racism and sexism, and the effects of unemployment and economic dislocation in urban areas (see Chapter 5) are manifestations of economic inequality. For example, educational opportunities are unequally available to those along the social status ladder. The resulting educational inequalities affect not only life chances, but also whether schools are places that encourage or discourage delinquent behavior; the fact that students from economically disadvantaged backgrounds are more likely to drop out and get involved in delinquency; and how perceptions of economic aspirations and educational opportunities – one form of strain – may lead to involvement in delinquency. In general, radical theories offer an explanation of how the structural conditions of society affect individual-level pathways toward or away from delinquency (Lynch and Stretesky, 2001).

A radical model of adolescent subcultures, moral rhetoric, and delinquency

Herman and Julia Schwendinger (1985) used Marxist ideas about economic relationships to develop a model of adolescent subcultures. Accepting the radical theory view that the contradictions of capitalism lead to an ideology that opportunities for economic advancement are real and that a culture of individualism is needed to take advantage of these opportunities, they argued that adolescents normally find themselves in particular groups – or subcultures – that variously reinforce this ideology. Reflecting the period and location of their research (1960s California), they identified various adolescent groups such as Greasers, Surfers, and Athletes. Each group developed a greater or lesser attachment to the individualistic ideology of capitalism. Moreover, because capitalism inculcates an ideology of commodity exchange, moral obligations are perceived as exchange relations among individuals. This leads to indifference to other people's welfare unless a person's self-interests are involved.

The Schwendingers found that there are multiple values that guide adolescent behavior. Because of the self-interested, narcissistic, and selfish nature that arises from capitalism, delinquent youths use egoistic values to "neutralize" (see Chapter 7) a guilty conscience ("I was getting even with the shop owner for charging such high prices"), instrumental values to point out that harming others is a natural consequence of a tough, competitive, world ("He was a punk who should've fought back or we wouldn't have had to beat his face in"), and other forms of neutralization. These are reinforced by group membership and often become integrated into a group's identity. As dictated by capitalism, adolescent groups have to compete for property – such as defending one's neighborhood – and honor. However, some delinquents may not even need these justifications; it is sufficient to simply note that the culture of indifference caused by capitalism makes obligations not to harm others irrelevant. Moreover, many delinquents engage in illegal enterprises that mirror legitimate businesses. In brief, capitalism produces competitive instincts, alienated youths, and several forms of inequality, all of which lead to delinquent behavior.

An integrated structural-Marxist theory of delinquency

Mark Colvin and John Pauly (1983) drew upon structural-Marxist theory to develop an explanation of delinquency. Recognizing that radical theories are by nature integrated theories,[4] Colvin and Pauly attempted to combine insights from structural Marxism and control theories of delinquency. To begin, they agreed with the Schwendingers that capitalism breeds relentless competition. The class structure that develops out of capitalism is also antagonistic and authoritarian, so control structures must be developed to bond societal members together. Two opposing forces have thus developed under capitalism: Class antagonism threatens to tear society apart, whereas control structures try to hold it together.

The various classes that have developed under capitalism include a managerial and supervisory class. Those in this class control the means of production, but also lack the final control that the owners have. There is also a floating surplus population that must always work for others, and a stagnant surplus population that is chronically unemployed. The amount of control that people have, and what they are subjected to, depends on their location in this class structure. They may exercise three forms of control. (1) In the more competitive lower-class positions workers are threatened with dismissal if they do not comply with job requirements. Members of the surplus population are ready to replace workers if positions become available. This creates a coercive bond between workers and companies. (2) Better-organized workers are controlled through technological means. These workers are encouraged to look for opportunities to advance through the company hierarchy, thus promoting competition and an uneasy bond to the organization. (3) Middle managers, professionals, and skilled craftsmen are controlled through the bureaucracy. Bureaucratic control is designed to create a sense of company unity and commitment. These workers have a more positive outlook toward their work and sense a greater feeling of control over their lives.

Similar to Hagan's argument, control structures in the workplace affect control structures in the home. Thus, workers under a coercive control structure at work tend to use such control in their family relations. On the other hand, workers with freedom in the workplace use more flexible control strategies at home. Children, by interacting with parents, learn "that one acts toward authority out of fear or calculation of external consequences or out of a sense of internalized respect or commitment" (Colvin and Pauly, 1983, p.535).

Thus, lower-class workers tend to impart negative bonds to their children wherein coercion is the norm. This tends to alienate children. Their parents also practice more punitive and less consistent discipline, which increases negative bonds. However, workers who enjoy greater autonomy raise children mainly through affection and good communication. They promote idealism in their children, and their discipline styles tend to be more consistent. As children enter school their control experiences in the home affect their behaviors. Negatively bonded children are more apt to be labeled as troublemakers and are less motivated to achieve. Poorer schools tend to rely on coercive controls to keep students in line. Finally, youths gravitate toward similar peers and this perpetuates the control structures experienced in the home and at school. The outcome is delinquency that is reinforced by peers.

In general, Colvin and Pauly's theory provides a good example of how macro-level processes affect relationships in families, schools, and peer groups. The notion that control structures at work affect control structures in the home is an attractive idea that has generated significant interest. Moreover, their model shows how structural Marxism can be used to develop theories of delinquency.

Research on integrated structural-Marxist theory

Research on Colvin and Pauly's theory has attempted to measure occupations in terms of power and authority in the workplace. For example, one categorization scheme used is:

- *Significantly low control*: (1) individuals unemployed for the previous year, (2) respondents living in public housing, and (3) receiving AFDC payments.
- *Low control*: (1) laborers, (2) farm laborers, (3) service workers, and (4) private household workers.
- *Medium control*: (1) clerical and kindred workers, (2) sales workers, (3) operatives and kindred, and (4) craftsworkers.
- *High control*: (1) professional, technical, and kindred workers and (2) managers, officials, and proprietors (Simpson and Ellis, 1994, p.471).

Research has found little evidence that the class-based control structures hypothesized by Colvin and Pauly translate from the workplace to the home. Rather, parents in occupations with low or medium control tend to provide conventional control efforts when raising children. However, adolescents who perceive that their families and schools exercise coercive control (parents are unfair and punitive; teachers do not explain themselves) rather than "normative" control (parents explain rules and actions well) are involved in more delinquent behaviors (e.g., Baron, 2009). In addition, coercive control is associated with low parent–child attachment (Messner and Krohn, 1990). Figure 10.3 provides a simplified version of this model. Other research has suggested that this type of model works better for female adolescents from lower-class positions, especially by showing that female adolescents from the surplus population are involved in more serious violence and theft (Simpson and Ellis, 1994). Nevertheless, the weak empirical links between the structural aspects of these models that rely on structural Marxist thought and the family- and school-based control efforts provide minimal support for Colvin and Pauly's theory. Rather, the research mainly supports social control theory or Patterson's coercive reinforcement model (see Chapter 7).

Promises and limitations of radical theories

It is easy to find examples of laws that appear to support capitalism, such as those that protect private property or that are designed to prevent fraud. However, there are also laws that protect workers from exploitation, such as minimum wage or health and safety laws. Focusing on adolescents, laws that protect them from workplace exploitation are common and restrict, for example, the number of hours they can work. A structural Marxist perspective is that these laws merely reinforce

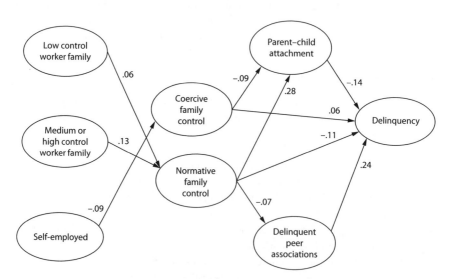

Figure 10.3 A test of integrated structural-Marxist theory of delinquency (adapted from Messner and Krohn, 1990, p.322). Note: Only the results for Caucasian males are shown. Portions of the model that address school characteristics are omitted.

the false ideology that capitalism is a fair economic system. This is an easy illusion to uncover because inequality is rampant in all capitalist societies (of course, socialist experiments, such as in the former Soviet Union and China, have not fared much better; see Burawoy, 2000).

An area where radical theory has fared well is in looking at how broad economic conditions are related to trends in crime. For example, higher levels of economic inequality are related to higher rates of violence among adolescents (Kramer, 2000). Nevertheless, too few studies have examined juvenile delinquency rates specifically to make any claims about radical theory's ability to explain general patterns of youth misbehaviors.

A more fruitful approach for radical theory is to address how economic conditions under capitalism affect social disorganization (see Chapter 5); the stresses and strains of adolescent life, especially among marginalized groups and when inequality is especially severe (see Chapter 6); and how learning is affected by the class-based background of parents and the way that schools are operated under conditions of inequality (see Chapter 7). Moreover, radical theorists point out that one of the negative consequences of capitalism is that it breeds alienation, or feelings of powerlessness, meaninglessness, and isolation among a broad segment of the population. This is because workers are subordinate to the various products that are bought and sold under capitalism; the products are created through their labor but owned by the dominant class. Although this has not been studied adequately, it is fair to ask whether its macro- and micro-level aspects affect involvement in delinquent behavior. Alienation may also be seen as an aspect of strain theory, but it requires much more study to determine its potential links to crime and delinquency (Smith and Bohm, 2008).

In general, then, there have been too few radical models of delinquency to draw any definitive conclusions about whether the capitalist system or the high levels of inequality it presumably breeds is linked clearly to delinquency. Cross-national research does not show if delinquency is lower under socialism. However, there is some research that indicates that delinquency rates in Russia and China increased once they moved to a more market-driven economy (e.g., Feng, 2001). Whether this reflects economic influences, changes in state control, or other characteristics is uncertain, however.

Policy implications of conflict and radical theories

A criticism of conflict and radical theories is that they offer few practical solutions to the problem of juvenile delinquency. Rather, short of advocating the overthrow of the economic system, they seem to have little to offer. Still, some radical theorists have described policies that could work within a capitalist system. For instance, policies that equalize power so that one group does not dominate others might decrease alienation or strain, and consequently decrease delinquency. Reducing income inequality, helping the poor improve their political and economic standing, and advocating more conciliatory or mediational styles of conflict resolution – rather than relying on a court system that must produce a "winner"

– are promising ideas (Wozniak, 2009). Some justice scholars also recommend that capitalist societies need to reduce the competitiveness of the culture by moving from individualistic models of social order to *mutualist models*: those that appreciate our communal bonds rather than our individual tendencies. Mutualists do not oppose capitalism; instead they want a society that rejects coercion and favors voluntary cooperation, free exchange of products and ideas, and mutual aid. Their model of justice focuses on reconciliation rather than retribution (Cordella, 1991). Specific programs under these models involve diversion away from the criminal justice system and toward restorative justice and mediation programs designed to solve conflicts (see Chapter 9).

Radical theorists also argue that, since delinquency is rooted in deep societal inequalities, reducing inequality by redistributing income through changing tax codes, decreasing monetary fluctuations, guaranteeing health care to all people, reducing homelessness, providing jobs for marginalized workers, improving schools in impoverished areas and expanding higher educational opportunities for poor people, and reducing racial and ethnic discrimination should diminish the root causes of delinquent behavior. Moreover, expanding gun control, legalizing drugs and reducing illegal drug markets, prosecuting environmental criminals, and making the criminal justice system less discriminatory are additional steps advocated by radical theorists (see, for example, Lynch and Stretesky, 2001). Some of these may affect delinquency, such as improving schools and reducing inequality in general (Elrod, 2009), whereas others would likely not affect it much. For example, even under most proposed legalization schemes, the use of mind-altering substances would still be restricted to certain age groups.

Conclusions

Conflict and radical theories share the assumption that consensus models of social order are largely illusory. Instead, various groups in society compete for resources, with some gaining a disproportionate amount of wealth and capital goods. Adolescents – especially those with less power – may be pushed into delinquency because of various societal and cultural conflicts. Hagan's power-control theory and Colvin and Pauly's structural-Marxist theory suggest that the way power and authority are exercised in the workplace gets transferred to control efforts in the home. For Hagan, these affect risk preferences among adolescents. In particular, relative to girls, boys prefer more risk in patriarchal families where control efforts tend to focus on girls. In egalitarian families, where power is shared between husbands and wives, control efforts and risk preferences tend to be equal and so gender differences in delinquency narrower. Although key parts of power-control theory have not been supported by empirical research, it continues to offer a way to link gender and family control to the production of delinquency.

Colvin and Pauly's theory proposes that, when coercive control in low-status jobs is transferred to the home, youths learn that coercion is a way to gain things. This affects their school and peer relationships and increases the likelihood of delinquency. Although the key parts of this model that address the way control at work is transferred to the home have not been validated by empirical research, the notion that coercive relations between parents and children lead to delinquency has support, thus affirming propositions from coercive-reinforcement learning theories (see Chapter 7). Whether radical or conflict theories are needed to explain this association remains unclear, however.

Perhaps the main benefit of conflict and radical theories is that they shine a much brighter light than other theories on inequality in society and some of the ways it influences delinquent behavior. Moreover, their emphasis on the effects of competition and alienation are important for our understanding of delinquency. As we will see in the next chapter, these theories have also influenced new ideas about crime and delinquency.

11 Postmodern and feminist views of delinquency

Prologue

Jamie was a happy child. Even though her mother, Joyce, worked two jobs to make ends meet, they still spent time together. But this changed once Randy, Joyce's new boyfriend, started coming around. He worked as a manager at a small bank, wore nice suits, and drove a used but well-kept Volvo. Joyce couldn't believe her luck. She was a poor single mother, yet this well-established middle-class man wanted to see her.

On Jamie's twelfth birthday, Randy took them out for a day at the swimming pool. Jamie thought it was kind of creepy the way Randy looked at her and said, "You're developing into a beautiful young woman." A few days later, Joyce left Randy and Jamie in the house together alone. Randy made Jamie promise not to tell her mother or anyone else what he did to her. This abuse went on for about six months until Jamie told her best friend, Maggie. Maggie told her mother and word got around, eventually reaching Joyce. But she couldn't believe that Randy would do such a thing. She called Jamie a liar. After Randy was arrested, Joyce became especially vindictive. Either she wouldn't talk to Jamie or she yelled at her for minor infractions. The worst day of Jamie's life, up until that moment, was when her mother said she was marrying Randy when he was released from jail. Jamie couldn't take it and ran away to Chicago with Maggie. She was only 14 years old.

Soon after arriving in Chicago, Jamie and Maggie met Natasha, a beautiful girl of about 16. Natasha said they could stay at her place. She introduced them to her "sponsor" Leon. Soon, Jamie became one of Leon's "girls." She tried to leave after that first customer, but Leon choked her and said if she left him he'd kill her. Jamie didn't think she had a choice. By the time she was 18, Jamie had been arrested multiple times for prostitution, cocaine possession, and assault-and-battery (she stabbed two customers in the leg with a nail file after they refused to pay). She was also HIV-positive and had contracted hepatitis A (cf. Raphael, 2004).

Introduction

As mentioned in the last chapter, two relatively new perspectives on delinquency are postmodernism and feminism. Postmodernism offers an innovative way of looking at how our knowledge about individuals and behaviors – such as those that become known as delinquent – and the concepts we use to describe "reality" need to be *deconstructed* (to use a common term) to understand their sources and meanings. Postmodernism forces us to question whether any of our concepts of truth are valid; what the language we use ("delinquency") says about society and human relationships; and if the scientific method (see Chapter 1) merely gives an illusion of objectivity that conceals how researchers thrust their own notions of reality onto the subjects of their research (Milovanovic, 2003).

Feminism emerged over the last century as the place of women in society was questioned. Critics asked questions about why women were placed in subordinate positions. Why are their voices not heard more often when it comes to issues such as inequality and justice? Why are females less involved than males in most types of crime and delinquency? Is this because of biological differences? Alternatively, is it the result of a society that grants more power to one group? Feminists also studied women's experiences as victims of crimes and the types of crimes they experienced the most. They focused, in particular, on rape, domestic abuse, and sexual harassment as problems that have unique implications for women. Delinquency scholars have focused on the many girls who are exploited and abused and then turn to delinquency to escape their stressful environments. Some feminist scholars have also adopted postmodern ideas to argue that the knowledge gained through scientific methods is based on male domination and power.

This chapter addresses both postmodern and feminist perspectives on delinquency. Like conflict and radical theories, most of this work has focused on understanding the creation of criminal laws and factors that affect adult crime. However, there are ideas drawn from each that have been applied to adolescent behavior. Like the previous chapter, we begin with a general discussion of one perspective – postmodernism – followed by a discussion of research that has addressed it. After reviewing the next perspective – feminism – and research that has addressed it, we discuss the policy implications of each.

A brief introduction to postmodernism

Postmodernism is not a theory in itself, but rather an innovative way of seeing the social world. As its name implies, postmodernism follows modernism. The modern period developed as an emphasis on the scientific method swept across Europe and North America during the eighteenth and nineteenth centuries. Prior to this period, most people understood nature primarily in religious and supernatural terms. The earth was the center of the universe, God (or various supernatural beings) controlled events, and a hierarchical social order was the norm, with monarchs ruling over people. Modernity disrupted these traditions by arguing that science and rationality were the principal methods for understanding the world. The scientific method showed, for example, that the earth orbits the sun and many of the phenomena attributed to God or spirits had scientific explanations. Thus, science and the scientific method constituted the premier logical system for explaining how nature and people operated.

Modernism rose to new heights under thinkers such as Karl Marx, Sigmund Freud, and Charles Darwin. Their ideas generated a whole new way of thinking about society and people's place in it (see Chapters 3, 4, and 10). In particular, evolution became the accepted method of scientific thinking about all animals, including people. Humankind was evolving not only physiologically, but also socially, culturally, politically, and economically.

The support for modernism began to waver following World War II. The scientific method and evolutionary thinking were blamed for unprecedented destruction and suffering as the weapons of war killed millions, and despotic regimes – such as the Nazis – murdered millions more. Philosophers and social critics questioned the fundamental assumptions of evolutionary thinking and the scientific method. *Metanarratives*, those broad, overarching stories that were supposed to provide comprehensive explanations of society and its movements, such as those presented by Marx, Freud, or the Bible, were questioned and rejected (Lyotard, 1979). A new brand of skepticism about the scientific method became popular not just among philosophers, but also among literary scholars, artists, and social scientists. *Positivism*, which used the scientific method to discover "laws" governing human behavior, was criticized for attempting to discover "truth" at the expense of other methods and for falsely promoting objectivity. For example, postmodernists claimed that what is accepted as reality, truth, or even beauty is always historically and socially constructed, and is defined by more powerful segments in society. Notions of truth and knowledge are therefore often repressive, as powerful groups use political, social, and cultural means to suppress less powerful groups. As one postmodern alternative, reality is what is defined by the observer at the time it is observed. The scientific method, though valuable in some contexts, is simply one path leading to knowledge. The beliefs, opinions, and claims about knowledge by so-called experts are not any better or more valuable than anyone else's.

Postmodernists have developed a number of concepts to critique science and the concept of truth or knowledge. For example, the philosopher Foucault (2006 [1961]) contended that reason is simply another form of power and that it is continually recreated throughout history. The literary scholar and linguist Derrida (1976 [1967]) claimed that all language, whether spoken or written, is a form of what he termed "text" and its presumed "reality" is not apparent when we attempt to understand the meaning of the text as it appears on the page or as the writer may have interpreted it. Rather, the observer should attempt to *deconstruct* the text by dissecting the language in order to determine, perhaps, its fundamental meaning and the assumptions underlying it, but also to admit that meaning is irrelevant outside the observer/reader of the text. The practice of deconstruction is a way to read and interpret texts by exploring not their similarities, but their differences. An important point about text and language from a postmodern perspective is that they tend to reflect the views of more powerful elements in society (Milovanovic, 2003).

Another important concept in postmodernism is *hyperreality*: a network of images that appear to represent reality, but actually turn up empty without some external reference to make them appear real. The philosopher Baudrillard (1993) used this symbol of the imaginary nature of reality to criticize the presumed "truth" of radical theory terms such as *power, means of production*, and *political legitimacy* (see Chapter 10). These are simply representations of reality for which there is no underlying existence apart from their textual usage. Similarly, social theories, including delinquency theories, that are built on positivism and the scientific method are simply one set of "texts" that have no claim on superiority or privilege over any other "text" that might be used to discuss the behavior of individuals or groups (Allan and Turner, 2000).

Finally, postmodernists point out that social roles, identity, and identity formation have changed in recent decades. In the premodern and modern worlds, identity tended to be one- or two-dimensional as most people had a small number of roles to play. In our postmodern world, people tend to have multiple roles (Booker, 1999). These may shift from one social context to the next. The meanings and priorities of these multiple roles also vary as people age and take on new responsibilities (Sarup, 2005). Moreover, a sense of identity or identities is built by the power relations that people experience (Callero, 2003). For example, income inequality, sexism, racism, and other "isms" that are rooted in power relations affect individuals' ability to adopt or to discard identities. Other postmodernists, though, contend that there are no longer any clear identities; we are living in a period when identities hold little meaning and people are beginning to resist the labels applied by others (Sarup, 2005). It should be clear that this postmodern concern with identity has been influenced by symbolic interactionism (see Chapter 9).

This background review does not cover the entire terrain of postmodernism (Milovanovic, 1996). Nevertheless, since conflict and radical theories were covered in Chapter 10, it is useful to compare postmodernism to these theories on a number of dimensions.

- Whereas conflict and radical theories focus on social structure and how these affect crime and delinquency, postmodernism addresses primarily human subjects. It is a perspective on how language creates our understanding of "truth," "knowledge," and "power." The language used in court trials provides an example. Defendants and victim-witnesses are expected to use a language that conforms to legal discourse rather than employing their own expressions.
- Conflict and radical theories note that individuals and groups struggle over status or power. Postmodernism is concerned with conflicts over language and definitions of reality. Groups or individuals seek to control reality by making their language or ways of expression dominant and subjugating alternative languages and expressions. The term *juvenile delinquent*, for example, has come to evoke images of gangs, violence, or out-of-control adolescents who should be feared.
- The definition of delinquency is controlled by groups that have gained the most influence (conflict theory) or by those who own the means of production (radical theory). For postmodernists, these definitions are dictated by those who control *linguistic production*.

- Conflict theory does not necessarily accept absolute definitions of delinquent behavior, whereas radical theory sees violations of human rights as criminal. Postmodernists are skeptical about any claim that an activity or behavior is criminal or delinquent. Postmodernists might, for example, point out that the word *delinquent* is part of the *language game* by which certain ways of expression are privileged over others.
- Conflict and radical explanations of delinquency address the tendency to pursue economic and political interests, the inequitable distribution of resources, and, for radicals in particular, the greed and alienation generated by capitalism. Postmodernism focuses on how language is used to define delinquent behavior and how certain oppressed people or groups might use language and action in a way that is inconsistent with the dominant language (Arrigo and Bernard, 1997).

Given its reluctance to define or describe truth and knowledge, postmodernism does not yet offer – perhaps it never will – general theories of delinquent behavior. In fact, the language of "theory" is simply a privileged position in the language game. A useful approach for postmodernists is to deconstruct theories of delinquency and try to understand their assumptions and the biases and positions of authority of those who developed them. Thus, postmodernism may be able to tell us more about delinquency theorists than about delinquency.

Postmodernism does, however, offer some tools for developing a better understanding of delinquency. For example, postmodernists argue that elites in society (and their methods of inquiry) are given privileged positions when it comes to our understanding of morality. Less advantaged groups, who form the oppressed people in society, are given significantly less privilege: Their voices and stories, methods of inquiry, and relationships are diminished by elites. Researchers who fail to listen to them or simply place them in categories derived from survey questions are privileging their own positions with little legitimate reason. As Schwartz and Friedrichs (1994, p.230) claimed, "It is elitist to presume that we, as researchers and theoreticians, can explain something of the oppressed peoples of the world with our analyses, silencing their voices in favor of our own." Thus, a postmodern approach is more interested in listening to the voices of those who are called "delinquent." What is the language they use and how does it differ from our own? What is real to them? The point is not to excuse their behaviors, which may be harmful, but rather to examine how language operates among those in different positions from our own.

Of course, this runs the risk of privileging their voices, which is inappropriate to many postmodernists. In fact, postmodern criminology has been criticized for being out of touch with the "realities of life": It is easy to deconstruct theories of delinquency from such a critical viewpoint, but it is also easy to forget the actual human suffering that acts of violence produce (Schwartz and Friedrichs, 1994). Of course, one way around this dilemma is to give voice not only to the perpetrators and delinquency, but also to their victims. Oppression is clearly not just class-based or under the control of elite members of society, but also occurs whenever powerful individuals wield control over the less powerful. This can occur in economically disadvantaged neighborhoods as well as in elite private schools. Thus, listening to the stories of the victims of delinquency as well as delinquents and learning about their identities is a postmodern approach.

Postmodern approaches to delinquency

As mentioned earlier, many postmodernists see theory building as part of a positivist illusion that falsely claims a unique understanding of truth and knowledge. Nevertheless, some symbolic interactionist studies of delinquency have been influenced by postmodern thinking. For example, a recent body of research has interviewed youths living in disadvantaged neighborhoods and determined that many believe they have little access to conventional opportunities for success. They see little choice but to engage in unlawful behavior. The need to maintain respect through violence is a common value or *code* – an accepted and valued narrative – that many youths adopt because there are so few things that allow them to feel worthy and capable (Anderson, 2008). Studies using ethnographic techniques have shed light on other aspects of adolescent behaviors, such as by showing the "playful" nature of much delinquent behavior (Sato, 1988), how oppression is related to violent behaviors (Ness, 2004), and the opportunistic nature of drug trafficking among economically oppressed youths (Bourgois, 2003). The key is that these studies are based on research approaches that allow youths to express narratives of their "realities." There are also several important research projects that are based on postmodern ideas. Two of these, in particular, will give a flavor of how postmodernism has informed ideas about delinquency.

The attraction of sneaky thrills

Jack Katz's (1988) research relies on a postmodern notion: individuals have a need to create their identities in an uncertain and chaotic world; we can understand this need by listening to their stories (Schwartz and Friedrichs, 1994). Moreover, rather than assume that various pushes and pulls dictate behaviors, Katz argued that some youths deliberately adopt the role of a delinquent because they enjoy its rewards and find satisfaction in deviant behaviors. Many adolescents who fight or steal appreciate the powerful sense of the "sneaky thrills" that accompany these behaviors. Participating in "juvenile delinquency" is part of an unscripted performance that enhances their sense of identity as competent people who can get away with activities that other youths avoid. Fighting, robbing, and stealing offer a feeling of superiority; they are stronger and more capable than others. Hence, they have control over their identity rather than relying on others to define them. This is postmodern in the sense that these youths have subverted the identity label of delinquent and embraced their own identities. They have also adopted a language that is presumably under their control.

Cultural criminology

A second postmodern approach to understanding delinquency is known as *cultural criminology* (Ferrell, 2007). Cultural criminologists argue that delinquency is merely part of the larger cultural production of society. In general, culture includes the variety of symbols, language styles, works of art, musical preferences, mannerisms, ways of dressing, and other methods that communicate something about individuals and groups. Delinquent behavior is, in part, a way for adolescents to resolve various conflicts that have been caused by modern cultural and social conventions (Hayward, 2004). Cultural criminologists are particularly interested in how delinquent behaviors are frequently attempts to generate excitement, pleasure, and risk-taking to relieve the boredom and tedium of everyday life (Ferrell, 2007), but also as forms of creative expression (Williams, 2007). The tedium of modern everyday life is exemplified by the workplace, where cubicles and fluorescent lighting abound to create an atmosphere of alienation and sameness, workers are expected to meet steady goals of efficient production, and scientific management practices are heralded as the essence of bureaucratic capitalism.[1] School environments mimic these work environments. As Ferrell (2004, p.294) noted:

> Such situations [as offices, shopping malls, or schools] are boring precisely because they are systematically drained of human skill and possibility, devoid of the uncertainty and surprise that comes with human creativity. They share in the intentional erasure of human possibility, the preclusion of self-made variations in pace, meaning and intentionality; relentless in their governance of detail, they leave room for little but boredom in their effect . . . Excitement, it seems, is in reality a means to an end, a subset of what ultimately emerges as the antidote to modern boredom: human engagement.

As a way to escape boredom and creatively express their lives, adolescents attempt to find exciting alternatives. The term *edgework* describes their involvement in thrilling activities such as skateboarding or base-jumping, but also delinquent behaviors such as vandalism, shoplifting, and using drugs. These behaviors are indicative of having too few alternatives for meaningful expression. Adolescents live a world that is created by adults, with rules and values that reflect adult preferences. Delinquency is a way to creatively engage with the world and to escape a restrictive alienating adult world (Miller, 2005). It can offer adolescents meaning and identity, creating a cultural space wherein their lives play a central role and are not stripped of humanity or self-control (Ferrell, 1997).

In an example of cultural criminology, Ferrell (1998) studied freight train graffiti as a form of cultural expression. Consistent with postmodern thought, Ferrell identified graffiti as a form of anti-authoritarian, countercultural language production used by oppressed groups that have few resources. It allows them to create symbolic communities through hyperrealistic modes of expression and is part of a *postmodernism of resistance* (Foster, 1985). Freight train graffiti offers a way for subversive artists to produce a language that expands communication from face-to-face contact to a wider audience of people who share countercultural tendencies. The authorities may call these activities "destruction of property" or "defacement," but this is simply part of the language game that dominant groups use to oppress the creative expressions of others.

In general, studies of graffiti artists and thrill seekers show that some delinquent or other "misbehaviors" are part of modern culture; they are ways to express fundamental human needs and desires for creativity, autonomy, and self-expression. The methods used by cultural criminologists – primarily ethnographic approaches – are presumably better able to get at the expressive nature of delinquency through getting to know the subjects better.

Promises and limitations of postmodernism

Postmodernism provides a way to evaluate not just theories of and research on delinquency, but also a general method for criticizing how we understand human behavior in general. However, postmodernism has not yet had a substantial influence on our understanding of delinquency. Moreover, as mentioned earlier, it is difficult to consider a postmodern *theory* of delinquency since the point is not to explain particular behaviors, as many theorists attempt to do, but rather to deconstruct the discourses about delinquency. What do these tell us about oppression, language, and the seeming preoccupation with how adolescents are different from adults? Moreover, postmodern ideas about delinquency have called attention to the ways that adolescents attempt to create their own identity and social world in chaotic and difficult environments (Ferrell, 1997).

Nevertheless, critics of postmodernism have identified several limitations. Some argue, for example, that the advantages of positivism outweigh its limitations and that we risk falling into a trap they call "judgmental relativism" by rejecting the notion of objectivity. Judgmental relativism refers to the denial that there are *any* legitimate standards for judging between two claims. If this occurs, the fear is that *any* person's judgment about a phenomenon or policy option to solve problems is valid. Thus, research methods that attempt to be objective are preferable to what some scholars identify as "research anarchy" (e.g., Delanty, 1997). This is a false dichotomy, however, and most postmodernists would respond with two points. First, as described earlier, the objective nature of positivism is an illusion that should be investigated further. Second, investigating the voices of the oppressed or other "outsiders" is not the same as accepting all their knowledge claims as legitimate (Presser, 2009). Recognizing their viewpoints is valuable for understanding how language and the "realities" of their lives affect their behaviors.

Another criticism is that postmodernism spends too much time focusing on culture at the expense of other issues, such as agency, social structure, and solidarity among individuals (Delanty, 1997). Culture is an important part of human existence. However, there are aspects of social structure that affect how people behave; moreover, there is an element of agency in most behaviors that cannot be reduced to culture or language production (see Chapters 1 and 13). Just as postmodernists criticize an overreliance on structural explanations, they may be criticized for being too eager to embrace cultural explanations.

Perhaps the most important criticism of postmodern thought is that it risks ignoring the genuine suffering caused by delinquency. There is no doubt that many delinquent acts directly result in human pain and suffering (Schwartz and Friedrichs, 1994). Not only are there oppressed youths seeking to express themselves by resisting authority, but there are also human victims whose "reality" must be appreciated. It remains unclear what postmodernism in general and cultural criminology in particular offer to our understanding of why some youths choose – or are impelled – to cause this pain and suffering.

A brief introduction to feminist theory

In most cultures throughout history men have been dominant. Even in societies that encourage equality between men and women, an androcentric viewpoint has predominated. *Androcentrism* refers to ways of thinking that are centered on the male point of view, usually to the exclusion of women. Under androcentric systems, male norms and values become widely accepted and influence how social and cultural institutions operate. Androcentric cultures are *patriarchal*: men hold most of the power in society. Patriarchy justifies this dominance by claiming that there are innate biological and psychological differences between men and women. For example, some have claimed that women are not as analytical or logical as men, or not as well suited for leadership positions. According to critical social scientists, however, patriarchy and androcentrism are the result of power differentials. It is not that men are innately more capable of leadership; rather men have held power for so long that presumed differences between men and women have become accepted as normal (Rogers, 1978). Patriarchy is an example of how the superstructure (see Chapter 10) influences a particular ideology. From a postmodern perspective, it is a knowledge claim, for it stems from an elite group controlling the language that is used to define society.

Feminism refers to a movement that studies the respective roles of women and men in societies. It assumes that patriarchy exists and has often led to the exclusion and oppression of women. In particular, women's viewpoints and unique experiences are not appreciated by most of the institutions of modern society. A goal of feminist research is to study women's viewpoints and experiences to gain an understanding of how they have influenced societies, but also to help transform institutions so that women hold a more central and valued role (Beasley, 1999). Thus, feminism, like radical theory, is both a criticism of the existing order and a call for social change that will result is a more equitable society.

Although feminism is a broad movement, feminist theory has been classified into four types (Tong, 2008):

1   *Liberal feminism*: This position contends that traditional liberal principles of equality and freedom should dictate relationships between men and women. It is the form of feminism that bred the women's rights movement of the nineteenth and early twentieth centuries. This movement focused on equality

for women by arguing, among other things, that women should have full voting rights. Liberal feminist scholars study how socialization practices lead to gender differences and discrimination in schools, families, the workplace, and other institutions. There are actually two types of liberal feminism: *Libertarian feminism* emphasizes equality of freedom from coercive state power, and *egalitarian liberal feminism* highlights freedom – within reason – to live one's life as one chooses (Baehr, 2004).

2 *Socialist feminism*: This perspective draws upon the ideas of Karl Marx and others to describe the relationship between capitalism and patriarchy. Although not recognized by Marx, women are among the oppressed classes of society whose interests are subordinate to men and to the owners of the means of production (who are usually men). In particular, women are alienated in capitalism because their work as mothers and homemakers is not valued as highly as men's work (Walby, 1990). Gender equality will occur only when there is class equality; thus, capitalism must be overthrown and socialism put in its place.

3 *Radical or cultural feminism*: Radical feminists focus on patriarchy as the dominant mode of oppression. They argue that women's work is the key part of a patriarchal mode of reproduction that is at the center of all economic systems of production, whether feudalism, capitalism, or socialism. In all systems, men have exploited women for reproductive and other forms of labor (Harding, 1986). There must be a fundamental transformation in the social order that breaks away from the constraints of patriarchy.

4 *Postmodern feminism*: Postmodernism has been used to challenge radical and socialist theory's overemphasis on economic relationships as explanations for gender differences and oppression. A major problem is that the metanarrative of Marxism privileges the idea that domination and oppression have their roots in capitalism and patriarchy, yet generally ignore other problems such as racism and cultural imperialism. For many postmodernists the assumption of rationality that underlies other types of feminism is a fantasy and does not grasp that oppression is rooted not only in gender, but also in other conditions (Flax, 1987). This has led some feminist scholars to argue for greater recognition of sources of oppression based in gender, race, class, and ethnic and cultural origin (Hennessy and Ingraham, 1997)

Many feminists seek to promulgate a unique perspective to generate knowledge: *feminist epistemologies* (Smith, 1990). These emphasize the standpoint of women when conducting research (Harding, 2006). Many feminists also contend that positivistic research minimizes our understanding of gender, patriarchy, and oppression by assuming that there are objective social facts that can be gleaned in an unbiased manner. As an alternative, research should adopt more qualitative, ethnographic, and narrative approaches to studying women, gender roles, and the consequences of patriarchy (Daly, 2002). Women should be placed at the center of this research. As Naffine (1996, p.47) argued, "The value of drawing on women's experiences lies in the fact that women are direct eyewitnesses to their own lives. They are reporters of their own experiences, telling their own stories."

Feminist approaches to delinquency theory and research

Criminologists began to pay attention to female delinquency mainly in the 1960s and 1970s as the movement toward recognizing the subordinate role of women accelerated. As the so-called women's liberation movement picked up steam, scholars began to wonder what would happen if gender equality became a reality. Some criminologists adopted a liberal feminist viewpoint to predict that liberation would lead to more female delinquency as opportunities and socialization equalized. Simon (1975) argued that the increasing number of women in the workplace would lead to more property crime on account of more opportunities, but less violent crime on account of lower levels of frustration over being denied occupational opportunities.

This and related arguments became known as the *liberation hypothesis*. Evidence concerning this hypothesis has been mixed, however. Some sources indicate that the proportion of crimes committed by females increased during the late 1900s (Lynch, 2002), especially offenses that are frequently committed in the workplace, such as embezzlement, forgery, and fraud. However, other researchers contend that there has been only a slight change in the ratio of male to female crime and delinquency rates (e.g., Schwartz and Rookey, 2008). However, feminist theory has influenced other aspects of delinquency research. In particular, it has been used to (1) examine gender differences in delinquent behavior, (2) critique existing delinquency theories, and (3) construct new explanations of delinquency.

Research on gender and delinquency

Several studies in the 1970s and 1980s examined whether "masculine traits" – such as aggressiveness, independence, and competitiveness – are associated with delinquency. As implied by the liberation hypothesis, an underlying motivation for these studies was that, as women became more liberated, they would be more apt to adopt these "male" characteristics and thus become more involved in delinquency. However, there is mixed evidence that these traits are associated consistently with delinquency (e.g., Norland et al., 1981). Moreover, regardless of what this research shows, there are clearly gender-biased assumptions in this approach (Chesney-Lind and Eliason, 2006). Assuming that these traits are "male" or "masculine," or that passivity is a female trait that restrains delinquency (Chesney-Lind, 2006), is a reflection of androcentrism and a denial of female agency.

There is also research that compares delinquency theories to determine whether they are more predictive of male or female delinquency. Most studies suggest that a similar pathway exists for male and female delinquency, but others have shown some important differences. For example, Heimer and De Coster (1999) found that emotional bonds to families are important in reducing female delinquency, but that direct supervision is more important for reducing male delinquency. Research by Booth and colleagues (2008), though, showed that emotional bonds to parents are equally, but weakly, predictive of delinquency among girls and boys. Instead, prosocial activities, such as involvement in school, community, and religious activities, are negatively associated with delinquency for both groups. A study by Nofziger (2010) found that females exhibit greater self-control than males, and this explains why they report less delinquency.

Other studies have attempted to draw more explicitly from feminist perspectives on crime and delinquency. Research by Daigle and colleagues (2007), for instance, demonstrated that only one variable drawn from a "feminist perspective" distinguishes delinquency among boys and girls: depression. Symptoms of depression are positively associated with violent delinquency only among girls. Victimization experiences (also derived from a "feminist perspective") – which include domestic abuse – are positively associated with violent delinquency for both boys and girls. Daigle and colleagues thus concluded that the feminist perspective does not fully account for delinquency or gender differences in delinquent behavior.

Feminist critiques of delinquency theories

A general feminist critique of delinquency theories is that they fail to recognize that gender and patriarchy affect the socialization practices that influence adolescent behaviors, how formal and informal social control agencies treat youths, and how class and race are important determinants of structural and cultural relationships. Feminists are more apt to recognize these characteristics of culture and society and include them in their research (Chesney-Lind, 2006). Furthermore, as implied in the last section, most delinquency research takes an "add women and stir" approach (Chesney-Lind, 2006) by simply comparing females and males in empirical models. So, either we learn that males are more involved than females in delinquency, or that a few characteristics differentiate male and female delinquency.[2] However, it is rare to find a critical approach to this endeavor, one that attempts to figure out how adolescents think about or use gender or gender roles in determining their behaviors.

An example of a delinquency theory that attempts to take seriously patriarchal-based power relations in the home and workplace to examine male and female delinquency is power-control theory (see Chapter 10). Yet some argue that its view of patriarchy is woefully narrow and is measured mainly by the mother's workforce participation (Chesney-Lind, 2006). Moreover, the picture of the female adolescent in power-control theory is of a passive child who is simply the object of her mother's control. As Naffine (1987, p.69) argued:

> The conforming female emerges . . . as a grey and lifeless creature . . . . Gone is [social control theory's] rational and responsive agent, intelligently evaluating the risks and costs of crime . . . The law-abiding female is biddable rather than responsible. Hagan is thorough in his demolition of the agency of the female. Whereas [social control theory's] conforming male was positively attached to conventional others and thus positively solicitous of their welfare, Hagan's female seems unable to construct complex and caring relationships, even with her mother who subjects her to her control.

Although Hagan and colleagues (2002) have attempted to include measures of agency and gender-based norms in power-control theory (see Chapter 10), they address these among parents rather than among their children.

Another example of a feminist critique takes on Gottfredson and Hirschi's self-control theory (see Chapter 8). Flavin (2001) criticized these theorists' attempts to build a gender-neutral model. In particular, Gottfredson and Hirschi failed to note that mothers and fathers do not socialize in the same manner, nor do they treat male and female children as interchangeable. Rather, deep-seated gender norms and values influence parenting, especially of small children, but also of adolescents. A gendered theory of self-control would consider these aspects of parenting in greater detail, but would also explore if self-control is a distinct trait for male and female youths.

Feminist models of delinquency

An alternative to simply comparing males and females, according to feminist scholars, is to "theorize" gender. This includes an emphasis of the various complicated methods by which youths struggle with their gender identity and gender roles (Chesney-Lind, 2006). Two models of delinquency that emphasize these involve *blurred boundaries* and *masculinities*.

Blurred boundaries

Researchers have observed that many girls who run away from home, are arrested, or are in gangs have a history of sexual and physical abuse (e.g., Bottcher, 2001). Moreover, girls are more likely than boys to be the victims of sexual abuse, especially by family members. The sort of trauma these youths experience often leads to fear, depression, low self-worth, and, most importantly, anger and hostility (Schaffner, 1999, 2006). Some girls are forced onto the street as a result of this abuse, and may get involved in prostitution and theft to survive. Even though many try to avoid the label of delinquent, their survival often requires delinquent behavior.

At the core of this "blurred boundaries" model of victimization and delinquency is girls' sexuality (Pasko, 2008). In patriarchal cultures, the control girls have over their sexuality is tenuous and subject to the whims of parents and other adults. When the boundaries of acceptable sexuality are crossed, whether by their own choice or others' abuse, girls have traditionally been marginalized. The boundary violation may lead either to attempts to escape abusive situations, thus increasing the chances of delinquency, or to being placed under the supervision of social control agents. Either way, the result is marginalization.

Research showing a connection between abuse and neglect and delinquency, especially among girls, offers support for the blurred boundaries perspective. For instance, in a study of institutionalized delinquents, Belknap and Holsinger (2006) found that females report more abuse than males and are more likely to say that the abuse was related to their delinquent behavior. Moreover, their experience with sexual abuse is particularly high. This supports the blurred boundaries position that physical, emotional, and sexual abuse are particularly detrimental to female adolescents (e.g., Chesney-Lind, 2006). Similarly, Schaffner (1999) interviewed many troubled girls, including one who said she got "drunk and beat my girlfriend the same way my dad gets drunk and beats my mom" (p.58). Another mentioned that her abusive, alcoholic father had taught her to respond to violence with violence. These and other stories of violence in reaction to sexual harassment and family abuse are common among institutionalized girls.

However, it is also important to remember that many female delinquents do not have a history of abuse. On the other hand, many may experience abuse vicariously as they see their parents fighting or neighborhood violence. Others may get involved in delinquency for reasons that have been discussed in earlier chapters. Moreover, Daigle and colleagues (2007) determined that a measure of sexual abuse among females was, paradoxically, associated with less overall delinquency and was not associated with violent delinquency. They argued that victimization experiences should be seen as general explanations of delinquency and not just a factor in female delinquency. However, feminists have not declared that victimization is not a causal factor in male delinquency, only that certain types of victimization experiences – namely sexual abuse – especially affect the lives of many female adolescents (Chesney-Lind, 2006).

Masculinities

The second model is even more attentive to patriarchy because it focuses on how both males and females "do gender," or how they act in situations so that they may be considered "gender appropriate." For example, feminists have encouraged delinquency researchers to examine how male and female adolescents use masculinity *and* femininity. Moreover, delinquency provides one structurally permitted means of "establishing a man's masculinity when other channels for doing so are blocked due to one's race, ethnicity, class or age" (Flavin, 2001, p.276).

The basis of this model involves theories about *masculinities*. Connell (1995) argues that gender is not a biological condition or even an objective set of behaviors; rather it is what people actually do. The strategies that have historically allowed men to dominate women are known as *hegemonic masculinity*.[3] However, this is not the only type of masculinity; there are also *subordinate masculinities* that are dictated by hegemonic practices. When people "do gender" they are subscribing to some type of masculinity, or perhaps even a type of femininity, although this latter idea is not evident in Connell's writings. Hegemonic masculinity allows men in patriarchal societies to dominate labor market positions, control the government, and dictate the preferred norms, especially for handling conflict through aggression and violence rather than through negotiation and empathy. The institutions in a patriarchy – or what Connell terms *gender regimes* – support this system.

Hegemonic masculinity usually involves the most cherished ways of being a "man." Most men receive the benefits of patriarchy even when they do not deliberately draw upon it. This is known as *complicit masculinity* (Messerschmidt, 2000). Theories about masculinities have also noted that people of various racial, ethnic, and class configurations benefit or are placed in disadvantaged positions by different forms of masculinity. The various forms of masculinity are not equally available to people in all social positions. It should be clear that theories of masculinities draw heavily from feminist thought.

Not surprisingly, the notion of masculinities has been used to study male delinquency (e.g., Copes and Hochstetler, 2003; Messerschmidt, 2000). Messerschmidt (2000), in particular, proposed that delinquent behaviors often result when males use resources to show they are "manly," especially when other ways of "doing masculinity" are not available. The availability of alternative forms of masculinity may be especially restricted in poor neighborhoods or among marginalized boys for whom there is little hope to be successful through legitimate means. They are often left with no other masculinity than one that honors aggression, violence, and sexual exploitation. Moreover, violence is a way to verify self-respect and gain a high-status position; a way to "do gender" that celebrates a form of "manhood" on the streets.

Perhaps the most telling way that ideas about masculinities have informed delinquency research is in studies of girls in gangs. For many years, girls in gangs were seen as auxiliary members, usually as simply the girlfriends of male members. However, research on gang life has shown that this view is incorrect. There is actually considerable diversity in the gender make-up and the roles played by members. As noted earlier, female delinquents often have a history of abuse at home and many find alternative families and feel protected in gangs (Miller, 2008). Girls also often learn to express themselves through violence as part of their membership. They take on "violent" forms of masculinities not because they reject femininity, but because they are responding, directly and indirectly, to the abuse and marginalized status that sent them to the gangs in the first place (Bhana, 2008). Miller's (2001) research reinforces this point. Girls adopt and support masculinities that place them at a disadvantage in the gender hierarchy, yet this offers them protection and an honorable place in the gang. This is also an attractive alternative to their often disruptive and stressful home lives. Their close relations with other gang members provide an identity that they do not have with other girls, most of whom they learn to look down upon as feminine stereotypes. They often look for status through fighting with other girls and degrading them for their sexual behaviors (Artz, 1998). Many adolescent females absorb the patriarchally based idea that women are less worthy of respect in a society that generally marginalizes and oppresses women, thus they are more comfortable abusing other females through violence and harassment (Schaffner, 1999).

Promises and limitations of feminist theory

Feminism is a valuable perspective for critiquing traditional theories of delinquency and for understanding the role that gender plays in adolescent behavior. Since, like postmodernism, feminism actually comprises a theory cluster (Agger, 1998), there are various ways it could be used to inform explanations of delinquency. These include an emphasis on blurred boundaries involving sexual behavior, abuse, and delinquency; and addressing how masculinities and femininities affect male and female delinquency. There have also been some notable attempts by feminist researchers to explain why girls are less involved in delinquency than boys (e.g., Booth et al., 2008). Nevertheless, feminist theories have been used sparingly to develop specific models of delinquency.

As with postmodernism, there are some important critiques of feminist perspectives on delinquency. Perhaps the most compelling critiques have been offered by feminists themselves. For example, Daly (1998) argued that the notion of blurred boundaries is questionable because it does not consider human agency sufficiently. When a female adolescent physically assaults someone, should it be looked at mainly as a reaction to oppression or as the result of her own choice? One answer, of course, is that it is the result of a complex set of factors, one of which may be an oppressed condition. A second criticism is that feminist theory does not adequately address class, race, and ethnicity. As suggested earlier, some feminists note that women's experiences in a patriarchal culture are not uniform, but rather depend on sources of oppression based in gender, race, class, and ethnic and cultural origin (Hennessy and Ingraham, 1997). Caucasian middle-class women, for example, may experience some degree of indignity in patriarchal cultures, but it pales compared with what many poor women, immigrant women, or women of color experience. One could say the same about female adolescents, with some experiencing significantly more oppression and victimization than others. Hence, it is important to consider subgroups of girls to understand their experiences with victimization and delinquency.

A third criticism focuses directly on the notion of masculinities, in particular Messerschmidt's use of this concept to evaluate delinquency. Some critics argue that the notion that masculinities as one way of "doing gender" lead to delinquency is tautological. Presumably, adolescent males are involved in delinquency to verify their masculinity, but their offenses are somehow masculine because they are committed by men (Walklate, 2004). However, this is a better criticism of studies of masculine traits than it is of masculinities. Girls can also draw upon the masculinities that are part of their particular environment as they seek honor and respect. Thus, masculinities do not have to refer only to the male gender or the behaviors of boys.

A more important question is whether masculinities or blurred boundaries offer more valid explanations of delinquency than traditional theories. For example, are masculinities or other ways of "doing gender" simply learning or control mechanisms? Are they learned in the same way as other beliefs and values? Similarly, are certain forms of weak social bonding or a lack of self-control indicative of a form of masculinity (Hayslett-McCall and Bernard, 2002)? Is sexual abuse merely another stressor, albeit a serious one, for strain theory that leads to the delinquent behavior as females attempt to cope with their difficult lives (Baron, 2004)? Alternatively, is there something unique about the notion of masculinities, "doing gender," and blurred boundaries that makes explanations of delinquency more valid? The goal for feminist researchers is either to show how their theories offer a unique perspective on delinquency or to use an integrated theory-building approach (see Chapter 12) that combines their concepts with other models of delinquency (see, for example, Hayslett-McCall and Bernard, 2002). Moreover, a promising approach is to draw from radical or postmodern feminism to demonstrate how the metanarrative of patriarchy produces social and cultural conditions that affect female delinquency.

Policy implications of postmodernism and feminist theories

Some observers contend that postmodernists provide little practical policy guidance. There are some threads of postmodernist thought, however, that recommend general policies to end societal oppression. Some argue that simply changing policies that directly affect adolescent offenders is not sufficient; rather, broad social change is needed to improve people's lives. The key is changing language production away from discourses that reinforce differences among people to those that address similarities. It is discourses of difference that have led to social problems. As an alternative, there needs to be a language that promotes understanding, peace, and an environment where multiple discourses are acceptable. In general, language domination needs to end.

For feminist scholars, the policy implications depend on which type of feminism is advocated. For liberal feminists, equality of opportunity is the key; yet this might occur within the existing economic and political system. For social and radical feminists, however, the key is to end patriarchy. A system that equalizes opportunity, reduces the power of men, and appreciates the views of all women is necessary to overcome the historical tendency to privilege the position of men.

Some postmodern and feminist advocates suggest that a *peacemaking criminology* is needed that attempts to end human suffering by encouraging peace and justice for all people (Wozniak et al., 2008), and empowering the oppressed segments of society (Snider, 1998). The mutualist model discussed in Chapter 10 is one type of peacemaking approach. Some practical recommendations include:

1 Greater use of mediation to solve problems that divide delinquents from their victims;
2 Expand reliance on the principles of restorative justice (see Chapter 8);
3 Promote educational opportunities for all people, but especially those who have traditionally been oppressed or subordinate;
4 Provide more resources to decrease homelessness and assist not just the unemployed, but also those who fall outside the labor force; and
5 Combat the abuse that disproportionately affects girls and young women by educating men to respect women (McAlinden, 2005).

Some scholars have criticized peacemaking criminology as being out of touch with reality, and an abandonment of radical theory's emphasis on state power and suppression. They argue that it is simply a capitulation that would allow the oppressive forces of society to continue without opposition (Thomas et al., 2003). Others argue that peacemaking must be accompanied by a decrease in adversarialism – or the emphasis on winning in conflict situations – to be practical (Barak, 2005).

From a feminist perspective, perhaps the most essential policy initiative to prevent female delinquency is to develop programs to end sexual exploitation. As noted earlier, sexual abuse is the presumed cause of many female problems. Knopp (1991) pointed out that there is substantial variation across cultures in the risks of sexual abuse of women. Cultures with low rates of sexual abuse encourage that women be treated with respect and promote equality between men and women in all social institutions. Cultures that have sexual abuse problems tend to have more aggressive and competitive men, subordinate women in political and social roles, and define marriage in terms of men's "ownership" of women. Although large-scale cultural changes are difficult, Knopp noted that there are effective education programs designed to teach men to respect and value women. In the short term, aggressive enforcement of criminal laws against sexual abuse is needed, although in the long term programs that intervene early and treat victims with respect and compassion should be encouraged (Snider, 1998). Cognitive–behavioral therapy programs (see Chapter 4) also hold promise for preventing sexual abuse by changing the way male offenders think about females (Moster et al., 2008). Moreover, better victim services, offender restoration programs, and community alternatives to corrections are needed to avoid the worst consequences of the juvenile justice system (Verrecchia, 2009).

Conclusions

Postmodernism and feminist thought offer innovative ways of viewing delinquency and the justice system. Both ask us to question some fundamental beliefs about modern society. Postmodernists question the assumption of reality and knowledge. They also point out that the presumed infallibility of the scientific method is an illusion, so our most popular theories about delinquency are also illusions. Even the concept of delinquency is questionable: Is it simply a product of a language game that is dominated by more powerful segments of society? Are oppressed youths simply reacting to their conditions in a sensible way? Why are some acts so thrilling to some youths? Of course, irrespective of these questions, we must not ignore the genuine harm caused by some delinquent acts. Thus, listening to and learning from the perpetrators of these acts *and* their victims are equally important.

Feminist theories also pose difficult and stimulating questions, especially about the oppression of women. Too many girls fall victim to this oppression when they experience abuse by men. This system of abuse results from a patriarchal system that devalues women and gives the most power to adult men. It pushes many adolescents on a pathway that includes relationship problems, drug use, and delinquency. Some young women have to leave their homes and end up on the street, eventually being drawn into the juvenile justice system after being repeatedly exploited by men. The solution to this problem asks for a more equitable system for women that values their roles in society.

12 Integrating and elaborating theories of delinquency

Prologue

Amanda, Tony's mother, said that he was full of energy. His dad had left when Tony was about two years old; Amanda didn't know where he went. So she raised Tony and his sister Sam by herself. They were an interesting pair: Tony, who never seemed to stop moving, and Sam, who loved to read and write from a young age. Tony was tested for hyperactivity when he was five years old, but the doctor, who thought these types of diagnoses were ridiculous, told Amanda with a bit of contempt that Tony was a energetic boy and perhaps she couldn't understand this because she was a single woman.

Amanda often left Tony and Amanda for the evening when she went to her telemarketing job. When she was home, Amanda usually wanted to rest, so she spent very little time with her children. But Tony didn't mind; he'd found a group of older boys in the neighborhood who let him hang around. When he was 12 years old, Tony was picked up by the police with an older friend, Winston, for throwing rocks through the school windows. Amanda whipped him with an electrical cord and locked him in his room for the rest of the day. She also told him to stay away from Winston: "He's just trouble." But Tony, who seethed over the beating, snuck out that evening to drink wine with his friends.

The more Amanda punished him, the more Tony despised her and the more he hung out with his friends. He told his sister that the guys were like his family. Tony was soon kicked out of I.S. 10 – Horace Greeley Junior High for carrying an unloaded .32 caliber pistol that one of his friends let him borrow. Amanda tried to send him to live with her mother in Staten Island, but Tony ran away and went to stay with J.C., a 17-year-old who was the leader of a racist gang known as the Kaltyn Bluts. He stopped going to school and only went home to see Sam when Amanda was at work. He told Sam he felt free for the first time in his life. He had great friends who cared for him and he could go wherever he wanted (even though he never left Queens).

Tony was arrested for attempted murder after he almost killed a member of the Green Dragons, a well-known gang. But, since he was only 15 years old, he was sent to a juvenile facility in Brooklyn. After two years, he was released but had to go live with his mother. Tony left after less than a month, violating the conditions of his release. He was hiding out at Winston's apartment, helping sell cocaine when, based on an anonymous tip – which Tony figured was called in by his mother – the police raided early one morning. They arrested him for cocaine distribution. He was tried as an adult and sentenced to seven years at Gowanda in western New York. Sam comes to visit him once a month, but Amanda never shows up.

Introduction

Many delinquency theorists take a key characteristic or condition – such as social control – and build their main arguments around it. A common question is "How or why does some condition lead to delinquency?" However, it is natural to ask if only one factor is important. As shown earlier, the individual and social processes that lead to delinquency are complex and can involve many stages. Therefore, many experts have considered combinations of factors that result in delinquent behavior. Yet it is important to remember that simply throwing a bunch of concepts together does not result in a delinquency *theory* (see Chapter 1). Rather, an adequate theory describes the *mechanisms* that link specific factors to delinquency (Elster, 2007).

Some delinquency researchers have compared theories to see which offers a more valid explanation of misbehaviors. For example, is strain or self-control more predictive of delinquency? By testing competing theoretical claims, researchers try to determine which theory offers the best explanation. However, some argue that comparing theories is pointless. Instead, a better approach is to consider combining theories to offer a more powerful model of delinquency. This has been the goal of *theoretical integration*: combining two or more existing theories to explain some phenomenon. Another approach is to minimize the emphasis on theoretical traditions and focus instead on which risk factors are most predictive of delinquency (Bernard, 2001). Certain risk factors, such as low self-control (see Chapter 8), may be important for explaining individual-level delinquency, whereas others, such as low collective efficacy (see Chapter 5), may be important for explaining neighborhood-level differences in delinquency.

A distinct approach to modifying theories is to take an existing theory, such as social learning or bonding, and attempt to improve its ability to explain delinquency, perhaps by considering new ideas and research findings. This is known as *theoretical elaboration*. In this chapter, we shall learn about integrated and elaborated theories of delinquency, examine some research on both types, and consider some of their policy implications.

Theoretical integration

Theoretical integration became popular when researchers recognized that the strengths of several theories could be combined to form a new theory. Researchers argued, for instance, that integrating theories was the next logical step in understanding delinquency (Elliott et al., 1985). Previous studies had compared variables from different theories, but this sort of theoretical competition was fruitless because, even if one turned out to be a better predictor, it was still only modestly associated with delinquency. Therefore, the best approach is to determine if the main variables from different theories can be placed together in some fashion to construct a better general explanation of delinquency.

Although there are several ways to combine theories, one typology is to consider three general approaches:

1   end-to-end (sequential);
2   side-by-side (horizontal); and
3   up-and-down (combine different levels of abstraction) (Messner et al., 1989).

For example, an end-to-end approach might consider that, since delinquent peers are strongly correlated with delinquency, it is important to consider them in any good theory of delinquency. However, what leads to delinquent peers? Some argue that family relations affect whether adolescents are more or less likely to hang around delinquent friends. Figure 12.1 shows this model, which combines concepts from social bonding (families) and differential association (peers) theories.

Side-by-side integration involves dividing delinquency in some manner and then showing how specific theories predict certain aspects of delinquency. For example, social bonding theory may be more useful for explaining minor forms of delinquency, whereas general strain theory may be better at explaining violent behavior. Side-by-side integration is also useful for explaining delinquency among different groups. Figure 12.2 shows an example of a side-by-side integrated theory that involves social bonding theory and strain theory. The curved double-ended

Figure 12.1 A simple end-to-end integrated theory.

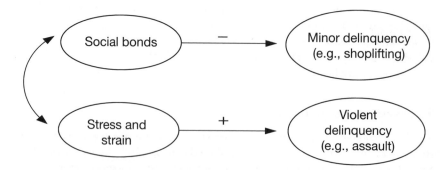

Figure 12.2 A simple side-by-side integrated theory.

arrow shows only that social bonds and strain are correlated, but does not make any claim of a causal connection.

A third type of theoretical integration is known as up-and-down. Up-and-down theories involve making an existing theory sufficiently broad so that it covers the arguments of other theories. Perhaps the best example of an up-and-down theory is social learning theory (see Chapter 7). Akers (1998) argued that most other theories of delinquency may be subsumed under social learning theory because learning is a necessary condition for delinquent behavior. For example, labeling works to produce secondary delinquency only if adolescents learn and internalize what others think of them.

Although these three types are useful, there are other ways to integrate theories. Recent attention to macro- vs. individual-level social processes may offer the most obvious way. For example, we might combine theories through *cross-level integration*: taking theories that address different levels and combining them to create a comprehensive explanation of delinquency. For instance, Agnew (2003) combined ideas about the impact of neighborhood factors with the effects of general strain (see Chapter 6). Figure 12.3 provides an illustration of this type of a cross-level integrated theory. Neighborhood violence affects stress and individual-level delinquency, perhaps because those neighborhoods that are violent have many other stressors and they also increase aggressiveness among residents. However, it also affects the association between strain and delinquency.

In the next few sections, we shall learn about some integrated theories of delinquency. Each has been subjected to some empirical testing. Furthermore, they were developed only after the researchers carefully considered how concepts from different theories might be combined.

An end-to-end integrated theory

Delbert Elliott, David Huizinga, and Susan Ageton (1985) developed the best-known integrated model of delinquency. Their main goal was to combine strain, social bonding, and social learning variables into a single theory that explained delinquency and drug use. They began by arguing that a lack of socialization,

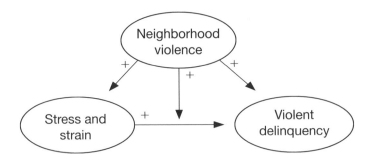

Figure 12.3 A simple cross-level integrated theory.

strain in the form of anticipated or actual failure to achieve valuable goals, and social disorganization weaken social bonds. Both strain and weak control affect later delinquency and drug use.

They also claimed that peers provide much of the support for delinquency. Therefore, Elliott and colleagues proposed that weak conventional bonds allow adolescents to become bonded to delinquent peers and these bonds directly result in delinquent behavior. Peers also provide beliefs (or definitions) and social support that favor delinquency. Hence, there are concepts from several theories in their integrated theory. Figure 12.4 provides an illustration.

An important issue addressed by these researchers involved what to do with the distinct assumptions of these theories. However, rather than try to reconcile them, Elliott and colleagues rejected bonding theory's assumption: "[the] assumption of constant motivation for deviance is unreasonable; . . . it is more reasonable to assume that the motivation for delinquency is not the same for everyone" (Elliott et al., 1985, p.39). Thus, they adopted the assumption of social learning theory that behaviors are learned and that learning to commit delinquent acts takes place most often in peer environments.

They subjected their model to a thorough empirical examination. Although there were some discrepancies across several empirical models, there was general support for most of their hypotheses. For example, Figure 12.5 shows the results when they examined serious offenses such as aggravated assault and robbery. Previous delinquency and associating with delinquent friends are the only direct antecedents of serious delinquent behavior. Strains in the home and in school are associated with modest decreases in family and school involvement, and increases in beliefs that deviant actions are acceptable. The strongest predictor of associating with delinquent friends is deviant beliefs, a concept derived from social bonding theory. Nevertheless, as mentioned earlier, this model may not provide a

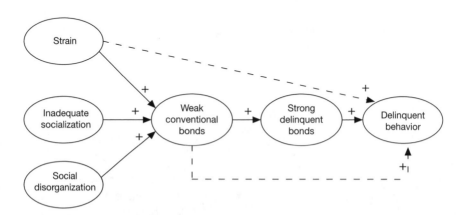

Figure 12.4 Elliott and associates' integrated model of delinquency (adapted from Elliott et al., 1985, p.66). Note: The solid lines indicate proposed causal relationships; the broken lines indicate traditional strain and control paths toward delinquency.

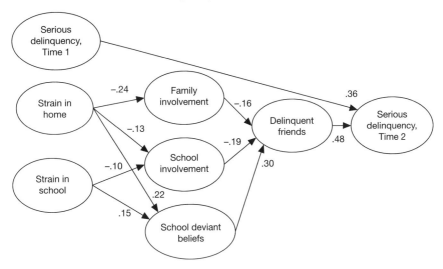

Figure 12.5 A test of Elliott and associates' integrated model of delinquency (adapted from Elliott et al., 1985, p.111).

valid test of strain theory since, as Bernard (2001) pointed out, it fails to address the aggregate-level arguments of this theory. Strain in the home and at school may simply reflect weak bonds or feelings of alienation rather than the kinds of mechanisms discussed by Merton or Cohen. In addition, it may appear as though the concept *beliefs* is drawn from social bonding theory, but, given that they measured these beliefs by asking adolescents whether they thought it was wrong to commit deviant acts, it is reasonable to label this variable as *definitions favorable to violation of law*, a differential association concept.

Social development theory

Another integrated model is David Hawkins and Joseph Weis's social development theory. These researchers were motivated to design a theory that would provide guidance on preventing delinquency. After considering a number of theories, Hawkins and Weis (1985) opted to combine aspects of social bonding and social learning. Bonding theory provides an explanation of how specific socializing units affect adolescent development by encouraging attachments, commitments, and beliefs in conventional values. Social learning theory emphasizes not just the units of socialization but also processes of socialization through positive and negative reinforcement. Moreover, this theory includes peer influences. Delinquent peers act to reinforce delinquent behavior, thus providing another source of socialization.

Figure 12.6 provides a diagram of the social development model. Note that it begins with opportunities for involvement and interaction. Hawkins and Weis argued that these opportunities are necessary to develop attachments,

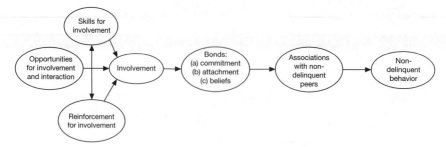

Figure 12.6 Social development theory of delinquency (adapted from Hawkins and Weis, 1985, p.79).

commitments, and beliefs, which then affect the likelihood of associating with delinquent peers. Yet these opportunities and interactions lead to involvement mainly if youths have sufficient skills and reinforcement for involvement. As with Elliott and colleagues' model, peer associations are the key direct influence on delinquent behavior. However, as shown in the figure, Hawkins and Weis also focused on non-delinquent peers and non-delinquent behavior because these are preferable outcomes.

Hawkins and colleagues have published several empirical examinations of social development theory that support its propositions (e.g., Catalano et al., 2005). For example, Huang and colleagues (2001) determined that prosocial socialization, which was measured by involvement in conventional activities, opportunities to engage in these activities, and a sense that parents reward adolescents for their work, lead to more bonding to parents. On the other hand, antisocial socialization leads to bonds to delinquent friends. Prosocial and antisocial socialization affect

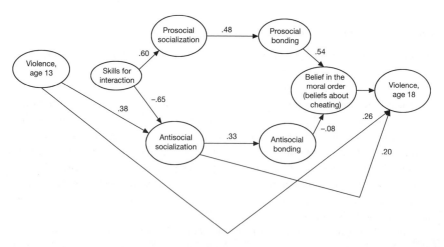

Figure 12.7 A test of social development theory (adapted from Huang et al., 2001, p.96). Note: Only statistically significant pathways are shown.

subsequent beliefs about cheating in school. The final outcome in their model is violent behavior at age 18, which is directly affected by beliefs, previous violent behavior, and antisocial bonds. Figure 12.7 shows the results of Huang and colleagues' final model.

Integrating social control and genetic risk factors

As discussed in Chapter 3, several genetic characteristics are associated with delinquency. However, it is important to remember that it is not genetics alone, but a complex set of genetic–environment interactions that increase the probability of delinquency among certain youths. In a model that integrates genetic risk factors and social bonds, Guo and colleagues (2008) claimed that certain genetic polymorphisms that are related to aggressiveness interact with social bonds and peer associations to produce a higher likelihood of delinquency. They suggested that social bonds can reduce whatever effect these genetic influences have on delinquency by restraining potential delinquents. However, low social bonds allow these conditions to increase involvement in delinquency. A simplified version of their model is presented in Figure 12.8.

Guo and his colleagues (2008) provided an empirical test to accompany their proposed integrated model. They tested adolescents for three genetic polymorphisms: DAT, DRD2, and MAO-A, which are associated with the neurotransmitter dopamine and MAO, an enzyme that is responsible for metabolizing

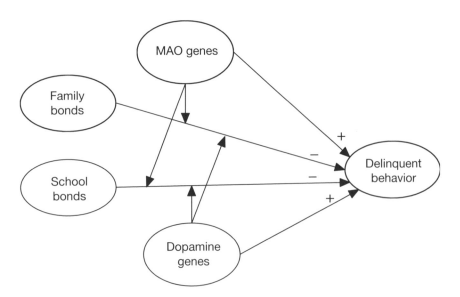

Figure 12.8 Integrated genetic and social bond model of delinquency (adapted from Guo et al., 2008, p.549). Note: The arrows pointing from the genes to the arrows indicate that they *modify* the association between bonds and delinquent behavior.

dopamine, serotonin, and norepinephrine (see Chapter 3 for more information). They also asked about family relationships, peer relationships, and school-related variables. In an empirical model that was loosely based on social bonding theory, they determined that these genes amplify the relationship between poor school performance and violent delinquency. Moreover, they found that having daily family meals – a type of family bond – dampens the association between low dopamine production or MAO deficiencies and delinquency. However, the combination of weak social bonds and these genes increases the likelihood of violent delinquency.

A focus on risk factors

Thomas J. Bernard (2001) proposed an alternative to comparing or integrating theories. He was critical of most attempts to combine theories of delinquency because (1) they make distinct and incompatible assumptions about human nature and (2) efforts to integrate have failed to appreciate the true form of these theories. By combining theories with incompatible assumptions, theorists are forced to choose one or another (as Elliott did), thus failing to genuinely utilize a particular theory (Hirschi, 1989). Most important, however, Bernard contended that those who have attempted to integrate strain theories with other theories have not realized that strain operates at the macro level. In general, then, theories such as Hirschi's social bond model and Merton's strain model cannot be combined because they explain delinquency at two different levels of abstraction.

As an alternative to theoretical integration, Bernard proposed a *risk factor* approach that focuses on variables rather than theories. Researchers should seek to determine which variables are best able to explain particular aspects of delinquency. Some variables may not explain any aspect of delinquency, so they may be discarded. Others may offer a good explanation for delinquent behavior among individuals regardless of the social environment. Still other variables may be best at explaining why certain communities have higher rates of delinquency (see Chapter 5). Bernard's point is that, rather than engaging in theory competition to see which is most valid, or combining dramatically different theories in one model, we should focus on specific variables derived from the theories and determine (1) what they purport to explain about delinquency and (2) whether they are successful (in a probabilistic sense) in explaining it.

What are some elements derived from theories and research projects that have proven useful in predicting delinquency at the individual and macro levels? Bernard (2001) pointed out that an important part of answering this question is to find elements that explain individual offending regardless of the social context and other elements that explain higher offending rates in certain areas or environments regardless of the type of people in them. He then offered a list of these various elements. For example, poor cognitive skills increase the chances of delinquency among individuals (Bennett et al., 2005), whereas a lack of jobs leads to higher rates of delinquency in some neighborhoods (Hoffmann, 2003).

Promises and limitations of theoretical integration

Although numerous studies have shown that aspects of integrated models are valid predictors of delinquency (e.g., Catalano et al., 2005; see also Chapter 3), there are important criticisms that have not been adequately addressed by those who support integration. First, several of these theories make distinct and incompatible assumptions about human nature. By combining them into one model, theorists are forced to adopt one assumption at the expense of the others. For instance, Elliott and associates' integrated theory is actually a learning theory since they claimed that it is socialization in groups that determines whether adolescents engage in delinquency

Second, even the most comprehensive of these models selects only certain elements of the theories. For instance, when considering learning theory, Elliott and colleagues included only peer associations in their model. Yet, as shown in Chapter 7, learning theories have many elements in addition to peer associations. There are a whole host of reinforcement and definitional factors that come into play. Without attention to these, it is difficult to see how blended models are truly integrated theories. Some of the most important explanatory components of these theories are left "on the cutting room floor" (Hirschi, 1989). Theoretical integration is thus not an accurate term; it is not the theories that are integrated, but rather a limited number of concepts drawn from the theories.

Third, as Bernard (2001) noted, integrated models tend to be flawed because they often fail to address the level of analysis. Moreover, pitting one theory against another is often fruitless because (1) each one may explain a small amount of variability in delinquency, and (2) they may explain different aspects of delinquency. Bernard's alternative, the risk factor approach, presumably solves these problems by moving away from theory competition and integration. It focuses on identifying particular factors that are associated with different aspects of delinquency and crime. Although this approach is promising and is common in other disciplines such as public health, it is not a strict theoretical method since prediction is more important than explanation (see Chapter 1). Thus, for scholars who use a strict definition of theory and wish to understand the mechanisms that link particular conditions and delinquency, a risk factor approach is not sufficient.

Theoretical elaboration

Terence P. Thornberry and others (e.g., Hirschi, 1989) have proposed that, as an alternative to theoretical integration, we focus on developing existing theories of delinquency. A common theme that can be seen throughout the preceding chapters is that there has been substantial progress in developing several theories of delinquency. For instance, Akers's social learning theory (see Chapter 7) is a significant advancement over previous learning theories, such as differential association. Moreover, over the last few years researchers have increased our understanding of how delinquency might be learned or deterred by considering important developments in neuroscience, cognitive science, and genetics. By continually improving the scope and significance of theories, better explanations of delinquency can be formulated without some of the drawbacks of theoretical integration.

Thornberry (1987, 1989) has developed a nicely structured framework for *theoretical elaboration*: the process of taking an existing theory and using new ideas and research to improve it. Accepting the assumptions and basic structure of a theory, the process of elaboration then attempts to construct a more thorough model by extending logically its basic propositions and linking them in a concise manner. This could entail revising certain propositions or introducing new ones. Scholars should also consider empirical studies that have addressed the theory, relevant philosophical discussions, and new strategies for studying delinquency. However, all this should be done within the basic confines of the theory. Moreover, some observers have recommended that theorists look outside their field for information that might be useful (Meier, 1989).

Interactional theory

Thornberry (1987) presented his own version of an elaborated theory, which he termed an *interactional theory of delinquency*. Interactional theory begins with the social control assumption that the fundamental cause of delinquency originates in weak social constraints over behaviors. Social controls develop over time as individuals and groups interact. Moreover, a weakening of social controls does not propel an adolescent directly into delinquency. It merely allows for a greater range of behavior, including misbehaviors. In order for delinquency to occur, an interactive process is required during which delinquent behaviors and delinquent values are adopted and reinforced.

Interactional theory includes six key concepts: attachment to parents, commitment to school, belief in conventional values, associations with delinquent peers, delinquent behavior, and delinquent values. These concepts interact across adolescence to increase or decrease the likelihood of delinquency. Unlike most previous theories, interactional theory proposes that the influences among the concepts are not in only one direction. Rather, a concept such as delinquent behavior can be influenced by, but also influence, commitment to school or attachment to parents. Thus, delinquency is not the end result in a chain of variables, but rather is embedded within a causal loop that includes the other key variables.

Figure 12.9 provides an illustration of interactional theory. Although there are separate models for different age groups, the figure shows only the model for mid-adolescence. Note that some of the associations go in both directions (reciprocal relationships). It is important to remember, though, that the assumptions and basic structure are derived from social bonding theory, but it has substantially elaborated this theory by (1) including delinquent peers associations and delinquent values, (2) addressing developmental changes by considering age differences, and (3) considering reciprocal relationships among the principal concepts. Thornberry (1987) argued that theorists should no longer consider, for example, attachment to parents and delinquency at one time point only. Instead they should address

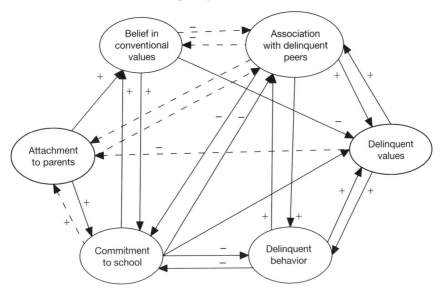

Figure 12.9 Interactional theory during middle adolescence (ages 14–16) (adapted from Thornberry, 1987, p.878). Note: Solid lines represent stronger effects; dashed lines represent weaker effects.

how attachment changes across adolescence, as well as how involvement in delinquency develops over time. Similarly, peer associations change substantially during adolescence. In sum, then, the interactional associations among several concepts across adolescence and into young adulthood must be evaluated in order to understand delinquent behavior.

Research on interactional theory

Almost 10 years after introducing his theory, Thornberry (1996) offered an appraisal of the research that had addressed aspects of it. Since, as mentioned earlier, the most innovative aspect of interactional theory involves reciprocal relationships among variables, he discussed 17 delinquency and crime studies that used data collected over time and explicitly included these types of relationships.

In general, Thornberry's review showed strong support for many aspects of interactional theory. For example, several studies have found that delinquent peer associations and delinquent behavior tend to reinforce one another over time. In fact, some studies suggest that the path from delinquent behavior to delinquent peers is stronger than the path from delinquent peers to delinquent behavior, although they are clearly mutually reinforcing (e.g., Matsueda and Anderson, 1998).

Thornberry has also worked with several colleagues to test aspects of interactional theory. In one study, they focused on the reciprocal associations among beliefs, delinquent peers, and delinquent behavior over a three-year period when most of the adolescents were between the ages of 13 and 17. They also examined peer reactions: the perceived responses of their friends to their involvement in delinquency (e.g., was it "okay" or "wrong"?). As they explained, peers can provide positive or negative reinforcements for behavior, so it is important to look at how friends might react to their delinquent behavior (Thornberry et al., 1994).

In this complex empirical examination, they determined the adolescents who hold beliefs that delinquent behavior is acceptable "tend to increase association[s] with delinquent peers and involvement in delinquency; in turn, these variables tend to consolidate further delinquent belief structures" (Thornberry, 1994, p.75). Thus, socialization is a two-way street and behaviors that may result from being socialized by peers also affect later peer relations. The results of their empirical model are presented in Figure 12.10.

Although Thornberry has directly linked interactional theory to social bonding theory, the empirical studies – especially the study represented in Figure 12.10 – have shown that it is at least as supportive of social learning theory (Matsueda, 1989). In fact, focusing on how peers socialize youths to engage in delinquency is clearly part of a learning process that seems antithetical to the assumption of social bonding theory that deviance and delinquency require no push, but rather are natural consequences of weak bonds to conventional institutions. Nonetheless,

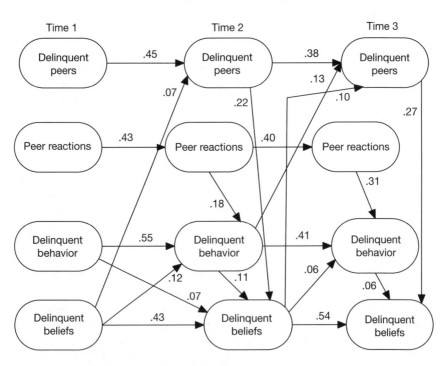

Figure 12.10 A test of interactional theory (adapted from Thornberry et al., 1994, p.68).
   Note: Only significant path coefficients are shown. The correlations among
   variables are omitted in Time 1.

interactional theory provides an important explanation of how delinquency not only is affected by but also affects relationships and values.

Control balance theory

Charles Tittle (1995) has developed a theory that elaborates several elements of existing theories of crime and delinquency to create a general theory of deviance. He disliked the label *theoretical elaboration*, preferring to call his approach *synthetic integration*. His *control balance theory* is based on a central concept that then adds additional concepts to fill out the theory. Tittle began by assuming that people are motivated to do some things because of fundamental needs (e.g., to eat) or culturally induced urges (e.g., to gain money). Sometimes, the things people wish to do are distasteful to others or are restricted by the social or physical environment. They may also be restricted by others who have the ability or authority to constrain their activities. There are always situations where people cannot do what they wish to do, so everyone is subject to some amount of control. Moreover, most people have some degree of control over the actions of others.

Another assumption of this theory is that people desire *autonomy*, or personal freedom. Thus, people attempt to escape the control they are subject to and exert their own control. This desire for autonomy is assumed to be constant across situations. Since people's own control and the potential control of others over them are variable, Tittle described a *control ratio*: a person's typical amount of control relative to being the object of others' controls. A particular control ratio may be balanced or imbalanced. Moreover, a person's control ratio varies from situation to situation. For example, the amount of control children have relative to their parents changes as they get older; by the time they reach adulthood, the balance favors much more control relative to parental control.

Tittle also claimed that, as relative controls become imbalanced, people become more likely to be motivated toward deviance. The likelihood of deviance also increases when goals are blocked. Although many people with control imbalances may be motivated to some extent, other elements are also needed. These include *provocation*: (1) being told what to do; (2) being treated unfairly by another person; (3) being overwhelmed by responsibilities; (4) having one's authority questioned; (5) being physically violated in some way; (6) being denied access to a place or denied some desired object; or (7) being subject to the hostility of another. These situations tend to remind people of their control imbalance, especially if they are lacking relative control in the particular situation. If these provocations elicit negative emotions – which they often do – and there are opportunities to react, then some physical response is likely to take place.

If there is control imbalance, motivation, provocation, and opportunity, most people will at least think about how to respond. Yet most people also realize that there is a cost to their response: Someone might fight back, the police might show up, or a parent might break out the paddle. In general, various *constraints* are present that affect the likelihood of a response. The more serious the contemplated action, the greater the control that the person is subject to. So, if Bob decides to poison his high school teacher, he must realize that state control will be severe: arrest, prosecution for homicide, and time in a youth lock-up or prison. Moreover, many people experience personal constraints, such as friendships, that may be jeopardized by deviant responses to provocation. The acts that people consider

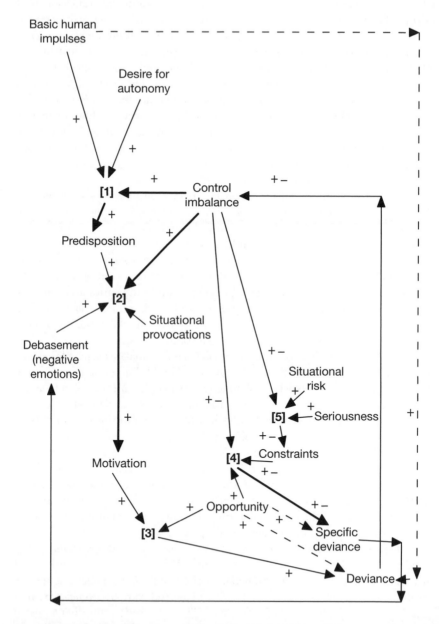

Figure 12.11 Control balance theory (adapted from Tittle, 1995, p.172).

are therefore based on (1) their control ratio; (2) the seriousness of the act; (3) the particular situation; (4) the nature of the provocation; (5) the strength of motivation; (6) the degree of negative emotion produced by the provocation; and (7) the constraints present at the time of the event. A diagram of this complex theory is presented in Figure 12.11.

The bracketed numbers in the diagram indicate that the particular influences converge to create conditions in favor of deviant acts. The darker arrows indicate that this influence is particularly strong. For instance, control imbalance is especially important when it converges with desire for autonomy and basic human impulses to create condition [1]. It is also highly important when it converges with predisposition, situational provocation, and debasement (negative emotions) to create condition [2]. Following the chain of arrows, notice that the stream ends with deviance and specific forms of deviance.

Where does delinquency come into play? On one extreme, people who have very little relative control may experience a submissive condition called *learned helplessness*; whereas on the other extreme those with substantial relative control adopt what Tittle termed a "decadent" lifestyle of wicked and exploitive pleasures. However, these two ends of the spectrum are rare. Instead, violent delinquency results when there is a relatively small deficit of control. Violence is an option because these people have almost as much control as others, so the probable response to their behaviors is not much of a deterrent. However, if some people have larger deficits than others, they are highly controlled and lashing out through violence is not a good option. Conformity, the most common outcome, results when control is relatively balanced. Yet there are also *contingencies* that affect responses to control imbalances and the other factors shown in Figure 12.11. These may intervene in the control balance process. There are many possible contingencies, such as cognitive perceptions and personality traits. For example, if a youth has a strong sense that violence is wrong and should be avoided, he will not fight even if provoked.

It should be apparent that control balance theory, though its central concept involves power and control, draws its general ideas from several theories of delinquency. However, it does this within the strict confines of a particular framework. Thus, although it is an integrated theory in one sense (Tittle, 1995), it is also an elaboration of a well-used core concept in criminological studies. Still, there are clearly elements of general strain, social control, rational choice, and opportunity theories.

Research on control balance theory

Control balance has been subjected to relatively few empirical tests, perhaps because its complexity makes it difficult to examine using survey methods. As an alternative, Piquero and Hickman (1999) developed a set of scenarios that identified various aspects of control balance and delinquency. For example, one scenario read:

Brian is standing in Shampoo, a dance club, with his friends drinking beer. Another patron, David, bumps into Brian from behind, causing him to spill beer all over his shirt and pants. Brian's friends can't help laughing at him. Brian turns around and David, smiling, says "sorry" and spins around to continue dancing with his friends. Brian taps David on the shoulder and says, "Hey, you just made me spill beer all over the place!" David stops dancing, stares directly into Brian's eyes and asks him, "Do you have a problem?" Brian says, "Yeah, why don't you get me another beer?" David pushes his finger into Brian's chest and asks, "Why don't you get on your knees and beg?" Brian hits David in the face with his fist, and a fight breaks out between them (p.236).

They then asked university students to consider the scenarios and whether they thought they would react in the same way as Brian. They also asked the respondents to report how much control they had in their friendships, school, families, and workplace, as well as how much control these environments had over them, in order to measure control balance. They found that it was not only those with control deficits who say they would react to the scenario in the same way as Brian, but also those who had a control surplus. Recall that Tittle proposed that those with a modest control deficit would be most likely to react with violence. Piquero and Hickman (1999) suggested that control deficits as well as surpluses often lead to aggressive acts, but for distinct reasons: Those with deficits feel they have little to lose and those with surpluses do not think they will lose their advantage in control over others by acting aggressively (see also Baron and Forde, 2007; Braithwaite 1997). However, as Tittle argued, someone with an especially large deficit in control tends to be dominated to such an extent that fear of retaliation by those with control deters an aggressive reaction.

Promises and limitations of theoretical elaboration

There are numerous examples of elaborated theories, many of which were discussed in earlier chapters. General strain theory and power-control theory, as well as several others, are elaborated theoretical models. In fact, it is difficult to find theories of delinquency that have been introduced in the last three decades that are not elaborated models in some sense, although integrated models are still common. Nevertheless, there are some limitations to the current elaborated models that should also be considered.

For example, although both interactional theory and control balance theory emphasize how controls affect delinquency, neither has considered the sources of control in genetic, biochemical, or cognitive variables, even though numerous studies have shown that these affect self-control, perceptions of others' intentions, and socialization. For instance, in Chapter 4 we learned that many aggressive youths have a perceptual bias that affects how they react to various situations (Dodge, 2003). They tend to think that others are hostile in social situations, consider fewer possible outcomes, and, when provoked, often think about a disproportionate number of aggressive outcomes. Thus, the way they perceive situations emphasizes hostile responses that others would not see. These youths also tend to think that reacting aggressively results in some favorable outcome for them (e.g., "I'll get respect by fighting"). Therefore, it is likely that the pathway that Tittle proposed is a consequence of cognitive processes that have their roots in early childhood and that may be affected by neurological characteristics or maltreatment (see Chapter 4). This does not invalidate control balance theory, but it does point toward the need for further elaboration.

Emphasizing control balance theory in particular, Braithwaite (1997) claimed that there are some theoretical issues that should be addressed. First, the theory should be based on the assumption that people simply seek control, regardless of how much they currently possess. Second, there is little reason to make distinctions between the forms of deviance; many people involved in one type of deviance – especially if it involves delinquency – are also involved in other types of these behaviors. Others have criticized the complexity of the theory, which makes it difficult to test. Moreover, the assumption that people seek autonomy, although it provides a simplification that makes it easier to build the theory, implies an ethnocentric, modernistic, and westernized view of human nature. Cultures bound more by interpersonal connections and social networks do not seem to match this assumption well. Thus, control balance's most fundamental assumption is not universalistic (Savelsberg, 1999).

Tittle (2004) responded to some of these criticisms by admitting that distinctions among some types of deviance were not necessary; they were based on speculation rather than valid research. Moreover, some forms of deviance that result from control balance, especially submissiveness, which Tittle reasoned would result from extreme deficits in control, are not always considered deviant. For example, some of the best soldiers are submissive to their superiors' authority, yet they are not deemed deviant. Tittle also argued that deviant behavior occurs along a continuum that is based on a new concept: *control balance desirability*. This refers to a combination of two concepts: (1) the likely effectiveness of a deviant act in altering one's control imbalance over the long term; and (2) whether the deviant act directly affects the victim. Control balance desirability is mainly a way to predict what type of deviant response a person uses in a particular situation. Returning to some of the factors that affect how control balance leads to deviant behavior (see Figure 12.11), the likelihood of committing a highly desirable control balance act occurs when:

a   there is a large control surplus;
b   there is opportunity to commit the act;
c   there are few constraints; and
d   the person has high self-control (see Chapter 8).

An undesirable act tends to occur when:

a   the person has a deficit in control (but not too much);
b   there is opportunity to commit the act;
c   there is significant constraint over committing alternative acts; and
d   the person has low self-control (Tittle, 2003, p.420).

Although control balance is a promising model for explaining a range of behaviors, including delinquency, the assumption of the need for autonomy remains problematic. In addition, it is important to realize that controls and bonds are often perceptual; that is, they may vary from person to person based on their subjective sense of control or relationships with conventional institutions. From a critical perspective (see Chapters 10 and 11), neither interactional theory nor control balance theory addresses the source of power and control in larger social structures, such as class, ethnicity, or patriarchy. Under what conditions are control and power most likely to be asserted over individuals and groups? It seems that, if theorists are genuinely interested in theoretical elaboration, answering this question is important. However, with the exception of a small number of critical theorists, few have attempted to tackle this issue.

Policy implications of integrated and elaborated theories of delinquency

Integrated and elaborated delinquency theories recommend many of the same policies as the theories from which they are derived. As mentioned in Chapter 8, for example, Gottfredson and Hirschi (1990, pp.272–273) claimed, "Policies directed toward enhancement of the ability of familial institutions to socialize children are the only realistic long-term state policies with potential for substantial crime reduction." This requires not only parents, but also "responsible adults committed to the training and welfare of the child" (p.272). However, if we accept the reasoning of interactional theory and the social development model that bonds to conventional social institutions may be strengthened during adolescence, policies that encourage parents and children to develop affectionate relations and commitments, and that provide parents with the tools they need to supervise their children's activities, furnish the best means for curbing involvement in delinquency. In particular, programs that emphasize parenting skills, even though they are often tied to social learning theories, offer a well-established way of helping families maintain close bonds. These programs train parents in effective discipline styles, teach them to reinforce prosocial behaviors, provide skills for more effective supervision, and train parents and children to communicate better. There is significant research that shows the effectiveness of these programs in reducing childhood misbehaviors and delinquent offending during adolescence.

Similarly, programs that encourage children and adolescents to develop and maintain strong bonds to schools and their communities may also help discourage delinquent behavior. Programs that provide after-school activities, that teach study skills to low-achieving students, and that help teachers to develop better relations with their students are designed in general to strengthen the bonds between adolescents and schools (Gottfredson et al., 2004).

Among the theories discussed in this chapter, social development theory has motivated the most intervention research because, as mentioned earlier, it was designed to inform intervention and prevention efforts. For example, the Seattle

Social Development Project, which was based directly on social development theory, included an intervention that had the following characteristics:

- train teachers to be more effective classroom managers;
- train teachers to give clear instructions about behavioral expectations, reinforce desirable student behaviors, and encourage cooperative learning;
- help students develop communication, negotiation, interpersonal problem solving, and conflict resolution skills, and identify the consequences of problem behaviors; and
- train parents to identify undesirable behaviors and to teach behavioral expectations, use consistent reinforcement strategies, and provide academic support skills.

Hawkins and colleagues' (2003, 2008) evaluations of this program found numerous positive effects. At age 18, six years after the program ended, those who took part in the intervention component had higher attachment to schools, better grades, and significantly less misbehaviors than those who were not part of the intervention. They also reported less violent behavior, less heavy alcohol use, and fewer sexual partners. A second follow-up when they were between the ages of 24 and 27 indicated that those who took part in the program 15 years earlier were more likely to have completed an Associate's degree and were less likely to have had a sexually transmitted disease. However, they were not less likely to use drugs, have a substance abuse problem, or engage in criminal behavior.

Given the novelty of control balance theory, its implications for policy are still tentative. Nevertheless, based on how control balance is measured and from what studies have demonstrated about its predictive capabilities, there are some potential programs that might be relevant. For instance, providing adolescents with some sense of control in their lives, but not too much, would presumably balance out their control surpluses and deficiencies and make deviant behaviors less likely. Some ways this might be done include offering protection from abuse and bullying to vulnerable youths, teaching youths to respect one another, and training youths and their families effective problem-solving techniques. Perhaps the most promising programs, however, are those that focus on contingencies. Recall that contingencies include conditions such as cognitive perceptions and personality traits. Therefore, programs might be developed to enhance those cognitive perceptions that minimize delinquency and provide treatment to youths who have personality traits that are most conducive to delinquency. Certain CBTs, such as those designed to reduce hostile attribution bias, might offer the most effective interventions (see Chapter 3).

Conclusions

Integrated and elaborated theories provide different ways of thinking about how to build models of delinquency. Integrated theories take the most promising concepts from existing theories and combine them into a model that should offer a more powerful explanation of delinquency. Elaborated theories are based on the idea that the full potential of existing theories has not yet been discovered. Rather than pulling them apart and putting them back together with other theories, this alternative approach is to use what we have learned since the theory was introduced to strengthen it.

Research addressing these theories has been promising. In particular, the notion that not only do relationships, beliefs, and commitments affect delinquency but also delinquency subsequently affects these bonds is of vital importance for understanding this behavior. These reciprocal loops have been found in a number of studies. Understanding how they operate may also offer some promising ways to prevent delinquency. If we can either stop youths from getting into these loops or pull them away through intervention then preventing delinquency is certainly possible. For example, programs that focus on building positive social bonds to families and schools and preventing negative bonds are one way of arresting the development of delinquency.

Since integration and elaboration, as well as Bernard's risk factor approach, are relatively new methods of theory building, it is too early to tell if one of them will become a preeminent model of theoretical development. Recent years have seen a substantial number of theories elaborated, such as strain theory and control theory; but there have also been some notable attempts to integrate theories. In the next chapter, we shall consider another movement that is related to both integration and elaboration. This involves creating developmental models that explain how delinquency and crime unfold across the lives of individuals.

13 Developmental theories of delinquency and crime

Prologue

The researchers came to interview Billy while he was in his late sixties, living in a one-bedroom apartment and working as a bus driver in Boston. Although he had held the job for three years, Billy felt uncomfortable, like something was going to go wrong soon. He figured if he could just win the lottery everything would be okay. Billy had been in and out of prison for most of his adult life. He had committed as many as 26 official delinquent and criminal offenses, was first incarcerated at age 15, and had spent more than half of his adult life in prison. Although Billy had been raised in a good, working class home by a mother and father, he liked playing in the streets and dropped out of school after the eighth grade. He then began to steal cars – they called it "hot-boxing" – with a friend. By age 15, Billy figured he had stolen about 50 cars. He had also started drinking and problems with alcohol continued to haunt Billy for most of his life.

Soon after he began to "hot-box" regularly, Billy was arrested and sent to the Industrial School for Boys, which seemed like "going to a farm" to him. He was arrested eight times by the time he was 25. After he began to rob people to get the "big money," Billy was labeled as one of the most dangerous inmates at the state prison. However, he didn't see himself as a violent person. Sure, he used a gun to rob people, but he said he never hurt anyone. Billy saw crime as an easy way to make money. There was also a sense of excitement to it: Billy described being shot by the police after escaping from reform school and about his part in a prison riot in the 1950s. His final arrest and conviction was for bank robbery at age 58.

Billy rarely held down a job for longer than a few months. Most were used only to make enough money to survive. He got married once when he was in his thirties, but his wife divorced him when he was in prison after about nine months of marriage. As a young adult, he tried to join the army, but was rejected because of his criminal record. Looking back on his life, Billy says that it was "a waste, a real waste." There seemed to be a lot of missed opportunities to turn his life around. But he didn't think he had a choice in the matter (Laub and Sampson, 2003, chapter 7).

Introduction

As discussed in the last chapter, an attractive approach to explaining delinquency has been to integrate theories or elaborate a particular theory. However, few theories offer explanations for the various stages of delinquency. For instance, can we explain why some adolescents begin to commit delinquent acts? Why do some get more and more involved in delinquency? What factors influence the majority of adolescents to end their involvement in delinquency? Although a few of the theories discussed earlier offer some ideas about these various stages, it has only been in the last couple of decades that theories have been elaborated to answer these questions.

The approaches that address such questions take elaboration in a new direction by focusing on the developmental aspects of theories. Many of the theories presented so far have been static: they do not explicitly consider how bonds, strain, reinforcement, or other factors change over time as young people mature physically, socially, emotionally, and psychologically. For example, we cannot expect a 12-year-old boy to react to family turmoil the same way as an 18-year-old young man. Developmental changes determine how many factors affect delinquent behaviors. In this chapter we consider some of the ways that theories of delinquency have been transformed into *developmental theories*.

However, given that development occurs over a substantial period of time, it is not sufficient to consider only delinquency. Rather, since the *life course*[1] consists of a number of stages running from early childhood to old age, theories should also consider conditions and behaviors that exist at these various stages. Developmental theorists consider, for example, how changes that occur in the transition from adolescence to young adulthood affect the likelihood of movement from delinquent to criminal. Moreover, since most individuals end their delinquent or criminal behavior at some point in their lives, developmental theorists study the reasons for *desistance* in the various transitions that occur as people enter or move through adulthood.

We shall begin with an overview of some general issues involving developmental theories and then present two theories that have been introduced to account for changes in delinquency and crime over the life course. These theories have even been extended to explain how conditions in families affect the likelihood that children and grandchildren will become involved in delinquency. After evaluating these theories, the policy implications are discussed.

The development of developmental theories

Motivated in part by Thornberry's (1987) interactional theory (see Chapter 12), but also by research in developmental psychology and longitudinal studies that follow people for many years, theorists have described how involvement in delinquency changes across adolescence and into young adulthood.[2] Moreover, the finding that delinquent behavior is often preceded by misbehavior during childhood suggests that looking at behavior over the life course is important. Developmental theories are elaborated theories since they often take a core concept, such as social bonding, examine how it changes over time, and determine whether this affects involvement in deviant behaviors.[3]

One of the key findings that generated an interest in studying the life course is that a relatively small number of youths tend to commit a disproportionate number of delinquent offenses. In particular, the Philadelphia Birth Cohort Study (1958–1988) and the Cambridge Study in Delinquent Development (1961–present) examined offending patterns among individuals as they aged from adolescence to adulthood. They determined that fewer than 20 percent of youths committed or were arrested for more than half of the offenses (Farrington, 1995; Wolfgang et al., 1987). What seemed to be a remarkable finding has been replicated in many other studies. Theorists thus argued that there are at least two types of juvenile offenders: adolescent-limited and life-course persistent. As described by Moffitt (1993), most adolescents who engage in delinquency – the *adolescent-limited offenders* – do so primarily during their middle to late teenage years, when peer influences are most powerful and parental influences have diminished. However, *life-course persistent offenders* – a relatively small group – engage in antisocial behavior during adolescence and continue to offend into adulthood, thus being involved in the most offenses. During childhood, they tend to be aggressive, impulsive, and experience one or more personality disorders (see Chapters 3 and 4).

Subsequent research indicated that there are as many as six juvenile groups, although the most common number of groups is between three and five (e.g., Broidy et al., 2003; Petts, 2009). Here is an example of four groups of adolescents:

1   This group of adolescents does not offend at all, or offends at such a low level that they are clearly conformists.
2   A second group of adolescents begins to engage in delinquency during their late childhood or early teenage years. They are moderately involved in a few types of offending but at about age 16 or 17 become less involved in delinquency.
3   This group gets involved in delinquency at about the same age, but the youths escalate to a higher rate of offending and, although they may decrease involvement as they get older, the rate of decrease is not as rapid as the previous group.
4   Finally, there is a group that begins offending at a relatively early age and is involved in offending in early and middle adolescence (ages 11–14). Unlike the other groups, these youths' offending diminishes only slightly during late adolescence, and it continues at a relatively high level into adulthood. Many of these people do not end their offending until they are in their late twenties or thirties (Nagin and Tremblay, 2005a). This latter group consists of the chronic or life-course persistent offenders.

Some studies have found additional groups, such as those who begin to offend later in adolescence and complete their offending "careers" in their early to middle twenties. Figure 13.1 shows a typical set of five adolescent trajectories.

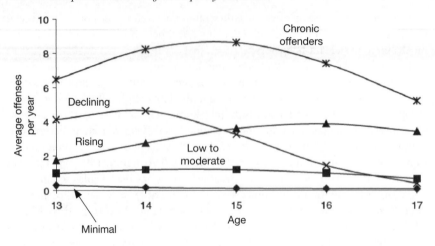

Figure 13.1 Trajectories of delinquency (adapted from Nagin and Tremblay, 2005a, p.96).

Since some youths continue to offend in adulthood, developmental theorists argue that there needs to be a much broader view of offending. A key issue question is: What happens in adulthood? Does this trajectory continue throughout life? Most research indicates that, even among chronic offenders, criminal involvement diminishes, ending by middle age. For example, Figure 13.2 shows the results of

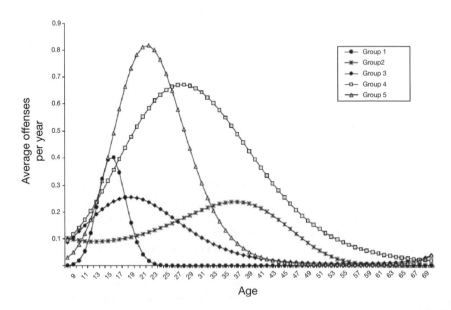

Figure 13.2 Trajectories of delinquency and crime, ages 7–70 (adapted from Laub and Sampson, 2003, p.105).

a study by Sampson and Laub (2003, 2005a) that used data initially gathered by the Gluecks (see Chapter 3). They identified five groups of offenders, one of which did not completely stop offending until they were in their forties and fifties. Thus, they desisted from crime even though they are labeled chronic (life-course persistent) offenders.

What factors predict these different offending trajectories? Using the Cambridge Study data mentioned earlier, Farrington and colleagues (2009) examined the lives of 411 men from ages 8 to 48. They found four groups of offenders, including persistent offenders who were convicted of offenses during adolescence and into adulthood. Some of the factors present during adolescence that predicted persistent offending included heavy alcohol use, hyperactivity, and harsh discipline by parents. Living in poor housing, low nonverbal IQ, high neuroticism, and anti-establishment attitudes during late childhood and adolescence predicted who would be in a group of late-onset offenders (began offending in late adolescence/early adulthood).

In addition, Moffitt (1993) suggested that life-course persistent offenders have an underlying genetic composition that affects involvement in delinquency and that this persists into adulthood. One study indicated that persistent offenders have deficits in spatial and verbal perception, memory problems, and neurocognitive impairments consistent with prefrontal cortex dysfunction (Raine et al., 2005) (see Chapter 3). A substantial proportion of these offenders may also meet the psychological criteria for severe CD and APD (see Chapter 4). All of these problems may affect behaviors during adolescence and adulthood.

From a theoretical standpoint, it is not sufficient to merely identify the existence of offending groups or independent risk factors, for this does not explain the development of delinquency and crime over the life course. Instead, theorists should develop theories of delinquent and criminal trajectories. Before discussing some theoretical models that have been used to elaborate developmental issues, however, it is helpful to review 10 key observations from research on offending over the life course. Farrington (2005b) argued that a valid developmental theory should be able to explain the following:

1   Involvement in offending tends to reach a peak between ages 15 and 19. This means that the highest proportion of adolescents within a specific age group (or *birth cohort*) is involved in some level of offending at these ages.
2   The most common ages for first initiating offending are between 8 and 14.
3   Youths who begin offending at an earlier age tend to have longer offending careers and be involved in a higher number of offenses. These are the life-course persistent offenders identified by Moffitt.
4   People who offend in childhood *and* adolescence have a higher likelihood of offending in adulthood. Although the types of offenses may change, the likelihood of offending in general remains roughly the same.
5   As mentioned earlier, a relatively small number of chronic offenders are involved in a large percentage of the delinquent and criminal acts that occur in any population of people.

6   Offenders are typically involved in several types of delinquent activities; they do not tend to specialize.

7   Delinquent and criminal acts are only part of a larger number of deviant behaviors that offenders – especially chronic offenders – are involved in. Thus, many offenders also engage in high-risk sex, heavy drug use, reckless driving, and aggressive behaviors.

8   During the adolescent years, offending tends to occur with others, whereas after age 20 more and more offenses are committed alone (see Piquero et al., 2007).

9   During adulthood, criminal activities are often used to obtain material goods or for revenge. The reasons for offending during adolescence are more diverse: to obtain goods, have fun, or relieve boredom, or out of anger.

10   The types of offenses that occur tend to accumulate up until early adulthood when specialization increases. Thus, a person might progress from petty theft to housebreaking to robbery during adolescence, but then specialize in robbery after entering adulthood.

Extending theories to explain developmental patterns of offending

There are several theories presented in earlier chapters that may be extended to account for developmental patterns of offending. After presenting some examples, we shall discuss in detail two specific development theories.

Recall that general strain theory (see Chapter 6) addresses how various negative experiences and relationships lead to anger and other emotions, which may then lead to delinquent behavior. Agnew (1997) explained stability of offending by focusing on aggressiveness. Aggressive youths tend to be treated poorly by others, interpret others' behaviors toward them as belligerent, and react with delinquent and criminal responses. This produces additional poor treatment by others, thus placing delinquency and strain in a reciprocal loop that is reinforced over time. As children enter adolescence they become more involved in misbehaviors because they enter a world where they have more social contacts and more is expected of them. This increases potential frustrations as they come across other people who may treat them negatively. They are physically stronger than when they were children, so they have more opportunities and motivation to react to negative treatment with aggressiveness and violence (Agnew, 2003). Adolescents also have more skills to escape aversive situations, such as by running away or fighting with parents. Finally, the end of offending occurs as adolescents are allowed additional freedoms when they enter adulthood. They have greater autonomy to associate with whomever they like, thus they can avoid those who treat them poorly. Moreover, the relative freedoms of adulthood allow more effective ways to cope with frustration and negative feelings than criminal behavior (Agnew, 1997; Hoffmann, 2010).

Social learning theory is perhaps best suited as a developmental theory since learning clearly takes place across the early life course, and reinforcement and behaviors affect one another over time (Akers, 1998; see Chapter 7). Brauer (2009) examined some developmental aspects of social learning theory and found that youths whose friends or parents reinforced theft or marijuana use tended to have substantially higher peak offending rates than other youths. However, *changes* in reinforcement did not predict later *changes* in theft or offending, thus suggesting that more work is needed to determine the developmental implications of social learning theory.

The *coercion–reinforcement* model discussed in Chapter 7 proposes that early parent–child interactions affect delinquency and antisocial conduct later in the child's life (Patterson and Yoerger, 1997). It is likely that the coercive interaction styles prevalent among juvenile offenders continue in adulthood and contribute to their involvement in criminal activities. In particular, Wiesner and colleagues (2007) argued that coercive interaction styles damage social relationships, whether in family or work settings, thus leading to failures to achieve adult goals (e.g., steady employment, marriage); create problems in school so that educational goals are not met; and often lead to a criminal record, thus making it more difficult to get a job. Failure to meet conventional goals reinforces the conditions that make criminal behavior attractive. Moreover, coercive interaction styles increase the likelihood that people rely on aggression or violence to solve problems. This process is not inevitable, however, since some people shift away from coercive styles, perhaps because they find a partner who helps them mature out of it or obtain therapy.

Symbolic interactionist theories of the life course have taken a different approach by focusing on the various identities that people adopt throughout their lives (see Chapter 9). For various reasons, such as informal labeling, a person could adopt a delinquent or criminal identity and actually become committed to this identity. Their agency and the social influences they experience affect which identities are adopted. Moreover, identities can change as life transitions take place, as people make choices about their lives, and as interactions with others influence how people view themselves and their interpersonal relationships (Ulmer, 2011).

An example of a developmental–symbolic interactionist model has been presented by Steffensmeier and Ulmer (2005). They argued that *commitment processes* result in persistent offending (at least during certain periods of time) as they encourage a desire for delinquent and criminal activities and as there are constraints on alternative behaviors. This process is influenced by the learning mechanisms discussed in Chapter 7 and by criminal and delinquent opportunities. Social structural conditions and social control (see Chapters 5 and 8) affect not only these opportunities, but may also limit alternatives to delinquency and crime. Steffensmeier and Ulmer introduced the term *commitment portfolio* to identify a person's personal and moral commitments to certain values and relationships. When delinquents and young criminals do not increase their conventional commitments over time (e.g., to marriage, parenting, or conventional jobs), they will typically develop a stronger criminal commitment portfolio, behave accordingly, and be classified as persistent offenders. However, it is important to remember that this process is difficult to predict since human agency allows various portfolios to be built.

Interactional theory as a developmental model of offending

As mentioned earlier, Thornberry's interactional model provided motivation for the increasing interest in developmental models. Moreover, he has extended it to consider not only delinquency, but also the transition into or away from adult crime. In fact, Thornberry (2005) argued that interactional theory can even explain intergenerational offending patterns. In terms of individual involvement in an offending career, he proposed that the interactions that lead to delinquent behavior during adolescence (see Figure 12.9) differ for adolescent-limited and life-course persistent offenders. Adolescent-limited offenders tend to experience relatively few problems in childhood. They get involved in delinquency perhaps because adolescence is a period when they are asserting their independence, which creates tension with their parents, thus decreasing attachments to parents. When this is coupled with reduced supervision during adolescence, these youths gravitate toward peer groups that reinforce behaviors such as drug use and minor forms of delinquency. Perhaps they are bored and get involved in delinquency as a form of thrill-seeking. In any event, the poor relations between these late starters and their parents do not usually persist for long. Some may continue offending, mainly because of associating with delinquent friends, but most enjoy better relations with parents as they get older. They also tend to have protective factors (e.g., low impulsivity, good school environments) that lead them away from delinquent behavior and toward prosocial lives. As their bonds to family members and schools get better in late adolescence, they exit their delinquent lives and enter conventional adult pathways.

However, life-course persistent offenders tend to experience ineffective parenting, impulsivity, and poor emotional control during childhood. Poor parenting and these psychological conditions are mutually reinforcing, thus leading to coercive interaction styles and aggressive behaviors. Ineffective parents often experience other problems, such as poverty, marginal employment, and residence in disorganized neighborhoods (Giordano, 2010). These increase the stress in the family and reinforce poor relations with their children. In many of these families various forms of abuse also occur. As they enter adolescence they become more severely involved in the interactional loops that form the basis of interactional theory. This intense involvement either multiplies or becomes stable, thus increasing delinquent behaviors. Moreover, many of these adolescents are rejected by conventional peers, so they gravitate toward delinquent peers. This reduces their ability to develop prosocial skills. These conditions have important consequences for their development. Many of these youths find themselves on a path toward "precocious adult milestones." These include having a child out of wedlock as a teenager (which is usually unplanned), failure to graduate from high school, and entering the full-time workforce early (usually in an unskilled, low-paying job). This makes it more difficult to escape the cycle described by interactional theory: Antisocial beliefs and poor attachments continue to influence involvement in offending. Continued involvement in offending reduces further the ability to create positive bonds to conventional others or develop prosocial beliefs. The end

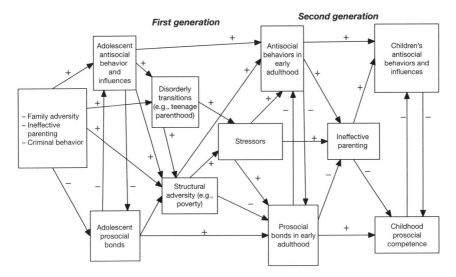

Figure 13.3 Interactional theory and intergenerational transmission of antisocial behaviors (adapted from Thornberry, 2005, p.181).

of their criminal career comes during adulthood, usually as the negative conditions that led to it in the first place end, when protective factors – such as marriage or job stability – eventually take hold, or even as treatment and intervention efforts are finally successful.[4]

An interesting aspect of Thornberry's developmental interactional theory is that it considers the intergenerational transmission of delinquency, crime, and antisocial behavior. He proposed that the same processes that lead to early offending produce poor parenting skills that then affect childrearing in the next generation. Figure 13.3 illustrates this process. Note, in particular, that adolescent prosocial bonds result in conventional life transitions and prosocial bonds in adulthood. However, antisocial behaviors and offending increase "disorderly" transitions and create structural adversities (e.g., poverty, unemployment) that then produce stressors in adulthood that lead to ineffective parenting. The next generation experiences this process all over again. This complex model demonstrates how delinquent and criminal behavior, ineffective parenting, and adversity are linked over time to influence intergenerational patterns of problem behaviors.

Research on developmental interactional theory

In a 15-year study, Thornberry (2005) demonstrated that positive parenting reduces the risk of delinquency, but delinquency predicts later negative life conditions such as poverty, homelessness, and single parenthood. Delinquency and negative life conditions predict poor parenting, which then leads to more delinquent behaviors among the next generation (see Figure 13.4).

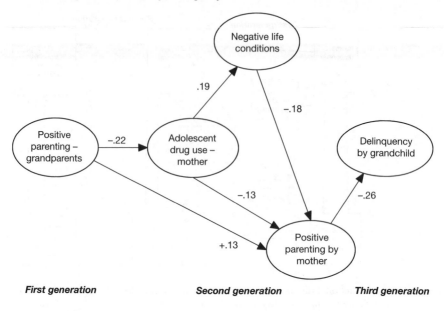

Figure 13.4 Intergenerational model of offending (adapted from Thornberry, 2005, p.187). Note: Only statistically significant pathways are shown.

An age-graded developmental theory of informal social controls and offending

Robert J. Sampson and John H. Laub (1993, 2005b) designed an age-graded developmental model of delinquency and crime that is primarily an elaboration of social bonding theory and offers a straightforward way to understand patterns of offending over the life course. Their motivation to build a theory was based on three criticisms of developmental research. First, focusing on different groups of offenders – dividing them into adolescent-limited and life-course persistent offenders or into four or five groups of adult persisters, late adolescent desisters, delayed starters, and so forth – implies that people find themselves in one group and then cannot change. Group-based models reify the categories while downplaying the realities of individual change. There is actually little solid evidence that these groups represent distinct life-course trajectories of offending; rather, they are statistical simplifications (Nagin and Tremblay, 2005b). Second, some theorists construct separate theories for these different groups or formulate different explanations for delinquency initiation, continuation, and desistance. Presumably, one could create distinct models for initiation, persistence, and desistance for each of the four or five trajectory groups! In general, there is a movement toward more specialized theories at the expense of general theories of delinquency and crime over the life course. Third, the tendency to combine concepts and mechanisms from different disciplines, such as genetics, developmental psychology, neuroscience, and sociology, has resulted in an overly complex picture of how delinquency begins and how it affects future criminal behavior.

As an alternative, Sampson and Laub (1993, 2005b) proposed a general approach that explains not only initiation of delinquency, but also continuity and desistance in adolescence and adulthood. They looked over almost the entire life span and tried to understand how delinquency emerges and why criminal behavior ends. Sampson and Laub maintained that persistence in crime from adolescence to adulthood occurs when there is a lack of social bonds, few structured activities, and individuals purposely have intentions to deviate from social norms. Desistance occurs when bonds, sufficient structured activities, and purposeful individual decision-making come together. Although there might be specific conditions that predict, say, violent or property crime in a given situation or among particular individuals, if we look across the life course these processes are generally in play.

Their theory is based on three main themes. First, social structural conditions (e.g., social class, residential instability; see Chapter 5) in childhood and adolescence influence informal family and school social controls, which then affect behaviors. As discussed in Chapter 8, social groups attempt to regulate members' behaviors by relying on formal and informal processes of control. Whereas formal mechanisms of control include state-run institutions (e.g., police, boys' homes), informal mechanisms include efforts by family members and schools to influence behaviors so they conform to the rules of society. It is these informal controls that have the most direct influence on delinquency. Second, there is a high probability, especially absent some sort of intervention or dramatic life change, that antisocial behaviors during childhood and adolescence continue into adulthood. These behaviors include not only violations of the law, but also transgressions of various norms, such as arguing, unstable interpersonal relationships, sexual promiscuity, and heavy drug and alcohol use. Third, informal social controls explain changes in adult offending regardless of risk factors that were present during childhood and adolescence. Thus, change is not only possible, but also probable. Among the majority of individuals, interventions and dramatic life changes – including initiation, continuation, and desistance of delinquent and criminal careers – are all affected primarily by informal social controls. As bonds change throughout the life course, there are consequent changes in behavior. Although theirs is a social bonding theory, Sampson and Laub rejected the arguments of Gottfredson and Hirschi that self-control and opportunities dictate delinquent and criminal behavior regardless of other social bonds.

Delinquency is caused generally by a lack of parental supervision, poor family disciplinary practices, and weak attachments between parents and children; poor attachments to schools; and delinquent friends. However, it is difficult during adolescence to separate delinquent behavior from delinquent friends since these behaviors often involve group activities. Thus, Sampson and Laub focused on family and school processes. They also rejected the argument that personality factors such as impulsivity generally place children and adolescents on a delinquent pathway. Instead, their research showed that informal social controls are more influential. Presumably even highly impulsive children can be steered toward conformity by strong informal controls in the family, at school, or in neighborhoods (see Lynam *et al.*, 2000).

Continuity of offending in early adulthood is explained by the way that delinquency can damage social bonds later in life. Delinquent behavior tends to weaken attachments to family members, evoke harsh discipline, and perhaps even diminish adult supervision. It is also associated with poor school performance and dropping out, thus reducing the controlling influence of schools. Hence, delinquent behavior, along with the structural deficiencies (e.g., poverty, family instability) that often accompany the lives of serious offenders, result in "cumulative disadvantages" that undermine later social bonds (Sampson and Laub, 1997b). Nevertheless, there is nothing inevitable about this process. Some juvenile offenders move onto a more conventional life trajectory in adulthood by developing stronger bonds to social institutions. The two major conditions that typically dictate this movement are job stability and marriage. In general, when offenders move into stable employment or a solid marriage they stop offending. Those who persist in offending, on the other hand, fail to develop relationships that furnish affectionate attachments, informal controls, or social support. Sampson and Laub referred to these people as "social nomads" who often have no permanent home, are in unstable marriages and jobs, and move in and out of jails, prisons, and mental institutions. But eventually even most of these nomads change their lives and end their "criminal careers." Figure 13.5 provides an illustration of this age-graded model of informal social control over the life course.

Sampson and Laub's theory emphasizes not only informal social controls, but an equally important factor: *human agency*. Some people actually embrace a delinquent and criminal lifestyle; many because they reject or resist the authority of others over their lives. Other people purposively discard this lifestyle, even when their informal social controls may appear weak. Many former offenders do not maintain that their behaviors resulted from systematic injustices or the way they were treated by their parents or teachers. Instead, they claim that they

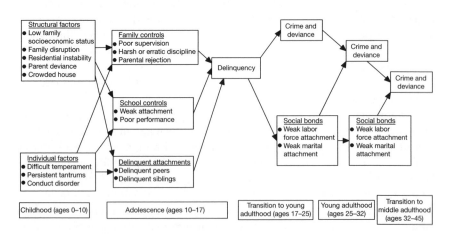

Figure 13.5 Age-graded theory of informal social control (adapted from Sampson and Laub, 1993, pp.244–245).

made conscious decisions whether or not to offend. In brief, then, changes in informal social controls and cumulative disadvantages do not completely explain delinquent and criminal careers because there is an element of purposeful human action, or agency, that dictates life choices. Notice that this is similar to a general point made by Matza in his theory of delinquency and drift (see Chapter 8).

Research on age-graded informal social control

A number of studies by Sampson and Laub, as well as others, find support for an age-graded theory of informal social control. For example, research indicates that the association between a disadvantaged family background (e.g., living in crowded homes, residential instability) or individual-level risks (e.g., poor emotional control) and delinquency is mostly mediated by poor social bonds such as low parental supervision and attachment, erratic or overly harsh parental discipline styles, and weak school attachment (e.g., Sampson and Laub, 1993, 2005a,b).

Moreover, having a good marriage, regardless of a spouse's offending behavior, is associated with subsequent reductions in offending (e.g., Maume et al., 2005; Sampson et al., 2006). This is particularly true for males, but less so for females (King et al., 2007). The reduction in offending may be caused by the informal controls that develop between spouses, the social support that is offered by a spouse, family commitments that leave little time for unstructured activities, changes in peer associations when former offenders no longer associate with friends who influence offending (Warr, 1998), or a transformation of one's identity from criminal to "family man" (Sampson et al., 2006).

Similarly, stable, quality employment is related to less offending in adulthood, although this tends to occur when offenders reach their late twenties. For those in their early twenties, employment has little effect, perhaps because it takes time for work stability to influence behavior and many low-risk people have just completed schooling before entering the workforce (Blokland and Nieuwbeerta, 2005). These various results from studies of delinquency and adult criminal behavior lend substantial support for several of the propositions that stem from Sampson and Laub's theory.

Promises and limitations of developmental theories

Developmental theories offer a way to understand not only the sources of delinquency in childhood, but also the transition from delinquency to adult criminal behavior. They also explain the consequences of delinquency for conventional life-course goals such as marriage and employment, and for problems such as divorce and poor mental and physical health in later life (Piquero et al., 2010). Moreover, these theories provide a way to understand the intergenerational transmission of delinquency and crime (Thornberry, 2005).

Although their popularity is undeniable, note that developmental theories do not satisfactorily explain all of the 10 findings about delinquency, crime, and the life course listed earlier in the chapter (Farrington, 2005b). For example, most have little to say about offense specialization or why it increases during adulthood. They also fail to explain why the reasons for offending tend to change from adolescence to adulthood.

A more general criticism has been offered by Gottfredson and Hirschi (1986), creators of self-control theory (see Chapter 8). They argued that (1) the relationship between age and delinquent/criminal behavior does not vary in virtually any environment or culture; (2) research using data collected over time has not advanced our understanding about what causes or predicts delinquency (or what factors are statistically associated with delinquency) beyond what we already knew from research based on one-time surveys; (3) and developmental theories are based on mistaken ideas about what causes what. Although there is not sufficient space to do justice to all of their criticisms, a brief overview will provide a flavor of the main points of contention.

First, most developmental theories are based on the fundamental assumption that there is variation in the relationship between age and delinquency/crime and that there are independent factors that can explain this variation. For example, some groups begin offending earlier than others, escalate to a higher level of offending, and do not stop offending for a long period of time. However, other groups – the adolescent-limited – begin later, offend less, and have substantially shorter "criminal careers." Assuming the presence of these and perhaps other groups, this implies that the age–crime relationship (which tends to look like a mountain, with the peak at about age 15 or 16) is different for various groups and, presumably, also across cultures that have, say, different levels of informal social control. Thus, we would expect a culture like Japan to have a different age–delinquency relationship from the United States because informal social controls are much stronger in Japan (Miller and Kanazawa, 2001). However, Gottfredson and Hirschi (1986) argued that there is not variation that can be tied to any factors, because the age variation exists regardless of the particular social or cultural group that one examines.

Second, if we compare the factors found to predict delinquency in one-time surveys with those found in studies that have followed people over time, they are virtually the same. For example, parental supervision, parent–child attachments, school attachment, gender, and pro-delinquent beliefs are consistent predictors of delinquency in both types of studies. Thus, we learn little from expensive life-course studies – or the developmental research that is based on these studies – that we did not know from one-time surveys of adolescents or adults. Gottfredson and Hirschi (1987) claimed that studies that collect data over time and across the life course are a waste of time and money (and theorizing!) because they tell us nothing that was not already known.

Third, developmental theories such as Sampson and Laub's or Thornberry's are based on a key misconception. Although there are some consistent predictors of offending across the life course, it is unclear whether these predictors *cause* delinquency and crime or are simply indicators of an underlying characteristic that produces both the predictors *and* delinquency or crime. Hirschi and Gottfredson (1995, 2000) asserted that self-control is the underlying characteristic that produces both. Those with weak self-control are impulsive, have a hard time delaying gratification, lack inhibitions, and do not think through the consequences of their actions. They get involved in short-sighted activities, such as delinquency, but also their lack of self-control means they are not successful in school, are not good conventional workers, and exasperate their parents. Thus, the consequences of low self-control are delinquency, crime, risky behaviors, weak attachments to parents, poor school performance, bad marriages, and failure to find suitable or long-term employment. We do not have to search for informal social controls that weaken during late childhood or early adolescence to understand initiation. Nor do we need to look at bonds that emerge in late adolescence or adulthood, such as good marriages or stable employment, to understand why offending stops. Rather, self-control, along with understanding how opportunities to offend diminish for many during adulthood (and physical skills decline), are all that is needed to understand delinquency and crime over the life course. So perhaps Billy, whom we met earlier, simply suffered from low self-control!

A number of researchers have countered that Hirschi and Gottfredson are wrong on all counts. In particular, there is evidence that the age–crime relationship differs across social groups and cultures (Greenberg, 1985); research that has collected data over time has demonstrated that delinquency affects conditions, such as attachments, beliefs, peer relationships, employment, and marriage, as much as it is affected by them (e.g., Thornberry and Krohn, 2001); and there are substantial differences in both the effects and types of informal social controls that are associated with subsequent delinquency and crime (Laub and Sampson, 2003).

Moreover, as mentioned in Chapter 8, critics of self-control theory point out that it is not a sufficient explanation of delinquent or criminal behavior. For example, one study found that the association between social bonds (such as good relations with parents), stable employment, or good romantic partnerships and less criminal behavior is strongest among those with low self-control (Wright et al., 2001). Figure 13.6 shows one of the results from this study. Hence, as Sampson and Laub (1995) argued, it appears that low self-control does not inevitably result in a criminal career when opportunities are present. Rather, strong conventional bonds can diminish involvement in delinquency and crime even among those with low self-control.

Although research has produced an impressive array of support for developmental delinquency theories, and relying on self-control theory may not quell the excitement over these explanations, there is still a need to consider what factors influence individuals to make the choices necessary to develop stronger bonds to social institutions. Moreover, what structural, interpersonal, and personal barriers exist that make access to bonding mechanisms, such as a good marriage or stable job, more difficult? Some observers argue that genetic characteristics influence self-control and bonding mechanisms (e.g., Beaver et al., 2010), thus indirectly affecting developmental trajectories. Laub and Sampson (2003), as well as symbolic interaction theorists (Ulmer, 2011), have emphasized human agency as a source of some of these choices; the conscious decisions that people make to

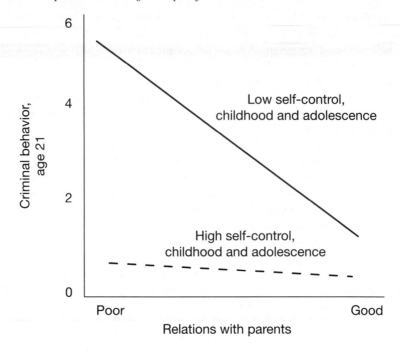

Figure 13.6 Self-control, relations with parents, and criminal behavior at age 21 (adapted from Wright et al., 2001, p.335).

change their behaviors are not explained fully by social factors, structural conditions, and opportunities. Thornberry's intergenerational theory suggests that the development of bonds necessary for a conventional life begins with parenting. When parents do not offer sufficient support and a stable environment, subsequent relational and educational goals are more difficult to achieve. This places youths at a disadvantage as they enter adulthood. Many experience negative conditions such as unemployment and single parenthood. Others are placed at a disadvantage by imprisonment, which negatively affects future employment opportunities (Western et al., 2001).

Critical theorists point out that there are broader structural forces at work, and these need to be considered by developmental theorists. Some observers argue, for instance, that, irrespective of previous socialization experiences, living in poverty or in an economically marginalized area makes conventional marriages and relationships difficult (Giordano, 2010). Moreover, what effect do macroeconomic changes have on family relations? As stable, well-paying jobs have been removed from urban areas over the last couple of decades, have there been alternative employment options for families that may be at risk because of poverty, low education, and single parenthood (Krivo and Peterson, 2004)? In addition, in a political climate that prides itself on getting "tough" on criminals, are social attitudes about former offenders so entrenched that they negatively affect programs that might provide them with jobs or educational opportunities?

Most developmental theories also do not consider whether there are differences by race, ethnicity, socioeconomic status, or other factors that are part of a stratified society. Are developmental theories sufficiently sensitive to gender-based experiences that may affect life-course outcomes? It seems unlikely that girls and boys experience the life course in the same way, or that social bonds, stressors, and socialization environments are equal for males and females (Moffitt et al., 2001; see also Chapter 11). For example, studies of incarcerated women show that child care, economic problems, and domestic violence often combine to lead some young mothers to get involved in criminal activities in order to avoid homelessness and feed their children (e.g., Moe, 2006). Since most of the responsibilities of parenting in poor communities fall on women, it is doubtful that women who are in the at-risk families described by developmental theorists have the same life-course experiences as men. As pointed out by Block and colleagues (2010), much of what we know about criminal careers, developmental trajectories, and groups of offenders is from studies of males. Few studies have addressed the life course of females, what their offending profiles may look like, or the relationship among experiences such as marriage, childrearing, employment, and criminal behavior.

Finally, what explains youths who have numerous disadvantages growing up yet end up on conventional life pathways? Are these the strained youths with the good personal and social resources (e.g., high self-efficacy, low anger) described by strain theorists (see Chapter 6)? What should we make of some youths who appear to have many of life's advantages yet end up on delinquent and criminal pathways? Perhaps agency does explain some of these cases, but attention to broader social conditions – as well as personal coping strategies, mental health, and interpersonal relationships – is also needed.

Policy implications of developmental theories

The policy options that stem from the theories described in this chapter are deceptively straightforward: If specialists can intervene to disrupt one or two of the pathways that leads to delinquency, then the risks of long-term problems can be reduced substantially. Rather than discuss all the many ways these interventions might occur, perhaps it is best to focus on an early point that all of these theories have in common: parent–child relationships. As discussed, for instance, in several previous chapters, there are several parent training programs that are effective in teaching the skills necessary to curb misbehaviors among children and adolescents (Piquero et al., 2009). These programs have sent trained nurses to the homes of pregnant women and new mothers to teach them positive parenting skills (Olds et al., 1998); provided social skills training to children in elementary school and to their parents (Tremblay et al., 2003), especially by using peer modeling and showing them how to reinforce prosocial behaviors; taught parents to supervise and discipline their children more effectively; and educated parents and adolescents to get along better, communicate more effectively, and avoid deviant peer influences (Spoth et al., 2001). It is interesting to note that, although some of the most prominent developmental theories are elaborations of social bonding theory, many of the most effective intervention programs are based on social learning principles (see, for example, Patterson et al., 2004).

In general, it appears that teaching positive parenting skills is a key way to curb the likelihood that a child or adolescent will enter one of the delinquent trajectories discussed earlier. School-based programs that teach positive skills such as conflict resolution, constructive peer relationships, and language competency are also effective in reducing delinquency and related misbehaviors, in improving later educational performance, and in reducing the risk of arrests and imprisonment in young adulthood (e.g., Reynolds et al., 2007). However, many intervention studies indicate that there is a group of incorrigible youths who do not respond well to intervention efforts. They continue to offend regardless of the characteristics or timing of programs. These youths are likely the chronic or persistent offenders who have been identified in many studies over the last 30 years. They may also be those discussed by Hirschi and Gottfredson (1995) as having especially low self-control, thus making intervention very difficult. Nevertheless, even those with low self-control can be shepherded toward more conventional behaviors when they have good relations with parents (Wright et al., 2001).

Although early intervention is the best way to prevent later delinquency and criminal behavior, research also suggests that it is rarely too late to intervene to move offenders onto a conventional life track. Offering good-quality employment opportunities is an effective method of intervention even for those with a long history of offending (Uggen and Wakefield, 2007). However, these various programs designed to get offenders on the right life-course track should also be informed by and sensitive to the realities of life; poverty, unemployment, victimization, and other problems are sometimes uncontrollable events that can return people to a life-course path toward delinquency and crime. Thus, broader structural measures that reduce these problems may also be needed to bring about the greatest reductions in delinquency and crime.

Conclusions

Developmental models are the "new wave" of delinquency theories. It is likely that these types of theories will continue to provide delinquency research with plenty of material over the next few years. The availability of data sets that have followed people for 20 or 30 years, the sophisticated statistical techniques that experts have developed, and the undeniable notion that people change and develop throughout their lives all contribute to an interest in how delinquency theories can be elaborated by looking across the life course and even across generations.

However, some principal questions that remain are whether these developmental issues are genuinely important for understanding changes in delinquency and crime, and whether trajectories of offending are meaningful and useful. To consider the second question first, even their most ardent advocates admit that delinquent trajectories are a simplifying device for considering how behaviors change over time. There is nothing deterministic and immutable about the groups, nor can we place youths neatly into one group or another. So whether they are useful is doubtful unless theory can be brought to bear to explain why they are significant and valid.

Of greater importance, though, is the question of what developmental theories can tell us about the true underlying causes of delinquency and crime across the life course. Are the presumed factors that predict changes in offending valid *causes* of delinquency and crime, or are they simply reflections of some underlying personality factor or low self-control? This is an important question because much money, time, and effort is being devoted to understanding how various conditions, such as parent–child attachments, school success, good marriages, and quality jobs, reduce involvement in delinquency and crime. However, if it is simply some personality disorder or self-control issue that causes both offending and these life-course transitions and conditions, researchers can spare themselves a lot of effort by focusing on early life-course intervention.

Notes

1 Theory and delinquency

1. An alternative explanation is that the police remove men's shirts to check for concealed weapons. This would invalidate the earlier claim, though, since the equation would now be *male + arrest = remove shirt*.
2. Actually, our theory may be more complex and allow other factors to predict delinquency.
3. They have not, however, been completely absent from these and other theories. For example, contemporary versions of strain theory address emotions such as frustration and anger (see Chapter 6). Some social control theorists include the role of agency in their models of crime and delinquency (see Chapter 13).

2 Deterrence and delinquency

1. The Supreme Court's decisions in both cases, including graphic descriptions of the crimes, can be found at *http://www.law.cornell.edu/supct*. Ewing (1992) has documented many other cases of young people who have committed homicide.
2. Since most of the research on delinquency uses the term *deterrence* rather than *rational choice* and there is such substantial overlap between these two perspectives, this chapter focuses mainly on concepts from and research on deterrence theory.
3. This pleasure might involve the money she gets for selling the drug, the excitement of being involved in a risky activity, or perhaps the objects that customers give her in exchange for the drug.
4. This is because, according to restrictive deterrence, "a person does not desist completely from offending because of risk of punishment, but instead curtails *the frequency of involvement*" (Nagin and Paternoster, 1991, p.567).
5. Chapters 3 and 4 will provide additional information about these areas of research. They are discussed briefly here because of their importance for our understanding of the role of deterrence theory among adolescents.

3 Biological theories of delinquency

1. The research on biochemicals is highly technical. The goal here is to provide a flavor of this research rather than an in-depth understanding of methods and results.
2. Consider how this research might be used to improve our understanding of deterrence among adolescents (Chapter 2).
3. Studies have also used brain scanning technology to determine physiological responses to stress.

4. This is part of the reasoning behind lie detector (polygraph) tests because lying presumably causes fluctuations in SC levels.

5 Communities and delinquency

1. Types of community explanations are often linked to social control, whereas types of people explanations are usually linked to socialization. However, there are exceptions. Shaw and McKay (1969 [1942]), for instance, focused on types of communities but then argued that characteristics of these communities impaired conventional socialization.
2. We shall learn more about collective efficacy later in the chapter.

6 The stresses and strains of adolescence

1. There is, of course, considerable variation in how people perceive the cultural message to make money. Some people may adopt it wholeheartedly, whereas others might reject it. Nevertheless, the general cultural message that wealth accumulation is a valuable goal is widespread.
2. Anger denotes much less of a persistent state of arousal than does hostility. When people get angry, the level of anger ebbs and flows depending on individual and environmental conditions. Hostility suggests a more stable trait that is more likely to be related to persistent frustration. Adolescents who are frustrated tend to develop feelings of hostility.
3. Merton (1959) identified the notion of opportunity structures as the most significant improvement to his original theory.

8 Control theories of delinquency

1. This is similar to the concept of self-efficacy (see Chapter 6).

10 Conflict and radical theories of delinquency

1. The term *critical theory* is often used as an umbrella term (or a "theory cluster"; see Agger, 1998, p.4) for these perspectives, which go by the names of constitutive, peacemaking, and anarchist (Schwartz and Friedrichs, 1994). Most critical theorists argue that (1) knowledge is constructed by researchers who are affected by their own assumptions about society and human behavior; (2) oppression needs to be recognized and opposed; and (3) domination is caused by unquestioned ideologies or allowing one group to dictate acceptable ideas and ideals (Agger, 1998). Critical theory also refers to a type of Marxist thought that sees culture as mainly a creation of the economic order. The capitalist ideology dictates what is considered culturally acceptable (Horkheimer and Adorno, 2002 [1947]).
2. These beliefs – or what the researchers called *schemas* – included statements such as "Men should make most of the important family decisions" and "It is best if a man works and the woman takes care of the family." Agreement with these statements indicates a more patriarchal schema or belief structure.
3. The term *structural Marxism* that is used in criminology is not identical to the structuralism associated with philosophers such as Althusser. Althusser's (1972) structural Marxist approach was interested more in arguing against a Marxist view that the economic base–superstructure generally dictates relationships in society. He emphasized, rather, economic, legal, educational, religious, and other "apparatuses" that must be considered in concert to determine the prevalent ideology of the state and how it influences thought and action.

4.   Although we address integrated theories in more depth in Chapter 12, one cannot avoid the notion of integration when considering radical theories.

11 Postmodern and feminist views of delinquency

1.   Films have offered some of the most amusing and tragic critiques of this modern environment, with examples such as *Fight Club* (1999) and *Wanted* (2008) showing that sterile office environments are implicated in the production of rebellious and criminal activities. These are cultural productions that stem from the recognition of how dehumanized modern society has become. The comic strip *Dilbert* has for years provided an amusing portrait of this modern workplace.

2.   The preceding chapters have included many examples of studies that have tested theories by gender. For instance, as discussed in Chapter 7, one study determined that girls are less delinquent than boys not because they have fewer delinquent peers, but mainly because girls are less likely to have pro-delinquent definitions (Mears et al., 1998). However, this leaves an important question unanswered: Why do girls report fewer of these definitions? A feminist approach would demand further investigation of this phenomenon.

3.   The term *hegemony* refers to the dominance of one social group or class over another, usually in cultural or other non-forceful ways, and with the consent of most of the people.

13 Developmental theories of delinquency and crime

1.   The life course involves a set of age-appropriate roles and social changes that occur over time and that are generally defined or sanctioned by one's culture. Researchers often use *trajectories* and *transitions* as two key terms in studying the life course. Trajectories are paths of development over one's life, such as going to school, getting married, having children, and retiring. Transitions are shifts marked by major events, such as graduating from high school or college (Sampson and Laub, 1993). In criminology, trajectories can include delinquent pathways and transitions can include beginning to commit delinquent acts.

2.   Several significant volumes on developmental theories have appeared in the last decade. These include volumes edited or authored by DeLisi and Beaver (2011), Farrington (2005a), Liberman (2008), Loeber and colleagues (2008), Piquero and colleagues (2007), and Thornberry and Krohn (2003).

3.   Although studying changes in delinquency and crime over the life course has been called *developmental criminology*, some also use the term *life-course theories* (see Farrington, 2005a). Others refer to this research as *life-course views of development* (Sampson and Laub, 2005a). This is because, whereas psychology has a long tradition of studying developmental issues, sociology has traditionally focused on the life course (Elder, 1998). Both of these traditions have also been placed under the criminal career paradigm (Piquero et al., 2003), a subcategory of criminology that studies how criminal behavior takes on the trappings of a career for some people. We shall use the term *developmental theories* in this chapter.

4.   Thornberry (2005) also described an offending pathway for late-onset delinquents ("late bloomers"). They tend to have risk factors that do not affect them until late adolescence (e.g., low intelligence, poor school performance that produces cumulative stress) or enjoy protective factors earlier in life (e.g., supportive parents) that are removed as they leave their homes or lose a parent.

References

Addad, Moshe, and Avraham Leslau. 1989. "Extraversion, Neuroticism, Immoral Judgment and Criminal Behavior." Medicine and Law 8: 611–622.

Agger, Ben. 1998. Critical Social Theories. Boulder, CO: Westview Press.

Agnew, Robert. 1985. "Social Control Theory and Delinquency: A Longitudinal Test." Criminology 23: 47–61.

Agnew, Robert. 1991. "A Longitudinal Test of Social Control Theory and Delinquency." Journal of Research in Crime and Delinquency 28: 126–156.

Agnew, Robert. 1992. "Foundations for a General Strain Theory of Crime and Delinquency." Criminology 30: 47–87.

Agnew, Robert. 1997. "Stability and Change in Crime over the Life Course: A Strain Theory Explanation." Advances in Criminological Theory 7: 101–131.

Agnew, Robert. 1999. "A General Strain Theory of Community Differences in Crime Rates." Journal of Research in Crime and Delinquency 36: 123–155.

Agnew, Robert. 2001. "Building on the Foundation of General Strain Theory: Specifying the Types of Strain Most Likely to Lead to Crime and Delinquency." Journal of Research in Crime and Delinquency 38: 319–361.

Agnew, Robert. 2003. "An Integrated Theory of the Adolescent Peak in Offending." Youth & Society 34: 263–299.

Agnew, Robert. 2006. Pressured into Crime: An Overview of General Strain Theory. New York: Oxford University Press.

Agnew, Robert. 2008. Juvenile Delinquency: Causes and Control. New York: Oxford University Press.

Agnew, Robert, and Helene Raskin White. 1992. "An Empirical Test of General Strain Theory." Criminology 30: 475–499.

Aichhorn, August. 1983 [1925]. Wayward Youth. Chicago: Northwestern University Press.

Akers, Ronald L. 1985. Deviant Behavior: A Social Learning Approach, Third Edition. Belmont, CA: Wadsworth Publishing.

Akers, Ronald L. 1991. "Self Control as a General Theory of Crime." Journal of Quantitative Criminology 7: 201–211.

Akers, Ronald L. 1998. Social Learning Theory and Social Structure: A General Theory of Crime and Deviance. Boston, MA: Northeastern University Press.

Akers, Ronald L. 2001. "Social Learning Theory." Pp.192–210 in Explaining Criminals and Crime, edited by Raymond Paternoster and Ronet Bachman. Los Angeles, CA: Roxbury Publishing.

Akers, Ronald L., and Gang Lee. 1996. "A Longitudinal Test of Social Learning Theory: Adolescent Smoking." Journal of Drug Issues 26: 317–343.

Akers, Ronald L., and Christine S. Sellers. 2008. Criminological Theories: Introduction, Evaluation, and Application, Fifth Edition. New York: Oxford University Press.

Allan, Kenneth, and Jonathan H. Turner. 2000. "A Formalization of Postmodern Theory." Sociological Perspectives 43: 363–385.

Almgren, Gunnar. 2005. "The Ecological Context of Interpersonal Violence: From Culture to Collective Efficacy." Journal of Interpersonal Violence 20: 218–224.

Althusser, Louis. 1972. "Ideology and Ideological State Apparatuses." Pp.127–187 in Lenin and Philosophy and Other Essays, edited by Louis Althusser. London: Monthly Review Press.

Amendola, A. Mark and Shana Scozzle. 2004. "Promising Strategies for Reducing Violence." Reclaiming Children and Youth 13: 51–53.

American Psychiatric Association (APA). 2000. Diagnostic and Statistical Manual of Mental Disorders, Fourth Edition, Text Revision (DSM-IV-TR®). Washington, DC: American Psychiatric Publishing, Inc.

Amnesty International USA. 2005. Stop Child Executions! Available electronically at: http://www.amnestyusa.org/abolish/juveniles/where.html.

Anderson, Craig A., Leonard Berkowitz, Edward Donnerstein, L. Rowell Huesmann, James D. Johnson, Daniel Linz, Neil M. Malamuth, and Ellen Wartella. 2003. "The Influence of Media Violence on Youth." Psychological Science in the Public Interest 4: 81–110.

Anderson, Craig A., Akiko Shibuya, Nobuku Ihori, Edward L. Swing, Brad J. Bushman, Akira Sakamoto, Hannah R. Rothstein, and Muniba Saleem. 2010. "Violent Video Game Effects on Aggression, Empathy, and Prosocial Behavior in Eastern and Western Countries: A Meta-Analytic Review." Psychological Bulletin 136: 151–173.

Anderson, Elijah. 1999. Code of the Streets: Decency, Violence, and the Moral Life of the Inner City. New York: W.W. Norton & Company.

Anderson, Elijah. 2008. "Against the Wall: Poor, Young, Black and Male." Pp. 1–27 in Against the Wall: Poor, Young, Black, and Male, edited by Elijah Anderson. Philadelphia: University of Pennsylvania Press.

Armstrong, Todd A., Shawn Keller, Travis W. Franklin, and Scott N. Macmillan. 2009. "Low Resting Heart Rate and Antisocial Behavior." Criminal Justice and Behavior 36: 1125–1140.

Arrigo, Bruce A., and Thomas J. Bernard. 1997. "Postmodern Criminology in Relation to Radical and Conflict Criminology." Critical Criminology 8: 39–59.

Arseneault, Louise, Richard E. Tremblay, Bernard Boulerice, Jean R. Séguin, and Jean-François Saucier. 2000. "Minor Physical Anomalies and Family Adversity as Risk Factors for Violent Delinquency in Adolescence." American Journal of Psychiatry 157: 917–923.

Artz, Sibylle. 1998. Sex, Power, and the Violent School Girl. New York: Teachers College Press.

Åsberg, Marie. 1994. "Monoamine Neurotransmitters in Human Aggressiveness and Violence: A Selective Review." Criminal Behaviour and Mental Health 4: 303–327.

Aseltine, Robert H., Susan Gore, and Jennifer Gordon. 2000. "Life Stress, Anger and Anxiety, and Delinquency: An Empirical Test of General Strain Theory." Journal of Health and Social Behavior 41: 256–275.

Austin, D. Mark, and Yoko Baba. 1990. "Social Determinants of Neighborhood Attachment." Sociological Spectrum 10: 59–78.

Avila, César, Isabel Cuenca, Vincente Félix, Maria-Antònia Parcet, and Ana Miranda. 2004. "Measuring Impulsivity in School-Aged Boys and Examining Its Relationship With ADHD and ODD Ratings." Journal of Abnormal Child Psychology 32: 295–304.

Baehr, Amy R. (Ed.). 2004. Varieties of Feminist Liberalism. Lanham, MD: Rowman and Littlefield.

Bahr, Stephen J., and John P. Hoffmann. 2008. "Religiosity, Peers, and Adolescent Drug Use." Journal of Drug Issues 38: 743–770.

Baier, Colin J., and Bradley R. Wright. 2001. " 'If You Love Me, Keep My Commandments': A Meta-Analysis of the Effect of Religion on Crime." Journal of Research on Crime and Delinquency 38: 3–21.

Bailey, Beth Nordstrom, Virginia Delaney-Black, Chandice Y. Covington, Joel Ager, James Janisse, John H. Hannigan, and Robert J. Sokol. 2004. "Prenatal Exposure to Binge Drinking and Cognitive and Behavioral Outcomes at Age 7 Years." American Journal of Obstetrics and Gynecology 191: 1037–1043.

Baird, Abigail A., Staci A. Gruber, Deborah A. Fein, Luis C. Maas, Ronald J. Steingard, Perry F. Renshaw, Bruce M. Cohen, and Deborah A. Yurgelun-Todd. 1999. "Functional Magnetic Resonance Imaging of Facial Affect Recognition in Children and Adolescents." Journal of the American Academy of Child and Adolescent Psychiatry 38: 195–199.

Baldwin, Scott A., and John P. Hoffmann. 2002. "The Dynamics of Self-Esteem: A Growth Curve Analysis." Journal of Youth and Adolescence 31: 101–113.

Bandura, Albert. 1986. Social Foundations of Thought and Action: A Social Cognitive Theory. Englewood Cliffs, NJ: Prentice Hall.

Bandura, Albert. 1991. "Social Cognitive Theory of Moral Thought and Action." Pp.45–103 in Handbook of Moral Behavior and Development, edited by William M. Kurtines and Jacob L. Gewirtz. Hillsdale, NJ: Lawrence Erlbaum.

Barak, Gregg. 2005. "A Reciprocal Approach to Criminology as Peacemaking: Between Adversarialism and Mutualism." Theoretical Criminology 9: 131–152.

Baron, Stephen W. 2004. "General Strain, Street Youth, and Crime: A Test of Agnew's Revised Theory." Criminology 42: 457–483.

Baron, Stephen W. 2009. "Differential Coercion, Street Youth, and Violent Crime." Criminology 47: 239–268.

Baron, Stephen W., and David R. Forde. 2007. "Street Youth Crime: A Test of Control Balance Theory." Justice Quarterly 24: 335–355.

Basham, Robert B. 1992. "Clinical Utility of the MMPI Research Scales in the Assessment of Adolescent Child Acting Out Behaviors." Psychological Assessment 4: 483–492.

Baudrillard, Jean. 1993. Symbolic Exchange and Death. Newbury Park, CA: Sage Publications.

Baumeister, Roy F., Joseph M. Boden, and Laura Smart. 1996. "Relation of Threatened Egotism to Violence and Aggression: The Dark Side of Self-Esteem." Psychological Review 103: 5–33.

Baumer, Eric P. 2007. "Untangling Research Puzzles in Merton's Multilevel Anomie Theory." Theoretical Criminology 11: 63–93.

Beasley, Chris. 1999. What is Feminism? An Introduction to Feminist Theory. Thousand Oaks, CA: Sage Publications.

Beauchaine, Theodore P., Emily Neuhaus, Sharon L. Brenner, and Lisa Gatzke-Kopp. 2008. "Ten Good Reasons to Consider Biological Processes in Prevention and Intervention Research." Development and Psychopathology 20: 745–774.

Beaver, Kevin M., and John Paul Wright. 2005. "Biosocial Development and Delinquent Involvement." Youth Violence and Juvenile Justice 3: 168–192.

Beaver, Kevin M., Christopher J. Ferguson, and Jennifer Lynn-Whaley. 2010. "The Association between Parenting and Levels of Self-Control: A Genetically Informed Analysis." Criminal Justice and Behavior 37: 1045–1065.

Beccaria, Cesare. 1985 [1764]. On Crimes and Punishment. New York: Macmillan Publishing Company.

Becker, Howard S. 1973. Outsiders: Studies in the Sociology of Deviance, Revised Edition. New York: Free Press.

Bedau, Hugo Adam. 2003. "Punishment." In Stanford Encyclopedia of Philosophy, edited by Edward N. Zalta. Available electronically at http://plato.stanford.edu/archives/sum2003/entries/punishment.

Beirne, Piers. 1988. "Heredity versus Environment: A Reconsideration of Charles Goring's The English Convict (1913)." British Journal of Criminology 28: 315–339.

Belknap, Joanne, and Kristi Holsinger. 2006. "The Gendered Nature of Risk Factors for Delinquency." Feminist Criminology 1: 48–71.

Bellair, Paul E., and Thomas L. McNulty. 2010. "Cognitive Skills, Adolescent Violence, and the Moderating Role of Neighborhood Disadvantage." Justice Quarterly 278: 538–559.

Bender, Kimberly. 2010. "Why Do Some Maltreated Youth Become Juvenile Offenders?" Children and Youth Services Review 32: 466–473.

Bennett, David S., and Theresa A. Gibbons. 2000. "Efficacy of Child Cognitive–behavioral Interventions for Antisocial Behavior: A Meta-Analysis." Child and Family Behavior Therapy 22: 1–15.

Bennett, Sarah, David P. Farrington, and L. Rowell Huesmann. 2005. "Explaining Gender Differences in Crime and Violence: The Importance of Social Cognitive Skills." Aggression and Violent Behavior 10: 263–288.

Bentham, Jeremy. 1996 [1789]. An Introduction to the Principles of Morals and Legislation. Oxford: Oxford University Press.

Bernard, Thomas J. 1983. The Consensus–Conflict Debate: Form and Content in Social Theories. New York: Columbia University Press.

Bernard, Thomas J. 1987. "Testing Structural Strain Theories." Journal of Research in Crime and Delinquency 24: 262–280.

Bernard, Thomas J. 2001. "Integrating Theories in Criminology." Pp. 335–346 in Explaining Criminals and Crime: Essays in Contemporary Criminological Theory, edited by Raymond Paternoster and Ronet Bachman. Los Angeles: Roxbury Publishing Company.

Bernburg, Jön G., and Marvin D. Krohn. 2003. "Labeling, Life Chances, and Adult Crime: The Direct and Indirect Effects of Official Intervention in Adolescence on Crime in Early Adulthood." Criminology 41: 1287–1318.

Bernburg, Jön G., Marvin D. Krohn, and Craig J. Rivera. 2006. "Official Labeling, Criminal Embeddedness, and Subsequent Delinquency: A Longitudinal Test of Labeling Theory." Journal of Research in Crime and Delinquency 43: 67–88.

Beyers, Jennifer M., Bates, John E., Pettit, Gregory S., and Dodge, Kenneth A. 2003. "Neighborhood Structure, Parenting Processes, and the Development of Youths' Externalizing Behaviors: A Multilevel Analysis." American Journal of Community Psychology 31: 35–53.

Bhana, Deevia. 2008. "'Girls Hit!' Constructing and Negotiating Violent African Femininities in a Working-Class Primary School." Discourse: Studies in the Cultural Politics of Education 29: 401–415.

Bishop, Donna M., and Charles E. Frazier. 1988. "The Influence of Race in Juvenile Justice Processing." Journal of Research in Crime and Delinquency 25: 242–263.

Bittman, Michael, Paula England, Nancy Folbre, Liana Sayer, and George Matheson. 2003. "Does Gender Trump Money? Bargaining and Time in Household Work." American Journal of Sociology 109: 186–214.

Blackwell, Brenda Sims. 2000. "Perceived Sanction Threats, Gender, and Crime: A Test and Elaboration of Power-Control Theory." Criminology 38: 439–488.

Blackwell, Brenda Sims, and Alex R. Piquero. 2004. "On the Relationship between Gender, Power Control, Self-Control, and Crime." Journal of Criminal Justice 33: 1–17.

Block, Carolyn Rebecca, Arjan A. J. Blokland, Cornelia van der Werff, Rianne van Os, and Paul Nieuwbeerta. 2010. "Long-Term Patterns of Offending in Women." Feminist Criminology 5: 73–107.

Blokland, Arjan A,J., and Paul Nieuwbeerta. 2005. "The Effects of Life Circumstances on Longitudinal Trajectories of Offending." Criminology 43: 1203–1240.

Blumer, Herbert. 1969. Symbolic Interactionism: Perspective and Method. Englewood Cliffs, NJ: Prentice-Hall.

Booker, Peter. 1999. Cultural Theory. London: Arnold.

Booth, Jeb A., Amy Farrell, and Sean P. Varano. 2008. "Social Control, Serious Delinquency, and Risky Behavior." Crime & Delinquency 54: 423–456.

Bostic, Jeff Q., David H. Rubin, Jefferson Prince, and Steven Schlozman. 2005. "Treatment of Depression in Children and Adolescents." Journal of Psychiatric Practice 11: 141–154.

Bottcher, Jean. 2001. "Social Practices of Gender: How Gender Relates to Delinquency in the Everyday Lives of High-Risk Youths." Criminology 39: 893–932.

Bourgois, Philippe. 2003. In Search of Respect: Selling Crack in El Barrio, Second Edition. New York: Cambridge University Press.

Boutwell, Brian B., and Kevin M. Beaver. 2010. "The Intergenerational Transmission of Low Self-Control." Journal of Research in Crime and Delinquency 47: 174–209.

Bowen, Gary L., and Van Dorn, Richard A. 2002. "Community Violent Crime Rates and School Danger." Children & Schools 24: 90–104.

Braga, Anthony A., David M. Kennedy, Elin J. Waring, and Anne Morrison Piehl. 2001. "Problem Oriented Policing, Deterrence, and Youth Violence: An Evaluation of Boston's Operation Ceasefire." Journal of Research in Crime and Delinquency 38: 195–225.

Brain, Paul Frederic. 1993. "Hormonal Aspects of Aggression and Violence." Pp.173–244 in Understanding and Preventing Violence, edited by Albert Reiss and Jeffrey Roth. Washington, DC: National Academy Press.

Braithwaite, John. 1989. Crime, Shame, and Reintegration. Cambridge: Cambridge University Press.

Braithwaite, John. 1997. "Charles Tittle's Control Balance and Criminological Theory." Theoretical Criminology 1: 77–97.

Braithwaite, John. 1999. "Restorative Justice: Assessing Optimistic and Pessimistic Accounts." Crime and Justice: An Annual Review of Research 25: 1–127.

Brauer, Jonathan R. 2009. "Testing Social Learning Theory Using Reinforcement's Residue: A Multilevel Analysis of Self-Reported Theft and Marijuana Use in the National Youth Survey." Criminology 47: 929–970.

Brendgen, Mara, Frank Vitaro, and William M. Bukowski. 2000. "Stability and Variability of Adolescents' Affiliation with Delinquent Friends: Predictors and Consequences." Social Development 9: 205–225.

Brennan, Patricia A., Emily R. Grekin, and Sarnoff A. Mednick. 2003. "Prenatal and Perinatal Influences on Conduct Disorder and Serious Delinquency." Pp.319–341 in Causes of Conduct Disorder and Juvenile Delinquency, edited by Benjamin B. Lahey, Terrie E. Moffitt, and Avshalom Caspi. New York: Guilford Press.

Brezina, Timothy, and Amie A. Aragones. 2004. "Devils in Disguise: The Contribution of Positive Labeling to 'Sneaky Thrills' Delinquency." Deviant Behavior 25: 513–535.

Brezina, Timothy, and Alex R. Piquero. 2007. "Exploring the Relationship between Social and Non-Social Reinforcement in the Context of Social Learning Theory." Pp.265–288 in Social Learning Theory and the Explanation of Crime, edited by Ronald L. Akers and Gary F. Jensen. New Brunswick, NJ: Transaction Publishers.

Brezina, Timothy, Alex R. Piquero, and Paul Mazerolle. 2001. "Student Anger and Aggressive Behavior in School: An Initial Test of Agnew's Macro-Level Strain Theory." Journal of Research in Crime and Delinquency 38: 362–386.

Brier, Norman. 1989. "The Relationship between Learning Disability and Delinquency: A Review and Reappraisal." Journal of Learning Disabilities 22: 546–553.

Broidy, Lisa. 2001. "A Test of General Strain Theory." Criminology 39: 9–35.

Broidy, Lisa, and Robert Agnew. 1997. "Gender and Crime: A General Strain Theory Perspective." Journal of Research in Crime and Delinquency 34: 275–306.

Broidy, Lisa M., Daniel S. Nagin, Richard E. Tremblay, John E. Bates, Bobby Brame, Kenneth A. Dodge, David Fergusson, John L. Horwood, Rolf Loeber, Robert Laird, Donald R. Lynam, Terrie E. Moffitt, Gregory S. Pettit, and Frank Vitaro. 2003. "Developmental Trajectories of Childhood Disruptive Behaviors and Adolescent Delinquency: A Six-Site, Cross-National Study." Developmental Psychology 39: 222–245.

Brook, Judith, Chenshu Zhang, and Pebbles Fagan. 2008. "Exposure to Parental Cigarette Smoking and Child Problem Behaviors: A Longitudinal Study." Journal of Child and Family Studies 17: 372–384.

Brown, Prudence, and Harold A. Richman. 1997. "Neighborhood Effects and State and Local Policy." Pp.164–181 in Neighborhood Poverty, Volume II: Policy Implications in Studying Neighborhoods, edited by Jeanne Brooks-Gunn, Greg J. Duncan, and J. Lawrence Aber. New York: Russell Sage Foundation.

Browning, Christopher R., Tama Leventhal, and Jeanne Brooks-Gunn. 2004. "Neighborhood Context and Racial Differences in Early Adolescent Sexual Activity." Demography 41: 697–720.

Browning, Katharine. 1999. Report to Congress on Juvenile Violence. Washington, DC: Office of Juvenile Justice and Delinquency Prevention, U.S. Department of Justice.

Burawoy, Michael. 2000. "Marxism after Communism." Theory and Society 29: 151–174.

Burgess, Ernest W. 1925. "The Growth of the City." Pp.142–155 in The City, edited by Robert Park, Ernest W. Burgess, and Roderick D. McKenzie. Chicago: University of Chicago Press.

Burgess, Robert L., and Ronald L. Akers. 1966. "A Differential Association–Reinforcement Theory of Criminal Behavior." Social Problems 14: 128–147.

Burke, Jeffrey D., Rolf Loeber, and Boris Birmaher. 2002. "Oppositional Defiant Disorder and Conduct Disorder: A Review of the Past 10 Years, Part II." Journal of the American Academy of Child and Adolescent Psychiatry 41: 1275–1293.

Burke, Jeffrey D., Irwin Waldman, and Benjamin B. Lahey. 2010. "Predictive Validity of Childhood Oppositional Defiant Disorder and Conduct Disorder." Journal of Abnormal Psychology 119: 739–751.

Burks, Virginia Salzer, Robert D. Laird, Kenneth A. Dodge, Gregory S. Pettit, and John E. Bates. 1999. "Knowledge Structures, Social Information Processing, and Children's Aggressive Behavior." Social Development 8: 220–236.

Bursik, Robert J. 1988. "Social Disorganization and Theories of Crime: Problems and Prospects." Criminology 26: 519–551.

Bursik, Robert J., and Harold G. Grasmick. 1993. Neighborhoods and Crime: The Dimensions of Effective Community Control. New York: Lexington Books.

Burton, Velmer S., and Francis T. Cullen. 1992. "The Empirical Status of Strain Theory." Journal of Crime and Justice 15: 1–30.

Burton, Velmer S., Francis T. Cullen, T. David Evans, and R. Gregory Dunaway. 1994. "Reconsidering Strain Theory: Operationalization, Rival Theories, and Adult Criminality." Journal of Quantitative Criminology 10: 213–239.

Butcher, James N., Susan Mineka, and Jill M. Hooley. 2004. Abnormal Psychology, Twelfth Edition. Boston, MA: Pearson Education.

Bynum, Evita G., and Ronald I. Weiner. 2002. "Self-Concept and Violent Delinquency in Urban African-American Adolescent Males." Psychological Reports 90: 477–486.

Callero, Peter L. 2003. "The Sociology of the Self." Annual Review of Sociology 29: 115–133.

Cancino, Jeffrey Michael. 2005. "The Utility of Social Capital and Collective Efficacy: Social Control Policy in Nonmetropolitan Settings." Criminal Justice Policy Review 16: 287–318.

Casey, B. J., Rebecca M. Jones, and Todd A. Hare. 2008. "The Adolescent Brain." Annals of the New York Academy of Sciences 1124: 111–126.

Caspi, Avshalom, Donald Lyman, Terrie E. Moffitt, and Phil A. Silva. 1993. "Unraveling Girls' Delinquency: Biological, Dispositional, and Contextual Contributions to Adolescent Misbehavior." Developmental Psychology 29: 19–30.

Caspi, Avshalom, Joseph McClay, Terrie E. Moffitt, Jonathan Mill, Judy Martin, Ian W. Craig, Alan Taylor, and Richie Poulton. 2002. "Role of Genotype in the Cycle of Violence in Maltreated Children." Science 297: 851–853.

Catalano, Richard F., Jisuk Park, Tracy W. Harachi, Kevin P. Haggerty, Robert D. Abbott, and J. David Hawkins. 2005. "Mediating Effects of Poverty, Gender, Individual Characteristics, and External Constraints on Antisocial Behavior: A Test of the Social Development Model and Implications for Developmental Life-Course Theory." Pp. 93–123 in Integrated Developmental and Life-Course Theories of Offending, edited by David P. Farrington. New Brunswick, NJ: Transaction Publishers.

Cernkovich, Stephen A., and Peggy C. Giordano. 1987. "Family Relationships and Delinquency." Criminology 25: 295–321.

Chamberlain, Patricia. 2003. Treating Chronic Juvenile Offenders: Advances Made through the Oregon Multidimensional Treatment Foster Care Model. Washington, DC: American Psychological Association.

Chapelle, Constance L. 2005. "Self-Control, Peer Relations, and Delinquency." Justice Quarterly 22: 89–106.

Chen, Aimin, Bo Cai, Kim N. Dietrich, Jerilynn Radcliffe, and Walter J. Rogan. 2007. "Lead Exposure, IQ, and Behavior in Urban 5–7 Year Olds: Does Lead Affect Behavior Only by Lowering IQ?" Pediatrics 119: e650–e658.

Chesney-Lind, Meda. 2006. "Patriarchy, Crime, and Justice: Feminist Criminology in an Era of Backlash." Feminist Criminology 1: 6–26.

Chesney-Lind, Meda, and Michele Eliason. 2006. "From Invisible to Incorrigible: The Demonization of Marginalized Women and Girls." Crime, Media, and Culture 2: 29–47.

Cleckley, Hervey. 1982. The Mask of Sanity. New York: New American Library.

Cloward, Richard A., and Lloyd E. Ohlin. 1960. Delinquency and Opportunity: A Theory of Delinquent Gangs. New York: Free Press.

Coccaro, Emil F. 1992. "Impulsive Aggression and Central Serotonergic System Function in Humans: An Example of a Dimensional Brain–Behavior Relationship." International Clinical Psychopharmacology 7: 3–12.

Cohen, Albert K. 1955. Delinquent Boys: The Culture of the Gang. Glencoe, IL: Free Press.

Colder, Craig R., and Eric Stice. 1998. "A Longitudinal Study of the Interactive Effects of Impulsivity and Anger on Adolescent Problem Behavior." Journal of Youth and Adolescence 27: 255–274.

Collins, Randall. 1990. "Conflict Theory and the Advance of Macro-Historical Sociology." Pp.68–87 in Frontiers of Social Theory, edited by George Ritzer. New York: Columbia University Press.

Colvin, Mark, and John Pauly. 1983. "A Critique of Criminology: Toward an Integrated Structural–Marxist Theory of Delinquency Production." American Journal of Sociology 89: 513–551.

Comte, August. 2007 [1848]. A General View of Positivism. London: Kessinger Publishing.

Connell, R. W. 1995. Masculinities. Berkeley: University of California Press.

Conway, Kevin P., and Joan McCord. 2002. "A Longitudinal Examination of the Relation between Co-Offending with Violent Accomplices and Violent Crime." Aggressive Behavior 28: 97–108.

Cooley, Charles Horton. 1902. Human Nature and the Social Order. New York: Charles Scribner's Sons.

Copes, Heith, and Andy Hochstetler. 2003. "Situational Construction of Masculinity among Male Street Thieves." Journal of Contemporary Ethnography 32: 279–304.

Cordella, J. Peter. 1991. "Reconciliation and the Mutualist Model of Community." Pp.30–46 in Criminology as Peacemaking, edited by Harold E. Pepinsky and Richard Quinney. Bloomington, IN: Indiana University Press.

Corman, Hope, and Naci Mocan. 2002. "Carrots, Sticks and Broken Windows." National Bureau of Economic Research (NBER) Working Paper 9061. Cambridge, MA: NBER.

Cornwall, Anne, and Harry N. Bawden. 1992. "Reading Disabilities and Aggression: A Critical Review." Journal of Learning Disabilities 25: 281–288.

Costello, Barbara J., and Paul R. Vowell. 1999. "Testing Control Theory and Differential Association: A Reanalysis of the Richmond Youth Data Project." Criminology 37: 815–842.

Covington, Jeanette, and Ralph B. Taylor. 1989. "Gentrification and Crime: Robbery and Larceny Changes in Appreciating Baltimore Neighborhoods during the 1970s." Urban Affairs Quarterly 25: 142–172.

Cressey, Donald. 1960. "Epidemiology and Individual Conduct: A Case Study from Criminology." Pacific Sociological Review 3: 47–58.

Crocker, Jennifer, and Brenda Major. 1989. "Social Stigma and Self-Esteem: The Self-Protective Properties of Stigma." Psychological Review 96: 608–630.

Cullen, Francis T. 1988. "Were Cloward and Ohlin Strain Theorists? Delinquency and Opportunity Revisited." Journal of Research in Crime and Delinquency 25: 214–241.

Cullen, Francis T., and John Paul Wright. 1997. "Liberating the Anomie-Strain Paradigm: Implications from Social-Support Theory." Pp.187–206 in The Future of Anomie Theory, edited by Nikos Passas and Robert Agnew. Boston, MA: Northeastern University Press.

Cullen, Francis T., John Paul Wright, Paul Gendreau, and D. A. Andrews. 2007. "What Correctional Treatment Can Tell Us about Criminological Theory: Implications for Social Learning Theory." Pp.339–362 in Social Learning Theory and the Explanation of Crime, edited by Ronald L. Akers and Gary F. Jensen. New Brunswick, NJ: Transaction Publishers.

Daigle, Leah E., Francis T. Cullen, and John Paul Wright. 2007. "Gender Differences in the Predictors of Juvenile Delinquency: Assessing the Generality–Specificity Debate." Youth Violence and Juvenile Justice 5: 254–286.

Daly, Kathleen. 1998. "Gender, Crime, and Criminology." Pp.85–108 in The Handbook of Crime and Punishment, edited by Michael Tonry. New York: Oxford University Press.

Daly, Kathleen. 2002. "Different Ways of Conceptualizing Sex/Gender in Feminist Theory and Their Implications for Criminology." Pp.277–284 in Criminological Theories: Bridging the Past to the Future, edited by Suzette Cote. Thousand Oaks, CA: Sage Publications.

Darwin, Charles. 1871. The Descent of Man. London: John Murray.

Dawson, George E. 1896. "A Study of Youthful Degeneracy." Pedagogical Seminary 4: 221–258.

Delanty, Gerard. 1997. Social Science: Beyond Constructivism and Realism. St. Paul: University of Minnesota Press.

DeLisi, Matt. 2009. "Psychopathy is the Unified Theory of Crime." Youth Violence and Juvenile Justice 7: 256–273.

DeLisi, Matt, and Kevin M. Beaver (Eds.). 2011. Criminological Theory: A Life-Course Approach. Boston: Jones and Bartlett Publishers.

Denno, Deborah W. 1990. Biology and Violence: From Birth to Adulthood. New York: Cambridge University Press.

Derrida, Jacques. 1976 [1967]. Of Grammatology. Baltimore, MD: Johns Hopkins University Press.

Desrichard, Olivier, and Virginie Denarié. 2005. "Sensation Seeking and Negative Affectivity as Predictors of Risky Behaviors: A Distinction between Occasional versus Frequent Risk-Taking." Addictive Behaviors 30: 1449–1453.

DiClemente, Ralph J., Gina M. Wingood, Richard Crosby, Catlainn Sionean, Brenda K. Cobb, Kathy Harrington, Susan Davies, Edward W. Hook, and M. Kim Oh. 2001. "Parental Monitoring: Association with Adolescents' Risk Behaviors." Pediatrics 107: 1363–1368.

Dietrich, Kim N., M. Douglas Ris, Paul A. Succop, Omer G. Berger, and Robert L. Bornschein. 2001. "Early Exposure to Lead and Juvenile Delinquency." Neurotoxicology and Teratology 23: 511–518.

DiLalla, Lisabeth Fisher. 2002. "Behavioral Genetics of Aggression in Children: Review and Future Directions." Developmental Review 22: 593–622.

Dishion, Thomas J., J. Mark Eddy, Eric Haas, Fuzhong Li, and Kathleen Spracklen. 1997. "Friendships and Violent Behavior during Adolescence." Social Development 6: 207–223.

Dishion, Thomas J., Marie-Helene Veronneau, and Michael W. Myers. 2010. "Cascading Peer Dynamics Underlying the Progression from Problem Behavior to Violence in Early to Late Adolescence." Development and Psychopathology 22: 603–614.

Dixon, David J. 1986. "On the Criminal Mind: An Imaginary Lecture by Sigmund Freud." International Journal of Offender Therapy and Comparative Criminology 30: 101–109.

Dodge, Kenneth A. 1991. "Emotion and Social Information Processing." Pp.159–181 in The Development of Emotion Regulation and Dysregulation, edited by Judy Garber and Kenneth A. Dodge. New York: Cambridge University Press.

Dodge, Kenneth A. 2003. "Do Social Information Processing Patterns Mediate Aggressive Behavior?" Pp.254–274 in Causes of Conduct Disorder and Juvenile Delinquency, edited by Benjamin B. Lahey, Terrie E. Moffitt, and Avshalom Caspi. New York: Guilford Press.

Dodge, Kenneth A. 2006. "Hostile Attribution Styles and the Development of Aggressive Behavior Problems." Development and Psychopathology 18: 791–814.

Dodge, Kenneth A., and David L. Rabiner. 2004. "Returning to Roots: On Social Information Processing and Moral Development." Child Development 75: 1003–1008.

D'Onofrio, Brian M., Amber L. Singh, Anastasia Iliadou, Mats Lambe, Christina M. Hultman, Martin Grann, Jenae M. Neiderhiser, Niklas Långström, and Paul Lichtenstein. 2010. "Familial Confounding of the Association between Maternal Smoking during Pregnancy and Offspring Criminality." Archives of General Psychiatry 67: 529–538.

Douglas, Heather E. 2009. "Reintroducing Prediction to Explanation." Philosophy of Science 76: 444–463.

Downey, Geraldine, Amy Lebolt, Claudia Rincon, and Antonio L. Freitas. 1998. "Rejection Sensitivity and Children's Interpersonal Difficulties." Child Development 69: 1074–1091.

Dunivant, Noel. 1982. The Relationship between Learning Disabilities and Juvenile Delinquency. Williamsburg, VA: National Center for State Courts.

Dunlop, Sally M., and Daniel Romer. 2010. "Adolescent and Young Adult Crash Risk: Sensation Seeking, Substance Use Propensity and Substance Use Behaviors." Journal of Adolescent Health 46: 90–92.

Durkheim, Émile. 2006 [1897]. On Suicide. Translated by Robin Buss. London: Penguin Books.

Elder, Glen H. 1998. "The Life Course as Developmental Theory." Child Development 69: 1–12.

Elliott, Delbert S., and Harwin L. Voss. 1974. Delinquency and Dropout. Lexington, MA: D.C. Heath and Company.

Elliott, Delbert, David Huizinga, and Susan S. Ageton. 1985. Explaining Delinquency and Drug Use. Beverly Hills, CA: Sage Publications.

Elliott, Delbert S., William Julius Wilson, David Huizinga, Robert J. Sampson, Amanda Elliott, and Bruce Rankin. 1996. "The Effects of Neighborhood Disadvantage on Adolescent Development." Journal of Research in Crime and Delinquency 33: 389–426.

Ellis, Lee. 1982. "Genetics and Criminal Behavior: Evidence through the End of the 1970s." Criminology 20: 43–66.

Ellis, Lee. 1992. "Monoamine Oxidase and Criminality: Identifying an Apparent Biological Marker for Antisocial Behavior." Journal of Research in Crime and Delinquency 28: 227–251.

Ellis, Lee. 2005. "A Theory Explaining Biological Correlates of Criminality." European Journal of Criminology 2: 287–315.

Elrod, Preston. 2009. "The Potential for Fundamental Change in Juvenile Justice: Implementing an Alternative Approach to Problem Youth." Pp.133–151 in Cutting the Edge: Current Perspectives in Critical/Radical Criminology and Criminal Justice, edited by Jeffrey Ian Ross. New Brunswick, NJ: Transaction Publishers.

Elster, Jon. 2007. Explaining Behavior: More Nuts and Bolts for the Social Sciences. New York: Cambridge University Press.

Emler, Nicholas, and Stephen Reicher. 2005. "Delinquency: Cause or Consequence of Social Exclusion?" Pp.211–241 in The Social Psychology of Inclusion and Exclusion, edited by Dominic Abrams, Michael A. Hogg, and José M. Marques. New York: Psychology Press.

Ennett, Susan T., Karl E. Bauman, Andrea Hussong, Robert Faris, Vangie A. Foshee, Li Cai, and Robert H. DuRant. 2006. "The Peer Context of Adolescent Substance Use: Findings from Social Network Analysis." Journal of Research on Adolescence 16: 159–186.

Erdley, Cynthia A., and Steven R. Asher. 1998. "Linkage between Children's Beliefs about the Legitimacy of Aggression and Their Behavior." Social Development 7: 321–339.

Evans, J., B. Reeves, H. Platt, A. Leibenau, D. Goldman, K. Jefferson, and D. Nutt. 2000. "Impulsiveness, Serotonin Genes and Repetition of Deliberate Self-Harm (DSH)." Psychological Medicine 30: 1327–1334.

Ewing, Charles Patrick. 1992. Kids Who Kill. New York: Avon.

Eysenck, Hans J. 1960. "Symposium: The Development of Moral Values in Children. The Contribution of Learning Theory." British Journal of Educational Psychology 30: 11–21.

Eysenck, Hans J. 1964. Crime and Personality. London: Routledge & Kegan Paul.

Eysenck, Hans J. 1970. Crime and Personality, Second Edition. London: Paladin Press.

Eysenck, Hans J. 1996. "Personality and Crime: Where Do We Stand?" Psychology, Crime and Law 2: 143–152.

Fagan, Jeffrey. 1996. "The Comparative Advantage of Juvenile versus Criminal Court Sanctions on Recidivism among Adolescent Felony Offenders." Law and Policy 18: 77–113.

Fang, Carolyn Y., Brian L. Egleston, Kathleen M. Brown, John V. Lavigne, Victor J. Stevens, Bruce A. Barton, Donald W. Chandler, and Joanne F. Dorgan. 2009. "Family Cohesion Moderates the Relation Between Free Testosterone and Delinquent Behaviors in Adolescent Boys and Girls." Journal of Adolescent Health 44: 590–597.

Farnworth, Margaret, and Michael Leiber. 1989. "Strain Theory Revisited: Economic Goals, Educational Means, and Delinquency." American Sociological Review 54: 263–274.

Farrington, David P. 1995. "The Development of Offending and Antisocial Behaviour from Childhood: Key Findings from the Cambridge Study in Delinquency Development." Journal of Child Psychology and Psychiatry 360: 929–964.

Farrington, David P. (Ed.). 2005a. Integrated Developmental and Life-Course Theories of Offending. New Brunswick, NJ: Transaction Publishers.

Farrington, David P. 2005b. "Introduction to Integrated Developmental and Life-Course Theories of Offending." Pp.1–13 in Integrated Developmental and Life-Course Theories of Offending, edited by David P. Farrington. New Brunswick, NJ: Transaction Publishers.

Farrington, David P., and Brandon C. Welsh. 2003. "Family-Based Prevention of Offending: A Meta-Analysis." Australian and New Zealand Journal of Criminal Justice 36: 127–151.

Farrington, David P., Maria M. Ttofi, and Jeremy W. Coid. 2009. "Development of Adolescence-Limited, Late-Onset, and Persistent Offenders from Age 8 to Age 48." Aggressive Behavior 35: 150–163.

Featherstone, Richard, and Mathieu Deflem. 2003. "Anomie and Strain: Context and Consequences of Merton's Two Theories." Sociological Inquiry 73: 471–489.

Felson, Richard B. 1992. "Kick 'Em When They're Down: Explanations of the Relationship between Stress and Interpersonal Aggression and Violence." Sociological Quarterly 33: 1–16.

Felson, Richard B., and Dana L. Haynie. 2002. "Pubertal Development, Social Factors, and Delinquency among Adolescent Boys." Criminology 40: 967–988.

Feng, Shuliang. 2001. "Crime and Crime Control in a Changing China." Pp. 123–131 in Crime and Social Control in a Changing China, edited by Jianhong Liu, Lening Zhang, and Stephen F. Messner. New York: Greenwood Press.

Ferguson, Christopher J., and John Kilburn. 2010. "Much Ado about Nothing: The Misestimation and Overinterpretation of Violent Video Games in Eastern and Western Nations: Comment on Anderson et al. (2010)." Psychological Bulletin 136: 174–178.

Ferrell, Jeff. 1997. "Youth, Crime, and Cultural Space." Social Justice 24: 21–38.

Ferrell, Jeff. 1998. "Freight Train Graffiti: Subculture, Crime, and Dislocation." Justice Quarterly 15: 587–608.

Ferrell, Jeff. 2004. "Boredom, Crime, and Criminology." Theoretical Criminology 8: 287–302.

Ferrell, Jeff. 2007. "Cultural Criminology." In Blackwell Encyclopedia of Sociology, edited by George Ritzer. New York: Blackwell Publishing.

Fight Club. 1999. Directed by David Fincher. Los Angeles, CA: Fox Pictures.

Finckenauer, James O. 1982. Scared Straight and the Panacea Phenomenon. Englewood Cliffs, NJ: Prentice Hall.

Finckenauer, James O., and P. W. Gavin. 1999. Scared Straight: The Panacea Phenomenon Revisited. Prospect Heights, IL: Waveland Press.

Fine, Gary Alan. 1990. "Symbolic Interactionism in the Post-Blumerian Age." Pp.117–157 in Frontiers of Social Theory, edited by George Ritzer. New York: Columbia University Press.

Fink, Arthur E. 1938. Causes of Crime: Biological Theories in the United States, 1800–1915. Philadelphia: University of Pennsylvania Press.

Finnegan, William. 1990. "Out There . . ." (Parts I and II). The New Yorker, September 10: 51–86 & September 17: 60–90.

First, Michael B., Allen Frances, and Harold Alan Pincus. 2004. DSM-IV-TR® Guidebook. Washington, DC: American Psychiatric Publishing, Inc.

Fishbein, Diana. 2001. Biobehavioral Perspectives in Criminology. Stamford, CT: Wadsworth/Thomson Learning.

Flavin, Jeanne. 2001. "Feminism in Mainstream Criminology: An Invitation." Journal of Criminal Justice 29: 271–285.

Flax, Jane. 1987. "Postmodernism and Gender Relations in Feminist Theory." Signs 12: 621–643.

Forgatch, Marion S., Gerald R. Patterson, David S. Degarmo, and Zintars G. Beldavs. 2009. "Testing the Oregon Delinquency Model with 9-Year Follow-Up of the Oregon Divorce Study." Development and Psychopathology 21: 637–660.

Foster, Hal (Ed.). 1985. Postmodern Culture. London: Pluto Press.

Foucault, Michel. 2006 [1961]. History of Madness. London: Routledge.

Freedman, Jonathan L. 2002. Media Violence and Its Effect on Aggression: Assessing the Scientific Evidence. Toronto: University of Toronto Press.

Freud, Sigmund. 1989a [1923]. The Ego and the Id. Translated by Joan Riviere. New York: W.W. Norton & Company.

Freud, Sigmund. 1989b [1912]. Totem and Taboo: Some Points of Agreement Between the Mental Lives of Savages and Neurotics. Translated by James Strachey. New York: W.W. Norton & Company.

Fritsche, Immo. 2005. "Predicting Deviant Behavior by Neutralization: Myths and Findings." Deviant Behavior 26: 483–510.

Furstenberg, Frank F., Thomas D. Cook, Jacquelynne Eccles, Glen H. Elder, and Arnold Sameroff. 1999. Managing to Make It: Urban Families and Adolescent Success. Chicago: University of Chicago Press.

Gau, Jacinta M., and Travis C. Pratt. 2008. "Broken Windows or Window Dressing? Citizens' (In)ability to Tell the Difference between Disorder and Crime." Criminology and Public Policy 7: 163–194.

Gaylord, Mark S., and John F. Galliher. 1988. The Criminology of Edwin Sutherland. New Brunswick, NJ: Transaction Publishers.

Ge, Xiaojia, Rand D. Conger, Remi J. Cardoret, Janae M. Neiderhiser, William Yates, Edward Troughton, and Mark A. Stewart. 1996. "The Developmental Interface between Nature and Nurture: A Mutual Influence Model of Child Antisocial Behavior and Parent Behaviors." Developmental Psychology 32: 574–589.

Gecas, Viktor. 1982. "The Self-Concept." Annual Review of Sociology 8: 1–33.

Genet, Jean. 1964 [1949]. The Thief's Journal. New York: Grove Press.

Giammanco, Marco, Garden Tabacchi, Santo Giammanco, Danila De Majo, and Maurizio La Guardia. 2005. "Testosterone and Aggressiveness." Medical Science Monitor 11: 136–145.

Gibbs, Carole, and Jennifer L. Melvin. 2008. "Structural Disadvantage and the Concentration of Environmental Hazards in School Areas: A Research Note." Crime, Law, and Social Change 49: 315–328.

Gibbs, Jack P. 1972. Sociological Theory Construction. Hinsdale, IL: The Dryden Press.

Gibbs, Jack P. 1975. Crime, Punishment and Deterrence. New York: Elsevier Science Ltd.

Gibson, Chris L., Alex R. Piquero, and Stephen G. Tibbetts. 2001. "The Contribution of Family Adversity and Verbal IQ to Criminal Behavior." International Journal of Offender Therapy and Comparative Criminology 45: 574–592.

Gibson, Chris L., Traci B. Poles, and Ronald L. Akers. 2011. "A Partial Test of Social Structure Social Learning: Neighborhood Disadvantage, Differential Association with Delinquent Peers, and Delinquency." Pp.133–148 in Criminological Theory: A Life-Course Approach, edited by Matt DeLisi and Kevin M. Beaver. Boston: Jones and Bartlett Publishers.

Gibson, Chris L., Christopher J. Sullivan, Shayne Jones, and Alex R. Piquero. 2010. "Does It Take a Village: Assessing Neighborhood Influences on Children's Self-Control." Journal of Research in Crime and Delinquency 47: 31–62.

Gibson, Mary. 2002. Born to Crime: Cesare Lombroso and the Origins of Biological Criminology. Westport, CT: Praeger Publishers.

Giedd, Jay N. 2008. "The Teen Brain: Insights from Neuroimaging." Journal of Adolescent Health 42: 335–343.

Gilligan, Carol. 1982. In a Different Voice: Psychological Theory and Women's Development. Cambridge, MA: Harvard University Press.

Giordano, Peggy C. 2010. Legacies of Crime: A Follow-Up of the Children of Highly Delinquent Girls and Boys. New York: Cambridge University Press.

Glueck, Sheldon, and Eleanor Glueck. 1950. Unraveling Juvenile Delinquency. New York: Commonwealth Fund.

Glueck, Sheldon, and Eleanor Glueck. 1956. Physique and Delinquency. New York: Harper.

Goddard, Henry Herbert. 1914. Feeble-Mindedness: Its Causes and Consequences. New York: The Macmillan Company.

Golub, Mari S., Gwen W. Collman, Paul M.D. Foster, Carole A. Kimmel, Ewa Rajpert-De Meyts, Edward O. Reiter, Richard M. Sharpe, Niels E. Skakkebaek, and Jorma

Toppari. 2008. "Public Health Implications of Altered Puberty Timing." Pediatrics 121: S218–230.

Gongaware, Timothy B., and Daniel Dotter. 2005. "Developing the Criminal Self: Mead's Social Psychology and Sutherland's Differential Association." Sociological Spectrum 25: 379–402.

Goring, Charles. 1913. The English Convict: A Statistical Study. London: His Majesty's Stationery Office.

Gottfredson, Denise C. 2001. Schools and Delinquency. New York: Cambridge University Press.

Gottfredson, Denise C., Stephanie A. Gerstenblith, David A. Soule, Shannon C. Womer, and Shaoli Lu. 2004. "Do after School Programs Prevent Delinquency?" Prevention Science 5: 253–266.

Gottfredson, Gary D., Denice C. Gottfredson, Allison Ann Payne, and Nisha C. Gottfredson. 2005. "School Climate Predictors of School Disorder: Results from a National Study of Delinquency Prevention in Schools." Journal of Research in Crime and Delinquency 42: 412–444.

Gottfredson, Michael R., and Travis Hirschi. 1986. "The True Value of Lambda Would Appear to be Zero: An Essay on Career Criminals, Criminal Careers, Selective Incapacitation, Cohort Studies, and Related Topics." Criminology 24: 312–234.

Gottfredson, Michael R., and Travis Hirschi. 1987. "Methodological Adequacy of Longitudinal Research on Crime." Criminology 25: 581–614.

Gottfredson, Michael R., and Travis Hirschi. 1990. A General Theory of Crime. Stanford, CA: Stanford University Press.

Gottfredson, Michael R., and Travis Hirschi. 2003. "Self-Control and Opportunity." Pp.5–19 in Control Theories of Crime and Delinquency, edited by Chester L. Britt and Michael R. Gottfredson. New Brunswick, NJ: Transaction Publishers.

Gourion, David, Céline Goldberger, Marie-Chantal Bourdel, Frank Jean Bayle, Henri Lôo, and Marie-Odile Krebs. 2004. "Minor Physical Anomalies in Patients with Schizophrenia and Their Parents: Prevalence and Pattern of Craniofacial Abnormalities." Psychiatry Research 125: 21–28.

Grasmick, Harold G., Charles R. Tittle, Robert J. Bursik, and Bruce J. Arneklev. 1993. "Testing the Core Empirical Implications of Gottfredson and Hirschi's General Theory of Crime." Journal of Research on Crime and Delinquency 30: 5–29.

Greenberg, David F. 1976. "On One-Dimensional Marxist Criminology." Theory and Society 3: 611–621.

Greenberg, David F. 1985. "Age, Crime, and Social Explanation." American Journal of Sociology 91: 1–21.

Greenberg, David F. 1999. "The Weak Strength of Social Control Theory." Crime and Delinquency 45: 66–81.

Greenberg, David F., Robin Tamarelli, and Margaret S. Kelley. 2002. "The Generality of the Self-Control Theory of Crime." Pp.49–94 in Crime and Social Organization, edited by Elin Waring and David Weisburd. New Brunswick, NJ: Transaction Publishers.

Greenwood, Peter W. 2006. Changing Lives: Delinquency Prevention as Crime-Control Policy. Chicago: University of Chicago Press.

Greenwood, Peter W. 2008. "Prevention and Intervention Programs for Juvenile Offenders." Future of Children 18: 185–210.

Griffiths, Elizabeth, and George Tita. 2009. "Homicide in and around Public Housing: Is Public Housing a Hotbed, a Magnet, or a Generator of Violence for the Surrounding Community?" Social Problems 56: 474–493.

Gudjonsson, Gisli H. 1997. "Crime and Personality." Pp.142–164 in The Scientific Study of Human Nature: Tribute to Hans J. Eysenck at Eighty, edited by Helmuth Nyborg. New York: Pergamon.

Gudjonsson, Gisli H., and Jon Fridrik Sigurdsson. 2004. "Motivation for Offenders and Personality." Legal and Criminological Psychology 9: 69–81.

Guerra, Vito S., Steven R. Asher, and Melissa E. DeRosier. 2004. "Effect of Children's Perceived Rejection on Physical Aggression." Journal of Abnormal Child Psychology 32: 551–563.

Guo, Guang, Michael E. Roettger, and Tianji Cai. 2008. "The Integration of Genetic Propensities into Social-Control Models of Delinquency and Violence among Male Youths." American Sociological Review 73: 543–568.

Hagan, John. 1989. Structural Criminology. New Brunswick, NJ: Rutgers University Press.

Hagan, John, and Albert Palloni. 1990. "The Social Reproduction of a Criminal Class in Working-Class London, circa 1950–1980." American Journal of Sociology 96: 265–299.

Hagan, John, A. R. Gillis, and John Simpson. 1990. "Clarifying and Extending Power-Control Theory." American Journal of Sociology 95: 1024–1037.

Hagan, John, Bill McCarthy, and Holly Foster. 2002. "A Gendered Theory of Delinquency and Despair in the Life Course." Acta Sociologica 45: 37–46.

Hagedorn, John M. 1988. People and Folks. Chicago: Lakeview Press.

Harcourt, Bernard. 2001. Illusions of Order: The False Promise of Broken Windows. Cambridge, MA: Harvard University Press.

Harding, Sandra. 1986. The Science Question in Feminism. Ithaca, NY: Cornell University.

Harding, Sandra. 2006. Science and Social Inequality: Feminist and Postcolonial Issues. Chicago: University of Illinois Press.

Hartl, Emil M., Edward P. Monnelly, and Roland D. Elderkin. 1982. Physique and Delinquent Behavior: A Thirty-Year Follow-Up of William H. Sheldon's Varieties of Delinquent Youth. New York: Academic Press.

Hathaway, Starke R., and Elio D. Monachesi. 1963. Adolescent Personality and Behavior: MMPI Patterns of Normal, Delinquent, Dropout, and Other Outcomes. Minneapolis, MN: University of Minnesota Press.

Hawkins, J. David, and Joseph G. Weis. 1985. "The Social Development Model: An Integrated Approach to Delinquency Prevention." Journal of Primary Prevention 6: 73–97.

Hawkins, J. David, Rick Kosterman, Richard F. Catalano, Karl G. Hill, and Robert D. Abbott. 2008. "Effects of Social Development Intervention in Childhood 15 Years Later." Archives of Pediatrics and Adolescent Medicine 162: 1133–1141.

Hawkins, J. David, Brian H. Smith, Karl G. Hill, Rick Kosterman, Richard F. Catalano, and Robert D. Abbott. 2003. "Understanding and Preventing Crime and Violence: Findings from the Seattle Social Development Project." Pp. 255–312 in Taking Stock of Delinquency: An Overview of Findings from Contemporary Longitudinal Studies, edited by Terence P. Thornberry and Marvin D. Krohn. New York: Springer.

Hawthorne, Nathaniel. 1851. The Scarlet Letter. London: David Bogue.

Hay, Carter. 2001. "Parenting, Self-Control, and Delinquency: A Test of Self-Control Theory." Criminology 39: 707–736.

Hay, Carter, and William Forrest. 2008. "Self-Control and the Concept of Opportunity: The Case for a More Systematic Union." Criminology 46: 1039–1072.

Haynie, Dana L. 2002. "Friendship Networks and Delinquency: The Relative Nature of Peer Delinquency." Journal of Quantitative Criminology 18: 99–134.

Haynie, Dana L., Peggy C. Giordano, Wendy D. Manning, and Monica A. Longmore. 2005. "Adolescent Romantic Relationships and Delinquency Involvement." Criminology 43: 177–210.

Hayslett-McCall, Karen L., and Thomas J. Bernard. 2002. "Attachment, Masculinity, and Self-Control: A Theory of Male Crime Rates." Theoretical Criminology 6: 5–33.

Hayward, Keith J. 2004. City Limits: Crime, Consumer Culture and the Urban Experience. London: Glasshouse.

Healy, William. 1915. The Individual Delinquent: A Text-Book of Diagnosis and Prognosis for All Concerned in Understanding Offenders. Boston: Little, Brown, and Company.

Healy, William, and Augusta F. Bronner. 1926. Delinquents and Criminals: Their Making and Unmaking. New York: The Macmillan Company.

Heaven, Patrick C. L., and Michael Virgen. 2001. "Personality, Perceptions of Family and Peer Influences, and Males' Self-Reported Delinquency." Personality and Individual Differences 30: 321–331.

Heimer, Karen, and Stacy De Coster. 1999. "The Gendering of Violent Delinquency." Criminology 37: 277–318.

Heimer, Karen, and Ross L. Matsueda. 1994. "Role-Taking, Role Commitment, and Delinquency: A Theory of Differential Social Control." American Sociological Review 59: 365–390.

Hennessy, Rosemary, and Chrys Ingraham (Eds.). 1997. Materialist Feminism: A Reader in Class, Difference, and Women's Lives. New York: Routledge.

Herman, Madelynn M. 2002. Juvenile Justice Trends in 2002: Teen Courts – A Juvenile Justice Diversion Program. Williamsburg, VA: National Center for State Courts.

Higgins, George E. 2009. "Parental Criminality and Low Self-Control: An Examination of Delinquency." Criminal Justice Studies 22: 141–152.

Hirschi, Travis. 1969. Causes of Delinquency. Berkeley: University of California Press.

Hirschi, Travis. 1989. "Exploring Alternatives to Integrated Theories." Pp.37–50 in Theoretical Integration in the Study of Deviance and Crime: Problems and Prospects, edited by Steven F. Messner, Marvin D. Krohn, and Allen E. Liska. Albany: State University of New York Press.

Hirschi, Travis. 2004. "Self-Control and Crime." Pp. 537–552 in Handbook of Self-Regulation: Research, Theory, and Applications, edited by Roy F. Baumeister and Kathleen D. Vohs. New York: Guilford Press.

Hirschi, Travis. 2008. "Comment: Self-Control in the Lab." Pp.63–71 in Experiments in Criminology and Law: A Research Revolution, edited by Christine Horne and Michael J. Lovaglia. Lanham, MD: Rowman & Littlefield.

Hirschi, Travis, and Michael R. Gottfredson. 1995. "Control Theory and the Life-Course Perspective." Studies on Crime and Crime Prevention 4: 131–142.

Hirschi, Travis, and Michael R. Gottfredson. 2000. "In Defense of Self-Control." Theoretical Criminology 4: 55–69.

Hirschi, Travis, and Michael J. Hindelang. 1977. "Intelligence and Delinquency: A Revisionist Review." American Sociological Review 42: 571–587.

Hobbes, Thomas. 1962 [1651]. Leviathan, Or the Matter, Forme, and Power of a Commonwealth Ecclesiasticall and Civil. New York: Macmillan Publishers.

Hochstetler, Andy, Heith Copes, and Matt DeLisi. 2002. "Differential Association in Group and Solo Offending." Journal of Criminal Justice 30: 559–566.

Hoffmann, John P. 2003. "A Contextual Analysis of Differential Association, Social Control, and Strain Theories of Delinquency." Social Forces 81: 753–785.

Hoffmann, John P. 2008. "Illegitimate Opportunity Structures." Pp.471–472 in Encyclopedia of Social Problems, edited by Vincent N. Parrillo. Thousand Oaks, CA: Sage Publications.

Hoffmann, John P. 2009. "The Status of Strain Theory." Pp.156–168 in Criminological Theory: Readings and Retrospectives, edited by Heith Copes and Volkan Topalli. New York: McGraw-Hill.

Hoffman, John P. 2010. "A Life-Course Perspective on Stress, Delinquency, and Young Adult Crime." American Journal of Criminal Justice 25: 105–120.

Hoffmann, John P. and Timothy Ireland. 1995. "Cloward and Ohlin's Strain Theory Reexamined: An Elaborated Theoretical Model." Advances in Criminological Theory 6: 247–260.

Hoffmann, John P., and Timothy O. Ireland. 2004. "Strain and Opportunity Structures." Journal of Quantitative Criminology 20: 263–292.

Hooton, Earnest Albert. 1939. The American Criminal: An Anthropological Study. Cambridge, MA: Harvard University Press.

Horkheimer, Max, and Theodore W. Adorno. 2002 [1947]. Dialectic of Enlightenment: Philosophical Fragments. Stanford, CA: Stanford University Press.

Huang, Bu, Rick Kosterman, Richard F. Catalano, J. David Hawkins, and Robert D. Abbott. 2001. "Modeling Mediation in the Etiology of Violent Behavior in Adolescence: A Test of the Social Development Model." Criminology 39: 75–108.

Huesmann, L. Rowell, Leonard D. Eron, and Eric F. Dubow. 2002. "Childhood Predictors of Adult Criminality: Are All Risk Factors Reflected in Childhood Aggressiveness?" Criminal Behaviour and Mental Health 12: 185–208.

Huizinga, David, Terence P. Thornberry, Kelly E. Knight, Peter J. Lovegrove, Rolf Loeber, Karl Hill, and David P. Farrington. 2007. Disproportionate Minority Contact in the Juvenile Justice System: A Study of Differential Minority Arrest/Referral to Court in Three Cities. Report to the Office of Juvenile Justice and Delinquency Prevention, U.S. Department of Justice, Washington, DC.

Hunt, Morton. 1993. The Story of Psychology. New York: Doubleday.

Hutchings, Judy, Tracey Bywater, Dave Daley, Frances Gardner, Chris Whitaker, Karen Jones, Catrin Eames, and Rhiannon T Edwards. 2007. "Parenting Intervention in Sure Start Services for Children at Risk of Developing Conduct Disorder: Pragmatic Randomised Controlled Trial." British Medical Journal 334: 678–684.

Ireland, Timothy O., Carolyn A. Smith, and Terence P. Thornberry. 2002. "Developmental Issues in the Impact of Child Maltreatment on Later Delinquency and Drug Use." Criminology 40: 359–400.

Ireland, Timothy O., Terence P. Thornberry, and Rolf Loeber. 2006. "Adolescents in Public Housing: Is Stability or Change Related to Delinquent Behavior?" Pp.301–324 in Housing, Urban Governance, and Anti-Social Behaviour: Perspectives, Policy and Practice, edited by John Flint. Bristol, UK: The Policy Press.

Isen, Joshua. 2010. "A Meta-Analytic Assessment of Wechsler's P > V Sign in Antisocial Populations." Clinical Psychology Review 30: 423–435.

Ishikawa, Sharon S., and Adrian Raine. 2002. "Behavioral Genetics and Crime." Pp.81–110 in The Neurobiology of Criminal Behavior, edited by Joseph Glicksohn. Boston: Kluwer Academic Publishers.

Jacobs, Bruce A. 2010. "Deterrence and Deterrability." Criminology 48: 417–448.

Jang, Sung Joon, and Terence P. Thornberry. 1998. "Self-Esteem, Delinquent Peers, and Delinquency: A Test of the Self-Enhancement Hypothesis." American Sociological Review 63: 586–598.

Jarjoura, G. Roger, and Ruth A. Triplett. 1997. "The Effects of Social Area Characteristics on the Relationship between Social Class and Delinquency." Journal of Criminal Justice 25: 125–140.

Jencks, Christopher, and Susan E. Mayer. 1990. "The Social Consequences of Growing Up in a Poor Neighborhood." Pp.111–185 in Inner-City Poverty in the United States, edited by Laurence E. Lynn and Michael G. H. McGeary. Washington, DC: National Academy Press.

Jensen, Gary F. 1972. "Parents, Peers, and Delinquent Action: A Test of the Differential Association Perspective." American Journal of Sociology 78: 562–575.

Jensen, Gary F., and Ronald L. Akers. 2007. "'Taking Social Learning Global': Micro–Macro Transitions in Criminological Theory." Pp.9–38 in Social Learning Theory and the Explanation of Crime, edited by Ronald L. Akers and Gary F. Jensen. New Brunswick, NJ: Transaction Publishers.

Jensen, Gary F., and Kevin Thompson. 1990. "What's Class Got to Do with It? A Further Examination of Power-Control Theory." American Journal of Sociology 95: 1009–1023.

Jimerson, Jason B., and Matthew K. Oware. 2006. "Telling the Code of the Street: An Ethnomethodological Ethnography." Journal of Contemporary Ethnography 35: 24–50.

Johnson, Jeffrey G., Patricia Cohen, Elizabeth M. Smailes, Stephanie Kasen, and Judith S. Brook. 2002. "Television Viewing and Aggressive Behavior during Adolescence and Adulthood." Science 295: 2468–2471.

Junger, Marianne, and Maja Deković. 2003. "Crime as Risk-Taking: Co-occurrence of Delinquent Behavior, Health-Endangering Behaviors, and Problem Behaviors." Pp.213–248 in Control Theories of Crime and Delinquency, edited by Chester L. Britt and Michael R. Gottfredson. New Brunswick, NJ: Transaction Publishers.

Kaplan, Howard B. 1980. Deviant Behavior in Defense of Self. New York: Academic Press.

Kaplan, Howard B., Robert J. Johnson, and Carol A. Bailey. 1986. "Self-Rejection and the Explanation of Deviance: Refinement and Elaboration of a Latent Structure." Social Psychology Quarterly 49: 110–128.

Katz, Jack. 1988. Seductions of Crime: The Moral and Sensual Attractions of Doing Evil. New York: Basic Books.

Keen, Bradley, and David Jacobs. 2009. "Racial Threat, Partisan Politics, and Racial Disparities in Prison Admissions: A Panel Analysis." Criminology 47: 209–237.

Keenan, Kate, and Daniel S. Shaw. 2003. "Starting at the Beginning: Exploring the Etiology of Antisocial Behavior in the First Years of Life." Pp.153–181 in Causes of Conduct Disorder and Juvenile Delinquency, edited by Benjamin B. Lahey, Terrie E. Moffitt, and Avshalom Caspi. New York: Guilford Press.

Kelling, George L., and Catherine Coles. 1996. Fixing Broken Windows: Restoring Order and Reducing Crime in Our Communities. New York: Free Press.

de Kemp, Raymond A. T., Ron H. J. Scholte, Geertjan Overbeek, and Rutger C. M. E. Engels. 2006. "Early Adolescent Delinquency: The Role of Parents and Best Friends." Criminal Justice and Behavior 33: 488–510.

Kennedy, David M., Anne M. Piehl, and Anthony A. Braga. 1996. "Youth Violence in Boston: Gun Markets, Serious Youth Offenders, and a Use-Reduction Strategy." Law and Contemporary Problems 59: 147–196.

Kerr, Margaret, Håkan Stattin, and William J. Burk. 2010. "A Reinterpretation of Parental Monitoring in Longitudinal Perspective." Journal of Research on Adolescence 20: 39–64.

King, Ryn D., Michael Massoglia, and Ross MacMillan. 2007. "The Context of Marriage and Crime: Gender, the Propensity to Marry, and Offending in Early Adulthood." Criminology 45: 33–65.

Kirk, David S. 2008. "The Neighborhood Context of Racial and Ethnic Disparities in Arrest." Demography 45: 55–77.

Kling, Jeffrey R., Jeffrey B. Liebman, and Lawrence F. Katz. 2007. "Experimental Analysis of Neighborhood Effects." Econometrica 75: 83–119.

Kling, Jeffrey R., Jens Ludwig, and Lawrence R. Katz. 2005. "Neighborhood Effects on Crime for Female and Male Youth: Evidence from a Randomized Housing Voucher Experiments." Quarterly Journal of Economics 116: 607–654.

Knopp, Fay Honey. 1991. "Community Solutions to Sexual Violence: Feminist/Abolitionist Perspectives." Pp.181–193 in Criminology as Peacemaking, edited by Harold E. Pepinsky and Richard Quinney. Bloomington: Indiana University Press.

Kobak, Roger, Kristyn Zajac, and Seymour Levine. 2009. "Cortisol and Antisocial Behavior in Early Adolescence: The Role of Gender in an Economically Disadvantaged Sample." Development and Psychopathology 21: 579–591.

Kohlberg, Lawrence. 1973. Collected Papers on Moral Development and Moral Education. Cambridge, MA: Moral Education and Research Foundation, Harvard University Education Foundation.

Kohlberg, Lawrence. 1984. Essays on Moral Development: The Psychology of Moral Development. San Francisco, CA: Harper and Row.

Koita, Kiyofumi, and Ruth A. Triplett. 1998. "An Examination of Gender and Race Effects on the Parental Appraisal Process: A Reanalysis of Matsueda's Model of the Self." Criminal Justice and Behavior 25: 382–400.

Kornhauser, Ruth. 1978. Social Sources of Delinquency. Chicago: University of Chicago Press.

Kramer, Ronald C. 2000. "Poverty, Inequality, and Youth Violence." Annals of the American Academy of Political and Social Science 567: 123–139.

Kreager, Derek A. 2004. "Strangers in the Hall: Isolation and Delinquency in School Networks." Social Forces 83: 351–390.

Krivo, Lauren J., and Ruth D. Peterson. 2004. "Labor Market Conditions and Violent Crime among Youth and Adults." Sociological Perspectives 47: 485–505.

Krohn, Marvin D. 1986. "The Web of Conformity: A Network Approach to the Explanation of Delinquent Behavior." Social Problems 33: S81–S93.

Kroneman, Leoniek, Rolf Loeber, and Alison Hipwell. 2004. "Is Neighborhood Context Differently Related to Externalizing Problems and Delinquency for Girls Compared with Boys?" Clinical Child & Family Psychology Review 7: 109–123.

Lanctôt, Nadine, Stephen A. Cernkovich, and Peggy C. Giordano. 2007. "Delinquent Behavior, Official Delinquency, and Gender: Consequences for Adulthood Functioning and Well-Being." Criminology 45: 131–157.

Lander, Bernard. 1954. Toward an Understanding of Juvenile Delinquency. New York: Columbia University Press.

Lasley, James R. 1995. "Operation Cul-De-Sac: LAPD's Experiment in Total Community Policing." Pp.51–96 in Issues in Community Policing, edited by Duane Dukes and Peter C. Kratcoski. Cincinatti, OH: ACJS/Anderson Publishing.

Laub, John H., and Robert J. Sampson. 2003. Shared Beginnings, Divergent Lives: Delinquent Boys to Age 70. Cambridge, MA: Harvard University Press.

Lave, Charles A., and James G. March. 1975. An Introduction to Models in the Social Sciences. New York: Harper & Row Publishers.

LeBlanc, Linda A., and Loc Le. 1999. "Behavioral Treatment." Pp.197–218 in Advanced Abnormal Child Psychology, edited by Michel Hersen and Robert T. Ammerman. Mahwah, NY: Lawrence Erlbaum Associates.

LeBlanc, Line, Raymond Swisher, Frank Vitaro, and Richard E. Tremblay. 2008. "High School Social Climate and Antisocial Behavior: A 10 Year Longitudinal and Multilevel Study." Journal of Research on Adolescence 18: 395–419.

Lemann, Nicholas. 1988. "The Unfinished War." The Atlantic Monthly 262(6): 37–56.

Lemert, Edwin M. 1951. Social Pathology: A Systematic Approach to the Theory of Sociopathic Behavior. New York: McGraw-Hill.

Levine, Gene N., and Fernando Parra. 2000. "Gangbangers of East Los Angeles: Sociopsycho-Analytic Considerations." Journal of Gang Research 7: 9–12.

Levitt, Steven. 1998. "Juvenile Crime and Punishment." Journal of Political Economy 106: 1156–1185.

Li, Spencer De. 1999. "Legal Sanctions and Youths' Status Achievement: A Longitudinal Study." Justice Quarterly 16: 377–401.

Liberman, Akiva M. (Ed.). 2008. The Long View of Crime: A Synthesis of Longitudinal Studies. New York: Springer.

Liljeberg, Jenny Freidenfelt, Jenny M. Eklund, Marie Väfors Fritz, and Britt af Klinteberg. 2010. "Poor School Bonding and Delinquency over Time: Bidirectional Effects and Sex Differences." Journal of Adolescence, doi: 10.1016/j.adolescence.2010.03.008.

Lilly, J. Robert, Francis T. Cullen, and Richard A. Ball. 1994. Criminological Theory: Context and Consequences, Second Edition. Newbury Park, CA: Sage Publications.

Link, Bruce G., and Joanne C. Phelan. 2001. "Conceptualizing Stigma." Annual Review of Sociology 27: 363–385.

Lipsey, Mark W., and David B. Wilson. 1998. "Effective Intervention for Serious Juvenile Offenders: A Synthesis of Research." Pp.313–345 in Serious & Violent Juvenile Offenders: Risk Factors and Successful Interventions, edited by Rolf Loeber and David P. Farrington. Thousand Oaks, CA: Sage Publications.

Liska, Allen E. 1987. "A Critical Examination of Macro Perspectives on Crime Control." Annual Review of Sociology 13: 67–86.

Liu, Jianghong, Adrian Raine, Peter H. Venables, and Sarnoff A. Mednick. 2004. "Malnutrition at Age 3 Years and Externalizing Behavior Problems at Ages 8, 11, and 17 Years." American Journal of Psychiatry 260: 2005–2013.

Locke, John. 1975 [1690]. An Essay Concerning Human Understanding. Edited by Peter H. Nidditch. Oxford: Clarendon Press.

Loeber, Rolf, and Magda Stouthamer-Loeber. 1986. "Family Factors as Correlates and Predictors of Juvenile Conduct Problems and Delinquency." Crime and Justice: An Annual Review of Research 7: 29–149.

Loeber, Rolf, Jeffrey D. Burke, Benjamin B. Lahey, Alaina Winters, and Marcie Zera. 2000. "Oppositional Defiant Disorder and Conduct Disorder: A Review of the Past 10 Years, Part I." Journal of the American Academy of Child and Adolescent Psychiatry 39: 1468–1484.

Loeber, Rolf, David P. Farrington, Magda Stouthamer-Loeber, Helene Raskin White, and Evelyn Wei (Eds.). 2008. Violence and Serious Theft: Development and Prediction from Childhood to Adulthood. New York: Routledge.

LoGalbo, Anthony P., and Charlene M. Callahan. 2001. "An Evaluation of Teen Court as a Juvenile Crime Diversion Program." Juvenile and Family Court Journal 52: 1–11.

Lombroso, Cesare. 1876. L'Uomo delinquente. Milan: Hoepli.

Lombroso, Cesare. 1897. L'Uomo delinquente, Fifth Edition, Volume 2. Turin: Bocca.

Lombroso, Cesare. 1912. Crime: Its Causes and Remedies. Translated by Henry P. Horton. Boston: Little, Brown, and Company.

Lösel, Friedrich, Thomas Bliesener, and Doris Bender. 2007. "Social Information Processing, Experiences of Aggression in Social Contexts, and Aggressive Behavior in Adolescents." Criminal Justice and Behavior 34: 330–347.

Luna, Beatriz, Kristina E. Garver, Trinity A. Urban, Nicole A. Lazar, and John A. Sweeney. 2004. "Maturation of Cognitive Processes from Late Childhood to Adulthood." Child Development 75: 1357–1372.

Lynam, Donald R., Avshalom Caspi, Terrie E. Moffitt, Adrian Raine, Rolf Loeber, and Magda Stouthamer-Loeber. 2005. "Adolescent Psychopathy and the Big Five: Results from Two Samples." Journal of Abnormal Child Psychology 33: 431–443.

Lynam, Donald R., Avshalom Caspi, Terrie E. Moffitt, Per-Olof H. Wikström, Rolf Loeber, and Scott Novak. 2000. "The Interaction between Impulsivity and Neighborhood Context on Offending: The Effects of Impulsivity Are Stronger in Poorer Neighborhoods." Journal of Abnormal Psychology 109: 563–574.

Lynam, Donald R., Terrie E. Moffitt, and Magda Stouthamer-Loeber. 1993. "Explaining the Relation between IQ and Delinquency: Class, Race, Test Motivation, School Failure, or Self-Control?" Journal of Abnormal Psychology 102: 187–196.

Lynch, James P. 2002. Trends in Juvenile Offending: An Analysis of Victim Survey Data. Juvenile Justice Bulletin. Washington, DC: Office of Juvenile Justice and Delinquency Prevention, U.S. Department of Justice.

Lynch, Mary Ellen, Claire D. Coles, Tammy Corley, and Arthur Falek. 2003. "Examining Delinquency in Adolescents Differentially Prenatally Exposed to Alcohol: The Role of Proximal and Distal Causal Factors." Journal of Studies on Alcohol 64: 678–686.

Lynch, Michael J., and Raymond Michalowski. 2006. Primer in Radical Criminology: Critical Perspectives on Crime, Power, and Identity, Fourth Edition. Monsey, NY: Criminal Justice Press.

Lynch, Michael J., and Paul B. Stretesky. 2001. "Radical Criminology." Pp.267–286 in Explaining Criminals and Crime: Essays in Contemporary Criminological Theory, edited by Raymond Paternoster and Ronet Bachman. Los Angeles: Roxbury Publishing Company.

Lyotard, Jean-François. 1979. La Condition Postmoderne: Rapport Sur le Savoir. Paris: Minuit.

Mack, Kristin Y., Michael J. Lieber, Robert A. Featherstone, and Maria A. Monserud. 2007. "Reassessing the Family–Delinquency Association: Do Family Type, Family Processes, and Economic Factors Make a Difference?" Journal of Criminal Justice 35: 51–67.

Mahoney, Joseph L., and Håkan Stattin. 2000. "Leisure Activities and Adolescent Antisocial Behavior: The Role of Structure and Social Context." Journal of Adolescence 23: 113–127.

Maimon, David, and Christopher R. Browning. 2010. "Unstructured Socializing, Collective Efficacy, and Violent Behavior among Urban Youth." Criminology 48: 443–474.

Malmgren, Kimber, Robert D. Abbott, and J. David Hawkins. 1999. "LD and Delinquency: Rethinking the 'Link.'" Journal of Learning Disabilities 32: 194–200.

Marcus, Bernd. 2003. "An Empirical Examination of the Construct Validity of Two Alternative Self-Control Measures." Educational and Psychological Measurement 63: 674–706.

Marsh, Herbert W., Roberto H. Parada, Alexander Seeshing Yeung, and Jean Healy. 2001. "Aggressive School Troublemakers and Victims: A Longitudinal Model Examining the Pivotal Role of Self-Concept." Journal of Educational Psychology 93: 411–419.

Maruna, Shadd. 2001. Making Good: How Ex-Convicts Reform and Rebuild Their Lives. Washington, DC: American Psychological Association.

Maruna, Shadd, and Heith Copes. 2005. "What Have We Learned from Five Decades of Neutralization Research?" Crime and Delinquency: An Annual Review of Research 32: 221–320.

Marx, Karl. 1979 [1859]. Contribution to the Critique of Political Economy. New York: International Publishers.

Marx, Karl. 1999 [1867]. Capital. New York: Oxford University Press.

Masters, Roger D., and Myron J. Coplan. 1999. "A Dynamic, Multifactorial Model of Alcohol, Drug Abuse, and Crime: Linking Neuroscience and Behavior to Toxicology." Social Science Information 38: 591–624.

Masters, Roger D., Brian Hone, and Anil Doshi. 1998. "Environmental Pollution, Neurotoxicity, and Criminal Violence." Pp.13–48 in Environmental Toxicology: Current Developments, edited by J. Rose. New York: CRC Press.

Matsueda, Ross L. 1988. "The Current State of Differential Association Theory." Crime & Delinquency 34: 277–306.

Matsueda, Ross. 1989. "The Dynamics of Moral Beliefs and Delinquency." Social Forces 68: 428–457.

Matsueda, Ross L. 2001. "Labeling Theory: Historical Roots, Implications, and Recent Developments." Pp.223–241 in Explaining Criminals and Crime, edited by Raymond Paternoster and Ronet Bachman. Los Angeles, CA: Roxbury Publishing.

Matsueda, Ross L., and Kathleen Anderson. 1998. "The Dynamics of Delinquent Peers and Delinquent Behavior." Criminology 36: 269–308.

Matsueda, Ross L., and Karen Heimer. 1987. "Race, Family Structure, and Delinquency: A Test of Differential Association and Social Control Theories." American Sociological Review 52: 826–840.

Matsueda, Ross L., Derek A. Kreager, and David Huizinga. 2006. "Deterring Delinquents: A Rational Choice Model of Theft and Violence." American Sociological Review 71: 95–122.

Matthews, Shelley Keith, and Robert Agnew. 2008. "Extending Deterrence Theory: Do Delinquent Peers Condition the Relationship between Perceptions of Getting Caught and Offending?" Journal of Research in Crime and Delinquency 45: 91–118.

Matthys, Walter, Juliane M. Cuperus, and Herman Van Engeland. 1999. "Deficient Social Problem-Solving in Boys with ODD/CD, with ADHD, and with Both Disorders." Journal of the American Academy of Child and Adolescent Psychiatry 38: 311–321.

Mattson, Sarah N., Amy M. Schoenfeld, and Edward P. Riley. 2001. "Teratogenic Effects of Alcohol on Brain and Behavior." Alcohol Research and Health 25: 185–191.

Matza, David. 1964. Delinquency and Drift. New York: John Wiley & Sons.

Maume, Michael O., Graham C. Ousey, and Kevin Beaver. 2005. "Cutting the Grass: A Reexamination of the Link between Marital Attachment, Delinquent Peers and Desistance from Marijuana Use." Journal of Quantitative Criminology 21: 27–53.

Mayhew, Henry. 1967 [1861]. London Labour and the London Poor: A Cyclopaedia of the Condition and Earnings of Those That Will Work, Those That Cannot Work, and Those That Will Not Work. Four Volumes. New York: Frank Cass & Company.

McAlinden, Anne-Marie. 2005. "The Use of Shame with Sexual Offenders." British Journal of Criminology 45: 373–394.

McCart, Michael R, Paul E Priester, W. Hobart Davies, and Razia Azen. 2006. "Differential Effectiveness of Behavioral Parent-Training and Cognitive–Behavioral Therapy for Antisocial Youth: A Meta-Analysis." Journal of Abnormal Child Psychology 34: 527–543.

McCarthy, Bill. 1996. "The Attitudes and Actions of Others: Tutelage and Sutherland's Theory of Differential Association." British Journal of Criminology 36: 135–147.

McCarthy, Bill, and Teresa Casey. 2008. "Love, Sex, and Crime: Adolescent Romantic Relationships and Offending." American Sociological Review 73: 944–969.

McCarthy, Bill, John Hagan, and Todd S. Woodward. 1999. "In the Company of Women: Structure and Agency in a Revised Power-Control Theory of Gender and Delinquency." Criminology 37: 761–788.

McCloskey, Laura Ann, Aurelio José Figueredo, and Mary P. Koss. 1995. "The Effects of Systematic Family Violence on Children's Mental Health." Child Development 66: 1239–1261.

McCrae, Robert R., and Oliver P. John. 1992. "An Introduction to the Five-Factor Model and Its Applications." Journal of Personality 60: 175–215.

McGarrell, Edmund, and Natalie Kroovand Hipple. 2007. "Family Group Conferencing and Re-Offending among First-Time Juvenile Offenders: The Indianapolis Experiment." Justice Quarterly 24: 221–246.

McGloin, Jean Marie, and Lauren O'Neill Shermer. 2009. "Self-Control and Deviant Peer Network Structure." Journal of Research in Crime and Delinquency 46: 35–72.

McGloin, Jean Marie, Travis C. Pratt, and Jeff Maahs. 2004. "Rethinking the IQ–Delinquency Relationship: A Longitudinal Analysis of Multiple Theoretical Models." Justice Quarterly 21: 603–635.

McNulty, Thomas L., and Paul E. Bellair. 2003. "Explaining Racial and Ethnic Differences in Serious Adolescent Violent Behavior." Criminology 41: 709–748.

Mead, George Herbert. 1934. Mind, Self, and Society. Chicago: University of Chicago Press.

Mearns, Andrew. 1970 [1883]. The Bitter Cry of Outcast London: An Inquiry into the Condition of the Abject Poor. London: Frank Cass & Company.

Mears, Daniel P., Matthew Ploeger, and Mark Warr. 1998. "Explaining the Gender Gap in Delinquency: Peer Influence and Moral Evaluations of Behavior." Journal of Research in Crime and Delinquency 35: 251–266.

Mednick, Sarnoff A. 1977. "A Biosocial Theory of the Learning of Law-Abiding Behavior." Pp.1–8 in the Biosocial Bases of Criminal Behavior, edited by Sarnoff A. Mednick and Karl O. Christiansen. New York: Gardner Press.

Mednick, Sarnoff A., and Elizabeth Kandel. 1988. "Genetic and Perinatal Factors in Violence." Pp.121–134 in Biological Contributions to Crime Causation, edited by Terrie E. Moffitt and Sarnoff A. Mednick. Boston, MA: Kluwer Academic.

Meier, Robert F. 1989. "Deviance and Differentiation." Pp.199–212 in Theoretical Integration in the Study of Deviance and Crime: Problems and Prospects, edited by Steven F. Messner, Marvin D. Krohn, and Allen E. Liska. Albany: State University of New York Press.

Menard, Scott. 1997. "A Developmental Test of Cloward's Differential-Opportunity Theory." Pp.142–186 in The Future of Anomie Theory, edited by Robert Agnew and Nikos Passas. Boston, MA: Northeastern University Press.

Merton, Robert K. 1938. "Social Structure and Anomie." American Sociological Review 3: 672–682.

Merton, Robert K. 1959. "Social Conformity, Deviation, and Opportunity Structures: A Comment on the Contributions of Dubin and Cloward." American Sociological Review 24: 177–189.

Merton, Robert K. 1968. Social Theory and Social Structure, Enlarged Edition. New York: Free Press.

Messerschmidt, James W. 2000. Nine Lives: Adolescent Masculinities, the Body, and Violence. Boulder, CO: Westview Press.

Messner, Steven F. 1988. "Merton's 'Social Structure and Anomie': The Road Not Taken." Deviant Behavior 9: 33–53.

Messner, Steven F., and Marvin D. Krohn. 1990. "Class, Compliance Structures, and Delinquency: Assessing Integrated Structural–Marxist Theory." American Journal of Sociology 96: 300–328.

Messner, Steven F., Marvin D. Krohn, and Allen E. Liska (Eds.). 1989. Theoretical Integration in the Study of Deviance and Crime: Problems and Prospects. Albany: State University of New York Press.

Mill, John Stuart. 1884. A System of Logic, Ratiocinative, and Inductive, Being a Connected View of the Principles of Evidence and the Methods of Scientific Investigation. London: Longmans, Green, and Company.

Miller, Alan S., and Satoshi Kanazawa. 2001. Order by Accident: The Origins and Consequences of Group Conformity in Contemporary Japan. Boulder, CO: Westview Press.

Miller, Edgar. 2002. "Brain Injury as a Contributory Factor in Offending." Pp.137–153 in The Neurobiology of Criminal Behavior, edited by Joseph Glicksohn. Boston, MA: Kluwer Academic Publishers.

Miller, Jody. 2001. One of the Guys: Girls, Gangs, and Gender. New York: Oxford University Press.

Miller, Jody. 2008. Getting Played: African American Girls, Urban Inequality, and Gendered Violence. New York: NYU Press.

Miller, Walter. 2005. "Adolescents on the Edge: The Sensual Side of Delinquency." Pp.153–171 in Edgework: The Sociology of Risk-Taking, edited by Stephen Lyng. New York: Routledge.

Milner, Joel S. 2000. "Social Information Processing and Child Physical Abuse: Theory and Research." Pp. 39–84 in Nebraska Symposium on Motivation, Volume 45, edited by David J. Hansen. Lincoln: University of Nebraska Press.

Milovanovic, Dragan. 1996. "Postmodern Criminology: Mapping the Terrain." Justice Quarterly 13: 567–610.

Milovanovic, Dragan. 2003. An Introduction to the Sociology of Law, Third Edition. Monsey, NY: Criminal Justice Press.

Mitchell, Jim, Richard A. Dodder, and Terry D. Norris. 1990. "Neutralization and Delinquency: A Comparison by Sex and Ethnicity." Adolescence 25: 98–103.

Mithaug, Dennis E. 2000. Learning to Theorize. Thousand Oaks, CA: Sage Publications.

Mocan, H. Naci, and Daniel I. Rees. 2005. "Economic Conditions, Deterrence, and Juvenile Crime: Evidence from Micro Data." American Law and Economics Review 7: 319–349.

Moe, Angela M. 2006. "Women, Drugs, and Crime." Criminal Justice Studies 19: 337–352.

Moffitt, Terrie E. 1993. "Adolescence-Limited and Life-Course Persistent Antisocial Behavior: A Developmental Taxonomy." Psychological Review 100: 674–701.

Moffitt, Terrie E. 2003. "Life-Course-Persistent and Adolescence-Limited Antisocial Behavior: A 10-Year Research Review and a Research Agenda." Pp.49–75 in Causes of Conduct Disorder and Juvenile Delinquency, edited by Benjamin B. Lahey, Terrie E. Moffitt, and Avshalom Caspi. New York: Guilford Press.

Moffitt, Terrie E., and Phil A. Silva. 1988. "IQ and Delinquency: A Direct Test of the Differential Detection Hypothesis." Journal of Abnormal Psychology 97: 330–333.

Moffitt, Terrie E., Gary L. Brammer, Avshalom Caspi, J. Paul Fawcett, Michael Raleigh, Arthur Yuwiler, and Phil Silva. 1998. "Whole Blood Serotonin Relates to Violence in an Epidemiological Study." Biological Psychiatry 43: 446–457.

Moffitt, Terrie E., Avshalom Caspi, Michael Rutter, and Phil A. Silva. 2001. Sex Differences in Antisocial Behaviour: Conduct Disorder, Delinquency, and Violence in the Dunedin Longitudinal Study. Cambridge: Cambridge University Press.

Moore, Mignon R. 2003. "Socially Isolated? How Parents and Neighbourhood Adults Influence Youth Behaviour in Disadvantaged Communities." Ethnic and Racial Studies 26: 988–1005.

Morash, Merry, and Meda Chesney-Lind. 1991. "A Reformulation and Partial Test of the Power-Control Theory of Delinquency." Justice Quarterly 8: 347–377.

Morton, Todd L., and Kelly L. Farris. 2002. "MMPI-A Structural Summary Characteristics of Male Juvenile Delinquents." Assessment 9: 327–333.

Mosher, Clayton. 1999. "The Reaction to Black Violent Offenders in Ontario – 1892–1961: A Test of the Threat Hypothesis." Sociological Forum 14: 635–658.

Moster, Aviva, Dorota W. Wnuk, and Elizabeth L. Jeglic. 2008. "Cognitive Behavioral Therapy Interventions with Sex Offenders." Journal of Correctional Health Care 14: 109–121.

Nadder, T. S., M. Rutter, J. L. Silberg, H. H. Maes, and L. J. Eaves. 2002. "Genetic Effects on the Variation and Covariation of Attention Deficit–Hyperactivity Disorder (ADHD) and Oppositional-Defiant Disorder/Conduct Disorder (ODD/CD) Symptomatologies across Informant and Occasion of Measurement." Psychological Medicine 32: 39–53.

Naffine, Ngaire. 1987. Female Crime: The Construction of Women in Criminology. Sydney: Allen & Unwin.

Naffine, Ngaire. 1996. Feminism and Criminology. Philadelphia: Temple University Press.

Nagin, Daniel S. 1998. "Criminal Deterrence Research at the Outset of the Twenty-First Century." Crime and Justice: A Review of Research 23: 1–42.

Nagin, Daniel S., and Raymond Paternoster. 1991. "The Preventive Effects of the Perceived Risk of Arrest: Testing an Expanded Conception of Deterrence." Criminology 29: 561–587.

Nagin, Daniel S., and Greg Pogarsky. 2001. "Integrating Celerity, Impulsivity, and Extralegal Sanction Threats into a Model of General Deterrence: Theory and Evidence." Criminology 39: 865–892.

Nagin, Daniel S., and Richard E. Tremblay. 2005a. "What Has Been Learned from Group-Based Trajectory Modeling? Examples from Physical Aggression and Other Problem Behaviors." The Annals of the American Academy of Political and Social Science 602: 82–117.

Nagin, Daniel S., and Richard E. Tremblay. 2005b. "Developmental Trajectory Groups: Fact or Useful Statistical Fiction?" Criminology 43: 873–904.

Nas, Coralijn N., Bram Orobio De Castro, and Willem Koops. 2005. "Social Information Processing in Delinquent Adolescents." Psychology, Crime and Law 11: 363–375.

Negriff, Sonya, Michelle T. Fung, and Penelope K. Trickett. 2008. "Self-Rated Pubertal Development, Depressive Symptoms and Delinquency: Measurement Issues and Moderation by Gender and Maltreatment." Journal of Youth and Adolescence 37: 736–746.

Nelson, Eric E., Ellen Leibenluft, Erin McClure, and Daniel S. Pine. 2005. "The Social Re-orientation of Adolescence: A Neuroscience Perspective on the Process and Its Relation to Psychopathology." Psychological Medicine 35: 163–174.

Ness, Cindy D. 2004. "Why Girls Fight: Female Youth Violence in the Inner City." Annals of the American Academy of Political and Social Science 595: 21–48.

Newman, Graeme. 1985. The Punishment Response. Albany, NY: Harrow and Heston.

Nigg, Joel T., and Cynthia L. Huang-Pollock. 2003. "An Early Onset Model of the Role of Executive Functions and Intelligence in Conduct Disorder/Delinquency." Pp.227–253 in Causes of Conduct Disorder and Juvenile Delinquency, edited by Benjamin B. Lahey, Terrie E. Moffitt, and Avshalom Caspi. New York: Guilford Press.

Nix, Robert L., Ellen E. Pinderhughes, Kenneth A. Dodge, John E. Bates, Gregory S. Pettit, and Steven A. McFadyen-Ketchum. 1999. "The Relation between Mothers' Hostile Attribution Tendencies and Children's Externalizing Behavior Problems: The Mediating Role of Mothers' Harsh Discipline Practices." Child Development 70: 896–909.

Nofziger, Stacey. 2008. "The 'Cause' of Low Self-Control." Journal of Research in Crime and Delinquency 45: 191–224.

Nofziger, Stacey. 2010. "A Gendered Perspective on the Relationship between Self-Control and Deviance." Feminist Criminology 5: 29–50.

Norland, Stephen, Randall C. Wessel, and Neal Shover. 1981. "Masculinity and Delinquency." Criminology 19: 421–433.

Norris, Michael, Sarah Twill, and Chigon Kim. 2010. "Smells Like Teen Spirit: Evaluating a Midwestern Teen Court." Crime & Delinquency, doi: 10.1177/0011128709354037.

Novak, Kenneth J., and Charlotte L. Seiler. 2001. "Zoning Practices and Neighborhood Physical Disorder." Criminal Justice Policy Review 12: 140–163.

Nye, F. Ivan. 1958. Family Relationships and Delinquent Behavior. New York: John Wiley & Sons.

O'Connor, Thomas G., Kirby Deater-Deckard, David Fulker, Michael Rutter, and Robert Plomin. 1998. "Genotype–Environment Correlations in Late Childhood and Early Adolescence: Antisocial Behavioral Problems and Coercive Parenting." Developmental Psychology 34: 970–981.

O'Keefe, Suzanne, and Roger Dunstan, 2001. Evaluation of California's Enterprise Zones. Sacramento: California Research Bureau.

O'Sullivan, Arthur. 2005. "Gentrification and Crime." Journal of Urban Economics 57: 73–85.

Oh, Joong-Hwan. 2005. "A Dynamic Approach to Population Change in Central Cities and Their Suburbs, 1980–1990: Crime, Employment, and Spatial Proximity." American Journal of Economics and Sociology 64: 663–681.

Olds, David, Charles R. Henderson, Robert Cole, John Eckenrode, Harriett Kitzman, Dennis Luckey, Lisa Pettitt, Kimberly Sidora, Pamela Morris, and Jane Powers. 1998. "Long-Term Effects of Nurse Home Visitation on Children's Criminal and Antisocial Behavior." Journal of the American Medical Association 280: 1238–1244.

Osgood, D. Wayne, and Jeff M. Chambers. 2000. "Social Disorganization outside the Metropolis: An Analysis of Rural Youth Violence." Criminology 38: 81–115.

Oxford English Dictionary. 2010. Third Edition. Available electronically at: http://www.oed.com.

Palmer, Emma J. 2003. "An Overview of the Relationship between Moral Reasoning and Offending." Australian Psychologist 38: 165–174.

Palmer, Emma J., and Clive R. Hollin. 2001. "Sociomoral Reasoning, Perceptions of Parenting and Self-Reported Delinquency in Adolescents." Applied Cognitive Psychology 15: 85–100.

Pardini, Dustin A., John E. Lochman, and Paul J. Frick. 2003. "Callous/Unemotional Traits and Social-Cognitive Processes in Adjudicated Youths." Journal of the American Academy of Child and Adolescent Psychiatry 42: 364–371.

Pardini, Dustin, Jelena Obradovic, and Rolf Loeber. 2006. "Interpersonal Callousness, Hyperactivity/Impulsivity, Inattention, and Conduct Problems as Precursors to Delinquency Persistence in Boys: A Comparison of Three Grade-Based Cohorts." Journal of Clinical Child & Adolescent Psychology 35: 46–59.

Park, Robert. 1936. "Human Ecology." American Journal of Sociology 42: 1–15.

Pasko, Lisa. 2008. "The Wayward Girl Revisited: Understanding the Gendered Nature of Juvenile Justice and Delinquency." Sociology Compass 2/3: 821–836.

Paternoster, Raymond, and LeeAnn Iovanni. 1989. "The Labeling Perspective and Delinquency: An Elaboration of the Theory and an Assessment of the Evidence." Justice Quarterly 6: 359–394.

Paternoster, Raymond, and Ruth Triplett. 1988. "Disaggregating Self-Reported Delinquency and Its Implications for Theory." Criminology 26: 591–625.

Patrick, Steven, Robert Marsh, Wade Bundy, Susan Mimura, and Tina Perkins. 2004. "Control Group Study of Juvenile Diversion Programs: An Experiment in Juvenile Diversion – The Comparison of Three Methods and a Control Group." Social Science Journal 41: 129–135.

Patterson, Gerald R., and Thomas J. Dishion. 1985. "Contributions of Families and Peers to Delinquency." Criminology 23: 63–77.

Patterson, Gerald R., and Karen Yoerger. 1997. "A Developmental Model for Late-Onset Delinquency." Pp.119–177 in Motivation and Delinquency: Nebraska Symposium on Motivation, Volume 44, edited by D. Wayne Osgood. Lincoln: University of Nebraska Press.

Patterson, Gerald R., David DeGarmo, and Marion S. Forgatch. 2004. "Systematic Changes in Families Following Prevention Trials." Journal of Abnormal Child Psychology 32: 621–633.

Patterson, Gerald R., Thomas J. Dishion, and Karen Yoerger. 2000. "Adolescent Growth in New Forms of Problem Behavior: Macro and Micro-Peer Dynamics." Prevention Science 1: 3–13.

Patterson, Gerald R., John B. Reid, and Thomas J. Dishion. 1992. Antisocial Boys. Eugene, OR: Castalia Publishing.

Payne, Allison Ann, Denise C. Gottfredson, and Gary D. Gottfredson. 2003. "Schools as Communities: The Relationships among Communal School Organization, Student Bonding, and School Disorder." Criminology 41: 749–777.

Pearl, Judea. 2000. Causality: Modeling, Reasoning, and Inference. New York: Cambridge University Press.

Petrosino, Anthony, Carolyn Petrosino-Turpin, and James Finckenauer. 2000. "Well-Meaning Programs Can Have Harmful Effects! Lessons from Experiments of Programs Such as Scared Straight." Crime & Delinquency 46: 354–379.

Petts, Richard J. 2009. "Family and Religious Characteristics' Influence on Delinquency: Trajectories from Adolescence to Young Adulthood." American Sociological Review 74: 465–483.

Piaget, Jean. 1966 [1932]. The Moral Judgment of the Child. New York: Free Press.

Pinker, Steven. 1999. How the Mind Works. New York: W.W. Norton.

Pinker, Steven. 2002. The Blank Slate: The Denial of Human Nature and Modern Intellectual Life. New York: Viking Press.

Piquero, Alex R., and Jeff A. Bouffard. 2007. "Something Old, Something New: A Preliminary Examination of Hirschi's Redefined Self-Control." Justice Quarterly 24: 1–27.

Piquero, Alex R., and Matthew Hickman. 1999. "An Empirical Test of Tittle's Control Balance Theory." Criminology 37: 319–342.

Piquero, Alex R., David P. Farrington, and Alfred Blumstein. 2003. "The Criminal Career Paradigm." Crime and Justice: An Annual Review of Research 30: 359–506.

Piquero, Alex R., David P. Farrington, and Alfred Blumstein. 2007. Key Issues in Criminal Career Research: New Analyses of the Cambridge Study in Delinquent Development. New York: Cambridge University Press.

Piquero, Alex R., David P. Farrington, Daniel S. Nagin, and Terrie E. Moffitt. 2010. "Trajectories of Offending and Their Relation to Life Failure in Late Middle Age: Findings from the Cambridge Study in Delinquent Development." Journal of Research in Crime and Delinquency 47: 151–173.

Piquero, Alex R., David P. Farrington, Brandon C. Welsh, Richard Tremblay, and Wesley G. Jennings. 2009. "Effects of Early Family/Parent Training Programs on Antisocial Behavior & Delinquency: A Systematic Review." Journal of Experimental Criminology 5: 83–120.

Piquero, Nicole Leeper, and Miriam D. Sealock. 2010. "Race, Crime, and General Strain Theory." Youth Violence and Juvenile Justice, doi: 10.1177/1541204009361174.

Plomin, Robert, and Kathryn Asbury. 2005. "Nature and Nurture: Genetic and Environmental Influences on Behavior." Annals of the American Academy of Political and Social Science 600: 86–98.

Plomin, Robert, John C. DeFries, Gerald E. McClearn, and Peter McGuffin. 2000. Behavioral Genetics, Fourth Edition. New York: Worth Publishers.

Pogarsky, Greg. 2002. "Identifying Deterrable Offenders: Implications for Research on Deterrence." Justice Quarterly 19: 431–452.

Pogarsky, Greg, KiDeuk Kim, and Raymond Paternoster. 2005. "Perceptual Change in the National Youth Survey: Lessons for Deterrence Theory and Offender Decision-Making." Justice Quarterly 22: 1–29.

Ponce, Ninez A., Katherine J. Hoggatt, Michelle Wilhelm, and Beate Ritz. 2005. "Preterm Birth: The Interaction of Traffic-Related Air Pollution with Economic Hardship in Los Angeles Neighborhoods." American Journal of Epidemiology 162: 140–148.

Pope, Carl E., and Howard N. Snyder. 2003. Race as a Factor in Juvenile Arrest. Juvenile Justice Bulletin. Washington, DC: Office of Juvenile Justice and Delinquency Prevention.

Popma, Arne, Theo A. H. Doreleijers, Lucres M. C. Jansen, Stephanie H. M. Van Goozen, Herman Van Engeland, and Robert Vermeiren. 2007. "The Diurnal Cortisol Cycle in Delinquent Male Adolescents and Normal Controls." Neuropsychopharmacology 32: 1622–1628.

Popper, Karl R. 1968. The Logic of Scientific Discovery, Second Edition. New York: Harper & Row Publishers.

Porter, Roy. 1994. London: A Social History. Cambridge, MA: Harvard University Press.

Pratt, Travis C., and Francis T. Cullen. 2000. "The Empirical Status of Gottfredson and Hirschi's Theory of Crime: A Meta-analysis." Criminology 38: 931–964.

Pratt, Travis C., and Francis T. Cullen. 2005. "Assessing Macro-Level Predictors and Theories of Crime: A Meta-analysis." Crime and Justice 32: 373–450.

Pratt, Travis C., Francis T. Cullen, Kristie R. Blevins, Leah E. Daigle, and Tamara D. Madensen. 2007. "The Empirical Status of Deterrence Theory: A Meta-analysis." Pp.367–396 in Taking Stock of Delinquency: An Overview of Findings from

Contemporary Longitudinal Studies, edited by Francis T. Cullen, John Paul Wright, and Kristie R. Blevins. New Brunswick, NJ: Transaction Publishers.

Pratt, Travis C., Michael G. Turner, and Alex R. Piquero. 2004. "Parental Socialization and Community Context: A Longitudinal Analysis of the Structural Sources of Low Self-Control." Journal of Research in Crime and Delinquency 41: 219–243.

Presser, Lois. 2009. "The Narratives of Offenders." Theoretical Criminology 13: 177–200.

Pulsipher, Ian. 2005. Evaluating Enterprise Zones: NCSL/Annie E. Casey Partnership on Family Economic Success. Washington, DC: National Conference of State Legislators.

Quay, Herbert. 1987. Handbook of Juvenile Delinquency. New York: John Wiley & Sons.

Quinney, Richard. 1974. Critique of the Social Order. Boston: Little, Brown, and Company.

Raaijmakers, Quinten A. W., Rutger C. M. C. Engels, and Anne Van Hoof. 2005. "Delinquency and Moral Reasoning in Adolescence and Young Adulthood." International Journal of Behavioral Development 29: 247–258.

Rafter, Nicole. 2004. "The Unrepentant Horse-Thrasher: Moral Insanity and the Origins of Criminological Thought." Criminology 42: 979–1008.

Ragin, Charles C. 1994. Constructing Social Research: The Unity and Diversity of Method. Thousand Oaks, CA: Pine Forge Press.

Raine, Adrian. 1993. The Psychopathology of Crime: Criminal Behavior as a Clinical Disorder. San Diego, CA: Academic Press.

Raine, Adrian. 2002. "Biosocial Studies of Antisocial and Violent Behavior in Children and Adults: A Review." Journal of Abnormal Child Psychology 30: 311–326.

Raine, Adrian. 2008. "From Genes to Brain to Antisocial Behavior." Current Directions in Psychological Science 17: 323–328.

Raine, Adrian, and Jianghong Liu. 1998. "Biological Predispositions to Violence and Their Implications for Biosocial Treatment and Prevention." Psychology, Crime & Law 4: 107–125.

Raine, Adrian, Laura Baker, and Jianghong Liu. 2006. "Biological Risk Factors for Antisocial and Criminal Behavior." Pp.83–107 in Crime and Schizophrenia: Causes and Cures, edited by Adrian Raine. New York: Nova Science Publishers.

Raine, Adrian, Terrie E. Moffitt, Avshalom Caspi, Rolf Loeber, Magda Stouthamer-Loeber, and Don Lynam. 2005. "Neurocognitive Impairments in Boys on the Life-Course Persistent Antisocial Path." Journal of Abnormal Psychology 114: 38–49.

Raine, Adrian, Peter H. Venables, and Mark Williams. 1990. "Relationships between Central and Autonomic Measures of Arousal at Age 15 Years and Criminality at Age 24 Years." Archives of General Psychiatry 47: 1003–1007.

Raine, Adrian, Peter H. Venables, and Mark Williams. 1996. "Better Autonomic Conditioning and Faster Electrodermal Half-Recovery Time at Age 15 Years as Possible Protective Factors against Crime at Age 29 Years." Developmental Psychology 32: 624–630.

Raphael, Jody. 2004. Listening to Olivia: Violence, Poverty and Prostitution. Boston: Northeastern University Press.

Rebellon, Cesar J., Murray A. Straus, and Rose Medeiros. 2008. "Self-Control in Global Perspective: An Empirical Assessment of Gottfredson and Hirschi's General Theory within and across 32 National Settings." European Journal of Criminology 5: 331–362.

Reckless, Walter C. 1961. The Crime Problem, Third Edition. New York: Appleton-Century-Crofts.

Redding, Richard E. 2003. "The Effects of Adjudicating and Sentencing Juveniles as Adults." Youth Violence and Juvenile Justice 1: 128–155.

Reebye, Pratibha, Marlene M. Moretti, Vaneesa J. Wiebe, and Jocelyne C. Lessard. 2000. "Symptoms of Posttraumatic Stress Disorder in Adolescents with Conduct Disorder: Sex Differences and Onset Patterns." Canadian Journal of Psychiatry 45: 746–751.

Reiss, Albert J. 1951. "Delinquency as a Failure of Personal and Social Controls." American Sociological Review 16: 196–207.

Reiss, Albert J. 1986. "Why are Communities Important in Understanding Crime?" Pp.1–33 in Communities and Crime, edited by Albert J. Reiss and Michael Tonry. Chicago: University of Chicago Press.

Revelle, W. 1997. "Extraversion and Impulsivity: The Lost Dimension?" Pp.189–212 in The Scientific Study of Human Nature: Tribute to Hans J. Eysenck at Eighty, edited by Helmuth Nyborg. New York: Pergamon.

Reyna, Valerie F., and Frank Farley. 2006. "Risk and Rationality in Adolescent Decision Making: Implications for Theory, Practice, and Public Policy." Psychological Science in the Public Interest 7: 1–44.

Reynolds, Arthur J., Judy A. Temple, Suh-Ruu Ou, Dylan L. Robertson, Joshua P. Mersky, James W. Topitzes, and Michael D. Niles. 2007. "Effects of a School-Based, Early Childhood Intervention on Adult Health and Well-being: A 19-Year Follow-up of Low-Income Families." Archives of Pediatric and Adolescent Medicine 161: 730–739.

Robinson, William S. 1950. "Ecological Correlation and the Behavior of Individuals." American Sociological Review 15: 351–357.

Rodney, Renai S. 2004. "Am I My Mother's Keeper? The Case against the Use of Juvenile Arrest Records in One-Strike Public Housing Evictions." Northwestern University Law Review 98: 739–772.

Rogan, Walter J., and James H. Ware. 2003. "Exposure to Lead in Children: How Low Is Low Enough?" New England Journal of Medicine 348: 1515–1516.

Rogers, Susan Carol. 1978. "Women's Place: A Critical Review of Anthropological Theory." Comparative Studies in Society and History 20: 123–162.

Roper v. Simmons. 2005. 125 S.Ct. 1183.

Rose, Steven R. 1997. "Analysis of Juvenile Court Diversion Program." Journal of Offender Rehabilitation 24: 153–161.

Ross, Ian Simpson. 1995. The Life of Adam Smith. Oxford: Clarendon Press.

Rousseau, Jean-Jacques. 1974 [1755]. Discourse on the Origin and Basis of Inequality among Men. Reprinted pp.125–202 in The Essential Rousseau. Translated by L. Blair. New York: New American Library.

Rowe, David C. 1986. "Genetic and Environmental Components of Antisocial Behavior: A Study of 265 Twin Pairs." Criminology 24: 513–532.

Rowe, David C. 2002. Biology and Crime. Los Angeles, CA: Roxbury Publishing.

Rucklidge, Julia J., Anthony P. McLean, and Paul Bateup. 2010. "Criminal Offending and Learning Disabilities in New Zealand Youth: Does Reading Comprehension Predict Recidivism?" Crime & Delinquency 56: 1–20.

Sampson, Robert J. 2000. "A Neighborhood-Level Perspective on Social Change and the Social Control of Adolescent Delinquency." Pp. 178–190 in Negotiating Adolescence in Times of Social Change, edited by Lisa Crockett and Rainer Silbereisen. New York: Cambridge University Press.

Sampson, Robert J. 2001. "Crime and Public Safety: Insights from Community-Level Perspectives on Social Capital." Pp.89–114 in Social Capital and Poor Communities, edited by Susan Saegert, J. Phillip Thompson, and Mark R. Warren. New York: Russell Sage Foundation.

Sampson, Robert J., and W. Byron Groves. 1989. "Community Structure and Crime: Testing Social Disorganization Theory." American Journal of Sociology 94: 774–802.

Sampson, Robert J., and John H. Laub. 1993. Crime in the Making: Pathways and Turning Points through Life. Cambridge, MA: Harvard University Press.

Sampson, Robert J., and John H. Laub. 1995. "Understanding Variability in Lives through Time: Contributions of Life-Course Criminology." Studies in Crime and Crime Prevention 4: 143–158.

Sampson, Robert J., and John H. Laub. 1997a. "Unraveling the Social Context of Physique and Delinquency: A New, Long-Term Look at the Gluecks' Classic Study." Pp.175–188 in The Biosocial Bases of Violence, edited by Adrian Raine, Patricia A. Brennan, David P. Farrington, and Sarnoff A. Mednick. New York: Plenum Press.

Sampson, Robert J., and John Laub. 1997b. "A Life-Course Theory of Cumulative Disadvantage and the Stability of Delinquency." Pp. 133–161 in Developmental Theories of Crime and Delinquency, edited by Terence P. Thornberry. New Brunswick, NJ: Transaction Publishers.

Sampson, Robert J., and John H. Laub. 2003. Crime in the Making: Pathways and Turning Points through Life. Cambridge, MA: Harvard University Press.

Sampson, Robert J., and John H. Laub. 2005a. "A Life-Course View of the Development of Crime." The Annals of the American Academy of Political and Social Science 602: 12–45.

Sampson, Robert J., and John H. Laub. 2005b. "A General Age-Graded Theory of Crime: Lessons Learned and the Future of Life-Course Criminology." Pp.165–181 in Integrated Developmental and Life-Course Theories of Offending, edited by David P. Farrington. New Brunswick, NJ: Transaction Publishers.

Sampson, Robert J., and Stephen W. Raudenbush. 1999. "Systematic Social Observation of Public Spaces: A New Look at Disorder in Urban Neighborhoods." American Journal of Sociology 105: 603–651.

Sampson, Robert J., and Stephen W. Raudenbush. 2004. "Seeing Disorder: Neighborhood Stigma and the Social Construction of 'Broken Windows.'" Social Psychology Quarterly 67: 319–342.

Sampson, Robert J., John H. Laub, and Christopher Wimer. 2006. "Does Marriage Reduce Crime? A Counterfactual Approach to within-Individual Causal Effects." Criminology 44: 465–508.

Sampson, Robert J., Jeffrey D. Morenoff, and Thomas Gannon-Rowley. 2002. "Assessing 'Neighborhood Effects': Social Processes and New Directions in Research." Annual Review of Sociology 28: 443–478.

Sampson, Robert J., Stephen W. Raudenbush, and Felton Earls. 1997. "Neighborhoods and Violent Crime: A Multilevel Study of Collective Efficacy." Science 277: 918–924.

Sandstrom, Marlene J., and Rachel Jordan. 2008. "Defensive Self-Esteem and Aggression in Childhood." Journal of Research in Personality 42: 506–514.

Santiago, Anna M., George C. Galster, and Kathryn L. S. Pettit. 2003. "Neighbourhood Crime and Scattered-Site Public Housing." Urban Studies 40: 2147–2163.

Sari, Youssef, and Feng C. Zhou. 2004. "Prenatal Alcohol Exposure Causes Long-Term Serotonin Deficit in Mice." Alcoholism: Clinical and Experimental Research 28: 941–948.

Sarnecki, Jerzy. 2001. Delinquent Networks: Youth Co-offending in Stockholm. New York: Cambridge University Press.

Sarup, Madan. 2005. Identity, Culture, and the Postmodern World. Edinburgh: Edinburgh University Press.

Sato, Ikuya. 1988. "Play Theory of Delinquency: Toward a General Theory of 'Action.'" Symbolic Interaction 11: 191–212.

Savage, Joanne. 2004. "Does Viewing Violent Media Really Cause Criminal Violence? A Methodological Review." Aggressive Behavior 10: 99–128.

Savelsberg, Joachim J. 1999. "Human Nature and Social Control in Complex Society: A Critique of Charles Tittle's Control Balance." Theoretical Criminology 3: 331–338.

Scared Straight! 20 Years Later. 1999. TV documentary. Directed by Arnold Shapiro. Los Angeles: Arnold Shapiro Productions.

Schaffner, Laurie. 1999. "Violence and Female Delinquency: Gender Transgressions and Gender Invisibility." Berkeley Women's Law Journal 14: 40–65.

Schaffner, Laurie. 2006. Girls in Trouble with the Law. New Brunswick, NJ: Rutgers University Press.

Schmidt, Louis A., Nathan A. Fox, and Dean H. Hamer. 2007. "Evidence for a Gene–Gene Interaction in Predicting Children's Behavior Problems: Association of Serotonin Transporter Short and Dopamine Receptor D4 Long Genotypes with Internalizing and Externalizing Behaviors in Typically Developing 7-Year-Olds." Development and Psychopathology 19: 1105–1116.

Schur, Edwin M. 1971. Labeling Deviant Behavior: Its Sociological Implications. New York: Harper & Row.

Schwartz, Jennifer, and Bryan D. Rookey. 2008. "The Narrowing Gender Gap in Arrests: Assessing Competing Explanations Using Self-Report, Traffic Fatality, and Official Data on Drunk Driving, 1980–2004." Criminology 46: 637–671.

Schwartz, Martin D., and David O. Friedrichs. 1994. "Postmodern Thought and Criminological Discontent: New Metaphors for Understanding Violence." Criminology 32: 221–246.

Schwendinger, Herman, and Julia R. Siegel Schwendinger. 1985. Adolescent Subcultures and Delinquency. New York: Praeger Publishers.

Scott, Elizabeth S. 2000. "The Legal Construction of Adolescence." Hofstra Law Review 29: 547–590.

Scott, Elizabeth S., and Thomas Grisso. 2005. "Developmental Incompetence, Due Process, and Juvenile Justice Policy." North Carolina Law Review 83: 793–851.

Sealock, Miriam D., and Sally S. Simpson. 1998. "Unraveling Bias in Arrest Decisions: The Role of Juvenile Offender Type-Scripts." Justice Quarterly 15: 427–457.

Sears, Alan. 2005. A Good Book, in Theory. Orchard Park, NY: Broadview Press.

Segalowitz, S. J., and Patricia L. Davies. 2004. "Charting the Maturation of the Frontal Lobe: An Electrophysiological Strategy." Brain and Cognition 55: 116–133.

Sharkey, Patrick, and Robert J. Sampson. 2010. "Destination Effects: Residential Mobility and Trajectories of Adolescent Violence in a Stratified Metropolis." Criminology 48: 639–681.

Shaw, Clifford R. 1951. The Natural History of a Delinquent Career. Philadelphia: Albert Saifer.

Shaw, Clifford R., and Henry D. McKay. 1969 [1942]. Juvenile Delinquency and Urban Areas. Chicago: University of Chicago Press.

Sheldon, William H. 1949. Varieties of Delinquent Youth: An Introduction to Constitutional Psychiatry. New York: Harper & Brothers Publishers.

Shields, Ian W., and Georga C. Whitehall. 1994. "Neutralization and Delinquency among Teenagers." Criminal Justice and Behavior 21: 223–235.

Shimamura, Arthur P. 2002. "Memory Retrieval and Executive Control Processes." Pp.210–220 in Principles of Frontal Lobe Function, edited by Donald T. Stuss and Robert T. Knight. London: Oxford University Press.

Shoham, S. Giora. 1979. "Labeling and Beyond: Social Stigma Revisited." Pp.44–88 in New Paths in Criminology: Interdisciplinary and Intercultural Explorations, edited by Sarnoff Mednick and S. Giora Shoham. Lexington, MA: Lexington Books.

Shoham, S. Giora, and Giora Rahav. 1982. The Mark of Cain: The Stigma Theory of Crime and Social Explorations. New York: St. Martins Press.

Shoham, S. Giora, and Mark C. Seis. 1993. A Primer in the Psychology of Crime. Albany, NY: Harrow and Heston Publishers.

Shore, Heather. 1999. Artful Dodgers: Youth and Crime in Early Nineteenth-Century London. Woodbridge, UK: Boydell Press.

Short, James F. 1964. "Gang Delinquency and Anomie." Pp.98–127 in Anomie and Deviant Behavior, edited by Marshall Clinard. New York: Free Press.

Shrek. 2001. Directed by Andrew Adamson and Vicky Jenson. Burbank, CA: Dreamworks Studios.

Sica, Alan (Ed.). 1998. What Is Social Theory? Malden, MA: Blackwell Publishers.

Siegler, Robert S. 2005. "Children's Learning." American Psychologist 60: 769–778.

Siever, Larry J. 2008. "Neurobiology of Aggression and Violence." American Journal of Psychiatry 165: 429–442.

Simon, Rita J. 1975. Women and Crime. Lexington, MA: Lexington Books.

Simons, Ronald L., Yi-Fu Chen, Eric A. Stewart, and Gene H. Brody. 2003. "Incidents of Discrimination and Risk for Delinquency: A Longitudinal Test of Strain Theory with an African-American Sample." Justice Quarterly 20: 827–854.

Simpson, Sally S., and Lori Ellis. 1994. "Is Gender Subordinate to Class? An Empirical Assessment of Colvin and Pauly's Structural Marxist Theory of Delinquency." Journal of Criminal Law and Criminology 85: 453–480.

Singer, Simon I., and Murray Levine. 1988. "Power-Control Theory, Gender, and Delinquency: A Partial Replication with Additional Evidence on the Effects of Peers." Criminology 26: 627–647.

Skinner, B. F. 1953. Science and Human Behavior. New York: Macmillan.

Skogan, Wesley G. 1990. Disorder and Decline: Crime and the Spiral of Decay in American Neighborhoods. Berkeley, CA: University of California Press.

Small, Mario Luis, and Katherine Newman. 2001. "Urban Poverty after the Truly Disadvantaged: The Rediscovery of the Family, the Neighborhood, and Culture." Annual Review of Sociology 27: 23–45.

Smit, Evelien, Jacqueline Verdurmen, Karin Monshouwer, and Filip Smit. 2008. "Family Interventions and Their Effect on Adolescent Alcohol Use in General Populations: A Meta-analysis of Randomized Controlled Trials." Drug and Alcohol Dependence 97: 195–206.

Smith, Adam. 1991 [1776]. Inquiry into the Nature and Causes of the Wealth of Nations. Amherst, NY: Prometheus Books.

Smith, Dorothy. 1990. The Conceptual Practices of Power: A Feminist Sociology of Knowledge. Evanston, IL: Northwestern University Press.

Smith, Hayden P., and Robert M. Bohm. 2008. "Beyond Anomie: Alienation and Crime." Critical Criminology 16: 1–15.

Snider, Laureen. 1998. "Feminism, Punishment, and the Potential of Empowerment." Pp.246–261 in Criminology at the Crossroads: Feminist Readings in Crime and Justice, edited by Kathleen Daly and Lisa Maher. New York: Oxford University Press.

Snyder, Jim, Lew Bank, and Bert Burraston. 2005. "The Consequences of Antisocial Behavior in Older Male Siblings for Younger Brothers and Sisters." Journal of Family Psychology 19: 643–653.

South, Scott J., and Steven F. Messner. 2000. "Crime and Demography: Multiple Linkages, Reciprocal Relations." Annual Review of Sociology 26: 83–106.

Spergel, Irving. 1967. "Deviant Patterns and Opportunities of Pre-adolescent Negro Boys in Three Chicago Neighborhoods." Pp.38–54 in Juvenile Gangs in Context, edited by Malcolm W. Klein. Englewood Cliffs, NJ: Prentice-Hall.

Spoth, Richard L., Cleve Redmond, and Chungyeol Shin. 2001. "Randomized Trial of Brief Family Interventions for General Populations: Adolescent Substance Use Outcomes 4 Years Following Baseline." Journal of Consulting and Clinical Psychology 69: 627–642.

Stanford v. Kentucky. 1989. 109 S. Ct. 2969.

Stark, Rodney. 1996. "Religion as Context: Hellfire and Delinquency One More Time." Sociology of Religion 57: 163–173.

Steffensmeier, Darrell J., and Jeffrey T. Ulmer. 2005. Confessions of a Dying Thief: Understanding Criminal Careers and Illegal Enterprise. New York: Aldine de Gruyter.

Steinberg, Laurence. 2004. "Risk Taking in Adolescence: What Changes, and Why?" Annals of the New York Academy of Sciences 1021: 51–58.

Stewart, Eric A., and Ronald L. Simons. 2010. "Race, Code of the Street, and Violent Delinquency: A Multilevel Investigation of Neighborhood Street Culture and Individual Norms of Violence." Criminology 48: 569–605.

Stewart, Eric A., Ronald L. Simons, Rand D. Conger, and Laura V. Scaramella. 2002. "Beyond the Interactional Relationship between Delinquency and Parenting Practices: The Contribution of Legal Sanctions." Journal of Research in Crime and Delinquency 39: 36–59.

Stiles, Beverly L., Xiaoru Liu, and Howard B. Kaplan. 2000. "Relative Deprivation and Deviant Adaptations: The Mediating Effects of Negative Self-Feelings." Journal of Research in Crime and Delinquency 37: 64–90.

Stryker, Sheldon. 1994. "Identity Theory: Its Development, Research Base, and Prospects." Studies in Symbolic Interaction 16: 9–20.

Sukhodolsky, Denis G., Howard Kassinove, and Bernard S. Gorman. 2004. "Cognitive–Behavioral Therapy for Anger in Children and Adolescents: A Meta-analysis." Aggression and Violent Behavior 9: 247–269.

Sullivan, Mercer L. 1989. Getting Paid. Ithaca, NY: Cornell University Press.

Sutherland, Edwin H. 1947. Principles of Criminology, Fourth Edition. Philadelphia: H.P. Lippincott.

Sutherland, Edwin H. 1973 [1942]. "Development of the Theory." Pp.13–29 in On Analyzing Crime, edited by Karl Schuessler. Chicago: University of Chicago Press.

Sutphen, Richard D., and Janet Ford. 2001. "The Effectiveness of a Teen Curfew Law." Journal of Sociology and Social Welfare 28: 55–78.

Sykes, Gresham M., and David Matza. 1957. "Techniques of Neutralization: A Theory of Delinquency." American Sociological Review 22: 664–670.

Tannenbaum, Frank. 1938. Crime and the Community. New York: Columbia University Press.

Teplin, Linda A., Karen M. Abram, Gary M. McClelland, Mina K. Dulcan, and Amy A. Mericle. 2002. "Psychiatric Disorders in Youth in Juvenile Detention." Archives of General Psychiatry 59: 1133–1143.

Thomas, Jim, Julie Capps, James Carr, Tammy Evans, Wendy Lewin-Gladney, Deborah Jacobson, Chris Maier, Scott Moran, and Sean Thompson. 2003. "Critiquing the Critics of Criminology as Peacemaking: Some Rather Ambivalent Reflections on the Theory of 'Being Nice.'" Pp.101–134 in Criminology, Conflict Resolution, and Restorative Justice, edited by Kieran McEvoy and Tim Newburn. New York: Palgrave Macmillan.

Thornberry, Terence P. 1987. "Toward an Interactional Theory of Delinquency." Criminology 25: 863–891.

Thornberry, Terence P. 1989. "Reflections on the Advantages and Disadvantages of Theoretical Integration." Pp.51–60 in Theoretical Integration in the Study of Deviance and Crime: Problems and Prospects, edited by Steven F. Messner, Marvin D. Krohn, and Allen E. Liska. Albany: State University of New York Press.

Thornberry, Terence P. 1996. "Empirical Support for Interactional Theory: A Review of the Literature." Pp.198–235 in Delinquency and Crime: Current Theories, edited by J. David Hawkins. New York: Cambridge University Press.

Thornberry, Terence P. 2005. "Explaining Multiple Patterns of Offending across the Life Course and across Generations." Annals of the American Academy of Political and Social Science 602: 156–195.

Thornberry, Terence P., and Marvin D. Krohn. 2001. "The Development of Delinquency: An Interactional Perspective." Pp.289–305 in Handbook of Youth and Justice, edited by Susan O. White. New York: Plenum.

Thornberry, Terence P., and Marvin D. Krohn. 2003. Taking Stock of Delinquency: An Overview of Findings from Contemporary Longitudinal Studies. New York: Springer.

Thornberry, Terence P., Alan J. Lizotte, Marvin D. Krohn, Margaret Farnworth, and Sung Joon Jang. 1994. "Delinquent Peers, Beliefs, and Delinquent Behavior: A Longitudinal Test of Interactional Theory." Criminology 32: 47–83.

Thrasher, Frederick M. 1927. The Gang. Chicago: University of Chicago Press.

Tittle, Charles R. 1995. Control Balance: Toward a General Theory of Deviance. Boulder, CO: Westview Press.

Tittle, Charles R. 2004. "Refining Control Balance Theory." Theoretical Criminology 8: 395–428.

Tittle, Charles, and Michael R. Welch. 1983. "Religiosity and Deviance: Toward a Contingency Theory of Constraining Effects." Social Forces 61: 653–682.

Tittle, Charles, David A. Ward, and Harold Grasmick. 2003. "Self-Control and Crime/ Deviance: Cognitive vs. Behavioral Measures." Journal of Quantitative Criminology 19: 333–365.

Tong, Rosemary Putnam. 2008. Feminist Thought: A More Comprehensive Introduction, Third Edition. Boulder, CO: Westview Press.

Topalli, Volkan. 2005. "When Being Good is Bad: An Expansion of Neutralization Theory." Criminology 43: 797–835.

Tremblay, Richard E., L. C. Mâsse, Linda Pagani, and Frank Vitaro. 1996. "From Childhood Physical Aggression to Adolescent Maladjustment: The Montreal Prevention Experiment." Pp.268–298 in Preventing Childhood Disorders, Substance Abuse, and Delinquency, edited by Ray D. Peters and Robert J. McMahon. Thousand Oaks, CA: Sage Publications.

Tremblay, Richard E., Benoist Schaal, Bernard Boulerice, Louise Arseneault, Robert Soussignan, and Daniel Pérusse. 1997. "Male Physical Aggression, Social Dominance, and Testosterone Levels in Puberty." Pp.271–291 in The Biosocial Bases of Violence, edited by Adrian Raine, Patricia A. Brennan, David P. Farrington, and Sarnoff A. Mednick. New York: Plenum Press.

Tremblay, Richard E., Frank Vitaro, Daniel Nagin, Linda Pagani, and Jean R. Séguin. 2003. "The Montreal Longitudinal and Experimental Study: Rediscovering the Power of Descriptions." Pp.205–254 in Taking Stock of Delinquency: An Overview of Findings from Contemporary Longitudinal Studies, edited by Terence P. Thornberry and Marvin D. Krohn. New York: Springer.

Turk, Austin T. 1964. "Toward Construction of a Theory of Delinquency." Journal of Criminal Law, Criminology, and Police Science 55: 215–229.

Turner, Jonathan H. 2003. The Structure of Sociological Theory, Seventh Edition. Chicago, IL: Wadsworth Press.

Turner, Jonathan H., Leonard Beeghley, and Charles H. Powers. 2002. The Emergence of Sociological Theory, Fifth Edition. Belmont, CA: Wadsworth Thomson Learning.

U.S. Department of Health and Human Services. 2006. About Head Start. Washington, DC: Administration for Children and Families, U.S. Department of Health and Human Services. Available electronically at: http://www.acf.hhs.gov/programs/hsb/about/index.htm.

Uggen, Christopher, and Sara Wakefield. 2007. "What Have We Learned from Longitudinal Studies of Work and Crime?" Pp.191–219 in The Long View of Crime: A Synthesis of Longitudinal Studies, edited by Akiva M. Liberman. New York: Springer.

Ulmer, Jeffrey T. 2011. "Symbolic Interactionism and Crime in the Life Course." Pp.211–226 in Criminological Theory: A Life-Course Approach, edited by Matt DeLisi and Kevin M. Beaver. Boston: Jones and Bartlett Publishers.

Ulmer, Jeffrey T., and Mindy S. Wilson. 2003. "The Potential Contributions of Quantitative Research to Symbolic Interactionism." Symbolic Interaction 26: 531–552.

Vaughn, Barry. 2007. "The Internal Narrative of Desistance." British Journal of Criminology 47: 390–404.

Vaughn, Michael G., Matt Delisi, Kevin M. Beaver, and John Paul Wright. 2009. "DAT1 and 5HTT are Associated with Pathological Criminal Behavior in a Nationally Representative Sample of Youth." Criminal Justice and Behavior 36: 1113–1124.

Vermeersch, Hans, Guy T'Sjoen, Jean-Marc Kaufman, and John Vincke. 2008. "The Role of Testosterone in Aggressive and Non-Aggressive Risk-Taking in Adolescent Boys." Hormones and Behavior 53: 463–471.

Vermeiren, Robert, Jef Bogaerts, Vladislav Ruchkin, Dirk Deboutte, and Mary Schwab-Stone. 2004. "Subtypes of Self-Esteem and Self-Concept in Adolescent Violent and Property Offenders." Journal of Child Psychology and Psychiatry 45: 405–411.

Verrecchia, P. J. 2009. "Female Delinquents and Restorative Justice." Women & Criminal Justice 19: 80–93.

Vitaro, Frank, Mara Brendgen, and Richard E. Tremblay. 2000. "Influence of Deviant Friends on Delinquency: Searching for Moderator Effects." Journal of Abnormal Child Psychology 28: 313–325.

Wadsworth, Sally J., and John C. DeFries. 2003. "Etiology of the Stability of Reading Performance from 7 to 12 Years of Age and Its Possible Mediation by IQ." Pp.49–61 in Nature, Nurture, and the Transition to Early Adolescence, edited by Stephen A. Petrill, Robert Plomin, John C. DeFries, and John K. Hewitt. New York: Oxford University Press.

Walby, Sylvia. 1990. Theorizing Patriarchy. Oxford: Basil Blackwell.

Waldie, Karen, and Otfried Spreen. 1993. "The Relationship between Learning Disabilities and Persisting Delinquency." Journal of Learning Disabilities 26: 417–423.

Waldrop, Mary F., Richard Q. Bell, Brian McLaughlin and Charles F. Halverson. 1978. "Newborn Minor Physical Anomalies Predict Short Attention Span, Peer Aggression, and Impulsivity at Age 3." Science 199: 563–565.

Walklate, Sandra. 2004. Gender and Crime: An Introduction, Second Edition. Portland, OR: Willan Publishing.

Wallace, John M., Ryoko Yamaguchi, Jerald G. Bachman, Patrick M. O'Malley, John E. Schulenberg, and Lloyd D. Johnston. 2007. "Religiosity and Adolescent Substance Use: The Role of Individual and Contextual Influences." Social Problems 54: 308–327.

Wanted. 2008. Directed by Timur Bekmambetov. Los Angeles, CA: Universal Pictures.

Wark, Gillian R., and Dennis L. Krebs. 1997. "Sources of Variation in Moral Judgment: Toward a Model of Real-Life Morality." Journal of Adult Development 4: 163–178.

Warner, Barbara D. 2003. "The Role of Attenuated Culture in Social Disorganization Theory." Criminology 41: 73–97.

Warr, Mark. 1998. "Life-Course Transitions and Desistance from Crime." Criminology 36: 183–216.

Warr, Mark. 2001. "The Social Origins of Crime: Edwin Sutherland and the Theory of Differential Association." Pp.182–191 in Explaining Criminals and Crime, edited by Raymond Paternoster and Ronet Bachman. Los Angeles, CA: Roxbury Publishing.

Warr, Mark. 2002. Companions in Crime: The Social Aspects of Criminal Conduct. New York: Cambridge University Press.

Warr, Mark. 2009. "Peers and Delinquency." Pp.383–404 in Handbook on Crime and Deviance, edited by Marvin D. Krohn, Alan J. Lizotte, and Gina Penly Hall. New York: Springer.

Warr, Mark, and Mark Stafford. 1991. "The Influence of Delinquent Peers: What They Say or What They Do?" Criminology 29: 851–866.

Weatherburn, Don, Bronwyn Lind, and Simon Ku. 1999. "Hotbeds of Crime: Crime and Public Housing in Urban Sydney." Crime & Delinquency 45: 256–271.

Western, Bruce, Jeffrey R. Kling, and David F. Weiman. 2001. "The Labor Market Consequences of Incarceration." Crime & Delinquency 47: 410–427.

White, Stuart F., and Paul J. Frick. 2010. "Callous-Unemotional Traits and Their Importance to Causal Models of Severe Antisocial Behavior in Youth." Pp.135–155 in Handbook of Child and Adolescent Psychopathy, edited by Randall T. Salekin and Donald R. Lynam. New York: Guilford Press.

Whitehead, Neil L. (Ed.). 2004. Violence. Sante Fe, NM: School of American Research Press.

Wiesner, Margit, Deborah M. Capaldi, and Gerald R. Patterson. 2007. "Development of Antisocial Behavior and Crime across the Life-Span from a Social Interactionist Perspective: The Coercion Model." Pp. 317–338 in Social Learning Theory and the Explanation of Crime, edited by Ronald L. Akers and Gary F. Jensen. New Brunswick, NJ: Transaction Publishers.

Wilcox, Pamela, Neil Quisenberry, Debra T. Cabrera, and Shayne Jones. 2004. "Busy Places or Broken Windows? Toward Defining the Role of Physical Structure and Process in Community Crime Models." Sociological Quarterly 45: 185–207.

Williams, Christopher R. 2007. "Potential Spaces of Crime: The Playful, the Destructive, and the Distinctively Human." Crime, Media, and Culture 3: 49–66.

Williams, Debra. 2005. "Englewood: Believing in Better Schools, a Better 'Quality of Life': A Long-Blighted South Side Community Gets an Overdue Shot of Renewal." Catalyst Chicago 16 (June): 15.

Wilson, James Q., and George E. Kelling. 1982. "Broken Windows: The Police and Neighborhood Safety." The Atlantic Monthly 249 (March): 29–38.

Woldoff, Rachael A. 2002. "The Effects of Local Stressors on Neighborhood Attachment." Social Forces 81: 87–116.

Wolfgang, Marvin E. 1972. "Cesare Lombroso." Pp.232–291 in Pioneers in Criminology, Second Edition, edited by Hermann Mannheim. Montclair, NJ: Patterson Smith.

Wolfgang, Marvin E., Robert M. Figlio, and Thorsten Sellin. 1987. Delinquency in a Birth Cohort. Chicago: University of Chicago Press.

Wozniak, John F. 2009. "Poverty and Peacemaking Criminology: Beyond Mainstream Criminology." Critical Criminology 16: 209–223.

Wozniak, John F., Michael C. Braswell, Ronald E. Vogel, and Kristie R. Blevins. 2008. Transformative Justice: Critical and Peacemaking Themes Influenced by Richard Quinney. Lanham, MD: Lexington Books.

Wright, Bradley R. Entner, Avshalom Caspi, Terrie E. Moffitt, and Phil A. Silva. 2001. "The Effects of Social Ties on Crime Vary by Criminal Propensity: A Life-Course Model of Interdependence." Criminology 39: 321–348.

Wright, John Paul, Kevin Beaver, Matt Delisi, and Michael Vaughn. 2008. "Evidence of Negligible Parenting Influences on Self-Control, Delinquent Peers, and Delinquency in a Sample of Twins." Justice Quarterly 25: 544–569.

Wyatt, Jennifer W., and Gustavo Carlo. 2002. "What Will My Parents Think? Relations among Adolescents' Expected Parental Reactions, Prosocial Moral Reasoning, and Prosocial and Antisocial Behaviors." Journal of Adolescent Research 17: 646–666.

Xie, Min, and David McDowall. 2008. "The Effects of Residential Turnover on Household Victimization." Criminology 46: 539–575.

Yaralian, Pauline S., and Adrian Raine. 2001. "Biological Approaches to Crime: Psychophysiology and Brain Dysfunction." Pp.57–72 in Explaining Criminals and Crime: Essays in Contemporary Criminological Theory, edited by Raymond Paternoster and Ronet Bachman. Los Angeles: Roxbury Publishing Company.

Young, Susan E., Andrew Smolen, John K. Hewitt, Brett C. Haberstick, Michael C. Stallings, Robin P. Corley, and Thomas J. Crowley. 2006. "Interaction between MAO-A Genotype and Maltreatment in the Risk for Conduct Disorder." American Journal of Psychiatry 163: 1019–1025.

Zalsman, Gil, and Alan Apter. 2002. "Serotogenic Metabolism and Violence/Aggression." Pp.231–250 in The Neurobiology of Criminal Behavior, edited by Joseph Glicksohn. Boston, MA: Kluwer Academic Publishers.

Zhang, Lening. 1997. "Informal Reactions and Delinquency." Criminal Justice and Behavior 24: 129–150.

Zingraff, Matthew T., Jeffrey Leiter, Matthew C. Johnsen, and Kristen A. Myers. 1994. "The Mediating Effect of Good School Performance on the Maltreatment–Delinquency Relationship." Journal of Research in Crime and Delinquency 31: 62–91.

Zuckerman, M. 1994. Behavioural Expressions and Biosocial Bases of Sensation Seeking. Cambridge: Cambridge University Press.

Index